Contemporary Issues
in Leadership

Contemporary Issues in Leadership

edited by William E. Rosenbach
and Robert L. Taylor

Foreword by David P. Campbell

Westview Press / Boulder and London

Published in 1984 in the United States of America by Westview Press, Inc., 5500 Central Avenue, Boulder, Colorado, 80301; Frederick A. Praeger, President and Publisher

Library of Congress Cataloging in Publication Data
Main entry under title:
Contemporary issues in leadership.
   1. Leadership—Addresses, essays, lectures.
I. Rosenbach, William E. II. Taylor, Robert L.
(Robert Lewis), 1939–
HM141.C69 1984   303.3′4   83-21820
ISBN 0-86531-727-5
ISBN 0-86531-728-3 (pbk)

Printed and bound in the United States of America

10 9 8 7 6 5 4 3 2 1

To Colleen and Aggie

Contents

Preface

Over the past ten years we have taught courses in leadership—individually and together—in a variety of organizational settings. On each occasion we renewed our own study of leadership and reflected on our personal roles as both followers and leaders. In our most recent joint teaching effort some four years ago, we again faced the elusiveness of the topic and, out of frustration, began a broad search for readings that captured the essence of leadership.

Soon we found ourselves conducting a systematic review of the literature of psychology, business, education, politics, history, sociology, philosophy, and the military. No one discipline could claim the truth; in fact, robust thinking on the topic was to be found in the popular press as well as in the realm of academe. We were astounded at the number of articles that had been written—the challenge was to select those that best presented a meaningful discussion of leadership without any disciplinary bias or special orientation. We had to make difficult choices, and in many instances excellent articles were omitted, articles that would have been included if we had had room for a larger selection.

The purpose of the resulting book is to describe the phenomenon of leadership and to identify what it is that makes a person an effective leader. We have avoided articles detailing specific models or themes; handbooks and texts that review the theoretical literature are readily available. We also excluded readings that reported the details of specific research projects or the complexities of research methodologies. Rather, we included those articles that provided an interdisciplinary overview of the key issues in leadership at different organizational levels from a variety of perspectives. Some of the articles are old, classics if you will; others are quite current. There is an interesting blend of scholarly and not-so-scholarly presentations, all well-written and thought-provoking.

There are five parts to the book. Part 1 explores the nature of the leadership paradox: Why is it that we cannot easily define leadership even though we recognize and appreciate it? In Part 2 leadership is contrasted with management, and in Part 3 we approach leadership from yet another point of view, introducing the concept of followership. (It is our belief that a thorough study of leadership must include a study of followership and its implications for leader succession.) The personal qualities of leadership are the focus of Part 4, in which we look at individual differences as they relate to leadership. Part 5 concludes with a discussion of whether the controversies of leadership have been resolved and, more important, whether they ever should be.

All too often scholars of various persuasions try to force leadership into rational empirical models, searching for a logic that does not exist. Other writers, however, consistently point to the intuitive, spontaneous qualities of leader behaviors outside the domain of models—qualities that relate to the individual and to the specific leadership situation. These two bodies of knowledge (i.e., empirical research literature versus the insightful writings of leaders, historians, and philosophers) can create polarities and frustrations.

We are well aware that our own academic knowledge has been tempered in the crucible of our daily leadership experiences. From that realization has come an appreciation of certain key ingredients involved in all leadership situations, including, but not being limited to, societal context, historical period, participants in the situation, tasks to be accomplished, and personalities of the leader and followers. All of these factors form the ambient light against which we must view and evaluate particular leadership models and studies as well as theoretical writings on the subject. We strongly believe that our examination of these factors provides a salient starting point for any study of leadership.

We are particularly indebted to the authors and publishers of the individual readings as well as to our students who, over the years, asked questions about leadership that we could not adequately answer. We wish to thank our colleagues and friends David Campbell, Bill Clover, and Bob Gregory for their advice and assistance and Sharon Weatherson and Helen Wilson for transforming our scribbled pages into a neatly typed manuscript. Finally, we appreciate the enthusiastic encouragement of the staff of Westview Press.

William E. Rosenbach
Robert L. Taylor

Foreword

Leadership has an elusive, mysterious quality about it. It is easy to recognize, hard to describe, difficult to practice, and almost impossible to create in others on demand. Perhaps no other topic has attracted as much attention from observers, participants, and philosophers—with so little agreement as to the basic facts.

It cannot even be adequately defined. Leadership means one thing to a 21-year-old platoon sergeant leading a small squad of soldiers on patrol through an eerie, pitch-black night deep in some hostile, foreign jungle; it means something quite different to an enlightened city mayor trying to deal simultaneously with a shrinking municipal budget and the need to refurbish a seedy, neglected center city.

Frequently, leaders are not even aware that they are leading. A United States senator is probably more motivated by political survival than by leadership when he or she works hard to corral enough votes to pass an important piece of legislation protecting agricultural subsidies for the home district, whether they be for cotton, corn, tobacco, or peanuts. Similarly, a scared but stubborn 16-year-old girl is hardly thinking about leadership while sitting, with dry mouth and moist palms, waiting to testify in front of her local school board. She wants equal access to the school's athletic facilities for both boys and girls, not because she sees herself as a leader, but simply because she sees the status quo as an odious situation.

The articles in this book reflect the breadth of this matter of perception. Rosenbach and Taylor have done an excellent job of selecting writings to maximize the range of opinions. No matter what you believe, you will find something here to support your viewpoint . . . and something else to contradict it.

The viewpoints of social scientists are especially well-represented here, and if you consider yourself a practicing leader, you may find this upsetting. Social scientists so often seem to be saying, "Well, that may work fine in practice, but how does it check out in theory?" There is as yet no single, dominant theory to help understand the multi-faceted concept of leadership. These articles highlight the major issues raised by people who have been putting leaders, managers, administrators, and executives under the microscope of scientific inquiry, but they offer no consensual solution. Indeed, a few authors even argue that leadership is irrelevant; the constraints are such that it doesn't matter who is leading.

One of the most constant issues in leadership discussions is whether leaders are born or made. Some individuals would have almost certainly left their stamp on history, no matter what their circumstances. Shakespeare's impact on the English language; Beethoven's legacy of great music; Michaelangelo's creations of great art; Napoleon's influence on war, law, and society; Churchill's impact on war and political geography—it is hard to imagine that these men would have lived unnoticed lives, no matter what their situation.

In contrast, many leaders seem captive to their time and situation. Would Gloria Steinem have achieved international prominence without the contemporary push for women's rights? Would Andy Warhol's pop art Campbell's Soup cans have become famous in any period less crazy than the 1960s? Could Martin Luther King, Jr., have stood out in an earlier time, before the conscience of the country had been activated by the distressing racial inequities documented on national television? Would Vince Lombardi have succeeded in a setting that didn't include the focusing discipline of physical violence? Perhaps leadership is merely an accidental collision between an appropriate person and a precipitating environment.

But only the most cynical observer can accept that analysis. The rest of us can see leadership happening routinely all around us or, equally impressive in a perverse way, can see the impact of its absence. Anyone who has ever been part of any disciplined human endeavor, be it military, athletic, musical, scientific, governmental, academic, or corporate, knows that some people strengthen the fabric of the enterprise just by their very presence. And further, those who strengthen it most are those whom others look to for guidance. In persuasive and all too common contrast, people in positions of power who do not provide the necessary guidance prove just as vividly, by the destructive nature of their passivity, the relevance of the concept of leadership.

Perhaps the most appealing reason for believing in the concept of leadership is that we all deeply want to believe that somewhere, some place, right now, leadership is happening. Somewhere great dreams are surely being energized, somewhere great thoughts are certainly being put into action, somewhere brilliant people must be managing the resources of the world for the betterment of us all. How else will wars be ended, will people be fed and housed, will children be educated, will great songs be written, will the edge of scientific knowledge be extended outward, will the ultimate frontier of space be explored?

For these events to happen, our resources must be mobilized and focused, and that leads me to at least a working definition of leadership: "Any action that focuses resources toward a beneficial end." Leadership is delivered through actions, through planning and implementing, through cajoling and rewarding, through persuasion and compromise, through detailing and demanding and driving ahead. The resources include the usual ones of people, money, time, and space, but also public opinion, media attention, legislative power, and a group's collective conscious— anything that can be mobilized for progress. Beneficial ends include higher profits, lower taxes, better health care, the elimination of war— an expansion in the total amount of love, beauty, happiness, or personal security experienced by each of us.

If your efforts lead, even faintly, to the above or similar ends, under this definition, you are a leader, and thus you will surely enjoy, and profit from, the viewpoints in this book.

David P. Campbell
Smith Richardson Senior Fellow,
The Center for Creative Leadership

Part One

LEADERSHIP: MYTH OR REALITY?

The term "leadership" is a relatively recent addition to the English language; it has been in use for fewer than 200 years. However, the root word "leader" has been in our literature for more than six centuries. Consequently, we have accumulated an impressive array of "facts" about leaders. But we still know very little about leadership itself.

Leadership, like happiness, success, or failure, means different things to different people. There are almost as many definitions of leadership as there are people who have attempted to describe the concept. We may not be able to adequately define it, we may fail at measuring it, but we seem to know good leadership when we see it. Leadership, one of the most observed and studied concepts in the modern world, is also one of the least understood of all social processes.

If there is a common thread running through the various approaches to the study of leadership, it is the aspect of social influence. However, attempts to clarify the process by which specific leaders in specific situations exert this influence have not been convincing. Profiles of leader behavior in its situational or organizational settings have little impact because of a dearth of commonly held assumptions. As a result, some scholars question whether the study of leadership is productive or worthwhile.

Society today seems to yearn for leadership to help counter economic and social crises, but candidates are often rejected because they cannot build a consensus among those waiting to be led. Many contemporary leaders find themselves impotent—their sphere of influence so severely constrained they cannot accomplish much, and the expectations of their followers are often unrealistic. The question becomes whether *anyone* can lead. The issues leaders must deal with are so complex that it seems no one can hope to do it all.

As problems and opportunities go unattended, the need for leadership intensifies. Yet, scholars have been unable to establish a theoretical groundwork, and the wide range of existing training programs contribute little to supplying our society with an actual leadership base. Is it realistic to think that we can find a working *concept* of leadership?

In "The Ambiguity of Leadership," (Chapter 1) Jeffrey Pfeffer questions whether leaders have any substantive influence on the performance of their organizations. Clearly, he contradicts the generally held notion that leaders are the major determinants of organizational success or failure. He argues that leaders are given too much credit for organizational success on the one hand, and too much blame when things go wrong on the other. Pfeffer suggests that we use organizationally irrelevant criteria to select our leaders, attributing causal relationships to social actions. In his opinion, it is this process of attributing leadership that should be the focus of study.

In Chapter 2, Michael Cohen and James March describe the position of college president as "Leadership in an Organized Anarchy" and posit that the ambiguities college presidents face are the same as those encountered by any formal leader. The authors identify four fundamental areas of ambiguity: purpose, power, experience, and success. These ambiguities are considered fundamental elements in most interpretations of leadership. The common metaphors of leadership and our tradition of personalizing history tend to confuse the issues of leadership by ignoring those basic ambiguities of leadership life, according to the authors. They conclude that the contributions of leaders may often be measured by their capacity for maintaining a creative interaction between foolishness and rationality; an idea that provides an interesting dilemma for those seeking a simple notion of leadership.

Edwin Hollander (Chapter 3) views leadership as a process of influence involving an ongoing transaction between leaders and followers in which there is always the potential for a crisis. In his article, "What Is the Crisis of Leadership?" he defines that crisis as a belief on the part of followers that they are not being treated fairly and are not being properly informed. The result is a psychological distance on the part of the followers—an absence of a "fair exchange"—that effectively robs leaders of their influence. Expectations are clearly a part of that "magic" that occurs between successful leaders and their followers.

In Chapter 4 Warren Bennis poses the question "Where Have All the Leaders Gone?" They are around, says Bennis, but it is difficult to recognize them. They're consulting, pleading, trotting about, temporizing, putting out fires, either avoiding or taking too much heat—and spending too much energy in the process. It is hard to recognize them because their authority and autonomy are being whittled away by forces over which they have little or no control. As a result, they resign or they burn out. Thus, at a time when the credibility of our leaders is at an all-time low, and when surviving leaders feel inhibited about exercising power, we badly need individuals who can lead. Bennis argues that the solution is not simple—leaders must develop vision, must be conceptualists with a sense of continuity and significance, willing to take risks. He insists that leaders must learn to be effective despite life's ambiguities and inconsistencies. The test of any leader is whether he or she can ride and direct the process of change and, by so doing, build new strengths in the process. If we agree with Bennis, we must decide whether current organizational structures are encouraging the development of these necessary behaviors.

In an attempt to summarize the conceptual nature of leadership, we turn to Michael Korda's "How to Be a Leader." Korda contends that we want leaders to be like us, but *better* than us. Because leaders must inspire us, they cannot always be pragmatists. Korda concludes that a leader is "the sum of us." But how, then, do we accurately describe "us"?

In "Leadership: A Challenge to Traditional Research Methods and Assumptions" (Chapter 6), Barbara Karmel suggests that researchers have failed to advance the understanding of leadership because they have employed inappropriate traditional methods and assumptions. She bemoans existing definitional confusion and the reliance on unproven, a priori assumptions for evaluating the dimensionality of the leadership concept. Karmel agrees with Pfeffer that the leadership concept is ambiguous, but she points out that this very ambiguity provides conceptual space to evolve a more fully developed understanding of leadership. To this end, she offers three propositions: (1) ambiguity in the definition of leadership is a consequence of the diversity of purposes for which research is conducted; (2) the underlying dimensionality of the leadership construct is dependent on these separate and diverse purposes; and (3) an improvement in leadership study depends on conceptual and empirical analysis of research purposes to provide a clearer view of the construct and to capture a wide array of exogenous variables presently ignored or treated as multiple contingencies.

The frustration of our initial inquiry is that we can come to no clear conclusion. Rather, our variety of perspectives only serves to highlight the need for each of us to realize that leadership as a concept is indeed characterized by ambiguity, inconsistency, and paradox. Leadership is an elusive concept, and the uncertainties associated with it are constantly challenged and enlivened by the realities of leadership's achievements. At this point, it is not important to embrace a standard definition; rather we must develop a conceptual framework within which we can address the leadership issues in the remainder of the book.

1

The Ambiguity of Leadership

JEFFREY PFEFFER

Leadership has for some time been a major topic in social and organizational psychology. Underlying much of this research has been the assumption that leadership is causally related to organizational performance. Through an analysis of leadership styles, behaviors, or characteristics (depending on the theoretical perspective chosen), the argument has been made that more effective leaders can be selected or trained or, alternatively, the situation can be configured to provide for enhanced leader and organizational effectiveness.

Three problems with emphasis on leadership as a concept can be posed: (a) ambiguity in definition and measurement of the concept itself; (b) the question of whether leadership has discernible effects on organizational outcomes; and (c) the selection process in succession to leadership positions, which frequently uses organizationally irrelevant criteria and which has implications for normative theories of leadership. The argument here is that leadership is of interest primarily as a phenomenological construct. Leaders serve as symbols for representing personal causation of social events. How and why are such attributions of personal effects made? Instead of focusing on leadership and its effects, how do people make inferences about and react to phenomena labelled as leadership (5)?

The Ambiguity of the Concept

While there have been many studies of leadership, the dimensions and definition of the concept remain unclear. To treat leadership as a

Reprinted by permission from *Academy of Management Review*, 2:1 (January 1977), pp. 104–112.

separate concept, it must be distinguished from other social influence phenomena. Hollander and Julian (24) and Bavelas (2) did not draw distinctions between leadership and other processes of social influence. A major point of the Hollander and Julian review was that leadership research might develop more rapidly if more general theories of social influence were incorporated. Calder (5) also argued that there is no unique content to the construct of leadership that is not subsumed under other, more general models of behavior.

Kochan, Schmidt, and DeCotiis (33) attempted to distinguish leadership from related concepts of authority and social power. In leadership, influence rights are voluntarily conferred. Power does not require goal compatibility—merely dependence—but leadership implies some congruence between the objectives of the leader and the led. These distinctions depend on the ability to distinguish voluntary from involuntary compliance and to assess goal compatibility. Goal statements may be retrospective inferences from action (46,53) and problems of distinguishing voluntary from involuntary compliance also exist (32). Apparently there are few meaningful distinctions between leadership and other concepts of social influence. Thus, an understanding of the phenomena subsumed under the rubric of leadership may not require the construct of leadership (5).

While there is some agreement that leadership is related to social influence, more disagreement concerns the basic dimensions of leader behavior. Some have argued that there are two tasks to be accomplished in groups—maintenance of the group and performance of some task or activity—and thus leader behavior might be described along these two dimensions (1, 6, 8, 25). The dimensions emerging from the Ohio State leadership studies—consideration and initiating structure—may be seen as similar to the two components of group maintenance and task accomplishment (18).

Other dimensions of leadership behavior have also been proposed (4). Day and Hamblin (10) analyzed leadership in terms of the closeness and punitiveness of the supervision. Several authors have conceptualized leadership behavior in terms of the authority and discretion subordinates are permitted (23, 36, 51). Fiedler (14) analyzed leadership in terms of the least-preferred-co-worker scale (LPC), but the meaning and behavioral attributes of this dimension of leadership behavior remain controversial.

The proliferation of dimensions is partly a function of research strategies frequently employed. Factor analysis on a large number of items describing behavior has frequently been used. This procedure tends to produce as many factors as the analyst decides to find, and permits the development of a large number of possible factor structures. The resultant factors must be named and further imprecision is introduced.

Deciding on a summative concept to represent a factor is inevitably a partly subjective process.

Literature assessing the effects of leadership tends to be equivocal. Sales (45) summarized leadership literature employing the authoritarian-democratic typology and concluded that effects on performance were small and inconsistent. Reviewing the literature on consideration and initiating structure dimensions, Korman (34) reported relatively small and inconsistent results, and Kerr and Schriesheim (30) reported more consistent effects of the two dimensions. Better results apparently emerge when moderating factors are taken into account, including subordinate personalities (50), and situational characteristics (23,51). Kerr, et al. (31) list many moderating effects grouped under the headings of subordinate considerations, supervisor considerations, and task considerations. Even if each set of considerations consisted of only one factor (which it does not), an attempt to account for the effects of leader behavior would necessitate considering four-way interactions. While social reality is complex and contingent, it seems desirable to attempt to find more parsimonious explanations for the phenomena under study.

The Effects of Leaders

Hall asked a basic question about leadership: is there any evidence on the magnitude of the effects of leadership (17, p. 248)? Surprisingly, he could find little evidence. Given the resources that have been spent studying, selecting, and training leaders, one might expect that the question of whether or not leaders matter would have been addressed earlier (12).

There are at least three reasons why it might be argued that the observed effects of leaders on organizational outcomes would be small. First, those obtaining leadership positions are selected, and perhaps only certain, limited styles of behavior may be chosen. Second, once in the leadership position, the discretion and behavior of the leader are constrained. And third, leaders can typically affect only a few of the variables that may impact organizational performance.

Homogeneity of Leaders

Persons are selected to leadership positions. As a consequence of this selection process, the range of behaviors or characteristics exhibited by leaders is reduced, making it more problematic to empirically discover an effect of leadership. There are many types of constraints on the selection process. The attraction literature suggests that there is a tendency for persons to like those they perceive as similar (3). In critical decisions such as the selections of persons for leadership positions, compatible styles of behavior probably will be chosen.

Selection of persons is also constrained by the internal system of influence in the organization. As Zald (56) noted, succession is a critical decision, affected by political influence and by environmental contingencies faced by the organization. As Thompson (49) noted, leaders may be selected for their capacity to deal with various organizational contingencies. In a study of characteristics of hospital administrators, Pfeffer and Salancik (42) found a relationship between the hospital's context and the characteristics and tenure of the administrators. To the extent that the contingencies and power distribution within the organization remain stable, the abilities and behaviors of those selected into leadership positions will also remain stable.

Finally, the selection of persons to leadership positions is affected by a self-selection process. Organizations and roles have images, providing information about their character. Persons are likely to select themselves into organizations and roles based upon their preferences for the dimensions of the organizational and role characteristics as perceived through these images. The self-selection of persons would tend to work along with organizational selection to limit the range of abilities and behaviors in a given organizational role.

Such selection processes would tend to increase homogeneity more within a single organization than across organizations. Yet many studies of leadership effect at the work group level have compared groups within a single organization. If there comes to be a widely shared, socially constructed definition of leadership behaviors or characteristics which guides the selection process, then leadership activity may come to be defined similarly in various organizations, leading to the selection of only those who match the constructed image of a leader.

Constraints on Leader Behavior

Analyses of leadership have frequently presumed that leadership style or leader behavior was an independent variable that could be selected or trained at will to conform to what research would find to be optimal. Even theorists who took a more contingent view of appropriate leadership behavior generally assumed that with proper training, appropriate behavior could be produced (51). Fiedler (13), noting how hard it was to change behavior, suggested changing the situational characteristics rather than the person, but this was an unusual suggestion in the context of prevailing literature which suggested that leadership style was something to be strategically selected according to the variables of the particular leadership theory.

But the leader is embedded in a social system, which constrains behavior. The leader has a role set (27), in which members have expectations for appropriate behavior and persons make efforts to modify the leader's behavior. Pressures to conform to the expectations of peers, subordinates, and superiors are all relevant in determining actual behavior.

Leaders, even in high-level positions, have unilateral control over fewer resources and fewer policies than might be expected. Investment decisions may require approval of others, while hiring and promotion decisions may be accomplished by committees. Leader behavior is constrained by both the demands of others in the role set and by organizationally prescribed limitations on the sphere of activity and influence.

External Factors

Many factors that may affect organizational performance are outside a leader's control, even if he or she were to have complete discretion over major areas of organizational decisions. For example, consider the executive in a construction firm. Costs are largely determined by operation of commodities and labor markets; and demand is largely affected by interest rates, availability of mortgage money, and economic conditions which are affected by governmental policies over which the executive has little control. School superintendents have little control over birth rates and community economic development, both of which profoundly affect school system budgets. While the leader may react to contingencies as they arise, or may be a better or worse forecaster, in accounting for variation in organizational outcomes, he or she may account for relatively little compared to external factors.

Second, the leader's success or failure may be partly due to circumstances unique to the organization but still outside his or her control. Leader positions in organizations vary in terms of the strength and position of the organization. The choice of a new executive does not fundamentally alter a market and financial position that has developed over years and affects the leader's ability to make strategic changes and the likelihood that the organization will do well or poorly. Organizations have relatively enduring strengths and weaknesses. The choice of a particular leader for a particular position has limited impact on these capabilities.

Empirical Evidence

Two studies have assessed the effects of leadership changes in major positions in organizations. Lieberson and O'Connor (35) examined 167 business firms in 13 industries over a 20 year period, allocating variance in sales, profits, and profit margins to one of four sources: year (general economic conditions), industry, company effects, and effects of changes in the top executive position. They concluded that compared to other factors, administration had a limited effect on organizational outcomes.

Using a similar analytical procedure, Salancik and Pfeffer (44) examined the effects of mayors on city budgets for 30 U.S. cities. Data on expenditures by budget category were collected for 1951–1968. Variance in amount and proportion of expenditures was apportioned to the year, the city, or the mayor. The mayoral effect was relatively small, with the city accounting for most of the variance, although the mayor effect was larger for expenditure categories that were not as directly connected to important interest groups. Salancik and Pfeffer argued that the effects of the mayor were limited both by absence of power to control many of the expenditures and tax sources, and by construction of policies in response to demands from interests in the environment.

If leadership is defined as a strictly interpersonal phenomenon, the relevance of these two studies for the issue of leadership effects becomes problematic. But such a conceptualization seems unduly restrictive, and is certainly inconsistent with Selznick's (47) conceptualization of leadership as strategic management and decision making. If one cannot observe differences when leaders change, then what does it matter who occupies the positions or how they behave?

Pfeffer and Salancik (41) investigated the extent to which behaviors selected by first-line supervisors were constrained by expectations of others in their role set. Variance in task and social behaviors could be accounted for by role-set expectations, with adherence to various demands made by role-set participants a function of similarity and relative power. Lowin and Craig (37) experimentally demonstrated that leader behavior was determined by the subordinate's own behavior. Both studies illustrate that leader behaviors are responses to the demands of the social context.

The effect of leadership may vary depending upon level in the organizational hierarchy, while the appropriate activities and behaviors may also vary with organizational level (26, 40). For the most part, empirical studies of leadership have dealt with first-line supervisors or leaders with relatively low organizational status (17). If leadership has any impact, it should be more evident at higher organizational levels or where there is more discretion in decisions and activities.

The Process of Selecting Leaders

Along with the suggestion that leadership may not account for much variance in organizational outcomes, it can be argued that merit or ability may not account for much variation in hiring and advancement of organizational personnel. These two ideas are related. If competence is hard to judge, or if leadership competence does not greatly affect organizational outcomes, then other, person-dependent criteria may be sufficient. Effective leadership styles may not predict career success when other variables such as social background are controlled.

Belief in the importance of leadership is frequently accompanied by belief that persons occupying leadership positions are selected and trained according to how well they can enhance the organization's performance. Belief in a leadership effect leads to development of a set of activities oriented toward enhancing leadership effectiveness. Simultaneously, persons managing their own careers are likely to place emphasis on activities and developing behaviors that will enhance their own leadership skills, assuming that such a strategy will facilitate advancement.

Research on the bases for hiring and promotion has been concentrated in examination of academic positions (e.g., 7, 19, 20). This is possibly the result of availability of relatively precise and unambiguous measures of performance, such as number of publications or citations. Evidence on criteria used in selecting and advancing personnel in industry is more indirect.

Studies have attempted to predict either the compensation or the attainment of general management positions of MBA students, using personality and other background information (21, 22, 54). There is some evidence that managerial success can be predicted by indicators of ability and motivation such as test scores and grades, but the amount of variance explained is typically quite small.

A second line of research has investigated characteristics and backgrounds of persons attaining leadership positions in major organizations in society. Domhoff (11), Mills (38), and Warner and Abbeglin (52) found a strong preponderance of persons with upper-class backgrounds occupying leadership positions. The implication of these findings is that studies of graduate success, including the success of MBA's, would explain more variance if the family background of the person were included.

A third line of inquiry uses a tracking model. The dynamic model developed is one in which access to elite universities is affected by social status (28) and, in turn, social status and attendance at elite universities affect later career outcomes (9, 43, 48, 55).

Unless one is willing to make the argument that attendance at elite universities or coming from an upper class background is perfectly correlated with merit, the evidence suggests that succession to leadership positions is not strictly based on meritocratic criteria. Such a conclusion is consistent with the inability of studies attempting to predict the success of MBA graduates to account for much variance, even when a variety of personality and ability factors are used.

Beliefs about the bases for social mobility are important for social stability. As long as persons believe that positions are allocated on meritocratic grounds, they are more likely to be satisfied with the social order and with their position in it. This satisfaction derives from the belief that occupational position results from application of fair and reasonable criteria, and that the opportunity exists for mobility if the person improves skills and performance.

If succession to leadership positions is determined by person-based criteria such as social origins or social connections (16), then efforts to enhance managerial effectiveness with the expectation that this will lead to career success divert attention from the processes of stratification actually operating within organizations. Leadership literature has been implicitly aimed at two audiences. Organizations were told how to become more effective, and persons were told what behaviors to acquire in order to become effective, and hence, advance in their careers. The possibility that neither organizational outcomes nor career success are related to leadership behaviors leaves leadership research facing issues of relevance and importance.

The Attribution of Leadership

Kelley conceptualized the layman as: "an applied scientist, that is, as a person concerned about applying his knowledge of causal relationships in order to *exercise control* of his world" (29, p. 2). Reviewing a series of studies dealing with the attributional process, he concluded that persons were not only interested in understanding their world correctly, but also in controlling it.

> The view here proposed is that attribution processes are to be understood not only as a means of providing the individual with a veridical view of his world, but as a means of encouraging and maintaining his effective exercise of control in that world (29, p. 22).

Controllable factors will have high salience as candidates for causal explanation, while a bias toward the more important causes may shift the attributional emphasis toward causes that are not controllable (29, p. 23). The study of attribution is a study of naive psychology—an examination of how persons make sense out of the events taking place around them.

If Kelley is correct that individuals will tend to develop attributions that give them a feeling of control, then emphasis on leadership may derive partially from a desire to believe in the effectiveness and importance of individual action, since individual action is more controllable than contextual variables. Lieberson and O'Connor (35) made essentially the same point in introducing their paper on the effects of top management changes on organizational performance. Given the desire for control and a feeling of personal effectiveness, organizational outcomes are more likely to be attributed to individual actions, regardless of their actual causes.

Leadership is attributed by observers. Social action has meaning only through a phenomenological process (46). The identification of certain organizational roles as leadership positions guides the construction of meaning in the direction of attributing effects to the actions of those positions. While Bavelas (2) argued that the functions of leadership, such as task accomplishment and group maintenance, are shared throughout the group, this fact provides no simple and potentially controllable focus for attributing causality. Rather, the identification of leadership positions provides a simpler and more readily changeable model of reality. When causality is lodged in one or a few persons rather than being a function of a complex set of interactions among all group members, changes can be made by replacing or influencing the occupant of the leadership position. Causes of organizational actions are readily identified in this simple causal structure.

Even if, empirically, leadership has little effect, and even if succession to leadership positions is not predicated on ability or performance, the belief in leadership effects and meritocratic succession provides a simple causal framework and a justification for the structure of the social collectivity. More importantly, the beliefs interpret social actions in terms that indicate potential for effective individual intervention or control. The personification of social causality serves too many uses to be easily overcome. Whether or not leader behavior actually influences performance or effectiveness, it is important because people believe it does.

One consequence of the attribution of causality to leaders and leadership is that leaders come to be symbols. Mintzberg (39), in his discussion of the roles of managers, wrote of the symbolic role, but more in terms of attendance at formal events and formally representing the organization. The symbolic role of leadership is more important than implied in such a description. The leader as a symbol provides a target for action when difficulties occur, serving as a scapegoat when things go wrong. Gamson and Scotch (15) noted that in baseball, the firing of the manager served a scapegoating purpose. One cannot fire the whole team, yet when performance is poor, something must be done. The firing of the manager conveys to the world and to the actors involved that success is the result of personal actions, and that steps can and will be taken to enhance organizational performance.

The attribution of causality to leadership may be reinforced by organizational actions, such as the inauguration process, the choice process, and providing the leader with symbols and ceremony. If leaders are chosen by using a random number table, persons are less likely to believe in their effects than if there is an elaborate search or selection process followed by an elaborate ceremony signifying the changing of control, and if the leader then has a variety of perquisites and symbols that distinguish him or her from the rest of the organization. Construction of the importance of leadership in a given social context is the outcome of various social processes, which can be empirically examined.

Since belief in the leadership effect provides a feeling of personal control, one might argue that efforts to increase the attribution of causality to leaders would occur more when it is more necessary and more problematic to attribute causality to controllable factors. Such an argument would lead to the hypothesis that the more the *context* actually effects organizational outcomes, the more efforts will be made to ensure attribution to *leadership*. When leaders really do have effects, it is less necessary to engage in rituals indicating their effects. Such rituals are more likely when there is uncertainty and unpredictability associated with the organization's operations. This results both from the desire to feel control in uncertain situations and from the fact that in ambiguous contexts, it is easier to attribute consequences to leadership without facing possible disconfirmation.

The leader is, in part, an actor. Through statements and actions, the leader attempts to reinforce the operation of an attribution process which tends to vest causality in that position in the social structure. Successful leaders, as perceived by members of the social system, are those who can separate themselves from organizational failures and associate themselves with organizational successes. Since the meaning of action is socially constructed, this involves manipulation of symbols to reinforce the desired process of attribution. For instance, if a manager knows that business in his or her division is about to improve because of the economic cycle, the leader may, nevertheless, write recommendations and undertake actions and changes that are highly visible and that will tend to identify his or her behavior closely with the division. A manager who perceives impending failure will attempt to associate the division and its policies and decisions with others, particularly persons in higher organizational positions, and to disassociate himself or herself from the division's performance, occasionally even transferring or moving to another organization.

Conclusion

The theme of this article has been that analysis of leadership and leadership processes must be contingent on the intent of the researcher. If the interest is in understanding the causality of social phenomena as realiably and accurately as possible, then the concept of leadership may be a poor place to begin. The issue of the effects of leadership is open to question. But examination of situational variables that accompany more or less leadership effect is a worthwhile task.

The more phenomenological analysis of leadership directs attention to the process by which social causality is attributed, and focuses on the distinction between causality as perceived by group members and causality as assessed by an outside observer. Leadership is associated with a set of myths reinforcing a social construction of meaning which legitimates leadership role occupants, provides belief in potential mobility for those not in leadership roles, and attributes social causality to leadership roles, thereby providing a belief in the effectiveness of individual control. In analyzing leadership, this mythology and the process by which such mythology is created and supported should be separated from analysis of leadership as a social influence process, operating within constraints.

References

1. Bales, R. F. *Interaction Process Analysis: A Method for the Study of Small Groups* (Reading, Mass.: Addison-Wesley, 1950).
2. Bavelas, Alex. "Leadership: Man and Function," *Administrative Science Quarterly*, Vol. 4 (1960), 491–498.
3. Berscheid, Ellen, and Elaine Walster. *Interpersonal Attraction* (Reading, Mass.: Addison-Wesley, 1969).
4. Bowers, David G., and Stanley E. Seashore. "Predicting Organizational Effectiveness with a Four-Factor Theory of Leadership," *Administrative Science Quarterly*, Vol. 11 (1966), 238–263.
5. Calder, Bobby J. "An Attribution Theory of Leadership," in B. Staw and G. Salancik (Eds.), *New Directions in Organizational Behavior* (Chicago: St. Clair Press, 1976), in press.
6. Cartwright, Dorwin C., and Alvin Zander. *Group Dynamics: Research and Theory*, 3rd ed. (Evanston, Ill.: Row, Peterson, 1960).
7. Cole, Jonathan R., and Stephen Cole. *Social Stratification in Science* (Chicago: University of Chicago Press, 1973).
8. Collins, Barry E., and Harold Guetzkow. *A Social Psychology of Group Processes for Decision-Making* (New York: Wiley, 1964).
9. Collins, Randall. "Functional and Conflict Theories of Stratification," *American Sociological Review*, Vol. 36 (1971), 1002–1019.

10. Day, R. C., and R. L. Hamblin. "Some Effects of Close and Punitive Styles of Supervision," *American Journal of Sociology*, Vol. 69 (1964), 499–510.
11. Domhoff, G. William. *Who Rules America?* (Englewood Cliffs, N.J.: Prentice-Hall, 1967).
12. Dubin, Robert. "Supervision and Productivity: Empirical Findings and Theoretical Considerations," in R. Dubin, G. C. Homans, F. C. Mann, and D. C. Miller (Eds.), *Leadership and Productivity* (San Francisco: Chandler Publishing Co., 1965), pp. 1–50.
13. Fiedler, Fred E. "Engineering the Job to Fit the Manager," *Harvard Business Review*, Vol. 43 (1965), 115–122.
14. Fiedler, Fred E. *A Theory of Leadership Effectiveness* (New York: McGraw-Hill, 1967).
15. Gamson, William A., and Norman A. Scotch. "Scapegoating in Baseball," *American Journal of Sociology*, Vol. 70 (1964), 69–72.
16. Granovetter, Mark. *Getting a Job* (Cambridge, Mass.: Harvard University Press, 1974).
17. Hall, Richard H. *Organizations: Structure and Process* (Englewood Cliffs, N.J.: Prentice-Hall, 1972).
18. Halpin, A. W., and J. Winer. "A Factorial Study of the Leader Behavior Description Questionnaire," in R. M. Stogdill and A. E. Coons (Eds.), *Leader Behavior: Its Description and Measurement* (Columbus, Ohio: Bureau of Business Research, Ohio State University, 1957), pp. 39–51.
19. Hargens, L. L. "Patterns of Mobility of New Ph.D.'s Among American Academic Institutions," *Sociology of Education*, Vol. 42 (1969), 18–37.
20. Hargens, L. L., and W. O. Hagstrom. "Sponsored and Contest Mobility of American Academic Scientists," *Sociology of Education*, Vol. 40 (1967), 24–38.
21. Harrell, Thomas W. "High Earning MBA's," *Personnel Psychology*, Vol. 25 (1972), 523–530.
22. Harrell, Thomas W., and Margaret S. Harrell. "Predictors of Management Success." *Stanford University Graduate School of Business, Technical Report No. 3 to the Office of Naval Research.*
23. Heller, Frank, and Gary Yukl. "Participation, Managerial Decision-Making, and Situational Variables," *Organizational Behavior and Human Performance*, Vol. 4 (1969), 227–241.
24. Hollander, Edwin P., and James W. Julian.. "Contemporary Trends in the Analysis of Leadership Processes," *Psychological Bulletin*, Vol. 71 (1969), 387–397.
25. House, Robert J. "A Path Goal Theory of Leader Effectiveness," *Administrative Science Quarterly*, Vol. 16 (1971), 321–338.
26. Hunt, J. G. "Leadership-Style Effects at Two Managerial Levels in a Simulated Organization," *Administrative Science Quarterly*, Vol. 16 (1971), 476–485.
27. Kahn, R. L., D. M. Wolfe, R. P. Quinn, and J. D. Snoek. *Organizational Stress: Studies in Role Conflict and Ambiguity* (New York: Wiley, 1964).
28. Karabel, J., and A. W. Astin, "Social Class, Academic Ability, and College 'Quality'," *Social Forces*, Vol. 53 (1975), 381–398.

29. Kelley, Harold H. *Attribution in Social Interaction* (Morristown, N.J.: General Learning Press, 1971).
30. Kerr, Steven, and Chester Schriesheim. "Consideration, Initiating Structure and Organizational Criteria—An Update of Korman's 1966 Review," *Personnel Psychology*, Vol. 27 (1974), 555–568.
31. Kerr, S., C. Schriesheim, C. J. Murphy, and R. M. Stogdill. "Toward A Contingency Theory of Leadership Based Upon the Consideration and Initiating Structure Literature," *Organizational Behavior and Human Performance*, Vol. 12 (1974), 62–82.
32. Kiesler, C., and S. Kiesler. *Conformity* (Reading, Mass.: Addison-Wesley, 1969).
33. Kochan, T. A., S. M. Schmidt, and T. A. DeCotiis. "Superior-Subordinate Relations: Leadership and Headship," *Human Relations*, Vol. 28 (1975), 279–294.
34. Korman, A. K. "Consideration, Initiating Structure, and Organizational Criteria—A Review," *Personnel Psychology*, Vol. 19 (1966), 349–362.
35. Lieberson, Stanley, and James F. O'Connor. "Leadership and Organizational Performance: A Study of Large Corporations," *American Sociological Review*, Vol. 37 (1972), 117–130.
36. Lippitt, Ronald. "An Experimental Study of the Effect of Democratic and Authoritarian Group Atmospheres," *University of Iowa Studies in Child Welfare*, Vol. 16 (1940), 43–195.
37. Lowin, A., and J. R. Craig. "The Influence of Level of Performance on Managerial Style: An Experimental Object-Lesson in the Ambiguity of Correlational Data," *Organizational Behavior and Human Performance*, Vol. 3 (1968), 440–458.
38. Mills, C. Wright. "The American Business Elite: A Collective Portrait," in C. W. Mills, *Power, Politics, and People* (New York: Oxford University Press, 1963), pp. 110–139.
39. Mintzberg, Henry. *The Nature of Managerial Work* (New York: Harper and Row, 1973).
40. Nealey, Stanley M., and Milton R. Blood. "Leadership Performance of Nursing Supervisors at Two Organizational Levels," *Journal of Applied Psychology*, Vol. 52 (1968), 414–442.
41. Pfeffer, Jeffrey, and Gerald R. Salancik. "Determinants of Supervisory Behavior: A Role Set Analysis," *Human Relations*, Vol. 28 (1975), 139–154.
42. Pfeffer, Jeffrey, and Gerald R. Salancik. "Organizational Context and the Characteristics and Tenure of Hospital Administrators," *Academy of Management Journal*, Vol. 20 (1977), in press.
43. Reed, R. H., and H. P. Miller. "Some Determinants of the Variation in Earnings for College Men," *Journal of Human Resources*, Vol. 5 (1970), 117–190.
44. Salancik, Gerald R., and Jeffrey Pfeffer. "Constraints on Administrator Discretion: The Limited Influence of Mayors on City Budgets," *Urban Affairs Quarterly*, in press.
45. Sales, Stephen M. "Supervisory Style and Productivity: Review and Theory," *Personnel Psychology*, Vol. 19 (1966), 275–286.

46. Schutz, Alfred. *The Phenomenology of the Social World* (Evanston, Ill.: Northwestern University Press, 1967).
47. Selznick, P. *Leadership in Administration* (Evanston, Ill.: Row, Peterson, 1957).
48. Spaeth, J. L., and A. M. Greeley, *Recent Alumni and Higher Education* (New York: McGraw-Hill, 1970).
49. Thompson, James D. *Organizations in Action* (New York: McGraw-Hill, 1967).
50. Vroom, Victor H. "Some Personality Determinants of the Effects of Participation," *Journal of Abnormal and Social Pscyhology*, Vol. 59 (1959), 322–327.
51. Vroom, Victor H., and Phillip W. Yetton. *Leadership and Decision-Making* (Pittsburgh: University of Pittsburgh Press, 1973).
52. Warner, W. L., and J. C. Abbeglin. *Big Business Leaders in America* (New York: Harper and Brothers, 1955).
53. Weick, Karl E. *The Social Psychology of Organizing* (Reading, Mass.: Addison-Wesley, 1969).
54. Weinstein, Alan G., and V. Srinivasan. "Predicting Managerial Success of Master of Business Administration (MBA) Graduates," *Journal of Applied Psychology*, Vol. 59 (1974), 207–212.
55. Wolfle, Dael. *The Uses of Talent* (Princeton: Princeton University Press, 1971).
56. Zald, Mayer N. "Who Shall Rule? A Political Analysis of Succession in a Large Welfare Organization," *Pacific Sociological Review*, Vol. 8 (1965), 52–60.

2

Leadership in an
Organized Anarchy

MICHAEL D. COHEN
JAMES G. MARCH

The college president faces four fundamental ambiguities. The first is the ambiguity of *purpose*. In what terms can action be justified? What are the goals of the organization? The second is the ambiguity of *power*. How powerful is the president? What can he accomplish? The third is the ambiguity of *experience*. What is to be learned from the events of the presidency? How does the president make inferences about his experience? The fourth is the ambiguity of *success*. When is a president successful? How does he assess his pleasures?

These ambiguities are fundamental to college presidents because they strike at the heart of the usual interpretations of leadership. When purpose is ambiguous, ordinary theories of decision making and intelligence become problematic. When power is ambiguous, ordinary theories of social order and control become problematic. When experience is ambiguous, ordinary theories of learning and adaptation become problematic. When success is ambiguous, ordinary theories of motivation and personal pleasure become problematic.

——— □ ———

Almost any educated person can deliver a lecture entitled "The Goals of the University." Almost no one will listen to the lecture voluntarily. For the most part, such lectures and their companion essays are well-intentioned exercises in social rhetoric, with little operational content.

Abridged from "Leadership in an Organized Anarchy" (pp. 195–234) from *Leadership and Ambiguity* by Michael D. Cohen and James G. March, 1974. Reprinted by permission of the Carnegie Commission on Higher Education.

Efforts to generate normative statements of the goals of a university tend to produce goals that are either meaningless or dubious. They fail one or more of the following reasonable tests. First, is the goal clear? Can one define some specific procedure for measuring the degree of goal achievement? Second, is it problematic? Is there some possibility that the organization will accomplish the goal? Is there some chance that it will fail? Third, is is accepted? Do most significant groups in the university agree on the goal statement? For the most part, the level of generality that facilitates acceptance destroys the problematic nature or clarity of the goal. The level of specificity that permits measurement destroys acceptance.

Efforts to infer the "real" objectives of a university by observing university behavior tend to be unsuccessful. They fail one or more of the following reasonable tests. First, is the goal uniquely consistent with behavior? Does the imputed goal produce the observed behavior and is it the only goal that does? Second, is it stable? Does the goal imputed from past behavior reliably predict future behavior? Although it is often possible to devise a statement of the goals of a university by some form of revealed preference test of past actions, such goal statements have poor predictive power.

The difficulties in imputing goals from behavior are not unique to universities. Experience with the complications is shared by revealed preference theorists in economics and psychology, radical critics of society, and functionalist students of social institutions. The search for a consistent explanation of human social behavior through a model of rational intent and an imputation of intent from action has had some successes. But there is no sign that the university is one of the successes, or very likely to become one.

Efforts to specify a set of consciously shared, consistent objectives within a university or to infer such a set of objectives from the activities or actions of the university have regularly revealed signs of inconsistency. To expose inconsistencies is not to resolve them, however. There are only modest signs that universities or other organized anarchies respond to a revelation of ambiguity of purpose by reducing the ambiguity. These are organizational systems without clear objectives; and the processes by which their objectives are established and legitimized are not extraordinarily sensitive to inconsistency. In fact, for many purposes the ambiguity of purpose is produced by our insistence on treating purpose as a necessary property of a good university. The strains arise from trying to impose a model of action as flowing from intent on organizations that act in another way.

College presidents live within a normative context that presumes purpose and within an organizational context that denies it. They serve on commissions to define and redefine the objectives of higher education. They organize convocations to examine the goals of the college. They accept the presumption that intelligent leadership presupposes the rational pursuit of goals. Simultaneously, they are aware that the process of choice in the college depends little on statements of shared direction. They recognize the flow of actions as an ecology of games (Long, 1958), each with its own rules. They accept the observation that the world is not like the model.

———— □ ————

Power is a simple idea, pervasive in its appeal to observers of social events. Like *intelligence* or *motivation* or *utility*, however, it tends to be misleadingly simple and prone to tautology. A person has power if he gets things done; if he has power, he can get things done.

As students of social power have long observed, such a view of power has limited usefulness. Two of the things the simple view produces are an endless and largely fruitless search for the person who has "the real power" in the university, and an equally futile pursuit of the organizational locale "where the decision is *really* made." So profound is the acceptance of the power model that students of organizations who suggest the model is wrong are sometimes viewed as part of the plot to conceal "the real power" and "the true locus of decision." In that particular logic the reality of the simple power model is demonstrated by its inadequacy.

As a shorthand casual expression for variations in the potential of different positions in the organization, *power* has some utility. The college president has more potential for moving the college than most people, probably more potential than any one other person. Nevertheless, presidents discover that they have less power than is believed, that their power to accomplish things depends heavily on what they want to accomplish, that the use of formal authority is limited by other formal authority, that the acceptance of authority is not automatic, that the necessary details of organizational life confuse power (which is somewhat different from diffusing it), and that their colleagues seem to delight in complaining simultaneously about presidential weakness and presidential willfulness.

The ambiguity of power, like the ambiguity of purpose, is focused on the president. Presidents share in and contribute to the confusion. They enjoy the perquisites and prestige of the office. They enjoy its excitement, at least when things go well. They announce important events. They appear at important symbolic functions. They report to the people. They accept and thrive on their own importance. It would be remarkable if they did not. Presidents even occasionally recite that "the buck stops here" with a finality that suggests the cliché is an observation about power and authority rather than a proclamation of administrative style and ideology.

At the same time, presidents solicit an understanding of the limits to their control. They regret the tendency of students, legislators, and community leaders to assume that a president has the power to do whatever he chooses simply because he is president. They plead the countervailing power of other groups in the college or the notable complexities of causality in large organizations.

The combination is likely to lead to popular impressions of strong presidents during good times and weak presidents during bad times. Persons who are primarily exposed to the symbolic presidency (e.g., outsiders) will tend to exaggerate the power of the president. Those people who have tried to accomplish something in the institution with presidential support (e.g., educational reformers) will tend to underestimate presidential power or presidential will.

The confusion disturbs the president, but it also serves him. Ambiguity of power leads to a parallel ambiguity of responsibility. The allocation of credit and blame for the events of organizational life becomes—as it often does in political and social systems—a matter for argument. The "facts" of responsibility are badly confounded by the confusions of anarchy; and the conventional myth of hierarchical executive responsibility is undermined by the countermyth of the nonhierarchical nature of colleges and universities. Presidents negotiate with their audiences on the interpretations of their power. As a result, during the recent years of campus troubles, many college presidents sought to emphasize the limitations of presidential control. During the more glorious days of conspicuous success, they solicited a recognition of their responsibility for events.

The process does not involve presidents alone, of course. The social validation of responsibility involves all the participants: faculty, trustees, students, parents, community leaders, government. Presidents seek to write their histories in the use of power as part of a chorus of history writers, each with his own reasons for preferring a somewhat different interpretation of "Who has the Power?"

College presidents attempt to learn from their experience. They observe the consequences of actions and infer the structure of the world from those observations. They use the resulting inferences in attempts to improve their future actions.

Consider the following very simple learning paradigm:

1. At a certain point in time a president is presented with a set of well-defined, discrete action alternatives.
2. At any point in time he has a certain probability of choosing any particular alternative (and a certainty of choosing one of them).
3. The president observes the outcome that apparently follows his choice and assesses the outcome in terms of his goals.
4. If the outcome is consistent with his goals, the president increases his probability of choosing that alternative in the future; if not, he decreases the probability.

Although actual presidential learning certainly involves more complicated inferences, such a paradigm captures much of the ordinary adaptation of an intelligent man to the information gained from experience.

The process produces considerable learning. The subjective experience is one of adapting from experience and improving behavior on the basis of feedback. If the world with which the president is dealing is relatively simple and relatively stable, and if his experience is relatively frequent, he can expect to improve over time (assuming he has some appropriate criterion for testing the consistency of outcomes with goals). As we have suggested earlier, however, the world in which the president lives has two conspicuous properties that make experience ambiguous even where goals are clear. First, the world is relatively complex. Outcomes depend heavily on factors other than the president's action. These factors are uncontrolled and, in large part, unobserved. Second, relative to the rate at which the president gathers experimental data, the world changes rapidly. These properties produce considerable potential for false learning.

We can illustrate the phenomenon by taking a familiar instance of learning in the realm of personnel policies. Suppose that a manager reviews his subordinates annually and considers what to do with those who are doing poorly. He has two choices: he can replace an employee whose performance is low, or he can keep him in the job and try to work with him to obtain improvement. He chooses which employees to replace and which to keep in the job on the basis of his judgment about their capacities to respond to different treatments. Now suppose that, in fact, there are no differences among the employees. Observed variations in performance are due entirely to random fluctuations. What would the manager "learn" in such a situation?

He would learn how smart he was. He would discover that his judgments about whom to keep and whom to replace were quite good. Replacements will generally perform better than the men they replaced; those men who are kept in the job will generally improve in their performance. If for some reason he starts out being relatively "humane" and refuses to replace anyone, he will discover that the best managerial strategy is to work to improve existing employees. If he starts out with a heavy hand and replaces everyone, he will learn that being tough is a good idea. If he replaces some and works with others, he will learn that the essence of personnel management is judgment about the worker.

Although we know that in the hypothetical situation it makes no difference what a manager does, he will experience some subjective learning that is direct and compelling. He will come to believe that he understands the situation and has mastered it. If we were to suggest to the manager that he might be a victim of superstitious learning, he would find it difficult to believe. Everything in his environment tells him that he understands the world, even though his understanding is spurious.

It is not necessary to assume that the world is strictly random to produce substantially the same effect. Whenever the rate of experience is modest relative to the complexity of the phenomena and the rate of change in the phenomena, the interpretation made of experience will tend to be more persuasive subjectively than it should be. In such a world, experience is not a good teacher. Although the outcomes stemming from the various learned strategies in the personnel management example will be no worse because of a belief in the reality of the learning, the degree of confidence a manager comes to have in his theory of the world is erroneously high.

College presidents probably have greater confidence in their interpretations of college life, college administration, and their general environment than is warranted. The inferences they have made from experience are likely to be wrong. Their confidence in their learning is likely to have been reinforced by the social support they receive from the people around them and by social expectations about the presidential role. As a result, they tend to be unaware of the extent to which the ambiguities they feel with respect to purpose and power are matched by similar ambiguities with respect to the meaning of the ordinary events of presidential life.

——— □ ———

Administrative success is generally recognized in one of two ways. First, by promotion: An administrator knows that he has been successful by virtue of a promotion to a better job. He assesses his success on the current job by the opportunities he has or expects to have to leave it. Second, by widely accepted, operational measures of organizational output: A business executive values his own performance in terms of a profit-and-loss statement of his operations.

Problems with these indicators of success are generic to high-level administrative positions. Offers of promotion become less likely as the job improves and the administrator's age advances. The criteria by which success is judged become less precise in measurement, less stable over time, and less widely shared. The administrator discovers that a wide assortment of factors outside his control are capable of overwhelming the impact of any actions he may take.

In the case of the college president all three problems are accentuated. As we have seen earlier, few college presidents are promoted out of the presidency. There are job offers, and most presidents ultimately accept one; but the best opportunity the typical president can expect is an invitation to accept a decent version of administrative semiretirement. The criteria of success in academic administration are sometimes moderately clear (e.g., growth, quiet on campus, improvement in the quality of students and faculty), but the relatively precise measures of college health tend neither to be stable over time nor to be critically sensitive to presidential action.

An argument can be made, of course, that the college president should be accustomed to the ambiguity of success. His new position is not, in this respect, so strikingly different from the positions he has held previously. His probable perspective is different, however. Success has not previously been subjectively ambiguous to him. He has been a success. He has been promoted relatively rapidly. He and his associates are inclined to attribute his past successes to a combination of administrative savoir-faire, interpersonal style, and political sagacity. He has experienced those successes as the lawful consequence of his actions. Honest modesty on the part of a president does not conceal a certain awareness of his own ability. A president comes to his office having learned that he is successful and that he enjoys success.

The momentum of promotion will not sustain him in the presidency. Although, as we have seen, a fair number of presidents anticipate moving from their present job to another, better presidency, the prospects are not nearly as good as the hopes. The ambiguities of purpose, power, and experience conspire to render success and failure equally obscure. The validation of success is unreliable. Not only can a president not assure himself that he will be able to lead the college in the directions in which others might believe, he also has no assurance that the same criteria will be applied tomorrow. What happens today will tend to be rationalized tomorrow as what was desired. What happens today will have some relation to what was desired yesterday. Outcomes do flow in part from goals. But goals flow from outcomes as well, and both goals and outcomes also move independently.

The result is that the president is a bit like the driver of a skidding automobile. The marginal judgments he makes, his skill, and his luck may possibly make some difference to the survival prospects for his riders. As a result, his responsibilities are heavy. But whether he is convicted of manslaughter or receives a medal for heroism is largely outside his control.

One basic response to the ambiguities of success is to find pleasure in the process of presidential life. A reasonable man will seek reminders of his relevance and success. Where those reminders are hard to find in terms of socially validated outcomes unambiguously due to one's actions, they may be sought in the interactions of organizational life. George Reedy (1970) made a similar observation about a different presidency: "Those who seek to lighten the burdens of the presidency by easing the workload do no occupant of that office a favor. The 'workload'—especially the ceremonial work load—are the only events of a president's day which make life endurable."

———— □ ————

The ambiguities that college presidents face describe the life of any formal leader of any organized anarchy. The metaphors of leadership and our traditions of personalizing history (even the minor histories of collegiate institutions) confuse the issues of leadership by ignoring the basic ambiguity of leadership life. We require a plausible basic perspective for the leader of a loosely coupled, ambiguous organization.

If we knew more about the normative theory of acting before thinking, we could say more intelligent things about the functions of management and leadership when organizations or societies do not know what they are doing. Consider, for example, the following general implications.

First, we need to reexamine the functions of management decision making. One of the primary ways in which the goals of an organization are developed is by interpreting the decisions it makes, and one feature of good managerial decisions is that they lead to the development of more interesting value premises for the organization. As a result, decisions should not be seen as flowing directly or strictly from a preexistent set of objectives. College presidents who make decisions might well view that function somewhat less as a process of deduction or a process of political negotiation, and somewhat more as a process of gently upsetting preconceptions of what the organization is doing.

Second, we need a modified view of planning. Planning can often be more effective as an interpretation of past decisions than as a program for future ones. It can be used as a part of the efforts of the organization to develop a new consistent theory of itself that incorporates the mix of recent actions into a moderately comprehensive structure of goals. Procedures for interpreting the meaning of most past events are familiar to the memoirs of retired generals, prime ministers, business leaders, and movie stars. They suffer from the company they keep. In an organization that wants to continue to develop new objectives, a manager needs to be tolerant of the idea that he will discover the meaning of yesterday's action in the experiences and interpretations of today.

Third, we need to reconsider evaluation. As nearly as we can determine, there is nothing in a formal theory of evaluation that requires that criteria be specified in advance. In particular, the evaluation of social experiments need not be in terms of the degree to which they have fulfilled our prior expectations. Rather we can examine what they did in terms of what we now believe to be important. The prior specification of criteria and the prior specification of evaluational procedures that depend on such criteria are common presumptions in contemporary social policy making. They are presumptions that inhibit the serendipitous discovery of new criteria. Experience should be used explicitly as an occasion for evaluating our values as well as our actions.

Fourth, we need a reconsideration of social accountability. Individual preferences and social action need to be consistent in some way. But the process of pursuing consistency is one in which both the preferences and the actions change over time. Imagination in social policy formation involves systematically adapting to and influencing preference. It would be unfortunate if our theories of social action encouraged leaders to ignore their responsibilities for anticipating public preferences through action and for providing social experiences that modify individual expectations.

Fifth, we need to accept playfulness in social organizations. The design of organizations should attend to the problems of maintaining both playfulness and reason as aspects of intelligent choice. Since much of the literature on social design is concerned with strengthening the rationality of decision making, managers are likely to overlook the importance of play. This is partly a matter of making the individuals within an organization more playful by encouraging the attitudes and skills of inconsistency. It is also a matter of making organizational structure and organizational procedures more playful. Organizations can be playful even when the participants in them are not. The managerial devices for maintaining consistency can be varied. We encourage organizational play by insisting on some temporary relief from control, coordination, and communication.

———— □ ————

Contemporary theories of decision making and the technology of reason have considerably strengthened our capabilities for effective social action. The conversion of the simple ideas of choice into an extensive technology is a major achievement. It is, however, an achievement that has reinforced some biases in the underlying models of choice in individuals and groups. In particular, it has reinforced the uncritical acceptance of a static interpretation of human goals.

There is little magic in the world, and foolishness in people and organizations is one of the many things that fail to produce miracles. Under certain conditions, it is one of several ways in which some of the problems of our current theories of intelligence can be overcome. It may be a good way, for it preserves the virtues of consistency while stimulating change. If we had a good technology of foolishness, it might (in combination with the technology of reason) help in a small way to develop the unusual combinations of attitudes and behaviors that describe the interesting societies of the world. The contribution of a college president may often be measured by his capability for sustaining that creative interaction of foolishness and rationality.

References

Adams, Jesse E., and Herman Lee Donovan: "The Administration and Organization in American Universities," *Peabody Journal of Education*, vol. 22, May 1945.

Allison, Graham T.: *Essence of Decision: Explaining the Cuban Missile Crisis*, Little, Brown and Company, Boston, 1971.

Baldridge, J. Victor (ed.): *Academic Governance: Research on Institutional Politics and Decision Making*, McCutchan Publishing Corporation, Berkeley, 1971.

Baldridge, J. Victor: *Power and Conflict in the University*, John Wiley & Sons, Inc., New York, 1971.

Beard, John L.: "A Study of the Duties Performed by College Administrators," Ph.D. dissertation in education, University of Texas at Austin, June 1948.

Bolman, Frederick de W.: *How College Presidents Are Chosen*, American Council on Education, Washington, D.C., 1965.

Bryan, William Lowe: "The Share of Faculty in Administration and Government," in Guy P. Benton (ed.), *Transactions and Proceedings of the National Association of State Universities in the United States*, Free Press Printing Company, Burlington, Vt., 1914.

Carnegie, Dale: *How to Win Friends and Influence People*, Simon and Schuster, New York, 1936.

Cohen, Michael D., James G. March, and Johan P. Olsen: "A Garbage Can Model of Organizational Choice," *Administrative Science Quarterly*, vol. 17, no. 1, pp. 1–25, March 1972.

Cyert, Richard M., and James G. March: *A Behavioral Theory of the Firm*, Prentice-Hall, Inc., Englewood Cliffs, N.J., 1963.

Demerath, Nicholas J., Richard W. Stephens, and R. Robb Taylor: *Power, Presidents, and Professors*, Basic Books, Inc., Publishers, New York, 1967.

Donovan, Herman Lee: "The State University Presidency: 1955," in C. P. McCurdy, Jr. (ed.) *Transactions and Proceedings of the National Association of State*

Universities in the United States, National Association of State Universities, Washington, D.C., 1955.

Faculty Efforts and Output Study, University of California, Berkeley, 1970.

Ferrari, Michael R.: *Profiles of American College Presidents,* Michigan State University Business School, East Lansing, 1970.

Foote, Caleb, Mayer, Henry, and Associates: *The Culture of the University— Governance and Education,* Jossey-Bass, Inc., San Francisco, 1968.

Frey, Frederick W.: "Comment: On Issues and Nonissues in the Study of Power," *American Political Science Review,* vol. 65, pp. 1081–1101, 1971.

Green, Paul E., and Frank J. Carmone: *Multidimensional Scaling and Related Techniques in Marketing Analysis,* Allyn and Unwin, Boston, 1970.

Hayes, Denis A., and James G. March: "The Normative Problems of University Governance," Assembly on University Goals and Governance, Stanford University, 1970. (Mimeographed.)

Hemphill, John K., and Herbert J. Walberg: *An Empirical Study of the College and University Presidents in the State of New York,* Regents Advisory Committee on Educational Leadership, Albany, 1966.

Hodgkinson, Harold L., and Richard L. Meeth (eds.): *Power and Authority* (Transformation of Campus Governance . . . Conference Papers) Jossey-Bass, Inc., San Francisco, 1971.

Hodgkinson, Harold L.: *Institutions in Transition: A Profile of Change in Higher Education,* McGraw-Hill Book Company, New York, 1971.

Iklé, Fred C.: *How Nations Negotiate,* Harper & Row, Publishers, Incorporated, New York, 1964.

Ingraham, Mark H.: *The Mirror of Brass: The Compensation and Working Conditions of College and University Administrators,* University of Wisconsin Press, Madison, 1968.

"The Invitational Seminar on Restructuring College and University Organization and Governance," *The Journal of Higher Education,* vol. 42, no. 6, pp. 421–542, June 1971.

Kerr, Clark: "Governance and Functions," *Daedalus,* vol. 99, no. 1, pp. 108–121, Winter 1970.

Kerr, Clark: "Presidential Discontent," in David C. Nichols (ed.), *Perspectives on Campus Tensions,* papers prepared for the Special Committee on Campus Tensions, American Council on Education, Washington, D.C., September 1970.

Kerr, Clark: *The Uses of the University,* Harvard University Press, Cambridge, Mass., 1963.

Klahr, David: "A Monte Carlo Investigation of the Statistical Significance of Kruskal's Nonmetric Scaling Procedure," *Psychometrika,* vol. 34, pp. 319–330, 1969.

Knode, Jay C: "Presidents of State Universities," *Scientific Monthly,* vol. 58, March 1944.

Kruse, S. A., and E. C. Beck: "Study of the Presidents of State Teachers Colleges and of State Universities," *Peabody Journal of Education,* pp. 358–361, May 1928.

Kruskal, J. B.: "Multidimensional Scaling by Optimizing Goodness of Fit to a Nonmetric Hypothesis," *Psychometrika,* vol. 29, pp. 1–28, March 1964.

Kruskal, J. B.: "Nonmetric Scaling: A Numerical Method," *Psychometrika*, vol. 29, pp. 115–129, June 1964.

Long, Norton A.: "The Local Community as an Ecology of Games," *American Journal of Sociology*, vol. 44, pp. 251–261, 1958.

McNeil, Kenneth, and James D. Thompson: "The Regeneration of Social Organizations," *American Sociological Review*, vol. 36, pp. 624–637, 1971.

McVey, Frank, and Raymond A. Hughes: *Problems of College and University Administration*, Iowa State College Press, Ames, 1952.

March, James G., and Herbert A. Simon: *Organizations*, John Wiley & Sons, Inc., New York, 1958.

March, James G. (ed.): *Handbook of Organizations*, Rand McNally & Company, Chicago, 1965.

March, James G.: "The Power of Power," in David Easton (ed.), *Varieties of Political Theory*, Prentice-Hall, Inc., Englewood Cliffs, N.J., 1966.

Mayhew, Lewis B.: *Arrogance on Campus*, Jossey-Bass, Inc., San Francisco, 1971.

Monson, C. H., Jr.: "Metaphors for the University," *Educational Record*, vol. 48, pp. 22–29, Winter 1967.

Perkins, James A.: *College and University Presidents: Recommendations and Report of a Survey*, New York State Regents Advisory Committee on Educational Leadership, Albany, 1967.

Peter, Laurence J.: *The Peter Principle*, William Morrow & Company, Inc., New York, 1969.

Rauh, Morton A.: *The Trusteeship of Colleges and Universities*, McGraw-Hill Book Company, New York, 1969.

Reedy, George E.: *The Twilight of the Presidency*, The World Publishing Company, New York, 1970.

Riesman, David: "Vicissitudes in the Career of the College President," Speech given at the dedication of the O. Meredith Wilson Memorial Library at the University of Minnesota, Minneapolis, May 13, 1969.

Selden, William K.: "How Long Is a College President?" *Liberal Education*, vol. 46, no. 1, pp. 5–15, March 1960.

Simon, Herbert A.: "The Job of a College President," *Educational Record*, vol. 48, no. 1, pp. 68–78, Winter 1967.

Singletary, Otis A. (ed.): *American Universities and Colleges*, American Council on Education, Washington, D.C., 1968.

Stephens, Richard W.: "The Academic Administration: The Role of the University President," Ph.D. dissertation, University of North Carolina, Chapel Hill, 1956.

Walton, Richard E., and Robert B. McKersie (eds.): *Behavioral Theory of Labor Negotiations*, McGraw-Hill Book Company, New York, 1965.

Warren, Luther E.: "A Study of the Presidents of Four-Year Colleges in the U.S.," *Education*, vol. 58, pp. 427–438, March 1938.

Weiner, Stephen S.: "Educational Decisions in an Organized Anarchy," Ph.D. dissertation, Stanford University, Stanford, Calif., 1972.

White, Harrison C.: *Chains of Opportunity: System Models of Mobility in Organizations*, Harvard University Press, Cambridge, Mass., 1970.

Wolfinger, Raymond: "Nondecisions and the Study of Local Politics," *American Political Science Review*, vol. 65, pp. 1063–1080, 1971.

Wolfinger, Raymond: "Rejoinder to Frey's 'Comments'," *American Political Science Review*, vol. 65, pp. 1102–1104, 1971.

3

What Is the
Crisis of Leadership?

EDWIN P. HOLLANDER

Leadership is critical to the health of a group, organization, or society. Given the expectations it raises, there is always the potential for a crisis of leadership to occur and to take on importance. The contemporary expression about a "lack of leadership" signals that importance and also indicates something about the general nature of the crisis. Recently, a friend used that phrase in describing the main problem in the organization in which she works. These words clearly conveyed a feeling of aimless drift and purposelessness, although little more was said.

Perhaps this malaise is a sign of existential alienation. However, whatever the label, there evidently are some expectations about leadership which are not being fulfilled and that may be characteristic of modern society, especially of the democratic form. Although leadership is present, even when it is "bad," the *process* called leadership very much depends upon the relationship between leader and followers. The leader is central to that process, and he or she is usually seen as the source of favorable or unfavorable features of the relationship and the results produced. But followers are not merely passive or inert, as the traditional view would have it. Leadership requires responsiveness, cooperation, and a distribution of labor. This fact necessitates a more active role for followers—"a piece of the action" in the vernacular—and its absence may be a basis for the current crisis.

One difficulty is the categorical quality of words. For instance, there is still a common notion that "the leader" and "the followers" fit into sharp categories. But this overlooks the facts. All leaders, some of the

Reprinted from *Humanitas*, 14:3 (November 1978), pp. 285–296, by permission of the author and publisher.

time and to some degree, are followers. And followers need not be cast immutably in non-leader roles. They may, and sometimes do, become leaders. Even though only some people can occupy the status of leader in a particular time and place, the qualities needed to be a leader are not possessed only by those persons. Furthermore, the leader cannot do everything, though he or she might try. In any group or organization, there are different leadership functions to be fulfilled, such as executive, problem-solver, arbitrator, and advocate. Being a leader is, therefore, a complex role, and these functions frequently require delegation among several people.

These points take on a particular significance when seen against the historical backdrop of thought and study regarding leadership. A mystique has for so long permeated the concepts of leader and leadership that it is essential to understand the basis for the more contemporary viewpoints. We turn now to a brief review of that development.

Leadership in Retrospect

Beginning with the venerable "great man" theory, there have been various approaches to leadership which have attracted interest over the years. The quintessential expression of this theory is in the statement by a contemporary philosopher that "all factors in history, save great men, are inconsequential."[1] Alternatively, an evaluation of the validity of this theory led an eminent sociologist to suggest that, if true, "the secret of greatness lies just in being born great. . . ."[2] His more serious conclusion was that greatness was determined by a combination of individual, social, and historical circumstances.[3]

Closely associated with this theory was the so-called "trait approach," stressing the personal qualities of those in leader roles. It was favored by psychologically oriented investigators who studied the personalities and other attributes of leaders.[4] These studies, mainly conducted during the first half of this century, dealt both with who becomes a leader and what qualities make a leader effective, sometimes disregarding the difference between the two. The assumption of an hereditary basis for leader qualities was also a feature of the classic trait approach, as in the work of Sir Francis Galton.[5]

A review of the findings from studies of leader traits showed such mixed results that other factors had to be considered.[6] This led to two interrelated developments. One was the study of the behavior of organizational leaders, initially through descriptive ratings by subordinates.[7] The other was the emergence of a "situational approach," emphasizing the characteristics of the particular situation and task in which the leader and followers were mutually involved.[8] The primary stress was on the demands made for particular leader characteristics there.

The situational approach gave needed attention to the varying demands made upon leaders and achieved a notable gain in putting to rest the trait-based conceptions of the past. However, it ran the risk of over-statement at the other extreme by tending to neglect the characteristics of leaders, when that was not the point at all. The situational approach also failed to distinguish between task demands and the structure, history, size and setting of different social entities. Furthermore, the leader and situation cannot be so sharply differentiated since followers see the leader as part of the situation, who also helps to shape and define it for them.[9]

An extension and refinement of the situational approach occurred through the relatively recent development of "contingency models."[10] These models attempt to specify what leader attributes are appropriate, for certain contingencies in the situation. They emphasize factors calling forth different leader attributes to achieve effectiveness. In one of these, for example, the amount of follower participation in making decisions is viewed as a function of various contingencies. Among these are the amount of information possessed by the leader *vis à vis* the followers, the importance of decision quality, the degree of structure in the problem, the followers' motivation to attain the objective represented by solving the problem, how much their acceptance is necessary to the implementation of the solution, and the probability that the leader's decision made alone will be accepted by the followers.[11]

Accordingly, while some decisions need to be made by the leader, there are conditions favoring greater follower participation. This particular model represents a break with the more traditional views of the leader-follower relationship which present an either-or contrast. One view asserts that the leader must do what he or she believes is the "right thing" without being overly influenced by followers. The other view is that leaders must take into account the followers' interests, needs, wishes, and so forth in setting goals and directing action. We see now that neither view can be applied universally, and that a variety of consid-erations enter the picture. In that vein, a parallel development in time was the "transactional approach."[12] It gave emphasis to the relationship between the leader and followers and the possibility of mutual influence.

Leadership as a Transaction

Leadership is a process, and not a person, but the leader is usually seen as the active agent who commands attention and influence. While the leader may have the power of position, influence depends more on persuasion than on coercion. A two-way influence process ordinarily is not characterized by the exercise or threat of force. Instead it involves a "social exchange" between the leader and those who are followers, which means that benefits are given and received as rewards. Social exchange also has to do with the expectations people have about fairness, equitable treatment, and what is just.[13]

In short, the leader gives something and gets something. He or she is usually expected to give direction producing successful results for the group, organization, or larger social entity. In return, the followers give the leader greater esteem, status, and the responsiveness which makes influence possible. However, some minimum degree of success is necessary for the leader's position to be supported, because a lack of success removes a major benefit which the leader can provide in a "fair exchange."[14]

Therefore, a fair exchange would be one where the leader performs well and deserves the advantages of status. If the leader fails to do well, especially because of an evident lack of effort, then followers are likely to have a sense of injustice. They may also be discontented if the leader seems to disregard their interests along the way. Furthermore, when a leader's poor performance results from not listening to followers, there may be a feeling among them that blunders are being made bacause the leader fails to "be in touch." Followers may feel left out and blame the leader for not maintaining the other end of the transaction with them. This constellation of feelings represents a major source of the crisis in leadership, especially with the followers who have become more exposed to the wider world through the cascade of mass communications.

Since leadership depends upon responsive followership, followers may justifiably feel that they have a vital role in the process. A counterpart to this is that poor leaders can create poor followers, insofar as the latter are not as much engaged and involved as they are capable of being. Therefore, a great waste of human potential can occur. One consequence is the despair that sets in when followers sense that gains are not being made, and opportunities are being lost, by an inept leader.

Ideally, the process of influence and counter-influence helps to use human talents and physical resources effectively for mutual goals. As already noted, any social entity has leadership in the sense of organized patterns of influence, even if it is poor leadership. The effectiveness of leadership depends on the character of this relationship of the leader and others involved in getting things accomplished. Poor leadership may result from many causes, including the leader's incompetence in moving on with the primary task, or the followers' failure to show some initiative. In general, groups carry out their functions best, and attain their goals, by having shared responsibilities for action and some delegation of authority.

In a simple transactional view, the leader directs communications to followers, to which they may react in various ways. The leader attempts to take account of the attitudes and needs of followers and they, in turn, evaluate the leader with particular regard to his or her responsiveness to these states. Especially pertinent are the followers' perceptions of the leader's effectiveness and how they perceive and evaluate the leader 's actions and motives. For instance, where the leader has the resources but routinely fails to deliver, there is bound to be dissatisfaction. If, as another example, the leader appears to be deviating from the accepted standards, such nonconformity may be tolerated initially, especially if it seems to be yielding productive outcomes. This is a feature of the "idiosyncrasy credit" model, which emphasizes sources of earned status and the leader's related latitude for innovation.[15]

The idiosyncrasy credit model confronts the apparent paradox that leaders are said to conform more to the group's norms and yet are also likely to be influential in bringing about innovations. Actually, these elements can fit together when seen as a matter of sequence. In the early contact between the leader, or would-be leader, and followers, credits are gained by signs of a *contribution to the group's primary task* and *loyalty to the group's norms*. As summary terms, these two factors are referred to as "competence" and "conformity."

The role of leader carries the *potential* to take innovative action in coping with new or altered demands. But how successful the leader is in effecting change depends upon the perceptions followers have of the leader's actions and related motivations. Accordingly, when a leader's nonconformity seems to produce *unsuccessful* outcomes, the leader is more vulnerable to blame.[16] It is as if the group said, "We expect good results from your actions. If you choose an unusual course, we will go along with you and give you some latitude. But you are responsible if the outcome is that the group fails to achieve its goals."

Given a fund of credits, an individual's assertions of influence become more acceptable. Furthermore, there is the expectation that, once accumulated, credits will be used to take actions which are in the direction of needed innovation. A failure to do so may result in the loss of credits.[17] The leader who "sits" on his or her credits may be seen as not fulfilling role obligations.

Credits exist only in the shared perceptions which group members gain of the others over time. But credits have operational significance in allowing later deviations which would otherwise be viewed negatively, if a person did not have a sufficient balance to draw upon. As a case in point, a newcomer to the group is poorly positioned to assert influence or take innovative actions. However, a particular individual may bring derivative credit from another group, based on his or her reputation. The credit concept may therefore apply to appointed leaders as well as to elected ones, even though followers are not the major source of legitimacy for appointed leaders.

The credit concept assumes that a process of evaluation goes on. This means, for instance, that maintaining a leader role depends on showing results that can be judged. The process may vary considerably from situation to situation, but ordinarily there are "validators" who have some basis for judging the adequacy of the leader's performance. However, even if the judgment is negative, it may not be possible to displace the leader. For example, a term of office may be involved, or a contractual arrangement. Also, the validators responsible for the leader's original placement in the position are likely to be unwilling to admit error.

This reluctance is even seen with an elected leader whose validators are the followers or constituents. They may have a sense of investment in the leader which makes them feel a greater responsibility for the leader's performance. When it is poor, there may be at least an initial rallying around to support the leader.[18] Deposing an elected leader can offer considerable hurdles, especially in the midst of a fixed term. The matter of a leader's legitimacy in the role is at stake, and this requires additional comment.

Leader Legitimacy and Authority

A leader's authority requires a legitimate basis. As suggested above, legitimacy may come through various sources—by appointment, election, or through the support of followers in a less formal way. However, whatever the source, legitimacy depends on the followers' perceptions about how the leader achieved his or her position. The essential point about legitimacy is that it produces the belief that the leader has the authority to exert influence.[19] Legitimacy can also be seen to derive from a person's office, that is, an assigned status, or from a person's own qualities. A parallel point was made by Thomas Jefferson in distinguishing between social status based on an aristocracy of inherited position and a "natural aristocracy" of talent. A person might be admired for high position but not for individual qualities, or vice versa. In either case, when viewed from a transactional standpoint, legitimacy is related to the followers' perceptions of the leader.

A further point about legitimacy is the fact that a leader's high office does not necessarily insure follower responsiveness. The leader's personal qualities still matter. For instance, the president of a company has a *position* of leadership, which carries the legitimacy of high office. It is greater than that of a supervisor. Yet the president might be unsuccessful in achieving the desired response from subordinates. The supervisor might show a greater *exercise* of leadership by a more affirmative subordinate response.[20] Fulfilling legitimacy through the use of authority, therefore, has a great deal to do with how followers respond to the leader's characteristics.

Authority can also be seen as a resource. The leader is expected to use it in meeting assigned responsibilities, just as the available material and personnel resources are there to be used. However, having authority is only a potential for action, and it may not be exercised for various reasons. Furthermore, as Chester Barnard long ago pointed out, followers will comply with an order only to the extent that: they understand it, believe on receiving it that it is not inconsistent with organizational goals or their own goals, and have the ability to comply with the order. Here again we see a stress on the importance of the followers' perception of the leader's legitimacy.[21]

In sum, there are several factors which support the legitimacy of a leader's role. These are the manner by which it is attained and the followers' perceptions of the leader's competence and motivation. The latter perceptions deal with performance, which means the outcomes resulting from the leader's actions. A favorable situation for the leader occurs, therefore, when the followers consider the leader's position to be valid, and approve of his or her performance in moving the group toward accepted goals.

In this regard, William Cowley many years ago made a distinction between leadership and headship.[22] He said that a leader who depends entirely on the authority of a legitimated office is relying on headship, and not leadership. Although "heads" are often called "leaders," they may have only the legitimacy of office. Without exercising authority through persuasion and influence, to achieve a program, there is not authentic leadership. Cowley acknowledged that ". . . a completely clean-cut distinction between leaders and headmen cannot always be made."[23] Some headmen, he said, are so clearly not leaders that everyone agrees that they are not. But others, to the contrary, may be more like leaders.

The point should be clear that office-holding is not the same as leading, and that one factor in the difference is whether a leader is persuasive in pursuing a program. However, persuasion alone will not do. It needs to be tempered by credibility and accountability. Failings in these respects can be seen as irresponsibility, which is another source of the crisis in leadership.

Credibility and Accountability

All problems are not of the leader's making, and all solutions do not depend upon the leader's wisdom or initiative. Yet, the leader's position is such that he or she is more often seen to be responsible for handling problems that arise and for finding solutions. Leaders not only have greater responsibility for the activities they direct; they also are the primary source of "social reality" for followers, which refers to a shared definition of the situation. In shaping social reality, the leader reduces uncertaintly for followers and gives them a basis for action. However, a leader's statements and behavior have a positive impact only to the extent that the leader maintains credibility.

Although the concept of credibility may seem elusive, it has been found to be comprised of two major elements, expertise and trustworthiness.[24] The so-called "credibility gap," which was said to have existed in recent presidencies, appears to have been caused more and more by a failure of trust. The leader needs to be trustworthy, most especially in fulfilling expectations by delivering on promises. Furthermore, there is a special significance to the presidency, because of the model it presents in the society at large.

The recent spate of critical commentary on the Carter presidency often centers on the failure to match performance to the expectations raised. Indeed, the public does not take well to being disappointed by a president who does not live up to high expectations, such as that for the "new Morality" of the post-Watergate era. The Burt Lance affair, with all of its denials, sounded too much like the "old cronyism," rather than the "new morality," and the president's credibility suffered on grounds of trust. The pity is that this problem can readily spill over into other areas and diminish the president's credits.

Unfortunately, in the late fall of 1977, a Harris poll found that a majority of people considered President Carter well-intentioned but wondered if he had the basic competence for the job. They felt that he suffered from inexperience and a failure to follow through.[25] This is a problem of expertise. Early in 1978, The Washington Post editorialized on the "Perceptions of the President," and opened by saying, "The Carter Administration is now beginning its second year but, oddly, a great many Americans still say they have no clear view of it. For them, Mr. Carter and his central purposes have not yet come into focus."[26] In another analysis, Thomas Ottenad, in the St. Louis Post-Dispatch, said that: "Carter's performance has suffered from an awkward approach which made him appear uncertain and, at times, floundering."[27] Although this may seem to be a matter of "style," it adversely affects the perceptions followers have of substance. There may be a sense that clarity of purpose is lacking. Such uncertainty undermines credibility and may increase frustration about the leader's accountability to followers.

Presidents and other leaders cannot evade the fundamental understanding that being a leader gives a person more influence over others and the prospect of having more control over expectations and events. It also means having greater visibility and recognition, as a person of higher status. All of this comes at a price, a vital part of which is represented in the idea of accountability. There are good reasons why leaders should be held to account for failures, inadequate effort, or inaction in the face of problems or evident threats to the well-being of the group, organization, or nation. However, leaders do find devices to avoid it in practice, such as resorting to the *appearance* of collective responsibility vested in a committee or board. There are, of course, real situations of shared authority, which can be a good thing in principle. What provokes annoyance is the manipulation of such committees to make them nothing more than a sham, thereby providing further disenchantment with leaders.

Returning to the earlier theme, the leader-follower transaction requires that there be at least the sense of a "fair exchange." A follower usually is not a disciple who is obliged to accept the master's view uncritically. More appropriately, the leader-follower relationship needs balance. The follower has to be able to know and use his or her own critical ability in deciding some matters. A pattern of accommodation and two-way influence is required to produce mutual trust and the likelihood of positive results.

Simply put, followers need to have a basis for believing that they are being treated fairly and being informed properly. Such a belief will increase their inclination to remain inside and participate, rather than putting themselves at a psychological distance and opting out. In the latter event, the crisis in leadership will most likely be perpetuated and grow worse.

References

1. S. Hook, *The Hero in History*, Boston: Beacon Press, 1955, p. 14.

2. G. Spiller, "The dynamics of greatness," *Sociological Review*, 1929, 21, p. 218.

3. *Ibid.*, p. 231.

4. C. A. Gibb, "Leadership," In G. Lindzey and E. Aronson (Eds.), *The Handbook of Social Psychology*, 2nd ed., Volume 4, Reading, Mass.: Addison-Wesley, 1968, pp. 205–282.

5. F. Galton, *Hereditary Genius: An Inquiry into its Laws and Consequences*, London: Macmillan, 1869.

6. R. M. Stogdill, "Personal Factors Associated With Leadership," *Journal of Psychology*, 1948, 25, pp. 35–71.

7. See, for example, E. A. Fleishman, "The Description of Supervisory Behavior," *Journal of Applied Psychology*, 1953, 37, pp. 1–6.

8. See especially J. K. Hemphill, *Situational Factors in Leadership*, Columbus: Ohio State University, Personnel Research Board, 1949; A. W. Gouldner, (Ed.), *Studies in Leadership*, New York: Harper, 1950, pp. 25–31; and E. P. Hollander, *Leaders, Groups, and Influence*, New York: Oxford University Press, 1964, Chapter 1.

9. E. P. Hollander and J. W. Julian, "Contemporary trends in the analysis of leadership processes," *Psychological Bulletin*, 1969, 71, pp. 387–397.

10. See, for example, F. E. Fiedler, "A Contingency Model of Leadership Effectiveness," In L. Berkowitz (Ed.), *Advances in Experimental Social Psychology*, Volume 1, New York: Academic Press, 1964; V. H. Vroom and P. W. Yetton, *Leadership and Decisionmaking*, University of Pittsburgh Press, 1973; R. J. House, "A path-goal theory of leader effectiveness," *Administrative Science Quarterly*, 1971, 16, pp. 321–338.

11. Vroom and Yetton, *op. cit.*

12. E. P. Hollander, "Conformity, Status, and Idiosyncrasy Credit," *Psychological Review*, 1958, 65, pp. 117–127; Hollander, 1964, *op. cit.*, Chapters 14–18; Hollander, *Leadership Dynamics: A Practical Guide to Effective Relationships*, New York: Free Press/Macmillan, 1978.

13. G. C. Homans, *Social Behavior: Its Elementary Forms*, Revised ed., New York: Harcourt Brace Jovanovich, 1974, Chapter 11.

14. T. O. Jacobs, *Leadership and Exchange in Formal Organizations*, Alexandria, Va.: Human Resources Research Organization, 1970, p. 80.

15. Hollander, 1958, *op. cit.*

16. R. Alvarez, "Informal reactions to deviance in simulated work organizations: a laboratory experiment," *American Sociological Review*, 1968, 33, pp. 895–912.

17. Hollander, 1958, *op. cit.*

18. E. P. Hollander, B. J. Fallon, and M. T. Edwards, "Some Aspects of Influence and Acceptability for Appointed and Elected Leaders," *Journal of Psychology*, 1977, 95, pp. 289–296.

19. E. P. Hollander and J. W. Julian, "Studies in Leader Legitimacy, Influence, and Innovation," In L. Berkowitz (Ed.), *Advances in Experimental Social Psychology*, Volume 5, New York: Academic Press, 1970, pp. 33–69; Hollander, 1978, *op. cit.*, Chapter 3.

20. D. Katz and R. L. Kahn, *The Social Psychology of Organizations*, New York: Wiley, 1966, p. 301.

21. C. I. Barnard, "A definition of authority," In R. K. Merton, A. P. Gray, B. Hockey, and H. C. Selvin (Eds.), *Reader in Bureaucracy*, Glencoe, Ill.: Free Press, 1952.

22. W. H. Cowley, "Three distinctions in the study of leaders," *Journal of Abnormal and Social Psychology*, 1928, 23, pp. 144–157.

23. *Ibid.*, p. 146.

24. C. I. Hovland, I. L. Janis, and H. H. Kelley, *Communication and Persuasion*, New Haven: Yale University Press, 1953.

25. H. Smith, "Problems of a Problem Solver," *The New York Times Magazine*, January 8, 1978, pp. 30ff. See especially page 32.

26. *The Washington Post*, February 15, 1978, p. A-22.

27. Ottenad, "Carter report card: The minuses pile up," *St. Louis Post-Dispatch*, December 25, 1977, p. C-1.

4

Where Have All
the Leaders Gone?

WARREN G. BENNIS

Where have all the leaders gone? They are, as a paraphrase of that
haunting song reminds us, "long time passing."

All the leaders whom the young respect are dead. F.D.R., who could
challenge a nation to rise above fear, is gone. Churchill, who could
demand and get blood, sweat, and tears, is gone. Eisenhower, the most
beloved leader since Washington, is gone. Schweitzer, who from the
jungles of Lambarene could inspire mankind with a reverence for life,
is gone. Einstein, who could give us that sense of unity in infinity, is
gone. Gandhi, the Kennedys, Martin Luther King, all lie slain, as if to
prove the mortal risk in telling us that we can be greater, better than
we are.

The landscape is littered with fallen leaders. A President re-elected
with the greatest plurality in history resigns in disgrace. The Vice
President he twice chose as qualified to succeed him is driven from
office as a common crook. Since 1973 the governments of all nine
Common Market countries have changed hands—at least once. In the
last year over a dozen major governments have fallen. Shaky coalitions
exist in Finland, Portugal, Argentina, Belgium, Holland, and Israel.
Minority governments rule precariously in Britain, Denmark, and Sweden.
In Ethiopia, the King of Kings died captive in his palace.

The leaders who remain, the successors and the survivors—the struggling corporate chieftains, the university presidents, the city managers
and mayors, the state governors—all are now seen as an "endangered
species," because of the whirl of events and circumstances beyond
rational control.

Reprinted with permission from *Technology Review*, 75:9 (March–April 1977), pp. 3–12.
Copyright © 1977.

There is a high turnover, an appalling mortality—whether occupational or actuarial—among leaders. In recent years the typical college president has lasted about four years; in the decade of the 1950s, the average tenure was over eleven years. Men capable of leading institutions often refuse to accept such pressures, such risks. We see what James Reston of the *New York Times* calls "burnt out cases," the debris of leaders. We see Peter Principle leaders rising to their final levels of incompetence. It has been said that if a Martian were to demand, "Take me to your leader," Earthlings would not know where to take him. Administrative sclerosis around the world, in political office, in all administrative offices breeds suspicion and distrust. A bumper sticker in Massachusetts summed it up: "Impeach Someone!"

In business the landscape is equally flat. The great leaders that come to mind—Ford, Edison, Rockefeller, Morgan, Schwab, Sloan, Kettering—are long gone. Nixon's business chums were either entrepreneurs "outside" the business Establishment, like Aplanalp the Aerosol King, or they had no widespread acceptance as business leaders or spokesmen. President Ford seemed to get on best with the Washington vice presidents of major corporations (a vice president syndrome as it were). *Fortune* magazine reveals the absence of business leaders in New York University's Hall of Fame. Of the ninety-nine individuals selected, only ten are business leaders.

The peril of the present situation is not exaggerated. Dr. John Platt, a scientist at the University of Michigan, recently stated what he considers to be the ten basic dangers to world survival. Of greatest significance was the possibility of some kind of nuclear war or accident which would destroy the entire human race. The second greatest danger is the possibility of a worldwide epidemic, famine or depression. He sees as the world's third greatest danger a general failure in *the quality of the management and leadership of our institutions.*

Where have all the leaders gone? Why have they become "endangered species?"

Falling Out of Control

Something's happened, that's clear; something that bewilders. As I write this, for example, it can be noted that our technology brings together, at 600 m.p.h. speeds, people who left Los Angeles, San Francisco, Denver, Chicago, Atlanta, at lunch, only to have them all blown to smithereens by a bomb left in a baggage locker at an airport.

It's as if mankind, to paraphrase Teilhard de Chardin, is *falling suddenly out of control of its own destiny.* Perhaps only a new Homer or Herodotus would be able, later on, to show us its patterns and designs, its coherences and contours. We still lack that historical view. What we hear and discern now is not one voice or signal but a confusing jim-jangle of cords. All we know for sure is that we cannot wait a generation for the historian to tell us what happened; we must try to make sense out of the jumble of voices now. Indeed, the first test for any leader today is to discover just *what* he or she does confront; only then will it be possible to devise the best ways of making that reality—the multiple realities—potentially manageable.

The most serious threat to our institutions and the cause of our diminishing sense of able leadership is the steady erosion of institutional autonomy. Time was when the leader could decide—period. A Henry Ford, an Andrew Carnegie, a Nicholas Murray Butler could issue a ukase—and all would automatically obey. Their successors' hands are now tied in innumerable ways—by governmental requirements, by various agencies, by union rules, by the moral and sometimes legal pressures of organized consumers and environmentalists. For example, before David Mathews became Secretary of Health, Education, and Welfare, and speaking as President of the University of Alabama, he characterized federal regulations as threatening to

> . . . bind the body of higher education in a Lilliputian nightmare of forms
> and formulas. The constraints emanate from various accrediting agencies,
> Federal bureaucracies, and state boards, but their effects are the same . . . a
> loss of institutional autonomy, and a serious threat to diversity, creativity,
> and reform. Most seriously, that injection of more regulations may even
> work against the accountability it seeks to foster, because it so dangerously
> diffuses responsibility.

The external forces that impinge and impose upon the perimeter of our institutions—the incessant concatenation of often contrary requirements—are the basic reasons for the loss of their self-determination. Fifty years ago this external environment was fairly placid, like an ocean on a calm day, forecastable, predictable, regular, not terribly eventful. Now that ocean is turbulent and highly inter-dependent—and makes tidal waves. In my own institution right now the key people for me to reckon with are not only the students, the faculty, and my own management group, but people external to the university—the city manager, city council members, the state legislature, accrediting and professional associations, the federal government, alumni, and parents. There is an incessant, dissonant clamor out there. And because the university is a brilliant example of an institution that has blunted and diffused its main purposes through a proliferation of dependence on "external patronage structures," its autonomy has declined to the point where our boundary system is like Swiss cheese. Because of these pressures, every leader must create a department of "external affairs," a secretary of state, as it were, to deal with external constituencies.

Accompanying all this is a new kind of populism, not the barn burners of the Grange days, not the "free silver" of Bryanism ("The crown of thorns"), but the fragmentation, the caucusization of constituencies. My own campus is typical; we have over 500 organized governance and pressure groups. We have a coalition of women's groups, a gay society, black organizations for both students and faculty, a veterans' group, a continuing education group for women, a handicapped group, a faculty council on Jewish affairs, a faculty union organized by the American Association of University Professors, an organization for those staff members who are neither faculty nor administrators, an organization of middle-management staff members, an association of women administrators, a small, elite group of graduate fellows.

This fragmentation, which exists more or less in all organizations, marks the end not only of community, a sense of shared values and symbols, but of consensus, an agreement reached despite differences. It was Lyndon Johnson's tragedy to plead, "Come let us reason together," at a time when all these groups scarcely wanted to *be* together, much less reason together.

These pressure groups are fragmented. They go their separate and often conflicting ways. They say: "No, we don't want to be part of the mainstream of America—we just want to be us," whether they're blacks, Chicanos, women, the third sex, or Menominee Indians seizing an empty Catholic monastery. They tell us that the old dream of "the melting pot," of assimilation does not work—or never was. They have never been *"beyond* the melting pot" (as Glazer and Moynihan wrote about it); they have been *behind* it.

So what we have now is a new form of politics—King Caucus, who has more heads than Cerberus, and contending Queens who cry, "Off with their heads!" as they play croquet with flamingos. It is *the politics of multiple advocacies*—vocal, demanding, often "out of sync" with each other. They represent people who are fed up with being ignored, neglected, excluded, denied, subordinated. No longer do they march on cities, on bureaus, or on organizations they view as sexist, racist, anti-Semitic, or whatever. Now, they file suit. The law has suddenly emerged as the court of first resort.

A Litigious Society:
"Is the Wool Worth the Cry?"

And so, we have become a litigious society where individuals and groups—in spectacularly increasing numbers—bring suits to resolve issues which previously might have been settled privately. A hockey player, injured in his sport, bypasses the institutional procedures to bring formal suit. The club owners are outraged that one of "its own" would take the case "outside." College students, unhappy with what they are learning on campus, are turning to the courts as well. A lawsuit against the University of Bridgeport may produce the first clear legal precedent. It was filed last spring by a woman seeking $150 in tuition, the cost of her books, and legal fees because a course required of secondary education majors was "worthless" and she "didn't learn anything." A law review has been sued for rejecting an article. In New Jersey, a federal judge has ordered twenty-eight state Senators to stand trial for violating the constitutional rights of the twenty-ninth member, a woman, by excluding her from their party caucus. They did so because, they claimed, she was "leaking" their deliberations to the press. In a Columbus, Ohio, test case, the U.S. Supreme Court recently ruled that secondary-school students may not be suspended, disciplinarily, without formal charges and a hearing, that the loss of a single day's education is a deprivation of property. A federal court in Washington has just awarded $10,000 to each of the thousands of May, 1970, anti-war demonstrators whom it found had been illegally arrested and confined at the behest of Attorney General Mitchell.

Aside from the merits of any particular case, the overriding fact is clear that the hands of all administrators are increasingly tied by real or potential legal issues. I find I must consult our lawyers over even small, trivial decisions. The university has so many suits against it (40 at last count) that my mother calls me, "My son, the defendant."

The courts and the law are, of course, necessary to protect individual rights and to provide recourse for negligence, breach of contract, and fraud. But a "litigious society" presents consequences that nobody bargained for, not the least the rising, visible expense of legal preparation plus the invisible costs of wasted time.

Far more serious than expense, however, is the confusion, ambiguity, and lack of subtlety of the law and what that does to institutional autonomy and leadership. To take the example of consumer protection, we see that lawsuits are forcing universities to insert a railroad-timetable disclaimer in their catalogues—e.g., "Courses in this catalogue are subject to change without notice"—in order to head off possible lawsuits. At the same time, the Federal Trade Commission is putting pressure on doctors, architects, lawyers, and other professionals to revise their codes of ethics forbidding advertising. The Buckley amendment, which permits any student to examine his own file, tends to exclude from the file any qualitative judgments which would provide even the flimsiest basis for a suit.

The confusion, ambiguity, and complexity of the law—augmented by conflicting court interpretations—tend toward institutional paralysis. Equally forbidding is the fact that the courts are substituting their judgments for the expertise of the institution. Justice may prevail but at a price to institutional leadership so expensive, as we shall see, that one has to ask if the "wool is worth the cry."

One for the Seesaw

The incessant external forces and the teeming internal constituencies, each with their own diverse and often contrary expectations, demands, and pressure, are difficult enough for any leader to understand, let alone control: at their best, leaders serve as quiet and efficient custodians.

The problem is made infinitely more complex when the goals and values of the internal and external forces seem not merely divergent, but irreconcilable. Their collision, or "boundary clash," tends to isolate or crush the "man at the top."

The College of Medicine of a large urban, but state affiliated, university accepts 187 applicants out of 8,000. Immediately some 23,000 people are angered, the rejected applicants and their parents. Although admissions decisions are the prerogative of the faculty, the president of the university finds himself deluged by phone calls and letters from parents, alumni, friends of the regents, and legislators. He feels, however, that "The president shouldn't butt in. . . ." Meanwhile, the issue grows more political. Disgruntled persons write their legislators. The legislators demand an informal commitment that the College of Medicine accept only state residents. Next they propose a bill that only state residents receive support. The president is forced to become involved. He talks to the governor, the legislators, and the media, and he amasses political support to oppose the state-only bill. Eventually, the bill is dropped.

The legislators provide a large share of the revenues of the university (which happens to be the University of Cincinnati—but it could be legion), and their support has a direct relation to how their constituents react to our internal decisions. Patronage structures blanket the social geography of our environment, as they do that of other institutions. Whether these structures consist of taxpayers or consumers, they are demanding, often fickle, and always want their way. In any case, their generosity or miserliness reflects the degree of respect which they feel for the institution, and whether they like what we're doing for them or their relatives. It's as simple as that.

Let me cite a classic confrontation between these internal and external constituencies, mirroring a divergence in their goals and values. It concerns the policy of "open admission" which has created bewilderment and confusion on many campuses. Open admission makes it difficult to understand what we're about, what our "basic" mission is. It makes it almost impossible to define with any precision the educational stands that we must take from time to time. It's hard to determine just what students need or want and what our responsibility to them should be. As one Appalachian student told his humanities professor: "Sure, I'll be glad to read Dante with you, as soon as everybody in my family has a pair of shoes."

The public's uneasiness is often verbalized through code words or phrases (at least according to my mail and the letters-to-the-editor columns) like "lowering of academic standards" or "cheapening the degree." These concerns often (but not always) reflect the public's foreboding about mass education and its concomitant, "equal opportunity" for minorities and women in higher education. While "Affirmative Action" is the mandated vehicle for implementing equal education and work opportunities, in practice it has proved to be more a case study of how difficult it is to force profound changes in an institution as complex, prestigious, slow-moving—and sensitive to economic forces— as a university.

Whatever the reality of Affirmative Action, some citizens are uneasy about this development and use the rhetoric of "lowering standards" or "quotas" to question sharply its validity. And to make matters more complicated, another, increasingly vocal, group feels dissatisfied at the seeming lack of progress. Each of these viewpoints is held by our various publics, and this in turn leads to a situation where "both sides" are dissatisfied with our progress—some because we are doing too little, others because we are trying too much. In either case, we are in the middle and neither side is happy with the university. Or its president.

The university is, in a sense, an anvil on which a fragmented society hammers.

Yes, provide a broad, liberal arts, humanistic education.

No, teach people practical things, so as to guarantee them jobs.

Yes, focus on research and education for the elite.

No, train dental technicians, hotel managers, accountants, but also provide professional education for lawyers, doctors, and engineers.

Yes, stop lowering academic standards, but be sure and enroll more minorities and the poor as a way of creating a more egalitarian society.

And also, while you're at it, provide compensatory education for those victimized by inadequate public schooling, provide opportunities for part-time students, especially for women caught in the homemaker's trap, provide continuing education as job enrichment for workers and executives, and, by the way, become the vehicle through which income redistribution can be achieved.

Obviously, we do not possess the resources to achieve all of these aims. We couldn't, even if we wanted to. By providing a complete menu for every taste we would inevitably and quickly alienate one or another public who would feel disaffected or threatened by one or another of our academic programs and would, actively or passively, turn off its support.

All of our institutions, both public *and* private, confront similar conflict between internal and external environments. In Cincinnati, Procter and Gamble and Federated Department Stores, two of our nation's most successful and well-managed enterprises, must now consider (indeed, are on occasion forced by law to consider) *both* external and internal conflicts, whether nitrates or price-labeling.

The root problem contains profound and grave consequences. It isn't only a matter of a loss of *consensus* over basic values; it is a *polarization* of these values. The university problem is basically a reflection of society's problems, a fact so obvious that we tend to forget it. Education and society are indivisible and cannot be detached from each other. Similarly, Business, with a large "B," is the concentrated epitome of our culture—and is inseparable from it. Coolidge was right that America's business *is* business, and Engine Charlie Wilson was not far wrong with his memorable "what's good for General Motors" remark: business thrives or sickens along with our nation's destiny. All of our institutional fates are correlated with our nation's.

What seems to have happened is this: the environmental encroachments and turbulence, the steady beat of litigation, the fragmentation of constituencies along with their new found eloquence and power, multiple advocacy, win-lose adversarial conflicts between internal and external forces—all of this—has led to a situation where our leaders are "keeping their heads below the grass," as L.B.J. once put it, or paralyzed, or resembling nothing so much as acrobatic clowns. Whatever metaphor one prefers, to grow and stay healthy an institution must strike a proper balance between openness to the environment and protection from too much permeability. Achieving the proper trading relationship without being colonialized is the delicate balance leaders must achieve.

Having to look both ways—in and out, back and forth—was the special gift of Janus, and is required for all leaders today. The "Janus Phenomenon" is a relatively new example of organizational turbulence and leadership optics. Today's leader is surrounded by constituent groups, from inside and outside, as well as by numerous individuals who at any moment, discovering some supposed mutual interest, may suddenly coalesce into some new constituency. In either case, people need slight stimulus to become vocal, organized advocates and activists.

The Cat's Cradle

We know what overstimulation by external forces does to an individual; a total reliance on external cues, stimuli, rewards, and punishments leads to an inability to control one's own destiny. People in this state tend to avoid any behavior for which there is no external cue. Without signals, they vegetate. With contrary signals, they either become catatonic—literally too paralyzed to choose, let alone *act* on a choice, for fear of risk—or, conversely, they lunge at anything and everything, finally contorting themselves into enervated pretzels.

When we apply this analysis to organizations and their leadership, we can observe the same effects. While these coercive political and legal regulations are more pronounced in the public sector than in the private sector, in the latter area the market mechanism has heretofore been the linking pin between the firm and environment, the source of feedback regarding rewards and punishments, and the reflection of the success or failure of decisions. Whether the organization is private or public, whether the controls are legitimate or not, there is only one natural conclusion: an excess of (even well-intended) controls will lead inexorably to lobotomized institutions.

What neither lawmakers nor politicians seem to realize is that law and regulation deal primarily with sins of commission. Sins of omission are more difficult to deal with, partly, as Kenneth Boulding points out, because it is just damned hard in practice to distinguish between honest mistakes and deliberate evil. Which is another way of saying that legitimate risk-taking can land you in jail. On the other hand, by "playing it safe," by living up to the inverted proverb, "Don't just do something, sit there," an institution, a leader, a person can avoid error, and if continued long enough, they can *almost* avoid living.

As the legal and political systems become increasingly concerned with sins of commission—a fact exemplified in the dramatic switch from *caveat emptor* to *caveat vendor*, in the deluge of consumer protection legislation, in malpractice suits, in the environmental protection movement, in the court decisions awarding damages to purchasers of faulty products—we can get to a point where no producer, no organization will do anything at all, like the California surgeons who quit operating on any but emergency patients. Why should they? The costs of uncertainty and honest mistakes are now unbearable and far too costly.

At my own and many other universities, for example, we are now in the process of rewriting our catalogues so carefully that it will be virtually impossible for any student (read: consumer) to claim that we haven't fulfilled our end of the bargain. At the same time, because we have to be so careful, we can never express our hopes, our dreams, and our bold ideas of what a university experience could provide for the prospective student. I suspect that in ten years or so, college catalogues, rarely a publication which faculty, students, or administrators are wild about in any case, will devolve into statements that resemble nothing more than the finely printed cautions and disclaimers on the back of airline tickets—just the opposite of what education is all about: an adventurous and exciting odyssey of the mind.

All this—all of the litigation, legislation, and *caveat vendor*—not only diminish the potency of our institutions, but lead to something more pernicious and possibly irrecoverable. We seek comfort in the delusion that all of our troubles, our failures, our losses, our insecurities, our "hangups," our missed opportunities, our incompetence can be located "somewhere else," can be blamed on "someone else," can be settled in the seamless, suffocating, and invisible "system." How convenient, dear Brutus.

Just think: at a certain point, following our current practices and national mood, any sense of individual responsibility will rapidly erode. And along with that, the volume of low-level "belly-aching" and vacuous preaching about "the system" will grow more strident. The result: those leaders who are around either will be too weak or will shy away from the inevitable risks involved in doing anything good, bad, or indifferent.

I am *not* arguing the case against regulations and controls. I am painfully conscious that some of them are necessary if we are to realize our nation's values (e.g., equality of opportunity for all); without them, I fear, our basic heritage would have long ago been indelibly corrupted. (And it is not hard to understand why campaign finances have come under control recently. How do we deal with Gulf's $12 million bribes, including one to L.B.J. in 1962 when he was Vice President?) I am also aware that many of our institutions have, through inactive, corrupt, and inhumane actions, brought on themselves regulations which today they claim are unnecessary.

All the same, when it comes to protecting people from their exploiters we have an extra responsibility to be so vigilant, so careful that we don't end up in a situation where *everyone* is enmeshed by a cat's cradle of regulations erratically tangled together with the filaments of "good intentions."

As Justice Brandeis put it many years ago:

> Experience should teach us to be most on guard to protect liberty when the governments' purposes are beneficent. Men born to freedom are naturally alert to repel invasion of their liberty by evil-minded rulers. The greatest dangers to liberty lurk in insidious encroachments by men of zeal, well-meaning, but without understanding.

Variations on a Theme

Memorandum to the People of Ohio's 13th Congressional District:

Summary: Being the Congressman is rigorous servitude, ceaseless en-slavement to a peculiar mix of everyone else's needs, demands and whims, plus one's own sense of duty, ambition or vanity. It is that from which Mrs. Mosher and I now declare our personal independence, to seek our freedom, as of January 3, 1977.

It is a Congressman's inescapable lot, his or her enslavement, to be never alone, never free from incessant buffeting by people, events, problems, decisions. . . . It is a grueling experience, often frustrating, discouraging, sometimes very disillusioning. . . . House debates, caucuses, briefings, working breakfasts, working lunches, receptions, dinners, homework study, and even midnight collect calls from drunks. . . . you name it!

I am for opting out. I shall not be a candidate for reelection in 1976.

Charles A. Mosher,
Representative
13th Congressional District
State of Ohio
December 19, 1975

The basic problem is that leaders are facing a set of conditions that seemed to take shape suddenly, like an unscheduled express train looming out of the night. Whoever would have forecast the post-Depression development in the public sector of those areas of welfare, social service, health, and education? Who, save for a Lord Keynes, could have predicted the scale and range of the multi-national corporations? Prophetically he wrote: "Progress lies in the growth and the recognition of semi-auton-omous bodies within the states. Large business corporations when they have reached a certain age and size, approximate the status of public corporations rather than that of the individualistic private enterprise."

The Keynesian prophecy is upon us. When David Rockefeller goes to London, he is greeted as if he were a chief of state (and some of his empires *are* bigger than many states). But in addition to the growth of semi-autonomous, often global, corporations which rival governments, we also have public-sector institutions which Keynes could scarcely have imagined. The largest employment sector of our society, and the one growing at the fastest rate, is local and state government. Higher education, which less than twenty years ago was 50 percent private–50 percent public, is now about 85 percent public and is expected to be 90 percent public by 1980. And, where a century ago 90 percent of all Americans were self-employed, today 90 percent work in what can be called bureaucracies, members of some kind of corporate family. They might be called "juristic" persons who work within the sovereignty of a legal entity called a corporation or agency. Juristic persons, not masters of their own actions, cannot place the same faith in themselves that self-employed persons did.

These are the problems of leadership today. We have the important emergence of a Roosevelt-Keynes revolution, the new politics of multiple advocacy, new dependencies, new constituencies, new regulatory controls, new values. And how do our endangered species, the leaders, cope with these new complications and entanglements? For the most part, they do not; that is, they are neither coping nor leading. One reason, I fear, is that many of us misconceive what leadership is about. Leading does not mean managing; the difference between the two is crucial. I know many institutions that are very well *managed* and very poorly *led*. They may excel in the ability to handle the daily routine, and yet they may never ask whether the routine should be done at all. To lead, the dictionary informs us, is to go in advance of, to show the way, to influence or induce, to guide in direction, course, action, opinion. To manage means to bring about, to accomplish, to have charge of or responsibility for, to conduct. The difference may be summarized as activities of vision and judgment versus activities of efficiency.

In his decisionmaking, the leader today is a multidirectional broker who must deal with four estates—his own management team, constituencies within his organization, forces outside his organization, and the media. While his decisions and actions affect the people of these four estates, their decisions and actions, too, affect him. The fact is that the concept of "movers and shakers"—a leadership elite that determines the major decisions—is an outdated notion. Leaders are as much the "shook" as the shakers. Whether the four estates force too great a quantity of problems on the leader or whether the leader takes on too much in an attempt to prove himself, the result is what I call "Bennis' First Law of Pseudodynamics," which is that routine work will always drive out the innovational.

When the well-known author, John Hersey, was permitted to sit for a week in the Oval Office and its antechambers, recording all he saw and heard, he counted (in five working days) more than 4,000 visitors—Indian tribal chiefs, bishops and rabbis, woolgrowers and cattlemen, labor leaders and businessmen, students, blacks—flowing through the President's office in an unending stream. Just to handle the millions of pieces of mail pouring in and out of the White House took some 250 employees. The daily "news summary" occupied six full-time staffers. To collect and screen the names of possible candidates for the 4,000 positions the President controls, there was a staff of 30. The speech-writing team, which turned out 746,000 words during Ford's first 10 months in office, numbered 13, and Ron Nessen's news staff included eight deputies plus 38 other assistants apparently needed to handle the 1,500 news correspondents covering the White House.

During Lincoln's presidency there was a total of 50 on the White House staff—and that included telegraph operators and secretaries. Roosevelt inherited three secretaries from Hoover; now there are over 3,000. During the Eisenhower and Kennedy years, the staff of the Office of the President increased 13 percent under each. L.B.J. increased his another 13 percent, and Nixon increased his by 25 percent in his first term. Unhappily, the White House overload can be duplicated over the entire corporate and public bureaucratic landscapes. Little wonder there are burnt-out cases or that Congressman Mosher should declare his independence from "rigorous servitude, ceaseless enslavement."

Leading Through Limits

We are now experiencing a transition period that may aptly be called an "era of limits." After the Club of Rome warned us of *The Limits of Growth,* the Arab petroleum boycott, soaring fuel costs, and the continuing energy crisis have confirmed the brutal fact that our national goals have outrun our present means. Some political and institutional leaders exploit this mood by turning the public's disenchantment with growth into a political asset. They want to follow the popular mood, rather than lead it.

The National Observer calls California's young Governor Edmund G. Brown "the hottest politician in America," and quotes him thus: "Growth in California has slowed down . . . the feeling is strongly antigrowth. Once people seemed to think there were no limits to the growth of California. Now Californians are moving to Oregon and Colorado. . . . There are limits to everything—limits to this planet, limits to government mechanisms, limits to any philosophy or idea. And that's a concept we have to get used to. Someone called it the Europeanization of America. That's part right. You take an empty piece of land and you fill it up with houses and soon the land is more scarce and the air is more polluted and things are more complicated. That's where we are today. . . ." *The National Observer* says his rhetoric works: "Over 90 percent of the people in California applaud his performance." (November 29, 1975, pp. 1, 16)

Compared with the grandiose rhetoric of a quarter-century about the apostolic conviction that size and scale plus technological "know-how" could solve all society's basic problems, the management of decline, as presented by Governor Brown, sounds at least respectably sane, and especially so when compared with a pronunciamento by one of the leaders of the European Economic Community, Dr. Sicco Mansholt: "More, further, quicker, richer are the watchwords of present day society. We must adapt to this for there is no alternative." *That* kind of rhetoric, especially when at brutal odds with present reality, denies the very nature of the human condition.

Thus, growing in popularity, and becoming more sophisticated in its approach, is a new movement. I call it "cameo leadership," which aspires to carve things well, but smaller. It preaches a "homecoming," a less complicated time, a communal life, a radical decentralization of organizational life, a return to Walden before the Pond was polluted, before the Coke stand made its appearance, before *Walden* itself was required reading . . . when things were compassable.

A chief spokesman for this counter-technology movement is E. F. Schumacher, a former top economist and planner for England's National Coal Board. In his book, *Small is Beautiful*, he writes: "We are poor, not demi-gods. . . . We have plenty to be sorrowful about, and are not emerging into a golden age. . . . We need a gentle approach, a non-violent spirit, and small is beautiful. . . ."

Governor Brown of California is an avid disciple of Dr. Schumacher's "Buddhist economics." Small *is* beautiful. Sometimes. Perhaps it is beautiful more often than big is beautiful. When big gets ugly, we see human waste, depersonalization, alienation, possibly disruption. When small gets ugly, which never crosses Schumacher's mind, it leads to a decentralization bordering on anarchy; also to poverty, famine, and disease.

Small is beautiful. The era of limits is upon us. Who can argue? Nevertheless, these are slogans as empty as they are both appealing and timely. Because they are appealing we fail to see that they represent no specific programs for change. In fact, rather than opening up the possibilities for solutions, they close them with brevity and an exclamation mark. Basically, they reflect the symptoms now afflicting us by setting rhetorical opposites against each other. Small is beautiful, so big must be ugly. A grain of sand may be more beautiful than a pane of glass. But must we trade the glass for sand (as well as the life expectancy of those protected by glass for that of a Bedouin out admiring that ultimate decentralization, the desert)?

The real point is not one of beauty. The real point is whether leaders can face up to and cope with our present crises, worries, and imperatives. The real problem is how we can lead institutions in a world of over three billion people, millions of whom will starve while other millions can't find work; and for many who do find work it's either boring or underpaid. Many whose work is exciting and provides meaning live with quiet desperation in armed fortresses in fear of "the others." The real question is: How do we provide the needed jobs, and, after that, how do we learn to lead so that people can work more cooperatively, more sensibly, more humanely with one another? How can we lead in such a way that the requisite interdependence—so crucial for human survival and economic resilience—can be realized in a humane and gentle spirit?

Coda

Where have all the leaders gone? They're consulting, pleading, trotting, temporizing, putting out fires, either avoiding—or, more often—taking too much heat, and spending too much energy in doing both. They are peering at a landscape of "bottom lines," ostentatiously taking the bus to work (with four bodyguards, rather than the one chauffeur they might need if they drove) to demonstrate their commitment to energy conservation. They are money changers lost in a narrow orbit. They resign. They burn out. They decide not to run or serve. They read Buddhist economics, listen to prophets of decentralization and then proceed to create new bureaucracies to stamp out old ones. (Nixon's "Anti-Big Government" one was bigger than Johnson's.) They are organizational Houdinis, surrounded by sharks or shackled in a water cage and manage to escape, miraculously, while the public marvels at the feat and then longs for something more than "disappearing acts." They are motivating people through fear, or by cautiously following the "trends," or by posing as Reality through adopting a "Let's Face It" cynicism. They are all characters in a dreamless society. Groping in the darkness, learning how to "retrench," as if that were an art like playing the violin. And they are all scared.

And who can blame them? Sweaty palms are understandable, even natural. That is the final irony. Precisely at the time when the trust and credibility of our leaders is at an all-time low and when survivors in leadership feel most inhibited in exercising the potentiality of power, we most need individuals who can lead. We need people who can shape the future, not just barely manage to get through the day.

There is no simple solution. But there are some things we must recognize:

• Leaders must develop the vision and strength to call the shots. There are risks in taking the initiative. The greater risk is to wait for orders. We need leaders at every level who can lead, not just manage.

• This means that institutions (and followers) have to recognize that they *need* leadership, that their need is for vision, energy, and drive, rather than for blandness and safety.

• This means that the leader must be a "conceptualist" (not just someone to tinker with the "nuts and bolts"). A conceptualist is more than an "idea man." He must have an entrepreneurial vision, a sense of perspective, the time and the inclination to think about the forces and raise the fundamental questions that will affect the destiny of both the institution and the society within which it is embedded.

• This means that he must have a sense of continuity and significance in order, to paraphrase the words of Shelley, to see the present in the past and the future in the present. He must, in the compelling moments of the present, be able to clarify problems—elevate them into understandable choices for the constituents—rather than exploit them; to define issues, not aggravate them.

In this respect leaders are essentially educators. Our great political leaders, such as Jefferson, Lincoln, and Wilson tried to educate the people about problems by studying the messy existential groaning of the people and transforming murky problems into understandable issues. A leader who responds to a drought by attacking the lack of rainfall is not likely to inspire a great deal of confidence. What we see today is sometimes worse: leaving the problem as a problem (e.g., "the economy" or "the energy crisis") or allowing the problem to get out of control until it sours and becomes a "crisis." What is essential, instead, are leaders who will get at the underlying issues and present a clear alternative. Dr. Martin Luther King, Jr. provided this perspective for black people. We sorely need the same leadership for the whole nation.

• A leader must get at the truth and learn how to filter the unwieldy flow of information into coherent patterns. He must prevent the distortion of that information by over-eager aides who will tailor it to what they consider to be his prejudices or vanities. The biggest problem of a leader—any leader—is getting the truth. Pierre du Pont said well in a long-ago note to his brother Irenée, "One cannot expect to know what will happen, one can only consider himself fortunate if he can know what *has* happened." The politics of bureaucracy tend to interfere with rather than facilitate truth gathering.

That's mainly true because the huge size of our organizations and the enormous overload burdening every leader make it impossible for him to verify all his own information, analyze all of his own problems, or always decide who should or should not have his ear or time. Since he must rely for much of this upon his key assistants and officers, he would not feel comfortable in so close and vital a relationship with men (women, unfortunately, would not even be considered!) who were not at least of kindred minds and of compatible personalities.

Of course, this is perfectly human, and up to a point understandable. But the consequences can be devastating for it means that the leader is likely to see only that highly selective information, or those carefully screened people that his key assistants decide he should see. And he may discover too late that he acted on information that was inadequate or inaccurate, or that he has been shielded from "troublesome" visitors who wanted to tell him what he should have known, or that he had been protected from some problem that should have been his primary concern.

Given the character of today's institutions with their multiple dependencies and advocacies, picking a team of congenial and compatible associates may be deadly, a replay of Watergate. The most striking thing and most obvious impression I remember from the early Watergate hearings is how much all the Nixon aides looked alike. I had trouble telling Dean from Magruder, Porter from Sloan, Strachan from Haldeman. In appearance, they are almost mirror images of the younger Nixon of the 1940s, as if they were that spiritual or ghostly double called doppelganger. It is easy enough to cry shame on Watergate without perceiving its interconnections with our own lives and organizations and, in lesser degree, our conduct.

For in too many institutions a very few people are filtering the facts, implicitly skewing reality, and selecting information that provides an inaccurate picture on which decisions may be based. Such skewing can affect history: Barbara Tuchman in her recent book on China tells how, in the 1940s, Mao Tse Tung wanted very much to visit Roosevelt, but Roosevelt cancelled the proposed meeting on the basis of incredibly biased information from Ambassador Pat Hurley. It was nearly thirty years later that another President sought out the meeting with Mao, which earlier conceivably could have averted many subsequent disasters.

So the leader cannot rely exclusively on his palace guards for information. Hard as it is to do, he must have multiple information sources and must remain accessible, despite the fact that accessibility in modern times seems one of the most under-rated political virtues. The Romans, who were the greatest politicians of antiquity, and probably also the busiest men, valued that quality highly in their leaders. Cicero, in praising Pompey, commented on his ready availability, not only to his subordinates, but to the ordinary soldiers in his command.

A later Roman historian recounted this even more telling anecdote about the Emperor Hadrian. The emperor, who at that time ruled almost the entire civilized world, was riding into Rome in his chariot when an old woman blocked his path. The woman asked him to hear a grievance. Hadrian brushed her aside, saying that he was too busy.

"Then you're too busy to be emperor," she called after him. Whereupon he halted his chariot and heard her out.

A pebble dropped in Watergate has its ripple throughout the complex organizational society, and by the same token it is the excesses, the concealments, the arrogance and half-truths of a thousand faceless doppelgangers, in innumerable large organizations, that make a Watergate, an Attica, a Selma possible.

• The leader must be a social architect who studies and shapes what is called the "culture of work"—those intangibles that are so hard to discern but are so terribly important in governing the way people act, the values and norms that are subtly transmitted to individuals and groups and that tend to create binding and bonding. In whatever goals and values the leader pursues he must proceed toward their implementation by designing a social architecture which encourages understanding, participation, and ownership of the goals. He must, of course, learn about and be influenced by those who will be affected by the decisions which contain the day-to-day realization of the goals. At the very least, he must be forever conscious that the culture can facilitate or subvert "the best laid plans. . . ."

The culture of an organization dictates the mechanisms by which conflict can be resolved, and how costly, humane, fair, and reasonable the outcomes will be. It can influence whether or not there is a "zero-sum" mentality that insists upon an absolute winner or an absolute loser or whether there is a climate of hope. There can be no progress without hope, and there can be no hope if our organizations view conflict as a football game, a win-lose (or possibly tie) situation. While zero-sum situations are extremely rare, most leaders (and followers) tend to respond to most conflicts as if there has to be only one winner and only one loser. In reality, organizations and nations are involved in a much different kind of contest, resembling not so much football as it does the remarkable Swedish game, Vasa Run, in which many take part, some reach the finish line earlier than others and are rewarded for it, but all get there in the end.

Lots of things go into producing a culture: the particular technology of the institution, its peculiar history and geography, the characteristics of the people, and its social architecture. The leader must understand these things; he must have the capacities of an amateur social anthropologist so that he can understand the culture within which he works and which he himself can have some part in creating and maintaining.

• The task of the leader is to lead. And to lead others he must first of all know himself. His ultimate test is the wise use of power. As Sophocles says in *Antigone:* "It is hard to learn the mind of any mortal, or the heart, till he be tried in chief authority. Power shows the man."

So he must learn, most of all, to listen to himself. He must integrate his ideal with his actions and, even when a crackling discrepancy exists, learn how to tolerate this ambiguity between the desirable and the necessary, but not so much tolerance that the margins between them become undiscernible. When that happens, the leader is unwittingly substituting an authentic ideal for an evasion of convenience. Soon he'll forget about the goal—and even feel "comfortable" with an illusion of progress. He must learn how to listen to understand, not to evaluate. He must learn to play, to live with ambiguity and inconsistency. And, most of all, the test of any leader is whether he can ride and direct the process of change and, by so doing, build new strengths in the process.

5

How to Be a Leader

MICHAEL KORDA

At a moment when we are waiting to see whether we have elected a President or a leader, it is worth examining the differences between the two. For not every President is a leader, but every time we elect a President we hope for one, especially in times of doubt and crisis. In easy times we are ambivalent—the leader, after all, makes demands, challenges the status quo, shakes things up.

Leadership is as much a question of timing as anything else. The leader must appear on the scene at a moment when people are looking for leadership, as Churchill did in 1940, as Roosevelt did in 1933, as Lenin did in 1917. And when he comes, he must offer a simple, eloquent message.

Great leaders are almost always great simplifiers, who cut through argument, debate and doubt to offer a solution everybody can understand and remember. Churchill warned the British to expect "Blood, toil, tears and sweat"; FDR told Americans that "the only thing we have to fear is fear itself"; Lenin promised the war-weary Russians peace, land and bread. Straightforward but potent messages.

We have an image of what a leader ought to be. We even recognize the physical signs: leaders may not necessarily be tall, but they must have bigger-than-life, commanding features—LBJ's nose and ear lobes, Ike's broad grin. A trademark also comes in handy: Lincoln's stovepipe hat, JFK's rocker. We expect our leaders to stand out a little, not to be like ordinary men. Half of President Ford's trouble lay in the fact that, if you closed your eyes for a moment, you couldn't remember his face, figure or clothes. A leader should have an unforgettable identity, instantly and permanently fixed in people's minds.

Special

It also helps for a leader to be able to do something most of us can't: FDR overcame polio; Mao swam the Yangtze River at the age of 72. We don't want our leaders to be "just like us." We want them to be like us but better, special, more so. Yet if they are *too* different, we reject them. Adlai Stevenson was too cerebral. Nelson Rockefeller, too rich.

Even television, which comes in for a lot of knocks as an image-builder that magnifies form over substance, doesn't altogether obscure the qualities of leadership we recognize, or their absence. Television exposed Nixon's insecurity, Humphrey's fatal infatuation with his own voice.

A leader must know how to use power (that's what leadership is about), but he also has to have a way of showing that he does. He has to be able to project firmness—no physical clumsiness (like Ford), no rapid eye movements (like Carter).

A Chinese philosopher once remarked that a leader must have the grace of a good dancer, and there is a great deal of wisdom to this. A leader should know how to appear relaxed and confident. His walk should be firm and purposeful. He should be able, like Lincoln, FDR, Truman, Ike and JFK, to give a good, hearty, belly laugh, instead of the sickly grin that passes for good humor in Nixon or Carter. Ronald Reagan's training as an actor showed to good effect in the debate with Carter, when by his easy manner and apparent affability, he managed to convey the impression that in fact he was the President and Carter the challenger.

If we know what we're looking for, why is it so difficult to find? The answer lies in a very simple truth about leadership. People can only be led where they want to go. The leader follows, though a step ahead. Americans *wanted* to climb out of the Depression and needed someone to tell them they could do it, and FDR did. The British believed that they could still win the war after the defeats of 1940, and Churchill told them they were right.

A leader rides the waves, moves with the tides, understands the deepest yearnings of his people. He cannot make a nation that wants peace at any price go to war, or stop a nation determined to fight from doing so. His purpose must match the national mood. His task is to force the people's energies and desires, to define them in simple terms, to inspire, to make what people already want seem attainable, important, within their grasp.

Above all, he must dignify our desires, convince us that we are taking part in the making of great history, give us a sense of glory about ourselves. Winston Churchill managed, by sheer rhetoric, to turn the British defeat and the evacuation of Dunkirk in 1940 into a major victory. FDR's words turned the sinking of the American fleet at Pearl Harbor into a national rallying cry instead of a humiliating national scandal. A leader must stir our blood, not appeal to our reason.

Fallacy

For this reason, businessmen generally make poor leaders. They tend to be pragmatists who think that once you've explained why something makes sense, people will do it. But history shows the fallacy of this belief. When times get tough, people don't want to be told what went wrong, or lectured, or given a lot of complicated statistics and plans (like Carter's energy policy) they don't understand. They want to be moved, excited, inspired, consoled, uplifted—in short, led!

A great leader must have a certain irrational quality, a stubborn refusal to face facts, infectious optimism, the ability to convince us that all is not lost even when we're afraid it is. Confucius suggested that, while the advisers of a great leader should be as cold as ice, the leader himself should have fire, a spark of divine madness.

He won't come until we're ready for him, for the leader is like a mirror, reflecting back to us our own sense of purpose, putting into words our own dreams and hopes, transforming our needs and fears into coherent policies and programs.

Our strength makes him strong; our determination makes him determined; our courage makes him a hero; he is, in the final analysis, the symbol of the best in us, shaped by our own spirit and will. And when these qualities are lacking in us, we can't produce him; and even with all our skill at image building, we can't fake him. He is, after all, merely the sum of us.

6

Leadership: A Challenge to Traditional Research Methods and Assumptions

Barbara Karmel

Joan Woodward tripped across a block of gold and labelled it "technology,"
and it made sense of otherwise hopeless data.

Paraphrased from Charles Perrow

Now and again, one stumbles across a metaphor so apt and so revealing that it seems to make sense of much more than the data. In this case, let us apply the meaning of Perrow's observation to the domain of leadership research. We have tripped over a block of gold, labelled it "leadership" and hope that it makes sense of both reality and the data. Reviewers of this domain are in substantial agreement that the whole history of research on leadership has led us to no clear conclusions and has provided little guidance in theory building (11, 18, 27). This article does not propose to review the early history of leadership (For a review, see Stogdill [31]), but to concentrate on recent research and suggest ways and means of moving into a productive future from a languishing present.

Two factors can be identified as primary contributors to the uncertain state of the art in leadership research. One, definitional confusion results from the confounding effects of environmental factors. Such diverse factors as interpretation of the scope of the leader's responsibilities, the vesting of formal authority, and structural characteristics of the organization play havoc with pursuit of a generalized and stable definition of this concept. Two, unrecognized and unacknowledged assumptions

Reprinted from *Academy of Management Review*, 3:3 (July 1978), pp. 475–482, by permission of the author and publisher.

have infiltrated the design of leadership studies, operationalization of the variable, and interpretation of findings.

This article systematically examines these two classes of problems and suggests ways and means of treating them in the design and interpretation of leadership studies, thus aiding in the evolution of the construct.

Problem Number 1: Definitional Confusion

Let us apply Perrow's metaphor to the problem of definitional confusion. Consider the possibility that the block of gold is not a block, but many blocks, and that leadership is not a single concept but, depending on the *purpose* of the investigation, a collection of concepts sharing the common theme, "behavior that makes a difference" in the purposive behavior of others (2, p. 238). This general theme does not provide a sufficient basis for definition and operationalization of the leadership variable but does establish boundaries of the domain. Within these boundaries, leadership can be conceptualized either as a process or as a determinant of behavior directed toward goals. This theme, or general agreement about a bounded area, should not be used to specify the configuration, size, or number of elements within. But neither should the data alone serve as the sole basis for determining the configuration, size, and number of elements. The former approach, conceptually based, is often attacked as impractical, unscientific, and idealistic; the latter, data-based, as raw empiricism without conceptual underpinning. This distinction between conceptually and operationally derived definitions is not new. It was eloquently stated in Golembiewski's *The Small Group* (10, pp. 283–290).

At one extreme in leadership research, House's charismatic theory (13) appears to define the bounded area and deduce its characteristics by phenomenological observation and inference about followers of some charismatic leaders. At the other extreme, the quasi-theory of leadership based on the Ohio State studies (2) rests on factor analytic analyses of raw data without a systematic attempt to link these factors in a nomological net. Even though these two approaches are in very different stages of evolution, they illustrate two distinct methods of attack, and may represent two different constructs having in common only the existence of a leader-follower relationship. It has been convenient to apply the label "leadership" to both, despite the very different purposes for which they were generated.

Thus the thorny path to a definition of leadership would be facilitated by understanding and delineating the investigator's purposes. Pfeffer asserts, "Analysis of the leadership process is contingent on the intent of the researcher" (24, p. 27). In summary comments at the SIU Fourth Biennial Leadership Symposium, Campbell stated: "The conceptualization of leadership cannot be divorced from the purpose for which it is considered" (3, p. 225). Thus, reduction of definitional confusion depends on establishing a classification of the *purposes* of research on leadership. For example, the practitioner asks how to train a leader; the behavioral scientist asks how to know a leader when you see one; the student asks how to be a leader; and the body politic asks "Where have all the leaders gone?" By context, we infer a different connotation to each use of the word "leader." The reader is invited to choose a synonym for the word "leader" in each of the examples above (e.g., manager, influencer, controller, father). It is consequently very difficult to settle on a single definition of leadership that is general enough to accommodate these many meanings and specific enough to serve as a functional guide to operationalization of the variable.

Even within the category of research qua research (the purpose is theory-building), a variety of sub-purposes may suggest different meanings and operationalizations of the variable. For example, operant theorists focus upon definitions such as "A leader is a manager of reinforcement contingencies" (29, p. 121). Scott (28) states that it is not necessary to have a complete description of follower behavior in order to analyze the structure of leader behavior. This perspective opts for a narrowly defined construct with minimum direct concern for exogenous variables and maximum clarity in experimental design.

Viewed from a more complex perspective, leadership can be defined in terms of dyadic and interactive behaviors of leader and follower, emphasizing evaluation of dynamic interindividual interaction. Group theorists add another element of complexity by using a broad interpretation of interaction, including group and inter-group relationships. Further along the complexity dimension are researchers who agree with Melcher that, "One cannot isolate leadership research from organizational research" (21, p. 98). Attempts to do so, according to this line of thought, inevitably result in a low percentage of explained variance due to artificial exclusion of environmental elements which impact directly on the leadership process. Karmel and Egan's study (16) of dimensionality of managerial performance included, but was not limited to, "leader behaviors" and reported results which are inconsistent with traditional leadership studies. This is not surprising since the purpose of the research was to investigate the full structure of managerial performance rather than measure specific leader behaviors determined *a priori*. In summary, a global definition of leadership, for all purposes, does not seem to be useful in advancing scientific inquiry; nor will scientific inquiry be facilitated by abandoning pursuit of definition. Therefore, the problem of definitional confusion should be attacked by specification and classification of the purposes for which inquiry is undertaken. This will require identification of underlying dimensions of purposes such as "need of the user" (e.g., practitioner, scientist, student, philosopher) or "complexity," extensiveness of the behavioral domain to be measured. A multi-dimensional classification of research purpose has potential to capture in a parsimonious fashion the effects of: (a) differences in sample sizes which preclude comparative analysis of competing operationalizations; (b) the myriad of environmental factors which impinge on some operationalizations but not others; (c) situation-specific factors; and (d) differences in level of analysis, perceptual vs. objective and individual vs. aggregate.

The reader may now believe that the introduction of research purpose as a stratification variable will further proliferate the operationalizations race. On the contrary, developments of a taxonomy of research purpose will facilitate weeding out of imprecise operationalizations and blending of those having similar purpose and content. In addition, under the umbrella of a purpose taxonomy it should be possible to determine *a priori* which operationalizations should be expected to show similar results and which should not. This is the keystone of theory-testing research. As stated by Smith, Kendall, and Hulin, "It is easy to make *post hoc* explanations, but we cannot extrapolate to new situations until we can classify them in some objective manner in relation to those situations which have already been studied" (30, p. 160).

Problem Number 2:
Unrecognized Research Assumptions

Some years ago in pursuit of knowledge about the leadership concept, a massive empirical effort was undertaken at Ohio State University (31). These studies resulted in identification of two dominant dimensions: Initiating Structure (IS) and Consideration (C). These two dimensions, loosely representing task and people, are the foundation for a broad range of leadership research, both in assumptions about dimensionality and in research instrumentation. The instrumentation (LBDQ, LOQ, SBDQ) emanating from the Ohio State studies has become endemic. Thus, we are in danger not only of developing a science of questionnaire behavior in lieu of leader behavior (3), we are also in danger of building an over-simplified, narrow, and unrealistic science of leadership based on the *assumption* about dimensionality which underlies a very significant proportion of current instrument development and research design. We are hooked on these two dimensions, by whatever name they are called, with no one but ourselves to blame. Leadership is one domain among many in organizational behavior where the absence of construct validation leaves us wide open to charges of undetected contamination in research results and deficiency in measurement techniques. The task and people dimensions as measured and defined by existing instruments may represent fully the real underlying phenomena, but we will not know until we construct instruments and develop observational techniques which are free of dimensional contamination and provide a scientific test of alternative hypotheses.

To support the charge that we are hooked on these two dimensions, consider their explicit presence in several "theories" of leadership. Theories X and Y (20), the Blake formulation (1), and several hundred studies based on the LBDQ (31, 32) are obvious cases in point. Each depends fundamentally on the two dimensions, people and task, out of which IS and C are made. Less obvious, but compellingly similar, is the Bowers and Seashore Four-Factory Theory (2), in which IS is captured by Work Facilitation and Goal Emphasis, and C is captured by Support and Interaction Facilitation. Path-goal theory (12) posits the two general elements of expectancy and valence. Expectancy rests on the assumption that individuals have a need for clarity (high EI and EII probabilities); valence assumes their need for satisfaction (achievement of desired objectives). If the word "structure" is substituted for clarity and "consideration" for satisfaction, we see a familiar pattern. Path goal prescriptions for leader behavior can then be interpreted as the leader's responsibility to facilitate fulfillment of followers' needs for structure and consideration. Since this is a process theory, it also posits a multiplicative relationship between the two dimensions and focuses on the follower's perception of what constitutes structure and consideration. Variations on the theme notwithstanding, the elements are the same.

With respect to the Fiedler contingency model (7), a parallel with IS and C can be demonstrated at two levels. One, the behavioral interpretation of LPC scores suggests a dimension from task-oriented to relationships (people)-oriented. The ancillary assumption of unidimensionality is even more restrictive than the IS and C formulation. Two, in later studies relating leader behavior and group effectiveness (8), Fiedler suggests that a relationships-oriented leader is more effective in situations of intermediate favorableness, i.e., a leader who is preoccupied with the group's needs for C rather than IS in a situation where things are neither very good nor very bad. In summary, the basic pattern of dimensionality in leadership "theories" is common; additional assumptions wrapped around the people and task dimensions give each theory a unique appearance.

Beyond the conceptual argument that IS and C are prominent in the major theoretical formulations, there is convincing numerical evidence of the pervasiveness of these dimensions. Studies which use variants of LBDQ are to be found in nearly every issue of every OB journal. There are variations and extensions such as Larson, Hunt, and Osborn's (19) creatively titled study of IS and C vs. IS or C and Durand and Nord's (6) extension to an evaluation of the effects of two personality characteristics on subordinates' perceptions of leader behavior. The confining assumption of IS and C dimensionality is demonstrated in Ilgen and Fugii's (15) study on validation of leader behavior descriptions. An "independent" measurement scale called Behavior Checklist is employed. The first seven of fourteen items are based on C and the second seven on IS. The behaviors captured by this scale are determined by and limited to the underlying IS and C dimensionality. Thus the term "validity" must be narrowly interpreted, and the validity test is confounded by dimensional commonality between independent and dependent variables.

In spite of, or perhaps because of, the high frequency of IS and C studies, Schriesheim, House, and Kerr (26) note that we are now encountering definitional problems depending on which operationalization of IS is used and that comparability among studies is poor. More and more studies are not necessarily better and better. Greene avers that "the most heavily investigated dimensions generally lack potential for significantly affecting behavior," and "leadership style dimensions are too few and too narrow in definition to be representative of outcomes of leader and subordinate interaction" (11, p. 58). The traditional IS and C scales assume a two-factor model to the exclusion of such dimensions as activity level, attribution characteristics, and importance. For example, judgments about leaders may be influenced by the physical "busy-ness" or psychological activation level of the leader, followers may prefer to attribute causality to the people who are their leaders rather than seemingly uncontrollable events, and the leadership function may be relatively unimportant in some situations. Dansereau states, "Major pratfalls seem likely when untested assumptions are made about how leaders behave" (5, p. 69), and Kerr suggests that we "stop assuming what really ought to be demonstrated . . ." (17, p. 152). Are we hooked on IS and C because instrumentation exists which produces quick studies and quick results?

There are studies designed for different purposes which utilize a different level of analysis and make different assumptions about dimensionality. Miner (22) recommends reconceptualization of leadership as control: hierarchical, professional, group and task. But do we need to throw out the baby (leadership) with the bath water (definitional confusion)? It may simply be that the control orientation is a different way to slice the theoretical pie, having a distinctly different underlying dimensionality. As Miner puts it, "We simply do not know what we want to know" (22, p. 198). House (13) posits the special case of leadership as charisma, in which being nurturant, possessing competence, and having high self-esteem appear to be the underlying dimensions, but these dimensions have been neither tested empirically nor subjected to an analysis of construct validity. Vroom and Jago (33) use a behavioral decision theory approach in which the dimensionality is not clear, but is clearly not IS and C. Does the dimensionality inferred in this model reflect its diagnostic purpose? A number of studies focus on role interpretations of leadership and consider "role making, taking and playing" (4, p. 185) as a continuous process, thus defining a functional dimensionality. Whether focused on control, charisma, diagnosis, or function, each model assumes a dimensionality by the very act of categorizing elements within the construct. But this dimensionality is not defended by analysis of the nomological net and not demonstrated empirically through a construct validation process. It is simply assumed.

Given the chaotic state of the art in leadership research, it is appropriate to consider ways and means of evaluating dimensionality of the concept without relying on instruments contaminated (or attenuated) by unproven, a priori assumptions. For example, two recent studies have utilized a non-metric multi-dimensional scaling (MDS) approach, one of the few analytical techniques which does not require use of existing leadership instruments. Both studies opt for a broad interpretation of leadership and hence would be expected to identify a larger perceptual space or domain within which leader behaviors are observed. An MDS study by Salancik et al. investigated leadership as an element in the social structure, that is, evaluation of the leader's "position in the social network of others" (25, p. 82). The empirically derived dimensionality of leadership included social status of the leader, responsibilities for work initiation, and organizational function. Work initiation is characterized as the prominence of the leader/manager in bringing work into the department, as distinct from handling the mechanics of processing work. Note that IS and C are not represented.

The Karmel and Egan study (16) found that style, role, behavior, and trait dimensions were used in making judgments about managerial performance. The major evaluative dimension which most closely resembles the traditional concept of leader behavior was termed "managerial competence" and was interpreted to reflect cognitive style. High competent managers appeared to be divergers (34) whose behaviors led peers and subordinates to see the manager as a problem-solver who thinks in big picture, assimilative terms. The low end of the competence dimension in this study contained both IS and C descriptors, with the obvious implication that IS and C are not useful concepts in discriminating between high and low competent managers. Other dimensions identified were purposefulness, role centrality and activity, none of which are explicitly included in traditional investigations, interpretations, or definitions of leadership. These two studies clearly illustrate the need for re-evaluation of the IS and C dimensions, based on careful specification of the purposes for which they are useful and the purposes for which they are misleading due to over-simplification of complex phenomena. We are led once again to the compelling conclusion that the purpose of the investigation (or the intent of the investigator) serves as a major contingency in conceptualization of leadership.

Conclusions and Interpretations

Pfeffer (24) is correct in asserting that the leadership concept is ambiguous. However, this very ambiguity provides conceptual space to evolve a more fully developed understanding of leadership. To this end, three propositions are offered.

P1: *Ambiguity in the definition of leadership is a consequence of diversity in the purposes for which research is conducted.*

The corollary of this proposition is that a topography of research purpose will provide a map or chart through ambiguous territory. This charting process is the path from a concept to a construct. The path which characterizes present research on leadership can be described as:

General Concept $\longrightarrow$ *Specific Operationalizations* $\overset{?}{=}$ *Constructs*

A more rigorous and defensible path, with higher probability of success in theory building, should take the form:

General Concept $\longrightarrow$ *Constructs* $\longrightarrow$ *Operationalization*

P2: *Underlying dimensionality of the leadership construct is dependent on these separate and diverse purposes.*

The corollary of this proposition is that no single model, perceptual or behavioral, adequately represents the full concept. However, *within* general clusters of purpose, an effort can be made to find consistent and parsimonious statements of dimensionality. An understanding of dimensionality within the concept must precede operationalization. The research path then takes the form:

$$\begin{array}{c} Purpose \\ \downarrow \end{array}$$

General Concept $\longrightarrow$ *Construct* $\longrightarrow$ *Dimensionality* $\longrightarrow$ *Operationalization*

P3: *An improved state of the art in leadership depends on conceptual and empirical analyses of research purpose.*

Further iterations of the historical trends in leadership research do not show promise for evolution, refinement, or validation of the construct. An intensive analysis of research purpose and its implications for application will provide a clearer view of the construct and capture a wide array of exogenous variables presently ignored or treated as multiple contingencies. Purpose holds a key to resolution of the definitional and operational dilemma with which leadership research is now confronted.

References

1. Blake, R. R., and J. S. Mouton. *The Managerial Grid* (Houston: Gulf, 1964).

2. Bowers, D. G., and S. E. Seashore. "Predicting Organizational Effectiveness with a Four-Factor Theory of Leadership," *Administrative Science Quarterly*, Vol. 11, No. 2 (1966), 238–263.

3. Campbell, J. P. "Summary Comments," in J. G. Hunt and L. L. Larson (Eds.), *Leadership: The Cutting Edge* (Carbondale, Ill. SIU Press, 1977).

4. Cummings, L. L. "Assessing the Graen/Cashman Model and Comparing It with Other Approaches," in J. G. Hunt and L. L. Larson (Eds.), *Leadership Frontiers* (Kent, Ohio: Comparative Administration Research Institute, 1975).

5. Dansereau, F., and McD. Dumas. "Pratfalls and Pitfalls in Drawing Inferences about Leader Behavior in Organizations," in J. G. Hunt and L. L. Larson (Eds.), *Leadership: The Cutting Edge* (Carbondale, Ill. SIU Press, 1977).

6. Durand, D. E., and W. R. Nord. "Perceived Leader Behavior as a Function of Personality Characteristics of Supervisors and Subordinates," *Academy of Management Journal*, Vol. 19, No. 3 (September 1976), 427–438.

7. Fiedler, F. E. *A Theory of Leadership Effectiveness* (New York: McGraw-Hill, 1967).

8. Fiedler, F. E. "Validation and Extension of the Contingency Model of Leadership Effectiveness: A Review of Empirical Findings," *Psychological Bulletin*, Vol. 76, No. 2 (1971), 128–148.

9. Fleishman, E. A., and E. F. Harris. "Patterns of Leadership Behavior Related to Employee Grievances and Turnover," *Personnel Psychology*, Vol. 15 (1962), 43–56.

10. Golembiewski, R. T. *The Small Group* (Chicago: University of Chicago Press, 1962).

11. Greene, C. N. "Disenchantment with Leadership Research: Some Causes, Recommendations and Alternative Directions," in J. G. Hunt and L. L. Larson (Eds.), *Leadership: The Cutting Edge* (Carbondale, Ill. SIU Press, 1977).

12. House, R. J. "A Path-Goal Theory of Leader Effectiveness," *Administrative Science Quarterly*, Vol. 16 (1971), 321–338.

13. House, R. J. "A 1976 Theory of Charismatic Leadership," in J. G. Hunt and L. L. Larson (Eds.), *Leadership: The Cutting Edge* (Carbondale, Ill. SIU Press, 1977).

14. Hunt, J. G., and L. L. Larson. *Leadership Frontiers* (Kent, Ohio: Comparative Administration Research Institute, 1975).

15. Ilgen, D. R., and D. S. Fugii, "An Investigation of the Validity of Leader Behavior Descriptions Obtained from Subordinates," *Journal of Applied Psychology,* Vol. 61, No. 5 (1976), 642–651.

16. Karmel, B., and D. M. Egan. "Managerial Performance: A New Look at Underlying Dimensionality," *Organizational Behavior and Human Performance,* Vol. 15 (1976), 322–334.

17. Kerr, S. "Substitutes for Leadership," *Proceedings of the American Institute for Decision Sciences,* 8th Annual Conference, San Francisco, California, 1976.

18. Korman, A. K. "Consideration, Initiating Structure, and Organizational Criteria—A Review," *Personnel Psychology,* Vol. 19 (1966), 349–362.

19. Larson, L. L., J. G. Hunt, and R. N. Osborn. "The Great Hi-Hi Leader Behavior Myth: A Lesson from Occam's Razor," *Academy of Management Journal,* Vol. 19, No. 4 (December 1976), 628–641.

20. McGregor, D. *The Human Side of Enterprise* (New York: McGraw-Hill, 1960).

21. Melcher, A. J. "Leadership Models and Research Approaches," in J. G. Hunt and L. L. Larson (Eds.), *Leadership: The Cutting Edge* (Carbondale, Ill. SIU Press, 1977).

22. Miner, J. B. "The Uncertain Future of the Leadership Concept," in J. G. Hunt and L. L. Larson (Eds.), *Leadership Frontiers* (Kent, Ohio: Comparative Administration Research Institute, 1975).

23. Perrow, Charles. "The Short and Glorious History of Organizational Theory," *Organizational Dynamics* (Summer 1973), 2–15.

24. Pfeffer, J. "The Ambiguities of Leadership," *Academy of Management Review* (January 1977), 104–112.

25. Salancik, G. R., B. J. Calder, K. M. Rowland, H. Leblebici, M. Conway. "Leadership as an Outcome of Social Structure and Process: A Multidimensional Analysis," in J. G. Hunt and L. L. Larson (Eds.), *Leadership Frontiers* (Kent, Ohio: Comparative Administration Research Institute, 1975).

26. Schriesheim, C., R. J. House, and S. Kerr. "Leader Initiating Structure: A Reconciliation of Discrepant Research Results and Some Empirical Tests," *Organizational Behavior and Human Performance,* Vol. 15 (1976), 297–321.

27. Schriescheim, C. A., and S. Kerr. "Theories and Measures of Leadership: A Critical Appraisal of Current and Future Directions," in J. G. Hunt and L. L. Larson (Eds.), *Leadership: The Cutting Edge* (Carbondale, Ill. SIU Press, 1977).

28. Scott, W. E. "Leadership: A Functional Analysis," in J. G. Hunt and L. L. Larson (Eds.), *Leadership: The Cutting Edge* (Carbondale, Ill. SIU Press, 1977).

29. Sims, H. P. "The Leader as Manager of Reinforcement Contingencies: An Empirical Example and a Model," in J. G. Hunt and L. L. Larson (Eds.), *Leadership: The Cutting Edge* (Carbondale, Ill. SIU Press, 1977).

30. Smith, P. C., L. M. Kendall, and C. L. Hulin. *The Measurement of Satisfaction in Work and Retirement* (Chicago: Rand McNally, 1969).

31. Stogdill, R. M. *Handbook of Leadership* (New York: The Free Press, 1974).

32. Stogdill, R. M., and A. E. Coons. *Leader Behavior: Its Description and Measurement* (Columbus: Ohio State University, Bureau of Business Research, 1957).

33. Vroom, V. H., and A. G. Jago. "Decision Making as a Social Process: Normative and Descriptive Models of Leader Behavior," *Decision Sciences* (December 1974), 160–186.

34. Wynne, B. E., and P. L. Hunsaker. "A Human Information-Processing Approach to the Study of Leadership," in J. G. Hunt and L. L. Larsons (Eds.), *Leadership Frontiers* (Kent, Ohio: Comparative Administration Research Institute, 1975).

Part Two

MANAGEMENT/ LEADERSHIP: WHAT'S THE DIFFERENCE?

Are there differences between management and leadership? To some people, the terms are synonymous; they argue that one cannot be a leader without being an effective manager and vice versa. Others differentiate management from leadership with firm conviction. To them, management is a clearly defined set of activities based on the use of learned tools and techniques, while leadership is a personality-based enigma with self-election growing out of a power or influence process.

There are many common elements in the various models of management proposed over the years. The concepts of *planning, organizing,* and exercising *control* dominate the literature. These functions or activities are, in themselves, the basis of the tools and techniques applied to the organizational resources of people, money, material, information, and time. Management success is evaluated in terms of effectiveness and efficiency of achieving organizational goals. These popular and commonly held principles stand in marked contrast to the vague and widely disputed concepts of leadership.

When it comes down to the actual behaviors necessary to be a good leader or a good manager, do such distinctions hold true? Successful leaders rarely achieve status in their organizations without paying attention to details, becoming immersed in the budgeting process, appraising the performance of subordinates and themselves, and participating in the political give-and-take of organizational life. David Campbell of The Center for Creative Leadership describes charismatic leaders without a management orientation as being cosmetic and without substance! He is convinced that leadership is recognized by most people only when there is a highly visible crisis or when there is some easily defined technological breakthrough—there is no leadership without a publicly visible event.

Yet, organizations continue to thrive because people plan, organize, and control resources wisely, reward excellence appropriately, and communicate effectively—in other words, do all the things called for by good management principles. Flamboyant, crisis-oriented leadership is certainly not the only way to assure organizational growth or survival.

In Part 2 our readings offer insights on whether the concern over similarities or distinctions between leadership and management is necessary. Chapter 7, "A Comprehensive Description of Managerial Work," by Henry Mintzberg, describes a manager as having two basic purposes. First, the manager must ensure that the organization produces its specific goods and services efficiently. Second, the manager must be certain that the organization serves the ends of those individuals who control it. Mintzberg defines ten interrelated roles performed by all managers. However, it is in one role—that of the leader—that the manager molds the image of the organization and directs its destiny. Leadership, then, is just one of many managerial roles, in Mintzberg's view.

In a popular *Harvard Business Review* article, "Managers and Leaders: Are They Different?" (Chapter 8) Abraham Zaleznik argues that, indeed, they are. A bureaucratic society that breeds managers may restrict the emergence of young leaders who need mentors and emotional interaction to develop. According to Zaleznik, managers and leaders differ in terms of personality, attitudes toward goals, conceptions of work, relationships with others, and senses of self. He contends that if organizations work at it they can develop leaders as well as managers.

Letters to the editor reacting to the Zaleznik article provide a companion piece (Chapter 9). The letter writers include key officers of some of this country's leading corporations. They present diverse responses to Zaleznik, each attempting to clarify the leader/manager issue.

In "Leadership and Headship: There Is a Difference," (Chapter 10) Charles Holloman makes an operational distinction between managerial headship and leadership. The former is characterized by authority relations, while the latter is viewed in terms of personal influence. Headship is maintained by a system of formal institutional authority directives, while leadership comes from group members and depends upon group acceptance of the appointed leader. Holloman basically helps us make a distinction between the person and the position that he or she holds.

In Chapter 11, written nearly twenty-five years ago, Alex Bavelas makes his own distinction between the idea of leadership as a personal quality and the idea of leadership as an organizational function. The first refers to a special combination of personal characteristics and leads us to consider qualities and abilities of the individual; the second approach focuses on the distribution of decision-making powers throughout an organization and leads us to consider the patterns of power and authority in organizations. According to Bavelas, the trend of management has been to remove as many of its decisions as possible from the realm of intuition to that of rational calculation. This new emphasis has not eliminated the role of personal leadership, writes Bavelas, but it has significantly redefined that role. The trend contains two serious threats. First, we may be systematically relinquishing the highest expression of personal leadership in favor of managerial expediency, which may be safer and more reliable but may yield at best only a high level of mediocrity. Second, having accepted the ordinary and improved its efficiency, we may be shunning the extraordinary, which could hold valuable skills we will sorely need to solve future problems. This remarkable article parallels contemporary writings that attempt to explain the larger dilemmas of our modern industrial society.

Chester Schriesheim, James Tolliver, and Orlando Behling write in "Leadership Theory: Some Implications for Managers" (Chapter 12), that leadership is a more specific process than management and more political in nature, implying that not every attempt at wielding leader-type influence will necessarily succeed. Other types of managerial behavior, in fact, may have a stronger influence on organizational effectiveness than those interpersonal efforts that are usually labeled "leadership." Furthermore, selection and training are not always de-terminants of leadership. Understanding how leadership evolves from personal interactions can help managers be more effective because they have more control over group behavior than they do over the more nonhuman aspects of their work. This situational nature of leadership and management activities may be changing as the actual situations change.

There do appear to be significant differences between leadership and management but the nature of these differences varies depending on how leadership is defined. Whether one concept is a subset of the other is not, we think, the issue. It is more important that we come to understand the individual and organizational variables involved. At the very least, we hope that the readings in Part 2 will clarify why confusion exists concerning the form and substance of management versus lead-ership.

7

A Comprehensive Description of Managerial Work

HENRY MINTZBERG

Definition and Basic Purposes

The manager is that person in charge of a formal organization or one of its subunits. He is vested with formal authority over his organizational unit, and this leads to his two basic purposes. First, the manager must ensure that his organization produces its specific goods or services efficiently. He must design, and maintain the stability of, its basic operations, and he must adapt it in a controlled way to its changing environment. Second, the manager must ensure that his organization serves the ends of those persons who control it (the "influencers"). He must interpret their particular preferences and combine these to produce statements of organizational preference that can guide its decision-making. Because of his formal authority the manager must serve two other basic purposes as well. He must act as the key communication link between his organization and its environment, and he must assume responsibility for the operation of his organization's status system.

Ten Working Roles

These basic purposes are operationalized through ten interrelated roles, performed by all managers. The roles fall into three groupings— three *interpersonal* roles, which derive from the manager's authority and status, three *informational* roles, which derive from the interpersonal roles and the access they provide to information, and four *decisional* roles, which derive from the manager's authority and information.

As *figurehead*, the simplest of managerial roles, the manager is a symbol, required because of his status to carry out a number of social, inspirational, legal, and ceremonial duties. In addition, the manager must be available to certain parties who demand to deal with him because of his status and authority. The *figurehead* role is most significant at the highest levels of the organizational hierarchy.

The *leader* role defines the manager's interpersonal relationships with his subordinates. He must bring together their needs and those of the organization to create a milieu in which they will work effectively. The manager motivates his subordinates, probes into their activities to keep them alert, and takes responsibility for the hiring, training, and promoting of those closest to him. The societal shift toward greater organizational democracy will cause managers to spend more time in the *leader* role.

The *liaison* role focuses on the manager's dealings with people outside his own organizational unit. He develops a network of contacts in which information and favors are traded for mutual benefit. The manager spends a considerable amount of time performing this role, first by making a series of commitments to establish these contacts, and then by engaging in various activities to maintain them. For some managers this role is paramount. In the managerial diad, for example, the chief executive generally focuses on outside work and the second in command concentrates on internal operations (notably the *leader* and the decisional roles). Line sales managers, because their orientation is external and interpersonal, give special attention to this role, and to the other two interpersonal roles as well.

Through the *leader* and *liaison* roles, the manager gains access to privileged information and he emerges as the "nerve center" of his organization. He alone has formal access to every subordinate in his own organization, and he has unique access to a variety of outsiders, many of whom are nerve centers of their own organizations. Thus the manager is his organization's information generalist, that person best informed about its operations and environment.

As *monitor* the manager continually seeks and receives internal and external information from a variety of sources to develop a thorough knowledge of his milieu. Because a good part of this information is current and nondocumented, the manager must take prime responsibility for the design of his own information system, which is necessarily informal. Managers in new jobs, particularly, spend considerable time on the *monitor* and *liaison* roles in order to build up their information systems and bring themselves up to the level of knowledge needed for effective strategy-making.

As *disseminator* the manager transmits some of his internal and external information to subordinates. In this way, he maintains their only access to certain privileged information. Some of this information is of a factual nature; some relates to the values of the organization's influencers.

As *spokesman* the manager transmits information to individuals outside his organizational unit. He acts in a public relations capacity, lobbies for his organization, informs key influencers, tells the public about the organization's performance, and sends useful information to his liaison contacts. Furthermore, the manager must serve outsiders as an expert in the industry or function in which his organization operates. Managers of staff groups, because their subunits are highly specialized and oriented to analysis, spend considerable time in this expert capacity as well as giving relatively more attention to the other informational roles.

Because of his formal authority and special information, the manager must take responsibility for his organization's strategy-making system— the means by which decisions important to his organizational unit are made and interrelated. Strategy is made through four decisional roles.

As *entrepreneur* the manager is responsible for the initiation and design of much of the controlled change in his organization. He continually searches for new opportunities and problems and he initiates improvement projects to deal with these. Once started, an improvement project may involve the manager in one of three ways. He may delegate all responsibility to a subordinate, implicitly retaining the right to replace him; he may delegate responsibility for the design work but retain responsibility for authorizing the project before implementation; or he may supervise the design work himself. Senior managers appear to maintain supervision at any one time over a large inventory of these projects. Each is worked on periodically, with each step followed by a period of delay during which the senior manager waits for the feedback of information or the occurrence of an event.

As *disturbance handler* the manager is required to take charge when his organization faces a major disturbance. Since each subordinate is charged with a specialized function, only the manager is able to intervene when the organization faces a novel stimulus that is unrelated to any particular function and for which it has no programmed response. In effect, the manager again acts as his organization's generalist—the problem-solver who can deal with any kind of stimulus. Disturbances may reflect an insensitivity to problems, but they may also result from the unanticipated consequences of bold innovation. Hence we may expect to find many disturbances in the work of managers of both innovative and insensitive organizations. One can also expect to find the *disturbance handler* role emphasized following a period of intense innovation; a period of major change must be followed by a period in which the change is consolidated. Furthermore, managers of small companies and those in line production jobs, especially at lower levels in the hierarchy, are likely to give the greatest attention to the *disturbance handler* role (and to the other decisional roles) because they tend to be most involved with the day-to-day maintenance of the workflow.

As *resource allocator* the manager oversees the allocation of all his organization's resources and thereby maintains control of its strategy-making process. He does this in three ways. First, by scheduling his own time the manager implicitly sets organizational priorities. Issues that fail to reach him fail to get support. Second, the manager designs the basic work system of his organization and programs the work of subordinates. He decides what will be done, who will do it, and what structure will be used. Third, the manager maintains ultimate control by authorizing, before implementation, all major decisions made by his organization. The authorization decisions are difficult ones to make; the issues are complex, but the time that can be devoted to them is short. The manager can ease the difficulty by choosing the person rather than the proposal. But when he must decide on the proposal, the manager makes use of loose models and plans that he develops implicitly from his nerve-center information. The models describe in a conceptual way a great variety of the internal and external situations that the manager faces. The plans—in the form of anticipated improvement projects— exist as his flexible vision of where the organization might go. Such plans serve as the common frame of reference against which he can evaluate, and hence interrelate, all proposals.

Finally, as *negotiator* the manager takes charge when his organization must have important negotiations with another organization. As *figurehead* he represents his organization, as *spokesman* he speaks for it, and as *resource allocator* he trades resources in real-time with the opposite party.

To summarize, the manager must design the work of his organization, monitor its internal and external environment, initiate change when desirable, and renew stability when faced with a disturbance. The manager must lead his subordinates to work effectively for the organization, and he must provide them with special information, some of which he gains through the network of contacts that he develops. In addition, the manager must perform a number of "housekeeping" duties, including informing outsiders, serving as *figurehead*, and leading major negotiations.

Thus, the popular view of the manager as the one who must take the broad view, do the unprogrammed work, and buttress the system where it is imperfect is only partly correct. Managers must also do their share of regular work and must involve themselves in certain ongoing organizational activities.

Basic Job Characteristics

It has been noted that the manager must take responsibility for the operation of his organization's strategy-making system, that he alone must find and process a significant amount of its important information, and that he must also perform a number of "housekeeping" duties. Added to all this is the open-ended nature of his job. There are no clear mileposts in the job of managing, never an indication that nothing more needs to be done for the moment, always the nagging thought that something could be improved if only the time could be found. Hence the manager's burden of responsibility is inherently great.

His problem is further compounded. The current and speculative nature of so much of the manager's information means that it is verbal. But the dissemination of verbal information is time-consuming. Hence the manager faces a "dilemma of delegation." He has unique access to much important information, but he lacks a formal and efficient means of disseminating it. The result is that the manager finds it difficult to delegate certain tasks with confidence, since he has neither the time nor the means to send along all the necessary information.

The net effect of all this is that the manager's time assumes a great opportunity cost. He carries this great burden of responsibility, yet he cannot easily delegate his tasks. As organizations become increasingly large and complex, this burden increases, particularly for senior managers. Unfortunately, these men cannot significantly increase their available time or significantly improve their abilities to manage. Hence the leaders of large complex bureaucracies face the real danger of becoming major obstructions in the flow of decisions and information.

These points explain a number of distinctive characteristics that can be observed in managerial work. The manager feels compelled to perform a great quantity of work and the pace he assumes is unrelenting. The manager seems to have little free time during the workday and he takes few breaks. Senior managers appear unable to escape from their work after hours because of what they take home and because their minds are constantly turned to their jobs.

The manager's activities are characterized by brevity, variety, and fragmentation. The vast majority are of brief duration, on the order of seconds for foremen and minutes for chief executives. A great variety of activities are performed, but with no obvious patterns. The trivial are interspersed with the consequential so that the manager must shift moods quickly and frequently. There is great fragmentation of work, and interruptions are commonplace. The characteristics of brevity and fragmentation, apparently present in virtually all managers' jobs, are most pronounced for those who are closest to the "action"—top managers of small organizations, managers at lower levels in the hierarchy, particularly in production jobs, and managers working in the most dynamic environments.

Interestingly, the manager shows signs of preference for brevity and interruption in his work. No doubt, he becomes conditioned by his workload. He develops an appreciation for the opportunity costs of his own time and he lives with an awareness that, no matter what he is doing, there are other, perhaps more important, things that he might do and that he must do. A tendency toward superficiality becomes the prime occupational hazard of the manager.

In choosing activities the manager gravitates where possible to the more active elements in his work—the current, the well-defined, the nonroutine. Very current information—gossip, hearsay, speculation—is favored; routine reports are not. Time scheduling reflects a focus on the definite and the concrete, and activities tend to deal with specific rather than general issues. These characteristics are clearly found in the activities of chief executives and most become even more pronounced at lower levels of the hierarchy. The manager's job is not one that breeds reflective planners; rather, it produces adaptive information manipulators who favor a stimulus-response milieu.

The manager's work is essentially that of communication and his tools are the five basic media—mail, telephone, unscheduled meetings, scheduled meetings and tours. Managers clearly favor the three verbal media, many spending on the order of 80 percent of their time in verbal contact. Some managers, such as those of staff groups, spend relatively more time alone. But the greatest share of the time of almost all managers is spent in verbal communication. The verbal media are favored because they are the action media, providing current information and rapid feedback. The mail, which moves slowly and contains little "live action" material, receives cursory treatment. Mail processing tends to be treated as a burden.

The informal media—the telephone and the unscheduled meeting— are generally used for brief contacts when the parties are well known to each other and when information or requests must be transmitted quickly. In contrast, scheduled meetings allow for more formal contacts, of longer duration, with large groups of people, and away from the organization. Of special interest is the flow of incidental, but often important, information at the beginning and end of scheduled meetings. Scheduled meetings are used for the special purposes of ceremony, strategy-making, and negotiation. Managers in large organizations and top managers of public organizations spend more time in scheduled meetings and other formal activities, while the work of lower-level managers and managers in dynamic environments tends to exhibit less formality.

Tours provide the manager with the opportunity to observe activity informally. Yet, managers apparently spend little time in this medium, perhaps because it involves nonspecific activity that is nonaction oriented.

An analysis of the characteristics of the manager's interactions with other people shows that he stands between his own organizational unit and an extensive network of contacts. These can include his unit's clients, suppliers, and associates, his peers and colleagues, and their superiors and subordinates. Non-line relationships are a significant component of every manager's job, generally consuming one-third to one-half of his contact time. Managers in large organizations appear to have greater ranges of these contacts and better communication patterns. Much of their horizontal communication, however, appears to be with small cliques of colleagues that serve as centers for specialized information. Subordinates consume about one-third to one-half of the manager's time. He interacts with a wide variety of subordinates, freely bypassing formal channels of authority to get the information he desires. Finally, the evidence suggests that managers spend relatively little time with their superiors, only about one-tenth of their contact hours.

It has been implied in a number of the above conclusions that the burden of his work results in the manager's being carried along by his job to a large extent. The evidence concerning who initiates the manager's contacts and what types of contacts he engages in would appear to bear this out. Nevertheless, the strong incumbent (in any but the most highly structured jobs) can control his own work in subtle ways. In the first place, he is responsible for many of his initial commitments which later lock him into a set of ongoing activities. In the second place, the strong manager can turn to his own advantage those activities in which he must engage; he can extract information, lobby for his causes, or implement changes.

An analysis of the roles further suggests a blend of duties and rights. The duties come with the roles of *figurehead, spokesman, disturbance handler,* and *negotiator.* But in the roles of *leader, entrepreneur,* and *resource allocator,* the manager has the opportunity to put his stamp on his organizational unit and set its course.

Science in the Job

The evidence suggests that there is no science in managerial work. That is to say, managers do not work according to procedures that have been prescribed by scientific analysis. Indeed, the modern manager appears to be basically indistinguishable from his historical counterparts. He may seek different information, but he gets most of it in the same old way, by word of mouth. He may make decisions dealing with modern technology, but he uses the same intuitive (that is, nonexplicit) procedures or "programs" in making them.

Managers use a whole repertoire of general-purpose programs in their work. Faced with a particular task, the manager chooses, combines, and sequences a set of programs to deal with it. We can identify a number of general-purpose programs—such as information dissemination, alternative selection, and negotiation. There are other general-purpose programs that are more difficult to isolate, such as those associated with the *leader* role. In addition, the manager has some special purpose programs. He uses one—the scheduling program—to control his activities and determine the sequence of tasks to be executed.

The current reality is that all these programs are locked in the manager's brain, not yet described by the management researcher. There can be no science of managing until these programs are demarcated, their contents specified, the set of them linked into a simulation of managerial work, and particular ones subjected to systematic analysis and improvement.

8

Managers and Leaders: Are They Different?

ABRAHAM ZALEZNIK

Most societies, and that includes business organizations, are caught between two conflicting needs: one for managers to maintain the balance of operations, and one for leaders to create new approaches and imagine new areas to explore. One might well ask why there is a conflict. Cannot both managers and leaders exist in the same society, or even better, cannot one person be both a manager and a leader? The author of this article does not say that is impossible but suggests that because leaders and managers are basically different types of people, the conditions favorable to the growth of one may be inimical to the other. Exploring the world views of managers and leaders, the author illustrates, using Alfred P. Sloan and Edwin Land among others as examples, that managers and leaders have different attitudes toward their goals, careers, relations with others, and themselves. And tracing their different lines of development, the author shows how leaders are of a psychologically different type than managers; their development depends on their forming a one-to-one relationship with a mentor.

What is the ideal way to develop leadership? Every society provides its own answers, defines its deepest concerns about the purposes, distributions, and uses of power. Business has contributed its answer to the leadership question by evolving a new breed called the manager. Simultaneously, business has established a new power ethic that favors collective over individual leadership, the cult of the group over that of personality. While ensuring the competence, control, and the balance of power relations among groups with the potential for rivalry, managerial leadership unfortunately does not necessarily ensure imagination, creativity, or ethical behavior in guiding the destinies of corporate enterprises.

Leadership inevitably requires using power to influence the thoughts and actions of other people. Power in the hands of an individual entails human risks: first, the risk of equating power with the ability to get immediate results; second, the risk of ignoring the many different ways people can legitimately accumulate power: and third, the risk of losing self-control in the desire for power. The need to hedge these risks accounts in part for the development of collective leadership and the managerial ethic. Consequently, an inherent conservatism dominates the culture of large organizations. In *The Second American Revolution*, John D. Rockefeller, 3rd. describes the conservatism of organizations: "An organization is a system, with a logic of its own, and all the weight of tradition and inertia. The deck is stacked in favor of the tried and proven way of doing things and against the taking of risks and striking out in new directions."[1]

Out of this conservatism and inertia organizations provide succession to power through the development of managers rather than individual leaders. And the irony of the managerial ethic is that it fosters a bureaucratic culture in business, supposedly the last bastion protecting us from the encroachments and controls of bureaucracy in government and education. Perhaps the risks associated with power in the hands of an individual may be necessary ones for business to take if organizations are to break free of their inertia and bureaucratic conservatism.

Manager Vs. Leader Personality

Theodore Levitt has described the essential features of a managerial culture with its emphasis on rationality and control:

> Management consists of the rational assessment of a situation and the systematic selection of goals and purposes (what is to be done?); the systematic development of strategies to achieve these goals; the marshalling of the required resources; the rational design, organization, direction, and control of the activities required to attain the selected purposes; and, finally, the motivating and rewarding of people to do the work.[2]

In other words, whether his or her energies are directed toward goals, resources, organization structures, or people, a manager is a problem solver. The manager asks himself, "What problems have to be solved, and what are the best ways to achieve results so that people will continue to contribute to this organization?" In this conception, leadership is a practical effort to direct affairs; and to fulfill his task, a manager requires that many people operate at different levels of status and responsibility. Our democratic society is, in fact, unique in having solved the problem of providing well-trained managers for business. The same solution stands ready to be applied to government, education, health care, and other institutions. It takes neither genius nor heroism to be a manager, but rather persistence, tough-mindedness, hard work, intelligence, analytical ability and, perhaps most important, tolerance and good will.

Another conception, however, attaches almost mystical beliefs to what leadership is and assumes that only great people are worthy of the drama of power and politics. Here, leadership is a psychodrama in which, as a precondition for control of a political structure, a lonely person must gain control of him or herself. Such an expectation of leadership contrasts sharply with the mundane, practical, and yet important conception that leadership is really managing work that other people do.

Two questions come to mind. Is this mystique of leadership merely a holdover from our collective childhood of dependency and our longing for good and heroic parents? Or, is there a basic truth lurking behind the need for leaders that no matter how competent managers are, their leadership stagnates because of their limitations in visualizing purposes and generating value in work? Without this imaginative capacity and the ability to communicate, managers, driven by their narrow purposes, perpetuate group conflicts instead of reforming them into broader desires and goals.

If indeed problems demand greatness, then, judging by past performance, the selection and development of leaders leave a great deal to chance. There are no known ways to train "great" leaders. Furthermore, beyond what we leave to chance, there is a deeper issue in the relationship between the need for competent managers and the longing for great leaders.

What it takes to ensure the supply of people who will assume practical responsibility may inhibit the development of great leaders. Conversely, the presence of great leaders may undermine the development of managers who become very anxious in the relative disorder that leaders seem to generate. The antagonism in aim (to have many competent managers as well as great leaders) often remains obscure in stable and well-developed societies. But the antagonism surfaces during periods of stress and change, as it did in the Western countries during both the Great Depression and World War II. The tension also appears in the struggle for power between theorists and professional managers in revolutionary societies.

It is easy enough to dismiss the dilemma I pose (of training managers while we may need new leaders, or leaders at the expense of managers) by saying that the need is for people who can be *both* managers and leaders. The truth of the matter as I see it, however, is that just as a managerial culture is different from the entrepreneurial culture that develops when leaders appear in organizations, managers and leaders are very different kinds of people. They differ in motivation, personal history, and in how they think and act.

A technologically oriented and economically successful society tends to depreciate the need for great leaders. Such societies hold a deep and abiding faith in rational methods of solving problems, including problems of value, economics, and justice. Once rational methods of solving problems are broken down into elements, organized, and taught as skills, then society's faith in technique over personal qualities in leadership remains the guiding conception for a democratic society contemplating its leadership requirements. But there are times when tinkering and trial and error prove inadequate to the emerging problems of selecting goals, allocating resources, and distributing wealth and opportunity. During such times, the democratic society needs to find leaders who use themselves as the instruments of learning and acting, instead of managers who use their accumulation of collective experience to get where they are going.

The most impressive spokesman, as well as exemplar of the managerial viewpoint, was Alfred P. Sloan, Jr. who, along with Pierre du Pont, designed the modern corporate structure. Reflecting on what makes one management successful while another fails, Sloan suggested that "good management rests on a reconciliation of centralization and decentralization, or 'decentralization with coordinated control'."[3]

Sloan's conception of management, as well as his practice, developed by trial and error, and by the accumulation of experience. Sloan wrote: "There is no hard and fast rule for sorting out the various responsibilities and the best way to assign them. The balance which is struck . . . varies according to what is being decided, the circumstances of the time, past experience, and the temperaments and skills of the executive involved."[4]

In other words, in much the same way that the inventors of the late nineteenth century tried, failed, and fitted until they hit on a product or method, managers who innovate in developing organizations are "tinkerers." They do not have a grand design or experience the intuitive flash of insight that, borrowing from modern science, we have come to call the "breakthrough."

Managers and leaders differ fundamentally in their world views. The dimensions for assessing these differences include managers' and leaders' orientations toward their goals, their work, their human relations, and their selves.

Attitudes Toward Goals

Managers tend to adopt impersonal, if not passive, attitudes toward goals. Managerial goals arise out of necessities rather than desires, and therefore, are deeply embedded in the history and culture of the organization.

Frederic G. Donner, chairman and chief executive officer of General Motors from 1958 to 1967, expressed this impersonal and passive attitude toward goals in defining GM's position on product development:

> To meet the challenge of the marketplace, we must recognize changes in customer needs and desires far enough ahead to have the right products in the right places at the right time and in the right quantity.
>
> We must balance trends in preference against the many compromises that are necessary to make a final product that is both reliable and good looking, that performs well and that sells at a competitive price in the necessary volume. We must design, not just the cars we would like to build, but more importantly, the cars that our customers want to buy.[5]

Nowhere in this formulation of how a product comes into being is there a notion that consumer tastes and preferences arise in part as a result of what manufacturers do. In reality, through product design, advertising, and promotion, consumers learn to like what they then say they need. Few would argue that people who enjoy taking snapshots *need* a camera that also develops pictures. But in response to novelty, convenience, a shorter interval between acting (taking the snap) and gaining pleasure (seeing the shot), the Polaroid camera succeeded in the marketplace. But it is inconceivable that Edwin Land responded to impressions of consumer need. Instead, he translated a technology (polarization of light) into a product, which proliferated and stimulated consumers' desires.

The example of Polaroid and Land suggests how leaders think about goals. They are active instead of reactive, shaping ideas instead of responding to them. Leaders adopt a personal and active attitude toward goals. The influence a leader exerts in altering moods, evoking images and expectations, and in establishing specific desires and objectives determines the direction a business takes. The net result of this influence is to change the way people think about what is desirable, possible, and necessary.

Conceptions of Work

What do managers and leaders do? What is the nature of their respective work? Leaders and managers differ in their conceptions. Managers tend to view work as an enabling process involving some combination of people and ideas interacting to establish strategies and make decisions. Managers help the process along by a range of skills, including calculating the interests in opposition, staging and timing the surfacing of controversial issues, and reducing tensions. In this enabling process, managers appear flexible in the use of tactics: they negotiate and bargain, on the one hand, and use rewards and punishments, and other forms of coercion, on the other. Machiavelli wrote for managers and not necessarily for leaders.

Alfred Sloan illustrated how this enabling process works in situations of conflict. The time was the early 1920s when the Ford Motor Co. still dominated the automobile industry using, as did General Motors, the conventional water-cooled engine. With the full backing of Pierre du Pont, Charles Kettering dedicated himself to the design of an air-cooled engine, which, if successful, would have been a great technical and market coup for GM. Kettering believed in his product, but the manufacturing division heads at GM remained skeptical and later opposed the new design on two grounds: first, that is was technically unreliable, and second, that the corporation was putting all its eggs in one basket by investing in a new product instead of attending to the current marketing situation.

In the summer of 1923 after a series of false starts and after its decision to recall the copper-cooled Chevrolets from dealers and customers, GM management reorganized and finally scrapped the project. When it dawned on Kettering that the company had rejected the engine, he was deeply discouraged and wrote to Sloan that without the "organized resistance" against the project it would succeed and that unless the project were saved, he would leave the company.

Alfred Sloan was all too aware of the fact that Kettering was unhappy and indeed intended to leave General Motors. Sloan was also aware of the fact that, while the manufacturing divisions strongly opposed the new engine, Pierre du Pont supported Kettering. Furthermore, Sloan had himself gone on record in a letter to Kettering less than two years earlier expressing full confidence in him. The problem Sloan now had was to make his decision stick, keep Kettering in the organization (he was much too valuable to lose), avoid alienating du Pont, and encourage the division heads to move speedily in developing product lines using conventional water-cooled engines.

The actions that Sloan took in the face of this conflict reveal much about how managers work. First, he tried to reassure Kettering by presenting the problem in a very ambiguous fashion, suggesting that he and the Executive Committee sided with Kettering, but that it would not be practical to force the divisions to do what they were opposed to. He presented the problem as being a question of the people, not the product. Second, he proposed to reorganize around the problem by consolidating all functions in a new division that would be responsible for the design, production, and marketing of the new car. This solution, however, appeared as ambiguous as his efforts to placate and keep Kettering in General Motors. Sloan wrote: "My plan was to create an independent pilot operation under the sole jurisdiction of Mr. Kettering, a kind of copper-cooled-car division. Mr. Kettering would designate his own chief engineer and his production staff to solve the technical problems of manufacture."[6]

While Sloan did not discuss the practical value of this solution, which included saddling an inventor with management responsibility, he in effect used this plan to limit his conflict with Pierre du Pont.

In effect, the managerial solution that Sloan arranged and pressed for adoption limited the options available to others. The structural solution narrowed choices, even limiting emotional reactions to the point where the key people could do nothing but go along, and even allowed Sloan to say in his memorandum to du Pont, "We have discussed the matter with Mr. Kettering at some length this morning and he agrees with us absolutely on every point we made. He appears to receive the suggestion enthusiastically and has every confidence that it can be put across along these lines."[7]

Having placated people who opposed his views by developing a structural solution that appeared to give something but in reality only limited options, Sloan could then authorize the car division's general manager, with whom he basically agreed, to move quickly in designing water-cooled cars for the immediate market demand. Years later Sloan wrote, evidently with tongue in cheek, "The copper-cooled car never came up again in a big way. It just died out, I don't know why."[8]

In order to get people to accept solutions to problems, managers need to coordinate and balance continually. Interestingly enough, this managerial work has much in common with what diplomats and mediators do, with Henry Kissinger apparently an outstanding practitioner. The manager aims at shifting balances of power toward solutions acceptable as a compromise among conflicting values.

What about leaders, what do they do? Where managers act to limit choices, leaders work in the opposite direction, to develop fresh approaches to long-standing problems and to open issues for new options. Stanley and Inge Hoffmann, the political scientists, liken the leader's work to that of the artist. But unlike most artists, the leader himself is an integral part of the aesthetic product. One cannot look at a leader's art without looking at the artist. On Charles de Gaulle as a political artist, they wrote: "And each of his major political acts, however tortuous the means or the details, has been whole, indivisible and unmistakably his own, like an artistic act."[9]

The closest one can get to a product apart from the artist is the ideas that occupy, indeed at times obsess, the leader's mental life. To be effective, however, the leader needs to project his ideas into images that excite people, and only then develop choices that give the projected images substance. Consequently, leaders create excitement in work.

John F. Kennedy's brief presidency shows both the strengths and weaknesses connected with the excitement leaders generate in their work. In his inaugural address he said, "Let every nation know, whether it wishes us well or ill, that we shall pay any price, bear any burden, meet any hardship, support any friend, oppose any foe, in order to assure the survival and the success of liberty."

This much-quoted statement forced people to react beyond immediate concerns and to identify with Kennedy and with important shared ideals. But upon closer scrutiny the statement must be seen as absurd because it promises a position which if in fact adopted, as in the Viet Nam War, could produce disastrous results. Yet unless expectations are aroused and mobilized, with all the dangers of frustration inherent in heightened desire, new thinking and new choice can never come to light.

Leaders work from high-risk positions, indeed often are temperamentally disposed to seek out risk and danger, especially where opportunity and reward appear high. From my observations, why one individual seeks risks while another approaches problems conservatively depends more on his or her personality and less on conscious choice. For some, especially those who become managers, the instinct for survival dominates their need for risk, and their ability to tolerate mundane, practical work assists their survival. The same cannot be said for leaders who sometimes react to mundane work as to an affliction.

Relations with Others

Managers prefer to work with people; they avoid solitary activity because it makes them anxious. Several years ago, I directed studies on the psychological aspects of career. The need to seek out others with whom to work and collaborate seemed to stand out as important characteristics of managers. When asked, for example, to write imaginative stories in response to a picture showing a single figure (a boy contemplating a violin, or a man silhouetted in a state of reflection), managers populated their stories with people. The following is an example of a manager's imaginative story about the young boy contemplating a violin:

> Mom and Dad insisted that junior take music lessons so that someday he can become a concert musician. His instrument was ordered and had just arrived. Junior is weighing the alternatives of playing football with the other kids or playing with the squeak box. He can't understand how his parents could think a violin is better than a touchdown.
>
> After four months of practicing the violin, junior has had more than enough, Daddy is going out of his mind, and Mommy is willing to give in reluctantly to the men's wishes. Football season is now over, but a good third baseman will take the field next spring[10]

This story illustrates two themes that clarify managerial attitudes toward human relations. The first, as I have suggested, is to seek out activity with other people (i.e. the football team), and the second is to maintain a low level of emotional involvement in these relationships. The low emotional involvement appears in the writer's use of conventional metaphors, even clichés, and in the depiction of the ready transformation of potential conflict into harmonious decisions. In this case, Junior, Mommy, and Daddy agree to give up the violin for manly sports.

These two themes may seem paradoxical, but their coexistence supports what a manager does, including reconciling differences, seeking compromises, and establishing a balance of power. A further idea demonstrated by how the manager wrote the story is that managers may lack empathy, or the capacity to sense intuitively the thoughts and feelings of others. To illustrate attempts to be emphatic, here is another story written to the same stimulus picture by someone considered by his peers to be a leader:

> This little boy has the appearance of being a sincere artist, one who is deeply affected by the violin, and has an intense desire to master the instrument.
>
> He seems to have just completed his normal practice session and appears to be somewhat crestfallen at his inabiility to produce the sounds which he is sure lie within the violin.
>
> He appears to be in the process of making a vow to himself to expend the necessary time and effort to play this instrument until he satisfies himself that he is able to bring forth the qualities of music which he feels within himself.
>
> With this type of determination and carry through, this boy became one of the great violinists of his day.[11]

Empathy is not simply a matter of paying attention to other people. It is also the capacity to take in emotional signals and to make them mean something in a relationship with an individual. People who describe another person as "deeply affected" with "intense desire," as capable of feeling "crestfallen" and as one who can "vow to himself," would seem to have an inner perceptiveness that they can use in their relationships with others.

Managers relate to people according to the role they play in a sequence of events or in a decision-making *process*, while leaders, who are concerned with ideas, relate in more intuitive and empathetic ways. The manager's orientation to people, as actors in a sequence of events, deflects his or her attention away from the substance of people's concerns and toward their role in a process. The distinction is simply between a manager's attention to *how* things get done and a leader's to *what* the events and decisions mean to participants.

In recent years, managers have taken over from game theory the notion that decision-making events can be one of two types: the win-lose situation (or zero-sum game) or the win-win situation in which everybody in the action comes out ahead. As part of the process of reconciling differences among people and maintaining balances of power, managers strive to convert win-lose into win-win situations.

As an illustration, take the decision of how to allocate capital resources among operating divisions in a large, decentralized organization. On the face of it, the dollars available for distribution are limited at any given time. Presumably, therefore, the more one division gets, the less is available for other divisions.

Managers tend to view this situation (as it affects human relations) as a conversion issue: how to make what seems like a win-lose problem into a win-win problem. Several solutions to this situation come to mind. First, the manager focuses others' attention on procedure and not on substance. Here the actors become engrossed in the bigger problem of *how* to make decisions, not *what* decisions to make. Once committed to the bigger problem, the actors have to support the outcome since they were involved in formulating decision rules. Because the actors believe in the rules they formulated, they will accept present losses in the expectation that next time they will win.

Second, the manager communicates to his subordinates indirectly, using "signals" instead of "messages." A signal has a number of possible implicit positions in it while a message clearly states a position. Signals are inconclusive and subject to reinterpretation should people become upset and angry, while messages involve the direct consequences that some people will indeed not like what they hear. The nature of messages heightens emotional response, and, as I have indicated, emotionally makes managers anxious. With signals, the question of who wins and who loses often becomes obscured.

Third, the manager plays for time. Managers seem to recognize that with the passage of time and the delay of major decisions, compromises emerge that take the sting out of win-lose situations; and the original "game" will be superseded by additional ones. Therefore, compromises may mean that one wins and loses simultaneously, depending on which of the games one evaluates.

There are undoubtedly many other tactical moves managers use to change human situations from win-lose to win-win. But the point to be made is that such tactics focus on the decision-making process itself and interest managers rather than leaders. The interest in tactics involves costs as well as benefits, including making organizations fatter in bureaucratic and political intrigue and leaner in direct, hard activity and warm human relationships. Consequently, one often hears subordinates characterize managers as inscrutable, detached, and manipulative. These adjectives arise from the subordinates' perception that they are linked together in a process whose purpose, beyond simply making decisions, is to maintain a controlled as well as rational and equitable structure. These adjectives suggest that managers need order in the face of the potential chaos that many fear in human relationships.

In contrast, one often hears leaders referred to in adjectives rich in emotional content. Leaders attract strong feelings of identity and difference, or of love and hate. Human relations in leader-dominated structures often appear turbulent, intense, and at times even disorganized. Such an atmosphere intensifies individual motivation and often produces unanticipated outcomes. Does this intense motivation lead to innovation and high performance, or does it represent wasted energy?

Senses of Self

In *The Varities of Religious Experience,* William James describes two basic personality types, "once-born" and "twice-born."[12] People of the former personality type are those for whom adjustments to life have been straightforward and whose lives have been more or less a peaceful flow from the moment of their births. The twice-borns, on the other hand, have not had an easy time of it. Their lives are marked by a continual struggle to attain some sense of order. Unlike the once-borns they cannot take things for granted. According to James, these personalities have equally different world views. For a once-born personality, the sense of self, as a guide to conduct and attitude, derives from a feeling of being at home and in harmony with one's environment. For a twice-born, the sense of self derives from a feeling of profound separateness.

A sense of belonging or of being separate has a practical significance for the kinds of investments managers and leaders make in their careers. Managers see themselves as conservators and regulators of an existing order of affairs with which they personally identify and from which they gain rewards. Perpetuating and strengthening existing institutions enhances a manager's sense of self-worth: he or she is performing in a role that harmonizes with the ideals of duty and responsibility. William James had this harmony in mind—this sense of self as flowing easily to and from the outer world—in defining a once-born personality. If one feels oneself as a member of institutions, contributing to their well-being, then one fulfills a mission in life and feels rewarded for having measured up to ideals. This reward transcends material gains and answers the more fundamental desire for personal integrity which is achieved by identifying with existing institutions.

Leaders tend to be twice-born personalities, people who feel separate from their environment, including other people. They may work in organizations, but they never belong to them. Their sense of who they are does not depend upon memberships, work roles, or other social indicators of identity. What seems to follow from this idea about separateness is some theoretical basis for explaining why certain individuals search out opportunities for change. The methods to bring about change may be technological, political, or ideological, but the object is the same: to profoundly alter human, economic, and political relationships.

Sociologists refer to the preparation individuals undergo to perform in roles as the socialization process. Where individuals experience themselves as an integral part of the social structure (their self-esteem gains strength through participation and conformity), social standards exert powerful effects in maintaining the individual's personal sense of continuity, even beyond the early years in the family. The line of development from the family to schools, then to career is cumulative and reinforcing. When the line of development is not reinforcing because of significant disruptions in relationships or other problems experienced in the family or other social institutions, the individual turns inward and struggles to establish self-esteem, identity, and order. Here the psychological dynamics center on the experience with loss and the efforts at recovery.

In considering the development of leadership, we have to examine two different courses of life history: (1) development through socialization, which prepares the individual to guide institutions and to maintain the existing balance of social relations; and (2) development through personal mastery, which impels an individual to struggle for psychological and social change. Society produces its managerial talent through the first line of development, while through the second leaders emerge.

Development of Leadership

The development of every person begins in the family. Each person experiences the traumas associated with separating from his or her parents, as well as the pain that follows such frustration. In the same vein, all individuals face the difficulties of achieving self-regulation and self-control. But for some, perhaps a majority, the fortunes of childhood provide adequate gratifications and sufficient opportunities to find substitutes for rewards no longer available. Such individuals, the "once-borns," make moderate identifications with parents and find a harmony between what they expect and what they are able to realize from life.

But suppose the pains of separation are amplified by a combination of parental demands and the individual's need to the degree that a sense of isolation, of being special, and of wariness disrupts the bonds that attach children to parents and other authority figures? Under such conditions, and given a special aptitude, the origins of which remain mysterious, the person becomes deeply involved in his or her inner world at the expense of interest in the outer world. For such a person, self-esteem no longer depends solely upon positive attachments and real rewards. A form of self-reliance takes hold along with expectations of performance and achievement, and perhaps even the desire to do great works.

Such self-perceptions can come to nothing if the individual's talents are negligible. Even with strong talents, there are no guarantees that achievement will follow, let alone that the end result will be for good rather than evil. Other factors enter into development. For one thing, leaders are like artists and other gifted people who often struggle with neuroses; their ability to function varies considerably even over the short run, and some potential leaders may lose the struggle altogether. Also, beyond early childhood, the patterns of development that affect managers and leaders involve the selective influence of particular people. Just as they appear flexible and evenly distributed in the types of talents available for development, managers form moderate and widely distributed attachments. Leaders, on the other hand, establish, and also break off, intensive one-to-one relationships.

It is a common observation that people with great talents are often only indifferent students. No one, for example, could have predicted Einstein's great achievements on the basis of his mediocre record in school. The reason for mediocrity is obviously not the absence of ability. It may result, instead, from self-absorption and the inability to pay attention to the ordinary tasks at hand. The only sure way an individual can interrupt reverie-like preoccupation and self-absorption is to form a deep attachment to a great teacher or other benevolent person who understands and has the ability to communicate with the gifted individual.

Whether gifted individuals find what they need in one-to-one relationships depends on the availability of sensitive and intuitive mentors who have a vocation in cultivating talent. Fortunately, when the generations do meet and the self-selections occur, we learn more about how to develop leaders and how talented people of different generations influence each other.

While apparently destined for a mediocre career, people who form important one-to-one relationships are able to accelerate and intensify their development through an apprenticeship. The background for such apprenticeships, or the psychological readiness of an individual to benefit from an intensive relationship, depends upon some experience in life that forces the individual to turn inward. A case example will make this point clearer. This example comes from the life of Dwight David Eisenhower, and illustrates the transformation of a career from competent to outstanding.[13]

Dwight Eisenhower's early career in the Army foreshadowed very little about his future development. During World War I, while some of his West Point classmates were already experiencing the war firsthand in France, Eisenhower felt "embedded in the monotony and unsought safety of the Zone of the Interior . . . that was intolerable punishment."[14]

Shortly after World War I, Eisenhower, then a young officer somewhat pessimistic about his career chances, asked for a transfer to Panama to work under General Fox Connor, a senior officer whom Eisenhower admired. The army turned down Eisenhower's request. This setback was very much on Eisenhower's mind when Ikey, his first-born son, succumbed to influenza. By some sense of responsibility for its own, the army transferred Eisenhower to Panama, where he took up his duties under General Connor with the shadow of his lost son very much upon him.

In a relationship with the kind of father he would have wanted to be, Eisenhower reverted to being the son he lost. In this highly charged situation, Eisenhower began to learn from his mentor. General Connor offered, and Eisenhower gladly took, a magnificent tutorial on the military. The effects of this relationship on Eisenhower cannot be measured quantitatively, but, in Eisenhower's own reflections and the unfolding of his career, one cannot overestimate its significance in the reintegration of a person shattered by grief. As Eisenhower wrote later about Connor,

> Life with General Connor was a sort of graduate school in military affairs
> and the humanities, leavened by a man who was experienced in his
> knowledge of men and their conduct. I can never adequately express my
> gratitude to this one gentleman. . . . In a lifetime of association with great
> and good men, he is the one more or less invisible figure to whom I owe
> an incalculable debt.[15]

Some time after his tour of duty with General Connor, Eisenhower's
breakthrough occurred. He received orders to attend the Command and
General Staff School at Fort Leavenworth, one of the most competitive
schools in the army. It was a coveted appointment, and Eisenhower
took advantage of the opportunity. Unlike his performance in high
school and West Point, his work at the Command School was excellent;
he was graduated first in his class.

Psychological biographies of gifted people repeatedly demonstrate the
important part a mentor plays in developing an individual. Andrew
Carnegie owed much to his senior, Thomas A. Scott. As head of the
Western Division of the Pennsylvania Railroad, Scott recognized talent
and the desire to learn in the young telegrapher assigned to him. By
giving Carnegie increasing responsibility and by providing him with
the opportunity to learn through close personal observation, Scott added
to Carnegie's self-confidence and sense of achievement. Because of his
own personal strength and achievement, Scott did not fear Carnegie's
aggressiveness. Rather, he gave it full play in encouraging Carnegie's
initiative.

Mentors take risks with people. They bet initially on talent they
perceive in younger people. Mentors also risk emotional involvment in
working closely with their juniors. The risks do not always pay off, but
the willingness to take them appears crucial in developing leaders.

Can Organizations Develop Leaders?

The examples I have given of how leaders develop suggest the
importance of personal influence and the one-to-one relationship. For
organizations to encourage consciously the development of leaders as
compared with managers would mean developing one-to-one relationships between junior and senior executives and, more important, fostering
a culture of individualism and possibly elitism. The elitism arises out
of the desire to identify talent and other qualities suggestive of the
ability to lead and not simply to manage.

The Jewel Companies, Inc., enjoy a reputation for developing talented
people. The chairman and chief executive officer, Donald S. Perkins, is
perhaps a good example of a person brought along through the mentor

approach. Franklin J. Lunding, who was Perkins's mentor, expressed the philosophy of taking risks with young people this way: "Young people today want in on the action. They don't want to sit around for six months trimming lettuce."[16]

The statement runs counter to the culture that attaches primary importance to slow progression based on experience and proved competence. It is a high-risk philosophy, one that requires time for the attachment between senior and junior people to grow and be meaningful, and one that is bound to produce more failures than successes.

The elitism is an especially sensitive issue. At Jewel the MBA degree symbolized the elite. Lunding attracted Perkins to Jewel at a time when business school graduates had little interest in retailing in general, and food distribution in particular. Yet the elitism seemed to pay off: not only did Perkins become the president at age 37, but also, under the leadership of young executives recruited into Jewel with the promise of opportunity for growth and advancement, Jewel managed to diversify into discount and drug chains and still remain strong in food retailing. By assigning each recruit to a vice president who acted as sponsor, Jewel evidently tried to build a structure around the mentor approach to developing leaders. To counteract the elitism implied in such an approach, the company also introduced an "equalizer" in what Perkins described as "the first assistant philosophy." Perkins stated:

> Being a good first assistant means that each management person thinks of himself not as the order-giving, domineering boss, but as the first assistant to those who 'report' to him in a more typical organizational sense. Thus we mentally turn our organizational charts upside-down and challenge ourselves to seek ways in which we can lead . . . by helping . . . by teaching . . . by listening . . . and by managing in the true democratic sense . . . that is, with the consent of the managed. Thus the satisfactions of leadership come from helping others to get things done and changed— and not from getting credit for doing and changing things ourselves.[17]

While this statement would seem to be more egalitarian than elitist, it does reinforce a youth-oriented culture since it defines the senior officer's job as primarily helping the junior person.

A myth about how people learn and develop that seems to have taken hold in the American culture also dominates thinking in business. The myth is that people learn best from their peers. Supposedly, the threat of evaluation and even humiliation recedes in peer relations because of the tendency for mutual identification and the social restraints on authoritarian behavior among equals. Peer training in organizations occurs in various forms. The use, for example, of task forces made up of peers from several interested occupational groups (sales, production, research, and finance) supposedly removes the restraints of authority on the individual's willingness to assert and exchange ideas. As a result, so the theory goes, people interact more freely, listen more objectively to criticism and other points of view and, finally, learn from this healthy interchange.

Another application of peer training exists in some large corporations, such as Philips, N.V. in Holland, where organization structure is built on the principle of joint responsibility of two peers, one representing the commercial end of the business and the other the technical. Formally, both hold equal responsibility for geographic operations or product groups, as the case may be. As a practical matter, it may turn out that one or the other of the peers dominates the management. Nevertheless, the main interaction is between two or more equals.

The principal question I would raise about such arrangements is whether they perpetuate the managerial orientation, and preclude the formation of one-to-one relationships between senior people and potential leaders.

Aware of the possible stifling effects of peer relationships on aggressiveness and individual initiative, another company, much smaller than Philips, utilizes joint responsibility of peers for operating units, with one important difference. The chief executive of this company encourages competition and rivalry among peers, ultimately appointing the one who comes out on top for increased responsibility. These hybrid arrangements produce some unintended consequences that can be disastrous. There is no easy way to limit rivalry. Instead, it permeates all levels of the operation and opens the way for the formation of cliques in an atmosphere of intrigue.

A large, integrated oil company has accepted the importance of developing leaders through the direct influence of senior on junior executives. One chairman and chief executive officer regularly selected one talented university graduate whom he appointed his special assistant, and with whom he would work closely for a year. At the end of the year, the junior executive would become available for assignment to one of the operating divisions, where he would be assigned to a responsible post rather than a training position. The mentor relationship had acquainted the junior executive firsthand with the use of power, and with the important antidotes to the power disease called *hubris*—performance and integrity.

Working in one-to-one relationships, where there is a formal and recognized difference in the power of the actors, takes a great deal of tolerance for emotional interchange. This interchange, inevitable in close working arrangements, probably accounts for the reluctance of many executives to become involved in such relationships. *Fortune* carried an interesting story on the departure of a key executive, John W. Hanley, from the top management of Proctor & Gamble, for the chief executive officer position at Monsanto.[18] According to this account, the chief executive and chairman of P&G passed over Hanley for appointment to the presidency and named another executive vice president to this post instead.

The chairman evidently felt he could not work well with Hanley, who, by his own acknowledgement, was aggressive, eager to experiment and change practices, and constantly challenged his superior. A chief executive officer naturally has the right to select people with whom he feels congenial. But I wonder whether a greater capacity on the part of senior officers to tolerate the competitive impulses and behavior of their subordinates might not be healthy for corporations. At least a greater tolerance for interchange would not favor the managerial team player at the expense of the individual who might become a leader.

I am constantly surprised at the frequency with which chief executives feel threatened by open challenges to their ideas, as though the source of their authority, rather than their specific ideas, were at issue. In one case a chief executive officer, who was troubled by the aggressiveness and sometimes outright rudeness of one of his talented vice presidents, used various indirect methods such as group meetings and hints from outside directors to avoid dealing with his subordinate. I advised the executive to deal head-on with what irritated him. I suggested that by direct, fact-to-face confrontation, both he and his subordinate would learn to validate the distinction between the authority to be preserved and the issues to be debated.

To confront is also to tolerate aggressive interchange, and has the net effect of stripping away the veils of ambiguity and signaling so characteristic of managerial cultures, as well as encouraging the emotional relationship leaders need if they are to survive.

Notes

1. John D. Rockefeller, 3rd., *The Second American Revolution* (New York: Harper & Row, 1973), p. 72.

2. Theodore Levitt, "Management and the Post Industrial Society," *The Public Interest,* Summer 1976, p. 73.

3. Alfred P. Sloan, Jr., *My Years with General Motors* (New York: Doubleday & Co. 1964), p. 429.

4. Ibid. p. 429.

5. Ibid. p. 440.

6. Ibid. p. 91.

7. Ibid. p. 91.

8. Ibid. p. 93.

9. Stanley and Inge Hoffmann, "The Will for Grandeur: de Gaulle as Political Artist," *Daedalus*, Summer 1968, p. 849.

10. Abraham Zaleznik, Gene W. Dalton and Louis B. Barnes, *Orientation and Conflict in Career*, (Boston: Division of Research, Harvard Business School, 1970), p. 326.

11. Ibid. p. 294.

12. William James, *Varieties of Religious Experience* (New York: Mentor Books, 1958).

13. This example is included in Abraham Zaleznik and Manfred F. R. Kets de Vries, *Power and the Corporate Mind* (Boston: Houghton Mifflin, 1975).

14. Dwight D. Eisenhower, *At Ease: Stories I Tell to Friends* (New York: Doubleday, 1967), p. 136.

15. Ibid. p. 187.

16. "Jewel Lets Young Men Make Mistakes," *Business Week*, January 17, 1970, p. 90.

17. "What Makes Jewel Shine so Bright," *Progressive Grocer*, September, 1973, p. 76.

18. "Jack Hanley Got There by Selling Harder," *Fortune*, November, 1976.

9

Managers and Leaders: Letters to the Editor

HARVARD BUSINESS REVIEW

Managers and Leaders

The sharp distinction between managers and leaders drawn by Abraham Zaleznik in "Managers and Leaders: Are They Different?" (May–June 1977) is useful as a study device, but in my view it overstates actual experience.

Leadership frequently stems from competence and example rather than from the use of power to influence others, and successful managers often display this kind of leadership. Although individuals may tend toward either "managerial" or "leadership" styles, I believe there is a greater ability to shift roles depending on specific circumstances than Zaleznik suggests in this article.

For example, although Alfred Sloan is portrayed in terms of managerial skills, he exercised strong leadership on appropriate occasions. However, I do agree that one of the great challenges for business today is to provide a climate where leadership characteristics can surface at various levels in an organization.

E. R. Kane,
President,
E. I. du Pont de Nemours & Company,
Wilmington, Delaware

. . . In general, the corporate organization structure does not produce man-to-man relationships and therefore is strong in developing managerial talent and not very strong in producing leaders. This, of course, presumes one agrees that there is a difference between managers and leaders. I do.

Zaleznik's observations explain why many of the more talented MBA and other professional school graduates incline toward joining a corporate unit of relatively small size.

Malcolm MacNaughton,
Chairman of the Board,
Castle & Cooke, Inc.,
Honolulu, Hawaii

. . . I disagree completely with the premise that distinguishes the manager from the leader and says, in effect, that an individual cannot fulfill both roles. This is nonsense.

Much of what is said in the article would be appropriate for a contrast between the "bureaucrat" and the "innovator" or "inventor." I would agree that these sets of characteristics are rarely, if ever, found in the same individual. I will grant that some of our *mature* industries are run by bureaucrats who have learned to excel only in moving up through the organizational structure.

However, in high-technology industries, the bureaucratic manager will not succeed. The competitors and the technology move too fast. A combination of strong leadership and excellent managerial capability is required for success.

J. Fred Bucy,
President,
Texas Instruments Incorporated,
Dallas, Texas

. . . Zaleznik is right, in my opinion, when he suggests that the structure of corporations and the conservative bias implicit in selection of managers in most corporations discourages the emergence of leaders, and I thought his suggestions for the development of "mentor" or one-on-one teaching relationships between executives and potential leaders worth considering.

On the other hand, it seems to me that his distinctions between managers and leaders are too sharp. Managers, in his definition, become the faceless, logical conservators and operators of a business, whereas leaders are defined more or less as creative, inward-looking artists. The successful leader is one who most often combines the creative charac-teristics with management skills. Surely the stability and judgment that go with being a good manager must also play a part in a leader's success.

T. H. Roberts, Jr.,
Chief Executive Officer
DeKalb AgResearch, Inc.,
DeKalb, Illinois

. . . Other than accepting his implied premise that there are more managers than leaders, I do not think Zaleznik has made much of a case for a necessary dichotomy between the two. In fact, he may have overstated his case.

I doubt that managerial responsibility inhibits leadership potential. Leaders cannot be effective without some respect for the role of the manager. (Leadership implies getting something accomplished.)

The example concerning President Eisenhower refers to motivation rather than leadership. He deliberately avoided confrontation and resolved most problems by choosing among individual independent views without taking full advantage of healthy colloquy with his subordinates.

The example of Eisenhower's stimulation by an individual (General Connor) is quite common in business and politics, but it is not unique or relevant to the argument distinguishing managers from leaders. History alone can evaluate his unwillingness to confront Senator McCarthy and his shocking attitude, which left serious wounds in the national psyche.

I would liken this to Pius XI's uncomfortable silence in the face of the murder of six million Jews. These were managerial decisions rather than ones of great leaders. Both the president and the pope let things happen and took their chances.

The Sloan-Kettering example is spurious. Sloan was not only an able manager but a brilliant conceptualist who developed the pricing structure of General Motors via the Cadillac-to-Chevrolet range of brands. He not only managed, he inspired a technique that eventually produced a 50% share of the automobile market.

Salvaging Kettering was a prudent managerial decision which any good businessman would have made when lucky enough to have one of the world's greatest engineering minds working for him. The fact that we have a Sloan-Kettering Institute indicates that Sloan not only understood Kettering's value as an inventor but regarded him as an associate worthy of any reasonable sacrifice short of the destruction of General Motors. Certainly Sloan's ability to manage did not inhibit his talent for imaginative leadership.

Zaleznik could have referred to the brilliance of Charles Revson or Abe Spanel of International Latex, who, despite their managerial quirks, were able to sustain organizations during turbulence and change and at the same time keep them moving forward. Too many of Zaleznik's examples simply indicate a use of tact to achieve a necessary end. Keeping Kettering happy, for instance, was essential to the growth of General Motors.

A more provocative example would have been the Truman-MacArthur decision. I would be interested in his evaluation of that as an example of the manager (Truman) versus the manager-leader (MacArthur).

The more I think about it, the more I believe that effective managers can become qualified to assume the role of true leaders. History is filled with individuals who have risen to the occasion when they had prepared minds.

One comment in the article struck me as particularly provocative and reasonable—leaders must be willing to be learners, gamblers, to break off intensive one-to-one relationships, and to go it alone. This is opposed to the usual managerial function, where blending becomes an essential ingredient for success. The "mentor relationship" in an environment of power will not necessarily produce leaders. I know of too many examples firsthand where exposure to authority and power has had little or no bearing when the individual was finally on his own.

Herbert L. Seegal,
President,
R. H. Macy & Co., Inc.
New York, New York

10

Leadership and Headship: There Is a Difference

CHARLES R. HOLLOMAN

It is a common notion that persons appointed to managerial or supervisory positions display leadership by virtue of their position in the hierarchy.[1] Industrial managers and military commanders, for example, have traditionally been referred to as leaders for no other reason than their position and title. Not only have they been described as leaders, but it has been presumed that they always exercised leadership behavior in directing the activities of their subordinates. The major shortcoming of this assumption is its failure to distinguish clearly between the static position of *headship* and the dynamic process of *leadership*.[2]

Mere occupancy of an office or position from which leadership behavior is expected does not automatically make the occupant a true leader. Such appointments can result in headship but not necessarily in leadership. While appointive positions of high status and authority are related to leadership, they are not the same thing. What is properly considered leadership is much more comprehensive than headship because leadership may or may not be exercised by persons appointed to formal positions of authority.

This paper focuses on the differences between headship and leadership in the hierarchical organization. The objective is to provide the supervisor with some useful leads for viewing and better understanding his relationships with his subordinates. In making this distinction between headship and leadership, the intent is to establish the idea that leadership is more a function of the group or situation than a quality which adheres to a person appointed to a formal position of headship.[3]

Reprinted by permission from *Personnel Administration*, 31:4 (July–August 1968), pp. 38–44.

Leadership: Natural and Appointed

Leadership is more than a position in an organization or the personal qualities of the person in that position. While position or personal qualities may enhance a person's chances of being accepted as a true leader, these factors alone do not constitute leadership. Leadership is a characteristic of the functioning of groups resulting from the interaction of leader, group, and situation. One of the more useful definitions of leadership has been offered by Stogdill. He has defined leadership as "... the process of influencing the activities of an organized group in its efforts toward goal setting and goal achievement."[4] Implied in this definition are three essential conditions which must exist before leadership can be presumed to take place. These are (1) the presence of a group, (2) a common task or objective, and (3) a differentiation of responsibility.

The last of these three conditions is perhaps in need of further clarification. In any group or organization, the persons who constitute the membership are usually differentiated as to the role they will play or the contribution they will make. This is necessary because of the many kinds of activity which are necessary for goal accomplishment. It is this distinction between roles that makes leadership both possible and necessary. Without it there is no opportunity or need for the would-be leader to supervise or coordinate the efforts of the group members toward goal accomplishment.

In voluntary organizations the elected leader is usually a natural leader who has emerged. According to Stogdill's definition of leadership, he is usually that person who most effectively influences group activities toward goal setting and goal achievement. He represents and articulates group goals and values to others, both within and outside the group. This is not the case in hierarchical organizations. Appointed supervisors in these organizations are not always natural leaders nor are they always able to function as such. Andrews has noted that "... a supervisor can be appointed to his organizational position by management, but he cannot, through appointment, be made the natural leader."[5] Appointments to these supervisory positions are based upon and supported by formal authority. They result in supervisory headship but not necessarily in leadership behavior by the appointee. Sometimes, as a consequence, the appointed supervisor is an individual who does not have group acceptance.

There are a number of theories of how the natural leader emerges into the leadership role. According to one theory, he may be elected or in some other way chosen by the group; or, according to another, he may purposefully take over the leadership role and be spontaneously accepted by the group. However he emerges into the leadership role, he must be perceived by the group as a means to the achievement of some recognized, desired goal. Group members willingly accept his direction because they believe that through following him they can satisfy their own personal needs as they achieve group goals. Regardless of the validity of their judgment, the person in the leadership role derives influence because the group believes that he can help them.

The natural leader in a voluntary organization is usually able to maintain his position as long as he is able to satisfy the members' needs for affiliation. He is responsible only to the membership of his group. The responsibility of the appointed leader, however, is two-directional. He is, in the first instance, responsible to a higher level of management for the achievement of specified organizational goals. At the same time, he is responsible to the group or activity of which he is a member. While he has obligations outside the group, he must also attempt to satisfy needs within the group.

Leadership Is Influence

In order to define the leader as that group member who is able to influence his followers to willingly cooperate in certain ways in working toward group goals, it is necessary to restrict the term leadership to situations in which the relationship between the leader and followers is voluntarily accepted by the members of the group. In a hierarchical organization the appointed head may rule, or dominate, or command; but unless those in the subordinate role have some choice to follow or not follow, there is no leadership. Where there is no choice, there is domination, the antithesis of leadership.[6] Thus, leadership results when the appointed head causes the members of his group to accept his directives without any apparent exertion of authority or force on his part. Through his ability to influence group action, he is able to create and use the power within the group; and his authority is received from the group.

The real problem facing the appointed supervisor is finding a pattern of leadership which recognizes the need for understanding and motivation without causing him to feel that his authority and control are being diluted.[7] Possible patterns of behavior range from authoritarian control on the one hand to true democratic leadership on the other. Under certain emergency conditions, it is sometimes necessary to employ the former means. When this is done, the relationship between the supervisor and his subordinates is an authority relationship. When, on the other hand, the mission is accomplished by the collective, integrated efforts and desires of all members of his work group, leadership is said to exist. The superior-subordinate relationship becomes a leader-follower relationship, and the authority of headship is replaced by the influence of the leader upon the group.

While the natural leader in a voluntary organization leads his followers, they exert a reciprocal influence upon him. The leader must always be aware of the needs and expectations of his followers and provide a reasonable measure of satisfaction of them. If he fails to do this, his followers will cease to support him and turn to another. Without followship, there can be no true leadership. It is the follower who accepts or rejects leadership acts on the part of the would-be leader. Thus, in a sense, followers are also leaders—they lead their leaders, select their leaders, and sometimes reject their leaders because they do not meet expectations.

Even though the appointed supervisor possesses formal authority, it usually remains within the discretion of the group members to choose the more decisive factor in their acceptance of his directives. That is, a subordinate can say, "I accept his direction of my activities because he is my legal supervisor. I have no choice but to obey." Or, he can say, "I accept his direction of my activities because I believe that he is best qualified to deal with our particular problems. Following him will help me to satisfy some of my own personal needs and wants." Whether the subordinate offers the former or the latter reason will depend upon the degree to which the supervisor has gained acceptance as the true leader of the group.

Headship, Leadership, and Authority

Within hierarchical organizations, a supervisor may be regarded as a person who has been designated to take charge of a specified number of persons, activities, or organizational elements. Used in this manner, the term supervisor refers not only to first-line supervisors and foremen, but also to managers and staff officers at higher levels. Supervisors are responsible for directing and coordinating the activities of others and are expected to carry out a specific part of the organization mission by getting subordinates to work toward specified goals.

There is evidence that the act of creating a supervisory position also creates a predisposition on the part of subordinates to accept the authority and directives of the occupant of that position. But it cannot be assumed that occupancy alone endows the supervisor with the ability to use that authority in a manner that will ensure the willing cooperation of subordinates. There are significant differences between achieving a headship position and the exercise of true leadership behavior. The appointed supervisor may very well be no more than what has been called the "headman."[8] Before the person in the appointed supervisory position can learn to function in a true leadership manner, he must be able to see the differences between his headship position and the leadership process.

In almost all hierarchical organization, the person in the headship or supervisory position is not selected by the group he is to lead, but is appointed by a higher level of the organization. He is placed in the supervisory position for the purpose of achieving the objectives of those who appointed him—objectives which may or may not be compatible with the personal goals of those persons whose activities he is supposed to direct. His authority is formal authority, and it comes not from the group being led but from those who appointed him to the position. This authority gives him the legal right to direct the activities of his subordinates, and they comply with his directives under threat of sanction.

The Limitations of Headship

When the supervisor is chosen by someone external to the group being led, there are special problems not usually felt by the natural leader in the voluntary organization. Most important of these problems is the fact that the appointed leader is not always free to choose his own methods of dealing with subordinates. When the conditions of the relationship between the appointed head and his subordinates are prescribed by the organization, the supervisor is prevented from functioning in a true leadership role. He is expected to succeed as a leader even though he does not always have the freedom to control the functional relationship between himself and his subordinates.

To view supervisors in hierarchical organizations as natural leaders is to overlook the organizational setting in which they work. The leadership function in these organizations is more limited than that of the natural leader. Every supervisory position is clothed with an expressed delegation of authority. It is exercised by virtue of rank and position and incorporates the idea that the person appointed as supervisor has the legal right to direct and that the subordinate has an enforceable duty to obey. The decisions of the superior guide the actions of the subordinate, and these decisions are made with the expectation that they will be accepted by the subordinate.

Persons appointed to these positions do occupy positions of *nominal* leadership; and if they possess sufficient status and power, they can secure obedience to their directives through the processes of domination. But status and power are not the same as leadership. This is not to say that appointed leaders do not have status and power; rather, it means that persons may have status and power without being true leaders. Conversely, it is also possible that certain persons will be able to exhibit true leadership even though they occupy a role in the organization other than that of the designated head. Headship can enforce compliance even though attempts to do so introduce resistance among subordinates. Leadership, on the other hand, is dependent upon voluntary followership; and without it there can be no leadership, though there may be obedience. While headship is imposed upon the group, leadership is generally accorded by the group being led.

Supervisors are appointed because of their technical or administrative qualifications more often than because of their leadership abilities or the fact that they have group acceptance. Appointments made on this basis usually reflect management's thinking about the relative importance of technical skills as compared to leadership attitudes and abilities. It is true that in planning and organizing work it is important for the supervisor to have sufficient knowledge of the job to make wise decisions. Without this knowledge the supervisor cannot be fully effective, and there is always the possibility that his subordinates would fail to respect him for not having it. The real danger of this situation, however, is in overlooking the fact that the basic responsibility of the supervisor is to supervise and direct the activities of others. When the technical aspects of the job are disproportionately emphasized, the problem of providing supervisory leadership receives correspondingly less attention.

At the present time, there appears to be little possibility of changing the traditional bases for appointing supervisors in hierarchical organizations. It is possible, however, and necessary, that the potential shortcomings of imposed headship be recognized.

The question remains as to the possible outcome of a situation in which an effective leader is appointed to a headship position. In this kind of situation, as it often happens, the two elements of headship and leadership are successfully fused. The appointed head is able to gain group acceptance and to establish within his work group those characteristics usually found only within voluntary groups. While many persons appointed to headship positions do function effectively in true leadership roles, it cannot be assumed that followership develops automatically. An appointed head cannot be regarded as a true leader unless his subordinates voluntarily accord him a measure of influence and power greater than formal authority alone permits.[9]

From Headship to Leadership

Although it has always been tempered by the necessities of human nature, formal supervision has traditionally been based upon authoritarian control. But there is today some evidence of a gradual shift being made in the authority systems of hierarchical organizations from domination to more indirect forms of control such as positive leadership and group consensus. Within military organizations, for example, there is emerging a new philosophy of leadership based more upon loyalty than upon military custom.[10] Loyalty presupposes obedience, but it indicates a wider latitude of initiative and freedom of action within the limitations of the situation.

Within both military and nonmilitary organizations there are two factors which can be identified as contributing to this shift in leadership emphasis and philosophy. First, there is the necessity for supervisors to consult and share authority with staff specialists on technological matters. They are not able to work as autonomously as they once were, and the fact that they must interact with others to get the job done means that they must consider the opinions and actions of others. Second, there is the increasing recognition that successful leadership depends more upon the supervisor developing and using the skills of motivation and understanding than upon delegating to him increased amounts of formal authority.

The appointed supervisor who aspires to be accepted as the true leader of his work group must establish and maintain relationships with his subordinates which approximate those found within voluntary groups. To do this he must be able to relate to them in terms of his being aware of and responsive to their personal needs and desires. Not only must he be able to perceive their needs and wants, but he must contribute something that will bring the group closer to its goals. He must be able to have his subordinates accept his directives for reasons other than the formal authority he possesses. To put it another way, he must be accepted by the group as a person they would have chosen had they been given the right to decide. A group free to choose its own leadership will tend to choose the person seen as being most capable of fulfilling their needs. Through their acceptance of him as their leader, they agree to follow him.

Leadership is always directed toward achieving goals desired by both the leader and the group being led, and control is exercised by all.[11] Under any other condition leadership becomes headship. To the extent that the appointed supervisor recognizes these differences between headship and leadership, the door is open for him to gain acceptance as a true leader.

Summary

This paper has presented an operational distinction between supervisory headship (authority relations or control by virtue of position) and leadership (leader-follower relations or personal influence). Headship is maintained by a system of formal institutional authority and directives; leadership is accorded from the members of the group being led and depends upon the acceptance of the appointed head by the group. In order to emphasize leadership behavior, the use of formal authority needs to be deemphasized. Appointed heads who aspire to acceptance as true leaders must establish and maintain relationships with subordinates which approximate those found within voluntary groups.

Notes

1. The views expressed herein are those of the author and do not necessarily reflect the views of the United States Air Force or the Department of Defense.

2. See Cecil A. Gibb, "Leadership," in Gardner Lindzey (Ed.), *Handbook of Social Psychology* (Reading, Mass.: Addison-Wesley, 1954), Vol. II, and Eugene L. Hartley and Ruth E. Hartley, *Fundamentals of Social Psychology* (New York: Alfred A. Knopf, 1961), Chap. XIX.

3. The term "group" is used here to refer to a congregation of persons who (1) interact with or are affected by the actions of others, (2) are psychologically aware of this interaction or effect, and (3) perceive themselves to be a group. Business and military organizations are special kinds of groups.

4. Ralph M. Stogdill, "Leadership, Membership, and Organization," *Psychological Bulletin*, 47:1–14, January 1950, p. 4.

5. Richard E. Andrews, *Leadership and Supervision* (Washington, D.C.: U.S. Civil Service Commission, Personnel Management Series No. 9, 1955), p. 23.

6. Paul Pigors, *Leadership or Domination* (Boston: Houghton Mifflin Co., 1935), p. 20.

7. For a comprehensive discussion of this problem, see Robert Tannenbaum and Warren H. Schmidt, "How To Choose a Leadership Pattern," *Harvard Business Review*, 36:95–101, March–April 1958.

8. W. H. Cowley, "Three Distinctions in the Study of Leadership," *Journal of Abnormal and Social Psychology*, 23:144–157, July–September 1928.

9. Peter M. Blau and W. R. Scott, *Formal Organizations* (San Francisco: Chandler Publishing Co., 1962), p. 141.

10. See Morris Janowitz, "Changing Patterns of Organizational Authority: The Military Establishment," *Administrative Science Quarterly*, 3:473–493, March 1959, and Brig. General Cecil E. Combs, "Loyalty: The Military Touch-Stone," *Air University Quarterly Review*, 7:30–36, Spring 1955.

11. Hubert Bonner, *Group Dynamics* (New York: The Ronald Press Co., 1959), p. 174.

11

Leadership:
Man and Function

ALEX BAVELAS

There is a useful distinction to be made between the idea of "leadership as a personal quality" and the idea of "leadership as an organizational function." The first refers to a special combination of personal characteristics; the second refers to the distribution throughout an organization of decision-making powers. The first leads us to look at the qualities and abilities of individuals; the second leads us to look at the patterns of power and authority in organizations. Both of these ideas or definitions of leadership are useful, but it is important to know which one is being talked about and to know under what conditions the two must be considered together in order to understand a specific organizational situation.

Early notions about leadership dealt with it almost entirely in terms of personal abilities. Leadership was explicitly associated with special powers. An outstanding leader was credited not only with the extensions of the normal abilities possessed by most men but with extraordinary powers, such as the ability to read men's minds, to tell the future, to compel obedience hypnotically. These powers were often thought of as gifts from a god, as conditional loans from a devil, or as the result of some accidental supernatural circumstance attending conception, birth, or early childhood. Today, claims of supernatural powers are made more rarely, but they are not entirely unknown. Of course, milder claims—tirelessness, infallibility of intuition, lightning-quick powers of decision—are made in one form or another by many outstandingly successful men. And when they do not make them for themselves, such claims

Reprinted from *Administrative Science Quarterly*, 4:4 (March 1960), pp. 491–498, by permission of *The Administrative Science Quarterly*.

are made for them by others, who, for their own reasons, prefer such explanations of success to other more homely ones.

Outright supernatural explanations of leadership have, in recent times, given way to more rational explanations. Leadership is still generally thought of in terms of personal abilities, but now the assumption is made that the abilities in question are the same as those possessed by all normal persons: individuals who become leaders are merely presumed to have them to a greater degree.

For many years attempts to define these abilities and to measure them failed. This was not only because the early techniques of measurement were primitive and unreliable, but for a more important reason. The traits that were defined as important for leadership were often nothing more than purely verbal expressions of what the researcher felt leaders *ought* to be like. Few of the many lists of traits that were developed had very much in common. Typical of the items that frequently appeared on such lists were piety, honesty, courage, perseverance, intelligence, reliability, imagination, industriousness. This way of thinking about leadership is still very common. It persists, not because it is helpful in analyzing and understanding the phenomenon of leadership, but because it expresses a deep and popular wish about what leaders *should* be like.

Modern trait research proceeds in a very different way. Leadership traits are no longer selected arbitrarily. They are, instead, largely derived from the results of tests that are carefully designed, administered, and interpreted. And the techniques of measurement and analysis which are applied to the data that are gathered have been extensively developed and refined. Numerous trait studies have been made of the physical, intellectual, and social characteristics of leaders. On various tests, persons who are leaders tend to be brighter, tend to be better adjusted psychologically, and tend to display better judgment. Studies that have concentrated on the social behavior of leaders show that they "interact" more than nonleaders. They tend to give more information, to ask for more information, and to take the lead in summing up or interpreting a situation.

Despite these accomplishments, the trait approach has in recent years been subjected to increasing criticism. A common objection is that the results are obtained by a method that requires an initial separation of people into "leaders" and "nonleaders" or "good leaders" and "not-so-good leaders." The validity of the distinguishing traits that come out of such work, the argument goes, can only be as good as the validity of the preliminary grouping of the persons being studied. All of this leads to the question, "On what basis is the initial separation of subjects made, and how is it justified?"

At first glance, this may appear a trivial and carping question. In fact, however, it is one of the most serious obstacles in the way of all leadership research. It is obviously impossible to define "good leaders" without reference to a system of values. To say that a man is a "good leader" means that his behavior and its consequences are held to be of greater worth than other behaviors and results.

What system of values shall the researcher adopt that is both scientifically acceptable and socially useful in distinguishing good or successful leaders from others? Many attempts have been made to find a suitable criterion, but the results have been generally unsatisfactory—not that it is difficult to find standards which are desirable and inspiring, but that such standards tend to be based, just as the early lists of traits were, on qualities that are difficult or impossible to measure. And often they just do not seem to "work." For example, there have been attempts to distinguish leaders from nonleaders in terms that rest essentially on moral and ethical considerations. It may be a significant commentary on our society that there appears to be no particular correlation between a man's ethics and morals and his power to attract followers.

It has been suggested that many of the philosophical difficulties that attend the definition of "good leader" can be avoided if one accepts the more limited task of defining "good executive." In business and industry, one would like to think, there should be practical, quantitative ways of making the distinction. Many attempts have been made in this direction. Reputation, financial success, hierarchical position, influence, and many other criteria have been tried without much satisfaction. The inadequacies of such standards are obvious to any experienced executive.

There is a second and more interesting objection that has been made to the trait approach. It is based not on the question of the accuracy or the validity of the assumptions that are made but upon the nature of the "traits" themselves. Traits are, after all, statements about personal characteristics. The objection to this is that the degree to which an individual exhibits leadership depends not only on *his characteristics* but also on the *characteristics of the situation* in which he finds himself. For example, a man who shows all the signs of leadership when he acts as the officer of a well-structured authoritarian organization may give no indication of leadership ability in a less structured, democratic situation. A man may become influential in a situation requiring deliberation and planning but show little evidence of leadership if the situation demands immediate action with no opportunity for weighing alternatives or thinking things out. Or, to take still another instance, a man may function effectively and comfortably in a group whose climate is friendly and cooperative but retreat and become ineffective if he perceives the atmosphere as hostile.

The case for the situational approach to leadership derives its strength from this fact: while organizations in general may exhibit broad similarities of structure and function, they also, in particular, show strong elements of uniqueness.

It is a matter of common observation that within any normal industrial organization, providing there has been a sufficient past, there will be found patterns of relationships and interactions that are highly predictable and highly repetitive. Some of these recurring situations will be unique to that organization. It is this uniqueness that is referred to when one speaks of the "personality" of a company. This is what a management has in mind when it selects a new member with an eye to how he will "fit in." The argument of the researcher who stresses the situational aspects of leadership is that these unique characteristics of an organization are often crucial in determining which of two equally competent and gifted men will become a "leader," and further that in the very same organization these unique patterns may change significantly at different levels of the hierarchy. The vary same "leadership abilities" that helped a man rise to the top may, once he is there, prove a positive detriment.

The status of trait and situational leadership research can be summed up in this way: (1) the broad similarities which hold for a great number of organizations make it possible to say useful things about the kind of person who is likely to become a leader in any of those organizations; and (2) the unique characteristics of a particular organization make it necessary to analyze the situational factors that determine who is likely to become a leader *in one particular organization.* To put it another way, when specific situational patterns are different from organization to organization, one cannot say what personal traits will lead to acknowledged leadership. Instead, one must try to define the leadership functions that must be performed in those situations and regard as leadership those acts which perform them. This point of view suggests that almost any member of a group may become its leader under circumstances that enable him to perform the required functions of leadership and that different persons may contribute in different ways to the leadership of the group.

In these terms we come close to the notion of leadership, not as a personal quality, but as an *organizational function.* Under this concept it is not sensible to ask of an organization, "Who is the leader?" Instead we ask, "How are the leadership functions distributed in this organization?" The distribution may be wide or narrow. It may be so narrow— so many of the leadership functions may be vested in a single person— that he is the leader in the popular sense. But in modern organizations this is becoming more and more rare.

What are these "leadership functions?" Many have been proposed: planning, giving information, evaluating, arbitrating, controlling, rewarding, punishing, and the like. All of these stem from the underlying idea that leadership acts are those which help the group achieve its objectives or, as it is also put, satisfy its "needs." In most face-to-face groups, the emergence of a leader can well be accounted for on this basis. That person who can assist or facilitate the group most in reaching a satisfactory state is likely to be regarded as the leader. If one looks closely at what constitutes assistance or facilitation in this sense, it turns out to be the making of choices or the helping of the group to make choices—"better" choices, of course.

But can the function of leadership be reduced simply to decision making or the facilitation of decision making? The objection can be raised that such a definition is much too wide to be useful. Every action, even every physical movement one makes, is after all "chosen" out of a number of possible alternatives. If when I am at my workbench I pick up a screwdriver in preference to a hammer, I am clearly making a choice; am I, by virtue of that choice, displaying leadership? Something is obviously wrong with the definition of leadership which imputes it to any act that can be shown to have involved a choice. Common sense would argue that customary, habitual, and "unconscious" actions, although they may logically contain elements of choice, should be separated from actions that are subjectively viewed by the person taking them as requiring a decision. Common sense would also argue that questions of choice that can be settled on the basis of complete information should be considered differently from questions of choice in which decisions must be taken in the face of uncertainty. And common sense would argue that some distinction should be made between decisions that, although made on equally uncertain grounds, involve very different orders of risk.

This is, of course, the implicit view of the practicing manager, and although it may contain very knotty problems of logic, it is the view that will be taken here. Stated in general terms, the position that will be taken is that organizational leadership consists of *uncertainty reduction.* The actual behavior through which this reduction is accomplished is the making of choices.

We saw above that not all choices are equally difficult or equally important. Some choices are considered unimportant or irrelevant and are ignored, and, of course, whole areas may be seen as so peripheral to the interests of the organization that they are not perceived as areas of choice at all. Other choices that *must* be made are so well understood that they become habitual and automatic. Some of these are grouped into more or less coherent bundles and given a job name. The employee learns to make them correctly as he becomes skilled in the job. In most job-evaluation plans, additional credit is given if the job requires judgment. This is a way of saying that there are choices remaining in the job that cannot be completely taken care of by instructions but must be made by the employee as they come along.

There are other choices which, although they are equally clear and habitual, are of a more general nature and do not apply just to a specific job but apply to all. These are customarily embodied in rules and procedures. Rules and procedures are, in this sense, decisions made in advance of the events to which they are to be applied. Obviously, this is possible and practical only to the extent that the events to which the rules and procedures apply can be foreseen, and the practical limit of their completeness and specificity depends on how these future events can be predicted.

Following this line of analysis, it is theoretically possible to arrange all the logically inherent choices that must be made in operating an industrial organization along scales of increasing uncertainty and importance. At some level in this hierarchy of choices, it is customary for management to draw a line, reserving for itself from that point on the duty and the privilege of making the required decisions.

Precisely where a management draws this line defines its scope. The way in which a management distributes the responsibility for making the set of choices it has thus claimed to itself defines its structure. What organizational leadership *is* and what kinds of acts constitute it are questions that can be answered only within this framework of scope and structure. In these terms leadership consists of the continuous choice-making process that permits the organization as a whole to proceed toward its objectives despite all sorts of internal and external perturbations.

But as every practicing manager knows, problems occasionally arise that are not amenable to the available and customary methods of analysis and solution. Although uncertain about which choice to make, a management may nevertheless have to make a decision. It is in situations of this kind that many of the popular traits attributed to leaders find their justification: quickness of decision, the courage to take risks, coolness under stress, intuition, and even luck. There is no doubt that quick, effective, and daring decisions are a highly prized commodity in a crisis, but just as precious a commodity is the art of planning and organizing so that such crises do not occur. The trend of management has been to remove as many of its decisions as possible from the area of hunch and intuition to that of rational calculation. More and more, organizations are choosing to depend less on the peculiar abilities of rare individuals and to depend instead on the orderly processes of research and analysis.

The occasions and opportunities for personal leadership in the old sense still exist, but they are becoming increasingly rare and circumscribed.

This new emphasis has not eliminated the role of personal leadership, but it has significantly redefined it. Under normal conditions of operation, leadership in the modern organization consists not so much in the making of decisions personally as it does of maintaining the operational effectiveness of the decision-making systems which comprise the management of the organization. The picture of the leader who keeps his own counsel and in the nick of time pulls the rabbit out of the hat is out of date. The popular stereotype now is the thoughtful executive discussing in committee the information supplied by a staff of experts. In fact, it may be that the brilliant innovator in the role of manager is rapidly becoming as much an organizational embarrassment as he is an asset.

This trend, reasonable though it may appear on the surface, conceals two serious dangers. First, we may be systematically giving up the opportunity of utilizing the highest expressions of personal leadership in favor of managerial arrangements which, although safer and more reliable, can yield at best only a high level of mediocrity. And second, having committed ourselves to a system that thrives on the ordinary, we may, in the interests of maintaining and improving its efficiency, tend to shun the extraordinary.

It is no accident that daring and innovation wane as an organization grows large and successful. On different levels this appears to have been the history of men, of industries, of nations, and even of societies and culture. Success leads to "obligations"—not the least of which is the obligation to hold what has been won. Therefore, the energies of a man or administration may be absorbed in simply maintaining vested interests. Similarly, great size requires "system," and system, once established, may easily become an end in itself.

This is a gloomy picture, because it is a picture of decay. It has been claimed, usually with appeals to biological analogies, that this is an inevitable cycle, but this view is, very probably, incorrect. Human organizations are not biological organisms; they are social inventions.

12

Leadership Theory: Some Implications for Managers

CHESTER A. SCHRIESHEIM
JAMES M. TOLLIVER
ORLANDO C. BEHLING

In the past seventy years more than 3,000 leadership studies have been conducted and dozens of leadership models and theories have been proposed.[1] Yet, a practicing manager who reads this literature seeking an effective solution to supervisory problems will rapidly become disenchanted. Although we have access to an overwhelming volume of leadership theory and research, few guidelines exist which are of use to a practitioner. Nevertheless, interest in leadership—and in those qualities which separate a successful leader from an unsuccessful one—remains unabated. In almost any book dealing with management one will find some discussion of leadership. In any company library there are numerous volumes entitled "Increasing Leadership Effectiveness," "Successful Leadership," or "How to Lead." Typical management development programs conducted within work organizations and universities usually deal with some aspect of leadership. This intensity and duration of writing on the subject and the sums spent annually on leadership training indicate that practicing managers and academicians consider good leadership essential to organizational success.

What is meant by leadership, let alone *good* leadership? Many definitions have been proposed, and it seems that most are careful to separate management from leadership. This distinction sometimes be-

Reprinted from *MSU BUSINESS TOPICS*, 22:2 (Summer 1978), pp. 34–40, by permission of the authors and publisher.

comes blurred in everyday conversations. The first term, *management*, includes those processes, both mental and physical, which result in other people executing prescribed formal duties for organizational goal attainment. It deals mainly with planning, organizing, and controlling the work of other people to achieve organizational goals.[2] This definition usually includes those aspects of managers' jobs, such as monitoring and controlling resources, which are sometimes ignored in current conceptualizations of leadership. *Leadership*, on the other hand, is a more restricted type of managerial activity, focusing on the interpersonal interactions between a leader and one or more subordinates, with the purpose of increasing organizational effectiveness.[3] In this view, leadership is a social influence process in which the leader seeks the voluntary participation of subordinates in an effort to reach organizational objectives. The key idea highlighted by a number of authors is that the subordinate's participation is voluntary.[4] This implies that the leader has brought about some change in the way subordinates want to behave. Leadership, consequently, is not only a specific process (more so than management), but also is undoubtedly political in nature. The political aspect of leadership has been discussed elsewhere, so at this point it suffices to note that a major implication of leadership's political nature is that such attempts at wielding influence will not necessarily succeed.[5] In fact, other types of managerial tasks may have a stronger influence on organizational effectiveness than those interpersonal tasks usually labeled leadership.[6]

Despite this shortcoming, the examination of leadership as it relates to interpersonal interactions is still worthwhile simply because managers may, in many cases, have more control over how they and their subordinates behave than over nonhuman aspects of their jobs (such as the amount and types of resources they are given). In addition, some information does exist concerning which leadership tactics are of use under various conditions. For this information to be of greatest use, however, practicing managers should have some concept of the direction leadership research has taken. Thus, before attempting to provide guidelines for practitioners, we shall briefly review major approaches to the subject of leadership and point out their weaknesses and limitations.

Basic Approaches to Leadership

Thinking concerning leadership has moved through three distinct periods or phases.

The Trait Phase. Early approaches to leadership from the pre-Christian era to the late 1940s emphasized the examination of leader characteristics (such as age and degree of gregariousness) in an attempt to identify a set of universal characteristics which would allow a leader to be effective in all situations. At first a few traits seemed to be universally important for successful leaders, but subsequent research yielded inconsistent results concerning these traits; in addition, research investigating a large number of other traits (about one hundred) was generally discouraging. As a result of this accumulation of negative findings and of reviews of this evidence, such as that conducted by R. M. Stogdill, the tide of opinion about the importance of traits for leadership effectiveness began to change.[7] In the late 1940s, leadership researchers began to move away from trait research. Contemporary opinion holds the trait approach in considerable disrepute and views the likelihood of uncovering a set of universal leadership effectiveness traits as essentially impossible.

The Behavioral Phase. With the fall of the trait approach, researchers considered alternative concepts, eventually settling on the examination of relationships between leader behaviors and subordinate satisfaction and performance.[8] During the height of the behavioral phase, dating roughly from the late 1940s to the early 1960s, several large research programs were conducted, including the Ohio State University leadership studies, a program of research which has received considerable publicity over the years.

The Ohio State studies started shortly after World War II and initially concentrated on leadership in military organizations. In one of these studies, a lengthy questionnaire was administered to B-36 bomber crews, and their answers were statistically analyzed to identify the common dimensions underlying the answers.[9] This analysis discovered two dimensions which seemed most important in summarizing the nature of the crews' perceptions about their plane commanders' behavior toward them.

Consideration was the stronger of the two factors, and it involved leader behaviors indicative of friendship, mutual trust, respect, and warmth.

The second factor was Initiation of Structure, a concept involving leader behaviors indicating that the leader organizes and defines the relationship between self and subordinates.[10]

In subsequent studies using modified versions of the original questionnaire, Consideration and Structure were found to be prime dimensions of leader behavior in situations ranging from combat flights over Korea to assembly line work.[11] In addition, studies were undertaken at Ohio State and elsewhere to compare the effects of these leader behaviors on subordinate performance and satisfaction. A high Consideration–high Structure leadership style was, in many cases, found to lead to high performance and satisfaction. However, in a number of studies dysfunctional consequences, such as high turnover and absenteeism, accompanied these positive outcomes. In yet other situations, different combinations of Consideration and Structure (for example, low Consideration–high Structure) were found to be more effective.[12]

Similar behaviors were identified and similar results obtained in a large number of studies, such as those conducted at the University of Michigan.[13] Although the display of highly Considerate–highly Structuring behavior was sometimes found to result in positive organizational outcomes, this was not true in all of the cases or even in most of them.[14] The research, therefore, clearly indicated that no single leadership style was universally effective, as the relationship of supervisory behavior to organizational performance and employee satisfaction changed from situation to situation. By the early 1960s this had become apparent to even the most ardent supporters of the behavioral approach, and the orientation of leadership researchers began to change toward a situational treatment.

The Situational Phase. Current leadership research is almost entirely situational. This approach examines the interrelationships among leader and subordinate behaviors or characteristics and the situations in which the parties find themselves. This can clearly be seen in the work of researchers such as F. E. Fiedler, who outlined one of the first situational models.[15]

Fiedler claims that leaders are motivated primarily by satisfaction derived from interpersonal relations and task-goal accomplishment. Relationship-motivated leaders display task-oriented behaviors (such as Initiating Structure) in situations which are favorable for them to exert influence over their work group, and they display relationship-oriented behaviors (such as Consideration) in situations which are either moderately favorable or unfavorable. Task-motivated leaders display relationship-oriented behaviors in favorable situations and task-oriented behaviors in both moderately favorable and unfavorable situations. Fiedler's model specifies that relationship-motivated leaders will be more effective in situations which are moderately favorable for the leader to exert influence, and that they will be less effective in favorable or unfavorable situations; the exact opposite is the case for task-motivated leaders. (They are the most effective in favorable or unfavorable situations and least effective in moderately favorable ones.) According to Fiedler, the favorableness of the situation for the leader to exert influence over the work group is determined by (1) the quality of leader–group member relations (the warmer and friendlier, the more favorable the situation); (2) the structure of the tasks performed by the leader's subordinates (the more structured, the more favorable); and (3) the power of the leader (the more power, the more favorable the situation).[16]

A number of other authors propose similar types of interactions among the leader, the led, and the situation. We will not review all these other models, but the situational model of Victor Vroom and Phillip Yetton deserves mention.[17] Their model suggests the conditions under which the leader should share decision-making power. Five basic leadership styles are recommended. These range from unilateral decisions by the leader to situations in which the leader gives a great deal of decision power to subordinates and serves as a discussion coordinator who does not attempt to influence the group. Which style is recommended depends upon the leader's "yes" or "no" response to seven quality and acceptability questions which are asked sequentially. In those cases where more than a single style is suggested, the leader is expected to choose between recommendations on the basis of the amount of time to be invested. While this model, as is the case with most of the situational models, has not been fully tested, the literature supports the basic notion that a situational view is necessary to portray accurately the complexities of leadership processes.

Organizational Implications

What does this discussion of leadership theory and research have to do with the practice of management?

Selection does not seem to be the primary answer to the organization's need to increase the pool of effective leaders. The results of the numerous trait studies summarized by Stogdill and others indicate that the search for universal personality characteristics of effective leaders is doomed.[18] This statement requires qualification, however. It should be recognized that the assertion concerns leadership effectiveness, which is only one aspect of managerial effectiveness. A manager may contribute to organizational effectiveness in many ways other than by being an effective leader. The role of selection in picking effective managers, as distinguished from effective leaders, consequently may be much greater. Furthermore, present disappointment with attempts at leader selection is derived from research which has sought to identify universal characteristics of effective leaders in all situations. Summaries such as Stogdill's demonstrate that leadership effectiveness is highly dependent upon the relationship between leader characteristics and the demands of particular situations, and thus universal approaches will not work. Exploration of leader traits as they relate to performance in particular situations may reveal that careful selection has some potential. Unfortunately, given the many situational factors which appear to influence leadership effectiveness, it seems unlikely that selection procedures will be able to follow typical actuarial (statistical) selection procedures.[19] (It appears almost impossible to gather enough individuals in identical jobs to do this.) However, this does not preclude the use of clinical (judgmental) techniques for selection of leaders.

A further limitation on selection procedures as ways of increasing the pool of effective managers and/or leaders within organizations is the dynamic nature of managerial jobs and managers' careers. If, as research seems to indicate, leadership success is situation-specific, then the continual and inevitable shifts in the nature of a manager's assignment and his or her movement from one assignment to another may make the initial selection invalid.

Another implication is that existing forms of leadership training appear to be inappropriate, based on the evidence outlined here. There are two reasons for this. First, the majority of such training programs are based upon the assumption that there exists one best way to manage. Great emphasis usually is placed on an employee-centered (Considerate) approach or one which combines a concern for employees with a concern for high output (Initiating Structure). For example, the Managerial Grid and its associated Grid Organizational Development Program are popular approaches to management and organizational development.[20] Both are based on the premise that a managerial style which shows high concern for people and high concern for production is the soundest way to achieve excellence, and both attempt to develop this style of behavior on the part of all managers.[21] Rensis Likert's "System-Four" approach to managerial and organizational development, although different from the Grid approach, also assumes that one best way to manage exists (employee-centered leadership).[22] Clearly, these ideas are in conflict with the evidence and with contemporary opinion.

The other limitation of leadership training is that it seems ineffective in changing the behavior of participants. Leadership training aimed not directly at leadership behavior itself, but at providing diagnostic skills for the identification of the nature of the situation and the behaviors appropriate to it, appears to offer considerable potential for the improvement of leadership effectiveness. Obviously, however, additional research is needed to identify the dimensions of situations crucial to leadership performance and the styles effective under various circumstances.

Fiedler's suggestion that organizations engineer the job to fit the manager also has potential.[23] However, the idea is impractical, if not utopian. Application of this approach is limited because we have not identified the crucial dimensions of situations which affect leadership performances. Also, while the overall approach may offer theoretical advantages when leadership is treated in isolation, it ignores dysfunctional effects on other aspects of the organization's operations. Leadership effectiveness cannot be the only concern of administrators as they make decisions about job assignments. They must consider other aspects of the organization's operations which may conflict with their attempts to make good use of leadership talent. Some characteristics of the job, task, or organization simply may not be subject to change, at least in the short run. Thus, engineering the job to fit the manager may increase leadership effectiveness, but this approach seems risky, at least for the foreseeable future.

It should also be noted that it is not unusual for work organizations to use traits and trait descriptions in their evaluations of both leadership and managerial performance. A quick glance at a typical performance rating form usually reveal the presence of terms such as *personality* and *attitude* as factors for individual evaluation. Clearly, these terms represent a modern-day version of the traits investigated thirty years ago, and they may or may not be related to actual job performance, depending upon the specifics of the situation involved. Thus, some explicit rationale and, it is hoped, evidence that such traits do affect managerial performance should be provided before they are included in performance evaluations. Just feeling that they are important is not sufficient justification.

Individual Implications

The implications of our discussion of leadership theory and research for individual managers are intertwined with those for the total organization. The fact that leadership effectiveness does not depend on a single set of personal characteristics with which an individual is born or which the individual acquires at an early age should provide a sense of relief to many managers and potential managers. Success in leadership is not limited to an elite, but can be attained by almost any individual, assuming that the situation is proper and that the manager can adjust his or her behavior to fit the situation. The process leading to effective leadership, in other words, is not so much one of changing the characteristics of the individual as it is one of assuring that he or she is placed in an appropriate situation or of teaching the individual how to act to fit the situation.

Thus, a manager's effectiveness can be improved through the development of skills in analyzing the nature of organizational situations—both task and political demands. Although it is difficult to provide guidelines, some recent research points to tentative prescriptions.[24]

Generally speaking, a high Consideration–high Structure style often works best. However, this approach cannot be used in all instances because dysfunctional consequences can result from such behaviors. For example, upper management sometimes gives highly considerate managers poor performance ratings, while in other instances high Structure has been related to employee dissatisfaction, grievances, and turnover. It sometimes will be necessary for a manager to choose between high Consideration and high Structure, and in these cases an individual's diagnostic ability becomes important.

If the diagnostician (manager) has little information, it is probably safe to exhibit high Consideration. Although it does not guarantee subordinate performance, its positive effects on frustration-instigated behavior—such as agression—are probably enough to warrant its recommendation as a general style. However, in some situations Structure probably should be emphasized, although it may mean a decrease in subordinate perceptions of Consideration. Although the following is not an exhaustive list of these exceptions, it does include those which are known and appear important. The individual manager, from a careful analysis of the situation, must add any additional factors that can be identified.

- *Emergencies or high-pressure situations.* When the work involves physical danger, when time is limited, or when little tolerance for error exists, emphasis on Initiating Structure seems desirable. Research has demonstrated that subordinates often expect and prefer high Structure in such instances.

- *Situations in which the manager is the only source of information.* When the leader is the only person knowledgeable about the task, subordinates often expect him or her to make specific job assignments, set deadlines, and generally engage in structuring their behavior. This does not mean that the leader cannot be considerate if this is appropriate.

- *Subordinate preferences.* There is limited evidence that some subordinates prefer high Structure and expect it, while other expect low Consideration and are suspicious of leaders who display high Consideration. Other preference patterns undoubtedly exist, and managers should attempt to tailor their behavior to each individual employee, as the situation dictates.

- *Preference of higher management.* In some instances, higher management has definite preferences for certain leadership styles. Higher management sometimes prefers and expects high Structure and low Consideration, and rewards managers for displaying this behavioral style. The manager should be sensitive to the desires of superiors, in addition to those of subordinates. While it is not possible to specify how these expectations may be reconciled if they diverge, compromise or direct persuasion might be useful.[25] Once again, the success of these methods probably will depend both upon the situation and the manager's skill. This leads to the last point—adaptability.

• *Leader ability to adjust.* Some managers will be able to adjust their behavior to fit the situation. For others, attempts to modify behavior may look false and manipulative to subordinates. In these instances, the manager probably would be better off keeping the style with which he or she is most comfortable.

Limitations and Conclusion

The situational approach avoids the major shortcomings of both the trait and behavioral approaches to leadership. However, the implicit assumption that hierarchical leadership is always important has recently come into question. Steven Kerr, for example, points out that many factors may limit the ability of a hierarchical superior to act as a leader for subordinates.[26] Factors such as technology (for example, the assembly line), training, clear job descriptions, and the like, may provide subordinates with enough guidance so that supervisor Structure may be unnecessary to ensure task performance. Also, jobs which are intrinsically satisfying may negate the need for supervisor Consideration, since Consideration is not needed to offset job dullness.

Another problem with the situational approach, and with leadership as a major emphasis in general, is that effective leadership may account for only 10 to 15 percent of the variability in unit performance.[27] While this percentage is certainly not trivial, it is clear that much of what affects performance in organizations is not accounted for by leadership. While studying and emphasizing leadership certainly has its merits, it could be argued that there is much to be gained by treating leadership effectiveness as but one component of managerial effectiveness. As an earlier publication emphasized:

> It is necessary to note that leadership is only one way in which the manager contributes to organizational effectiveness. The manager also performs duties which are *externally oriented* so far as his unit is concerned. For example, he may spend part of his time coordinating the work of his unit with other units. Similarly, not all of the manager's *internally oriented* activities can be labeled leadership acts. Some of them concern the physical and organizational conditions under which the work unit operates. For example, the manager spends part of his time obtaining resources (materials, equipment, manpower, and so on) necessary for unit operations. This is an essential internally oriented activity but hardly constitutes leadership. Clearly, the manager must perform a mix of internal and external activities if his unit is to perform well. Leadership is only one of the internal activities performed by managers.[28]

Thus, the manager should not overemphasize the importance of leadership activities, especially if this causes other functions to be neglected.

For managers to be effective as leaders, they must attempt to be politically astute and to tailor their behaviors, taking into account differences in subordinates, superiors, and situations. Leadership should be kept in perspective. Clearly, it is important, but it cannot be treated in isolation; the importance of leadership depends upon the situation, and the practicing manager must take this into account.

Notes

1. R.M. Stogdill, *Handbook of Leadership* (New York: The Free Press, 1974).

2. A. C. Filley, R. J. House, and Steven Kerr, *Managerial Process and Organizational Behavior,* 2nd ed. (Glenview, Ill.: Scott, Foresman, 1976). See also R. C. Davis, *Industrial Organization and Management* (New York: Harper 1957).

3. C. A. Gibb, "Leadership," in Gardner Lindzey and Elliot Aronson, eds., *The Handbook of Social Psychology* (Reading, Mass.: Addison-Wesley, 1969), vol. 4.

4. See, for example, R. H. Hall, *Organizations: Structure and Process* (Englewood Cliffs, N.J.: Prentice-Hall, 1972).

5. C. A. Schriesheim, J. M. Tolliver, and L. D. Dodge, "The Political Nature of the Leadership Process," unpublished paper, 1978.

6. For examples of other types of managerial tasks which may have more of an impact on organizations, see J. P. Campbell, M. D. Dunnette, E. E. Lawler, and K. E. Weick, *Managerial Behavior, Performance, and Effectiveness* (New York: McGraw-Hill, 1970).

7. R. M. Stogdill, "Personal Factors Associated with Leadership: A Survey of the Literature," *Journal of Psychology* 25 (January 1948): 35–71.

8. T. O. Jacobs, *Leadership and Exchange in Formal Organizations* (Alexandria, Va.: Human Resources Research Organization, 1970).

9. A. W. Halpin and B. J. Winer, "A Factorial Study of the Leader Behavior Descriptions," in R. M. Stogdill and A. E. Coons, eds., *Leader Behavior: Its Descriptions and Measurement* (Columbus: Bureau of Business Research, The Ohio State University, 1957).

10. Ibid., p. 42.

11. Stogdill and Coons, *Leader Behavior.*

12. Steven Kerr, C. A. Schriesheim, C. J. Murphy, and R. M. Stogdill, "Toward a Contingency Theory of Leadership Based upon the Consideration and Initiating Structure Literature," *Organizational Behavior and Human Performance* 12 (August 1974): 62–82.

13. See, for example, Daniel Katz, Nathan Maccoby, and Nancy Morse, *Productivity, Supervision and Morale in an Office Situation.* (Ann Arbor: Survey Research Center, University of Michigan, 1951).

14. Kerr et al., "Contingency Theory."

15. See F. E. Fiedler, "Engineer the Job to Fit the Manager," *Harvard Business Review* 43 (September–October 1965): 115–22.

16. F. E. Fiedler, *A Theory of Leadership Effectiveness* (New York: McGraw-Hill, 1967).

17. V. H. Vroom and P. W. Yetton, *Leadership and Decision-Making* (Pittsburgh, Pa.: University of Pittsburgh Press, 1973).

18. R. M. Stogdill, "Personal Factors."

19. Kerr et al., "Contingency Theory."

20. R. R. Blake and J. S. Mouton, *The Managerial Grid* (Houston, Texas: Gulf, 1964), and *Building a Dynamic Corporation Through Grid Organizational Development* (Reading Mass.: Addison Wesley, 1969).

21. Ibid., p. 63.

22. Rensis Likert, *New Patterns of Management* (New York: McGraw-Hill, 1961), and *The Human Organization: Its Management and Value* (New York: McGraw-Hill, 1967).

23. Fiedler, "Engineer the Job."

24. Kerr et al., "Contingency Theory."

25. See Filley, House and Kerr, *Managerial Process*, especially pp. 162–80; and George Strauss, "Tactics of Lateral Relations," in H. J. Leavitt and L. R. Pondy, eds., *Readings in Managerial Psychology*, 1st ed. (Chicago: University of Chicago Press, 1964), pp. 226–48.

26. Steven Kerr, "Substitutes for Leadership: Their Definition and Measurement," unpublished paper, 1978.

27. O. C. Behling and C. A. Schriesheim, *Organizational Behavior: Theory, Research and Application* (Boston: Allyn and Bacon, 1976).

28. Ibid., p. 294.

Part Three

FOLLOWERSHIP: A NECESSARY ELEMENT OF LEADERSHIP

Followers give legitimacy to the leadership role. If people do not believe that a leader has the authority to exert influence or if they cannot accept whatever authority a leader has, there cannot be successful leadership. Followership is often taken for granted. The failure to recognize the existence of reciprocal interdependencies between leader and followers can have grave consequences. These interdependencies are critical to leader success and they ensure, as well, an ongoing pattern of leadership development.

Followers' expectations are changing. Social, economic, and technological environments have created a better educated, more sophisticated constituency. Similarly, superior education, technical skill, and access to information are no longer solely within the purview of the leader. Today's leadership issues are more complex and leaders are expected to perform better. As a result, leaders are feeling the effects of a narrowing gap between their followers' competencies and their own abilities. Increasingly, leaders must actively involve followers in organizational decision-making. All of this suggests a need to *train followers* in how to communicate their expectations and expertise, to enhance their willingness to participate.

The group dynamics of leaders and followers in today's world revolve more on the group than on the leader. Yet leaders come from the ranks of the followers. One wonders whether the leader of tomorrow can be successful without having first learned the skills of followership. Many organizations find themselves adrift when a leader exits; subsequent leadership fails because of inadequate followership experience or because no formal mechanism existed to develop the next leader. Both roles are critical. Hence, the study of leadership must also include the dimension of followership, as it affects organizational success and serves as a prerequisite for effective leadership.

In Chapter 13, "Leadership Through Followership," William Litzinger and Thomas Schaefer present the thesis that effective leadership may be primarily an achievement of followers—that able leaders may emerge only from the ranks of able followers. They draw upon the philosophy of Aristotle, Plato, and particularly Hegel to support their argument that a good personal history of effective followership may be one of the most significant factors in leadership, although it is not by itself sufficient to ensure leadership success. Despite the fact that good followership is not the final determinant for successful leadership, Litzinger and Schaefer believe that followership deserves stronger consideration among the factors now attracting the attention of leadership theorists. (We happen to agree with them.)

"Leading Through the Follower's Point of View," by William Zierden (Chapter 14), shifts the attention of managers from the behavior of the leader to the basic questions that are presumed to exist in the minds of followers. A conceptual framework matches a situational or contingency approach with a set of questions representing a synthesis of possible situational elements. One should be aware, however, that translating a conceptual scheme into a specific leader behavior is more easily said than done, especially if the proposed behavior is different from customary behavior.

In Chapter 15, we turn to the topic of leadership succession, the planned or unplanned change of the formal leader of a group or organization. Gil Gordon and Ned Rosen review the relevant literature on the dynamics of the succession process and the implications for leadership and group effectiveness. The authors lay out a "prearrival-postarrival" model for analyzing leadership succession dynamics but also propose an alternate model that conceptualizes the succession process in terms of situational favorableness based on the linkage between leadership and group dynamics. Well-planned succession may be the only sure way of providing leadership continuity in our rapidly changing economic, social, and technological environment.

Leadership, followership, and the implications of succession planning are also examined by King Davis in "The Status of Black Leadership: Implications for Black Followers in the 1980s." Davis concludes that although leaders in the society at large may fit into one of James McGregor Burns's typologies (transformational or transactional leadership), the needs and experiences of the black population may dictate a greater emphasis on transformational leadership with high moral standards. Davis predicts that the most significant factor influencing the black movement will be the increasingly poor economic status of the nation in general and of the black population in particular. The inequities that have historically precipitated black social-change movements continue, but the form of those inequities has changed, according to Davis. He points out that many traditional black leaders have died without being replaced by effective successors, causing a decline in the number of followers. Davis predicts that the black population will identify and empower new leaders who solidify their relationship with their followers, thus legitimizing their leadership position and allowing them to aggressively work for the group's goals. He concludes by predicting a resurgence of a black movement characterized by protest, confrontation, economic pressure, and an independent cadre of transformational leadership.

In Chapter 17 Kathryn Moore describes the mentoring process by which leaders are developed from select followers. With great insight, Moore describes what mentors do and how the informal, idiosyncratic process can be effectively employed for leadership development. The mentor-protégé relationship is an intense, lasting relationship that changes the protégé's and, often, the mentor's life. Moore discusses how a mentor-protégé relationship develops and what the benefits and costs or risks are for the mentor, the protégé, and the organizations. Although she focuses on the college and university setting, the mentoring process she describes is applicable to all formal organizations.

Chapter 18 reflects on the heritage of the military and its unique contributions to the study of leadership. General Edward Meyer sees the need for a renaissance in the art of military leadership. In "Leadership: A Return to Basics," he calls for the creation of a climate in the Army wherein each individual can find meaning and fulfillment. This would mean enriching the relationship between the leader and the led, creating a bond sufficiently developed to withstand the rigors of combat. Meyer does make a distinction between leadership and management, arguing that the real challenge to leadership in today's Army is fostering the individual development and growth of the followers. These insights into the importance of followership reaffirm the tradition of disciplined military leadership, while acknowledging the changing relationship between leader and follower.

Leadership is not an isolated phenomenon; followership is indeed a necessary element of leader effectiveness. Only when the followers understand their role and give legitimacy to their leader does the leader's role become active and vital to the organization.

13

Leadership Through Followership

WILLIAM LITZINGER
THOMAS SCHAEFER

Not long ago, we posed a question to a group of officers, most of whom were on the West Point faculty, and many of whom were themselves graduates of the Academy. "Since developing leadership is what this place is all about," we asked, "how do you go about doing that task?" Their answer surprised us. "We begin by teaching them to be followers."

This insight prompted us to undertake a study, not of the nature of leadership (a subject which has been widely discussed), but of the notion that leadership may be chiefly an achievement of followers—that able leaders may emerge only from the ranks of able followers. Because of the genesis of our idea, we call it the West Point Thesis. Our concern is the developmental question of how leaders emerge and, particularly, how the mastery of followership may prepare and qualify one for leadership.

Contemporary authors seem to say little or nothing about what leaders must have done yesterday to become leaders today. Yet the ground of leadership can lie only in the leader's personal history.

Much earlier writers seem to have realized this. Plato's *Republic* analyzes what the king must do from his earliest years to become the sovereign. In the *Politics*, Aristotle laments the rarity of virtue among aspirants to statesmanship, and insists that only by training from youth may subjects grow to leadership. Much later, the philosopher Hegel required of the mature leader the most intimate understanding of his followers, achievable only by passage through the experience of servitude.

Reprinted by permission from *Business Horizons*, 25:5 (September–October 1982), pp. 78–81. Copyright © 1982 by the Foundation for the School of Business at Indiana University.

In his *Phenomenology of Mind*, Hegel so strongly affirms the mastery of followership as the sine qua non of leadership—our "West Point Thesis"—that an outline of his ideas is critical here.

Leadership/Followership

Hegel's "dialectic of master and slave" is a significant episode in the history of leadership theory. Leadership is possible, says Hegel, not only on the condition that followership has been learned, but on the more radical condition that the leader has known subjection and thralldom. The mature leader not only must have known the travail of the follower; he must here and now incorporate within himself all that the follower is. The school for leadership is indeed followership, a followership that is fully preserved within leadership, but transformed for having moved beyond itself. The leader, in short, must not merely have been a follower. He must, here and now, be a follower in the fullest sense; in a sense, paradoxically, that the follower cannot be. The leader is more a follower than the follower.

In the curious Hegelian dialectic, where opposites pass constantly into one another, the recognition that there is "followership in the leader" demands the recognition that there is "leadership in the follower." Believers in participative leadership would agree; "management by objectives," especially, through insisting that none manage "by objectives" who do not "control themselves," affirms a need for "leadership in the follower."[1] In MBO, leadership is a shared effort in which all, leader and follower alike, not only struggle for goals, but also set them. A central purpose of MBO is to substitute for the supervisor's role of judge that of "helper." This connects the "followership of the leader" with the "leadership of the follower." MBO receives "good grades" in the school of Hegel.

The paradoxes of Hegel's thought may be less unsettling when we recall how the Pope of the Catholic church designates his own leadership; he is "The Servant of the Servants of God." Where leader and follower alike are held to obedience to defined doctrine, neither may act on his own autonomous will alone. Leadership endures so long as it assumes a posture of humility, a spirit of followership.

Epitomizing the Group's Values

Argument from authority is notoriously weak. Plato and Aristotle, Hegel and others have propounded the "thesis," but does it prove out in practice?

In fact, many fine leaders *have* been excellent followers. The young Churchill distinguished himself as a faithful taker of orders, as did the young Bismarck, and the youthful Caesar. Even figures who are despised because they were not good followers of societal norms—such as Stalin, Hitler, Idi Amin—were good followers of some other code. Though he "marched to a different drummer," Hitler was an excellent "follower" of National Socialism in Germany. He was not above showing obsequiousness to those whom he judged to be arbiters of his rise to power. Mussolini, beloved of the Fascists, was a beast to the Allies, as was Ghengis Khan to the people of Europe.

The leader, then, appears to be a poor follower when judged by norms other than his own. When perceived in the context of his own organization, he is its obedient servant. Adversary organizations (gangs, revolutionary groups) demand more rigid conformity to group norms than do their legitimate counterparts. In prison societies, for example, an "inmate code" demands that leaders conform more perfectly to group norms than do their followers. Leaders who were notoriously "poor followers" of societal norms are typically heads of opposition groups that replaced, or threatened, another regime. They are, of course, poor followers of the enemy regime, but excellent followers of their own. "Mavericks," like Zapata, who became leaders, may appear to have been bad followers. They are, in fact, good followers of an orthodoxy other than the one by which the majority judges them. Zapata's organization exacted the strictest possible obedience from all, including Zapata himself.

Whether adversary or orthodox, an organization demands common acceptance of values. In this lies the link between obedience and command. The commander cannot break the link without destroying the legitimacy of his rule. Richard Nixon broke the link and had to relinquish command. In this sense, surely, followership is the school of leaders. To have internalized an organization's values, to have become, even, an embodiment of them, is to have the potential to be a leader. And, assuming an infallible awareness among the organization's members that one among them is an incarnation of its values, that member will be elected to leadership. No less certainly will abandonment of these values by the leader bring his decline and eventual fall.

There has been broad recognition of what we are calling the West Point Thesis throughout history. For centuries in China, leaders were chosen on the basis of their obedience to and knowledge of Confucian principles. The British Civil Service, like virtually all armies, has linked faithful service at the lower ranks to advancement to leadership. The idea, in fact, is inseparable from the conception of hierarchy. To stand at the pinnacle, one must have ascended some series of steps. Ascent demands not merely effort but upward progress. This occurs by gaining a foothold at each level, mastering each higher step. It requires the art of followership.

Applying the West Point Thesis

How might the West Point Thesis mesh with present-day concepts? Chester Barnard's well-known Acceptance Theory of Authority strongly asserts the followership-leadership link.

"The decision as to whether an order has authority or not lies with the persons to whom it is addressed, and does not reside in 'persons of authority' or those who issue these orders."[2]

With the ground of authority in the followers' granting or withholding obedience, leaders are constrained to lead in ways construed by followers to be consistent with the goals of the organization. "A person will accept a communication as authoritative only when . . . he believes that it is not inconsistent with the purposes of the organization," says Barnard. The leader, then, must also "follow," that is, follow goals as understood by those under him. Followers hold power over the leader since they judge whether the leader leads, that is, conducts them to their goal.

The leader turns out to *be* a follower, and "a truer follower than the followers" in that he is held to a greater fidelity in followership than are the followers. So great is the requirement of faithful followership for the leader that he ceases to exercise command the moment this "faith" is judged wanting by his followers. Such a situation arises when a command lies outside the "zone of indifference," that group of commands which are unquestionably acceptable. Presumably, if the follower perceives an order as conducive to the goal and *still* disobeys, the threat to organization is not nearly so great as it is when the leader commands action that does not conform to the goal. Again: mastery of followership is even more important in the leader than in the follower.

Barnard's ideas, then, support the West Point Thesis. Our thesis would illuminate the Acceptance Theory by focusing on the followership exercised by the leader. How is the leader's followership like, and how is it unlike, that of the followers? Pursuit of these questions could be fruitful in clarifying the Acceptance Theory, and in drawing out the meaning of the West Point Thesis. In any case, if followership as a subordinate is a propaedeutic for followership as a leader, then surely, as Aristotle claimed, "who would learn to command must first of all learn to obey." Theorists are well aware of the "reciprocality" between leader and follower, realizing that "poor" subordinates affect leadership style profoundly.

Yet the kind of follower the leader was may affect how he leads as significantly as the kinds of followers the leader now commands. We argue here that this dimension should be brought into any dialogue about leadership.

How might a more explicit awareness of "The West Point Thesis" enrich modern theories of leadership? We now grope for some idea of how "the thesis" might open some dimensions within existing theory.

"X- and Y-Style" Followership?

McGregor's distinction invites concern over which leadership style is best in particular circumstances. Whatever style may be appropriate, however, distinct styles of leadership must elicit distinct styles of followership. Appropriate types of followership will be expected as responses to, and support for, particular styles of leadership. Should we designate a follower's response to autocratic leaders as "X-style followership," or would the nuances of the concept require a separate designation? Whatever the answer, identifying followership styles seems a condition for understanding the kind of follower the leader was, which is crucial for knowing the kind of leader he is now. The most appropriate followership training needed for a specific style of leadership will probably depend on the style of leadership in question.

The ways in which the arts of followership and leadership are related will probably vary as a function of the degree of centralization, extent of specialization, type of technology, location on the product-life cycle trajectory, and other factors in the organization. A past mastery of followership probably would be increasingly important for leadership as one moves along a continuum from loosely controlled, decentralized organization to tightly controlled, centralized types. While the followership and leadership arts would prove always linked in some way, logic suggests that in the tightly structured organization the link would be very strong, while in the loosely structured organization, with decision-making at the lowest possible levels, the link would be found weaker.

Choice of a Followership Pattern

Does the "right" choice of a leadership pattern presuppose that subordinates must have learned to choose a "right" followership pattern? Is flexibility in the choice of "followership style" possible in anything like the way in which flexibility is possible in choosing one's leadership style? Although followership may be a necessary prelude to leadership in some organizations, is it necessary in all?

This last question prompts the reflection that, while a personal history of good followership may be one significant factor in leadership, it is not the final determinant of leadership success. Some mastery of followership is a *necessary* condition for leadership, but not a *sufficient* condition. A good record of followership is far from a guarantee that one will make a fine leader. Something more than being an "obedient servant" is needed to create the leader. There were others among the tribes of Israel as obedient as Moses, but none with his "fire."

Still, followership deserves a larger place among those items now attracting the attention of leadership theorists. The perennial affirmation of the idea through history should be enough to prompt more serious consideration of it. Its greater integration into contemporary theory will provide new insights into the phenomena of leadership.

Notes

1. In the chapter, "Management by Objectives and Self-Control" in *The Practice of Management* (New York: Harper and Row, 1954), Peter Drucker affirms this point strongly: "It [MBO] motivates the manager to action not because somebody tells him to do something . . . but because the objective needs of his task demand it. *He acts not because somebody wants him to but because he himself decides that he has to—he acts, in other words, as a free man.*" p. 136. (Italics are ours.)

2. Chester I. Barnard, *The Functions of the Executive* (Cambridge, Mass.: Harvard Press, 1938): 82.

14

Leading
Through the Follower's
Point of View

WILLIAM E. ZIERDEN

In organizational situations that require action, managers know that their response will involve what is generally referred to as leadership. In reflecting on such a situation they seek answers to the questions, "How should I manage?" and "How should I lead?"

Behavioral science approaches to such questions provide a range of responses to choose from. These responses differ in the extent to which the managers permit or depend on subordinates to exercise their own discretion as well as in the extent to which the managers show concern and provide support for each subordinate as an individual human being. The managers may reflect on the difference between Douglas McGregor's Theory X and Theory Y approaches, or try to identify a proper combination of concern for production and concern for people from the Managerial Grid® of Robert Blake and Jane Mouton, or possibly select a behavior on the continuum from boss-centered leadership to subordinate-centered leadership described in the classic article by Professors Tannebaum and Schmidt.

The manager who is up on the more recent treatments of leadership will recall the conclusion of today's theorists and researchers: that to be effective, a manager's behavior should be appropriate to the circumstances, implying different behaviors in different settings. The idea is that the manager's behavior should be contingent on at least four aspects of a situation.

Reprinted by permission of the publishers of *Organizational Dynamics*, Spring 1980. © 1980 by William E. Zierden. Published by AMACOM, a division of American Management Associations. All rights reserved.

1. *The nature of the people being managed.* In general it is proposed that the more experienced the subordinate, the more committed the subordinate to organizational goals, and the better the subordinate knows how to perform assigned work, the less the manager will have to provide direct guidance or strong emotional support.

2. *Characteristics of the work itself.* For structured, simple, repetitive tasks the manager has to see that rules and procedures are developed and followed. For complex, open-ended, ambiguous work something more must be added: a way of managing that encourages subordinates to be both creative and flexible.

3. *The relationship between manager and employees and the relationships among the employees.* Where good feelings and trust exist between manager and employees or among employees, the manager may depend on those employees to go along with the decisions or may depend on the employees to contribute in a cooperative and constructive manner to the decision making. In a case of poor relationships, a manager may have to resort to coercion and control in order to make things happen.

4. *The manager's personality and preferred management style.* With the exception of those who would match people to situations through personnel selection, most advocates of contingency approaches to selecting management behavior assume that managers can alter their behavior at will. But managers are influenced by their own personalities, their own ingrained rigidities and flexibilities. And they are also influenced by remembered managerial behavior that has proved useful in the past and is not easily put aside.

Recognizing the need for a contingency approach which integrates the various situational factors, and recalling the life-cycle theory of Paul Hersey and Ken Blanchard, the manager may attempt a combination of relationship behavior and task behavior to match the maturity exhibited by the employees. Or the manager may turn to a more structured method of selecting one of several autocratic or consultative approaches by using Victor Vroom's decision tree to diagnose the situation.

If we as managers were to consider these approaches to leadership, we would probably find that they help us clarify our own thinking, and if we were to attend a seminar on a particular theory, we would gain some insight about how our behavior, as seen by others, corresponds to one category of leader behavior or another.

Yet whichever conceptual framework we use as an aid in answering the questions "How should I manage?" and "How should I lead?" adapting our behavior to a situation is a difficult task. Managers must be able to execute a three-step process on demand: (1) analyze the situation, (2) select the appropriate behavior, and (3) perform the behavior effectively. This way of conceptualizing leadership, while probably best from a descriptive point of view, is problematic when we try to translate it into a prescription for action.

First, in analyzing the situation we must examine a large number of potentially interacting variables covering the people, the task, relationships, and our own personality. In considering the effects of the interplay among all these aspects of a situation, we may have to understand hundreds of relationships.

Second, as noted earlier, we must select and apply a conceptual model of leadership to the situational analysis and arrive at a prescribed set of behaviors.

Third, implicit in this approach is the idea that we as managers can translate a conceptual description or label for behavior (employee-centered, consultative, autocratic) into a mental image of what we would look like when behaving in that way, and then actually perform that behavior. This suggests that we should have a repertoire of behaviors and be able to shift from one to another at will.

Translating a conceptual scheme into a managerial behavior is more easily said than done, especially when we feel under pressure and the behavior being tried is different from our customary behavior. The ways of approaching the leadership question that are usually offered to managers, including most of those mentioned earlier here, have one underlying characteristic in common—they focus on our own behavior, thus increasing our self-consciousness. Even theories that take the subordinates and the situation into account seem ultimately to focus on the manager's own behavior and the extent to which this behavior conforms to a label (person-centered, task-oriented, consultative). As a practical matter, directing a manager's attention in this fashion seems to present two difficulties.

First, we managers must rely on information from the situation itself in order to obtain a view of our own behavior. Much of this information comes from the very people we are attempting to influence through this behavior. Thus it is at best difficult to develop an accurate perception of how we are behaving—or, for that matter, how we are seen to behave by others. This suggests that to the extent that we focus our attention on our own behavior, a search for information about this behavior may increase our self-consciousness to the point of being detrimental.

Second, the human mind seems limited as to the number of items of information it can handle in conscious memory at one time. Psychologists suggest that for most people the range is five to nine items. This implies that although managers may intuitively handle a great deal more complexity, they can consciously handle only a limited amount of complexity at one time.

This limitation suggests that managers who comprehend a complex model of situational leadership quite well when it is presented in a book or seminar may be hard put to keep a complex theory in mind on the job because the physiology of the brain does not permit simultaneous handling of the theory and all the dynamic stimuli in the situation. Thus when a situation is complex and dynamic, *consciously* undertaking the three-step process (analyze, select a behavior, behave) may be impossible. This seems particularly true when the required behaviors are different from the pattern of behavior that has been used repeatedly in the past. In practice, focusing primarily on one's own behavior may simply be adding to the confusion.

Reflecting on various conceptualizations of leadership, becoming more aware of one's managerial behavior, and practicing new managerial behaviors can help a manager develop flexible and appropriate approaches that can be integrated gradually into a behavioral repertoire. However, in most demanding situations the execution of this repertoire is for the most part intuitive. In the face of this, managers need some sort of conceptual touchstone that will help them focus on the realities of the situation at hand, and counter the tendency to apply an old or comfortable pattern of behavior inappropriately. What follows is a proposal for such a scheme and a suggestion that managers shift the relative emphasis in thinking about effective leadership from their own behavior to an inquiry into the state of mind of the subordinates.

Focusing on Subordinates: A Simple Framework

Suppose we manage or supervise a number of people and face a situation requiring a decision and action. Essentially we begin by asking: "How should I manage?" or "How should I lead?"

The initial answer to these questions should always be, *"It all depends . . . on what is to be achieved."* That is, the first step should be an explicit statement of objectives for the organization and for the people in it. These objectives should be elaborated along the three dimensions of performance, emotion, and growth and development.

Performance objectives are statements about products of work activity that are distinct and can be observed and counted or measured. These can take the form of financial or budget targets, project closing dates, sales volume, or the completion of any set of activities. Performance objectives can of course be established for organizations, groups of people, and individuals.

When we are thinking about performance objectives for individuals it is important to think in terms of specific behavior. We should be able to describe the behavior that is expected of an individual and the criteria that will be applied to determine when behavior is unacceptable.

Emotion refers to the attitudes and feelings of the employees. The idea is that managers should be explicit about how they want the employees to respond subjectively to the management and work process at any point along the way. This implies that we may see levels of job satisfaction or degrees of enthusiastic involvement in the work as appropriate objectives for our action. Or we may decide that the emotional state of employees is irrelevant to the task at hand and can be ignored. The point is that at the outset we should think how we want employees to respond emotionally, and we should identify the indicators we will use to determine whether they are in fact responding in this way. Indicators can range from the impressions we get in face-to-face contact with employees to aggregate measures such as absenteeism and grievance rates.

Growth and development objectives are explicit statements about what we expect of people in the organization as regards acquiring new skills, developing new ways of thinking, or increasing their ability to respond to new situations. Indicators of growth and development can be defined in terms of skill acquisition, such as the demonstrated ability to perform a variety of jobs; in terms of enrichment activities, such as working in different functional areas or participating on a product development team; or in terms of educational activities, including completion of college courses or participation in seminars covering technical advances in a field. Just as we did with performance and emotion objectives, in deciding how to manage in a given situation we should consider how many new and different things the employees will be required to do.

To say that managers should begin by making objectives explicit may seem old hat, yet it is emphasized for several reasons. First, commonly accepted definitions of leadership stress that *leading occurs only with respect to some goal*. That is, leaders influence followers toward some objective. Even though there may be involvement between manager and subordinates, without an objective such a relationship doesn't involve leadership, strictly speaking.

Second, and very important, by pausing to be explicit about objectives, we will increase the likelihood that our actions will be appropriate and responsive to the situation at hand, rather than merely a repeat of our earlier managerial behavior.

Third, the idea that the answer to the questions about how to manage or lead "all depends" is consistent with contingency or situational approaches to leadership, which is the direction supported by most of today's authorities in the field.

Finally, in situations involving complex organizational change most managers seem to set out to produce results along all three of the dimensions—performance, emotion, and growth and development. That is, managers expect employees to perform at a high level of effectiveness, want them to feel good about their work, and believe that they will acquire new skills or new ways of thinking in the process. Most managers are able to achieve results with respect to performance, many are able to create conditions within which employees can feel good about their work, and some are adept at assisting employees to develop. However, achieving positive results along all three dimensions simultaneously seems the most difficult of management challenges. Therefore, managers can only benefit by making objectives explicit. Of course, if they are unable to define objectives, their understanding of the situation must be improved in one way or another.

Four Basic Questions

Having specified objectives, managers should next turn their attention to the subordinates, with the notion that in any situation requiring managerial leadership, subordinates can be presumed to be seeking answers to one or more of four basic questions:

1. Where am I going?
2. How am I to get there?
3. Who will I be when I arrive?
4. Can I feel good about myself in the process? and, a subsidiary question,
5. How can I find answers to these questions?

The four basic questions have to be present in the thoughts, and possibly the behavior, of subordinates if they are to be open to influence by managers. This suggests that if subordinates are not seeking answers to these questions, they will not be interested in being led. If, in fact, employees are not seeking answers to these questions *and* their behavior is generating acceptable goals and objectives, managerial leadership is not required. Trying to lead under such circumstances is akin to trying to escort an elderly lady across the street when she doesn't want to go.

Simply put, then, managerial leadership can be viewed as managing in ways that will provide answers to these four basic questions, and in ways that will bring about the achievement of explicit objectives. The idea is that when all four questions are answered to the satisfaction of the subordinates, *and* when objectives are being met, leading is no longer necessary.

Taking the perspective of searching for ways to address these questions, as contrasted with focusing on the selection of a particular managerial behavior per se, offers an interesting approach to analyzing and making sense out of the myriad factors in any given situation, as follows.

The four questions can be considered indicators that the person asking the questions is experiencing stress in the form of the arousal people experience when they cannot clear up ambiguity, when their expectations are not met, or when they experience a threat to the view of themselves that they value and protect. From this perspective, leading is helping reduce the stress associated with any one of the four questions. This four-question framework is, in effect, a situational or contingency model viewed from the perspective of employees. (See Figure 1.)

In this model the subordinate perceives and is affected by the various multiple stimuli in the situation including the nature of the work, reward systems, organizational climate, and clarity of objectives. The subordinate is presumed to consciously and unconsciously synthesize these stimuli within the context of the subordinate's own personality. The *four basic questions*, posed in the mind of the subordinate, can be viewed as *summary statements* about the conclusions of this synthesis of the work environment. One way to look at it is that in producing the four basic questions, the subordinate performs a situational analysis for the manager. It is then up to the manager to use the questions as action guides.

For the manager, the four questions become similar to goals in management by objectives. Focusing on the four questions and attempting to do what is necessary to provide answers does not conceptually constrain the manager's behavior in some artificial way (for example, by a term like "person centered"). Rather, implicit in this approach is the recognition that managerial behavior is complex and much of it is intuitively guided. Therefore, the emphasis here is on answering the four questions, not on the manager's behavior per se. Obviously, the behavior of the manager and the needs of a subordinate are related. A manager's behavior will influence the subordinate and is therefore important. The perspective presented here does not suggest that managers can forget about their own behavior and its effect on subordinates. What is suggested is a conceptual focus that can be used to guide managers, a focus directed toward the subordinates rather than toward the managers themselves.

To apply the idea that the questions subordinates ask in a situation are guides for managerial action requires that managers decide which questions are being asked by drawing inferences from several sources. Principal among these sources are (1) what individual employees are

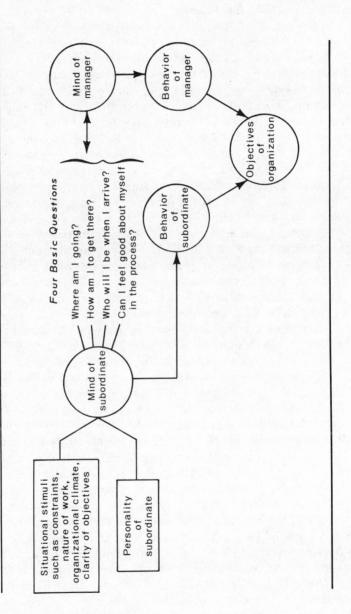

Figure 1

SITUATIONAL OR CONTINGENCY MODEL

heard to say, (2) what employees are observed to do, (3) how employees respond to questions put to them by the manager, and (4) how the manager reacts to the situation.

At the outset of the diagnosis, managers should make a careful distinction between (1) evidence that the employees are in fact asking the questions and (2) the managers' own opinion that the employees should be seeking answers to the questions. In the former case, the employees will in fact be exhibiting signs of *stress*—confusion, anxiety, frustration, dissatisfaction, even depression—thus showing that something is wrong. In the latter case, managers will have concluded from objective data, or intuitively, or otherwise, that the employees are not performing as they should. However, this conclusion may not be shared by the employees, and it is important to understand this difference in perceptions and experience of the situation before proceeding.

In assessing the four basic questions, managers should be on the lookout for signs of employee stress. In a general sense managers can ask, "Where is their energy going?" If employee energy is seen as going into activities other than those that will bring about the achievement of objectives, then the four questions should be examined in more depth.

Following is a broad description of each of the four questions, with indicators to look for as well as lines of inquiry to pursue when trying to determine what is on an employee's mind.

1. *Where am I going?* This question conveys the idea that a person requires a sense of purpose, a context, or a mental picture of the future to use as a point of reference for day-to-day thoughts and actions. This question has to do with specific goals and objectives. More important, it suggests that people need a more complex mental image of how they will fit into the organization in the future. Through this question, people seek a comprehensive picture of where they are headed and how they will relate to other people, things, and events as they pursue that end.

2. *How am I to get there?* This question suggests that employees need a set of specific thoughts and related behaviors that when performed will enable them to reach some goal, objective, or requirement of the job. The essence of signs of this question is that they can be related to the employees' sense of mastery of their work. Answers to this question should be easily translated into specific acts or descriptions of behavior. One way to look at it is that the question "Where am I going?" has to do with people's mental image of work and the organization in the future. This second question has to do with the link between that cognitive image and actual on-the-job behavior, the idea being that to be effective, people must transform the image into results.

3. *Who will I be when I arrive?* This question implies that people have within their cognitive structure an ideal view of themselves and

a mental picture of what they would like to be in the future. This can be thought of as their picture of themselves in the context of their wider view of the future. This picture is what is known as identity, and it serves to guide people as they think and behave each day. In many ways this ideal self does for people what well-articulated goals do for an organization. This idealized view is important, and people will attempt to protect it from external threat. In posing this question they are asking whether they will be able to maintain the integrity of this ideal self in the context of a given view of the future.

4. *Can I feel good about myself in the process?* Implicit in this question is the idea that as people work and participate in an organization they receive signals about how well they are performing and about their worth in the eyes of others in the organization. Messages about performance and worth come from many sources—from managers, peers, and customers; from objective measures of performance; from their own experience in doing the work. All this information helps form their concept of themselves at work, and this reality-based view is compared with the ideal view touched on earlier in discussing the third question. To the extent that the reality-based view and the ideal are discrepant, people experience an emotional *gap*, which can be viewed as a form of stress. One way of looking at it is that to experience this gap is synonymous with not feeling good about ourselves. Energy that goes into coping with the stress of not feeling good is energy that cannot be devoted to the job.

The Manager's Own Reaction
to the Situation

Since he both participates in and observes the employee's work situation, the manager's own responses to the situation can also serve as useful indicators of what may be needed. As managers we can look to ourselves for indications that we are asking one or more of the four questions just outlined. Such an analysis requires objectivity and a high degree of personal insight. To admit to ourselves that the situation is a source of stress may compel us to overcome a number of preconceptions about how we expect *ourselves* to respond emotionally in the managerial role. To the extent that we as managers are able to admit to not being completely sure about where the organization is headed or how it will get there—and to the extent that we are uncertain about our own place in the organization in the future, and do not anticipate that getting there will be a positive experience—providing answers to those same questions for our employees will be doubly difficult. In fact, insofar as we are unable to provide or work out answers for ourselves, particularly to questions about *where* and *how*, we may have to turn to others for assistance in developing those answers.

In the face of rapid, complex, or unanticipated change, both managers and subordinates are likely to ask the four questions to some degree. This should be especially true when the change implies dramatically new directions, jobs, or roles and the use of new skills or new techniques. In this regard we should be particularly sensitive to changes that require that we or our employees adopt new self-views in order to accommodate a new order of things. Whenever people are forced to give up some part of their ideal view of themselves in order to respond to an externally imposed change, it can be predicted that they will be seeking answers to one or more of the four questions, especially the questions concerning personal identity and self-worth.

When Employees Are Headed in the Wrong Direction

Thus far it has been suggested that when subordinates are asking the four basic questions, they are indicating a need for leadership. However, managers will have to stimulate the question-asking process when they conclude (1) that subordinate behavior is not leading to desired objectives and (2) that subordinates are not aware of this and are not showing signs of seeking leadership.

Managers will then have to initiate the process by introducing information that disconfirms a subordinate's expectations, bringing the subordinate to understand one or more of the following:

- That the goals of manager and subordinate are apparently not the same.
- That the subordinate's ways of attempting to reach the goals are not correct and will not be successful.
- That the subordinate's view of himself may not be attainable.
- That the subordinate's view of how well he or she is doing is not consistent with objective data or with the view held by the manager or others.

By communicating disconfirming information, managers can sensitize their subordinates to the need for change or can initiate an unfreezing process. The communication of such disconfirming information can stimulate an emotional response on the part of the subordinates in the form of anxiety, denial, and anger. Various writers have offered suggestions for minimizing or overcoming these psychological responses; however, short of changing behavior through behavior modification or some form of subterfuge, disconfirming information in one form or another is necessary if subordinates are to become open to leading. In general, emotional and behavioral resistance to disconfirming information will be lessened to the extent that employees see themselves as having some options in the matter, and some ability to influence the future course of events. Thus, all other things being equal, emotional and behavioral resistance can be reduced by having employees participate in developing new information about a situation, and by participating in making decisions about what should be done.

However, when employees are unable to see that they are headed in a wrong direction, a manager must be prepared to bring their attention to that fact even though the process may result in an angry, resistive response. In effect, such a response represents asking one or more of the four basic questions. Once this occurs a manager can begin to address the questions.

Some Approaches to Answering the Questions

To begin to develop answers to the four basic questions in the minds of employees, we should first specify our objectives along the dimensions of performance, emotion, and growth and development, as outlined earlier.

Next, we should address the fifth question inferred to be in the minds of our employees, "How can I find answers to the four basic questions?" At the outset we can choose between two fundamentally different approaches: (1) We can provide the answers directly or (2) we can involve the subordinates in developing answers to the questions.

In general terms, providing answers is a directive or authoritative approach, and involving subordinates in developing answers is a democratic or participative approach. The two are commonly viewed as falling on a continuum with direction and participation on opposite ends. A midpoint on the continuum is often labeled a consultative approach in which a manager asks employees for information, opinions, and ideas, but retains the right to make the final decision.

Most authorities agree that a directive approach is less time-consuming but can cause anger and resentment if subordinates do not agree with the directions given, whereas a participative approach can lead to commitment and understanding if the subordinates are in agreement with organizational objectives, but will often require more time for decision making.

Our use of a directive versus a participative approach might vary with respect to the four questions; for example, we might ourselves decide where, then ask subordinates to determine how. Either way, we should constantly ask ourselves:

- To what extent do they have answers to the four questions?
- How much do their answers differ from the ones we think they should have?
- Are they translating their answers into behavior that will reach organizational objectives?

With such an approach, leading can be viewed (and defined) as any act on the part of the manager that serves to provide employees with answers to one or more of the four basic questions. It follows that leading might come from several sources, including (1) the employees' manager; (2) the employees' peers and co-workers; (3) the employees' subordinates; (4) others, such as consultants or friends of the employees; and (5) the employees themselves.

With this view in mind, we become *leaders* only to the extent that we supply employees with answers to the questions. Since answers can come from the employees' peers, as well as from the employees themselves, we can lead by creating a process for the employees, and between employees and peers, by which answers to the four questions are developed. To create a process for answering the questions, instead of answering them directly, is to address our fifth, subsidiary question, "How can I find answers to these questions?" Therefore, creating a process qualifies as leading—as does answering the questions directly.

Answering the Four Basic Questions

In one sense, providing answers to the four basic questions is much of what managing people is all about. Complete answers would require an exhaustive treatment of the process of managing people. However, it is possible to sketch the form of approaches to answering the four questions by outlining some types of answers, the forms they might take, and various ways in which the answers might be communicated to an employee.

The idea that managers should communicate a vision, or picture of the organization in the future, seems to have been missed in the typical approaches to managerial leadership. Also, this is the area most frequently overlooked when managers initiate changes in their organizations— particularly managers at upper-middle and middle levels of organizational hierarchies.

To communicate a vision is to portray through words, media, and exemplary behavior a view of what the organization is to become, such that employees can transform that view into their own mental image of the future. Out of this imagery, employees can create broad goals and rules for governing their decision making and behavior in a wide range of situations. The most dramatic example of what is meant here was offered by Martin Luther King, Jr., in the speech that began, "I have a dream." On occasion when working with managers who are attempting to implement major changes in their organizations, I ask them to write a five-minute speech addressed to their employees, begining "I have a dream for this organization, and in that dream I see. . . ."

First, this exercise requires that managers clarify their expectations enough to put them into words.

Second, the process helps managers discover where their own view of the future is incomplete and to realize that without a vision of their own they will be hard put to offer one to others.

Third, by sharing their speeches, managers who will have to work together to implement a change come to understand what each has in mind, and through discussion and debate they develop a view of the organization that is more or less shared by all.

Fourth, out of the speeches managers can select key words or phrases that convey the essence of the vision they want to communicate. These words and phrases have included "innovative" (in an organization that was falling behind in its market), "be a professional" (in an organization where the quality of work had slipped, and where professionals had gradually taken on lower-level tasks that the new management wanted them to stop performing), and "a place where people are proud to work" (in an organization where morale had suffered).

In attempting to communicate a vision, managers should be prepared to do several things. First, they should repeat the words and phrases that characterize the vision over and over, face-to-face with employees, as well as through various communications media. Senior managers may become tired of the endless repetition, yet it is important that as many employees as possible hear the vision from them personally.

Second, and of critical importance, the managers must be willing and able to change the organization's structure, practices, policies, and reward systems so as to make these elements congruent with the picture communicated by the vision. This is called matching up the words and the music. It makes no sense to employees, for example, to hear about a new spirit of cooperation while working under a bonus scheme through which an individual employee or department profits most at the expense of a co-worker or another department.

Third, the managers should be prepared to pursue the vision for a long time despite employees who cannot comprehend what is being suggested, or who actively resist because the vision implies an unwanted change for them.

When discussing this concept of a vision, managers ask, "How will I know whan I have communicated one?" For one thing, they may use numerous measures of individual employee and departmental progress taken from the usual financial control systems, MBO targets, employee attitude surveys, and the like, to determine whether people in the organization are moving in the direction the managers have in mind.

For a second thing, to the extent that people appear to be putting less energy into seeking answers to the questions, "Where am I going?" and "Who will I be when I arrive?" the managers can infer that the vision is understood. A third answer is problematic with regard to providing managers with a clear-cut way to assess their efforts, but seems to convey the essence of what is meant by a vision. It is that an employee understands and accepts a vision when, in the face of a perplexing decision, the employee can say, "I know what the manager *would have me do* and that is what I will do."

When we as managers initiate changes yet fail to provide a new vision, employees are left seeking answers to the question, "Where am I going?" and have difficulty in developing an answer to "Who will I be when I arrive?" In practice, much management behavior seems devoted to defining operational objectives and structuring the work. From this perspective, one way to think of leadership style is in terms of how much of a manager's behavior is directed toward answering one or more of the four questions. The flexible managerial leader is capable of providing answers to a mix of the four basic questions as each situation and each subordinate may require.

The Challenge of Positive Energy Management

Recently the top managers of a major textbook publisher were changed by the management of its parent company. Although the publisher had been successful in its markets, holding its market share relative to its competitors, the new president and editor-in-chief (who were hired from outside the company) were charged with making the publishing company more aggressive—more marketing-oriented—and told to increase sales volume and market share in the process. Some visible evidence of progress in this direction was expected of them in 12 to 18 months.

The young and bright editor-in-chief quickly reviewed the lines of books: education, science, psychology, business. Each area was headed by a senior editor, a number of whom had been with the publisher for 15 years or more. These editors described their job and relationship with the prior management as personal, comfortable, and conducted by and large on the basis of mutual respect.

After examining the books in print and under development, and after lengthy discussions with the senior editors, the editor-in-chief concluded that the existing editorial organization could not develop new and innovative books, in particular books that would be interdisciplinary, at a pace that would meet the corporate sales and market share targets. Consequently, the editor-in-chief demoted several senior editors and promoted younger, seemingly more aggressive editorial managers in their stead.

With some fanfare he announced the creation of a special projects group. It was to be responsible for new products that were not within the established book lines, or that required editorial coordination across areas. By and large members of the existing editorial group were charged with the responsibility for improving the quality of their respective product lines, developing improved second editions, and developing the premier text in established academic fields where the topical outline for the top competing texts tended not to vary and a competitive edge was gained through superior graphics, teaching manuals, and other support materials.

The senior editors for the special projects group were hired from outside the company, and several promising junior editors were transferred to the new group from the old editorial areas.

In its second year of operation the special projects group was expected to contribute 5 percent to the sales of the total product line, a product line that was expected to grow by 30 to 40 percent a year.

Several months after the special projects group was staffed and operational, the editor-in-chief found himself spending more and more time with disgruntled senior editors from the established areas. He saw evidence of lack of cooperation between the old and new groups, and he felt that, if anything, the established editorial groups were even less effective at bringing new products into the pipeline than they had been in the past.

This example illustrates the most difficult challenge when a manager sets out to make changes or initiate action because circumstances dictate that something be done. The challenge goes like this: Assume that at any given moment an employee has limited energy to devote to psychological and physical activity and that, all other things being equal, a manager wants employees to direct as much of that energy as possbile toward the work and objectives of the manager's organization; the challenge then is to manage, to initiate action and change in such a way as to decrease the amount of energy the employees devote to seeking answers to the four basic questions, and to do so in such a way that an answer for one question does not dramatically increase the need for an answer to another.

What might the new editor-in-chief have done to reduce the impact of the change in demands and direction? He had several options:

1. He could have replaced most or all of the senior editors, hiring or promoting people who were thought able to build the product line.
2. He could have used a task force approach to new product development, pulling people from across the editorial areas and assigning senior editors to head the project teams. This would have required that the senior editors develop new skills and see their jobs differently.
3. He could have assigned some of the senior editors to the new project organization, making every effort to move those who were most interested in the new product directions.
4. He could have assigned to the senior editors the task of deciding how to implement the new product objectives. Such an effort could have taken place over a two- or three-day period set aside for that purpose.
5. He could have created a matrix organization with one or more members of each existing book-line area assigned to new product development, reporting both to their respective senior editors and to an editor in charge of new projects.

While probably none of these alternatives would initially have made the situation tension-free for the senior editors, in alternatives 2 through 5 the senior editors would have focused more of their energy on understanding their new roles and finding ways to carry out the new assignments, devoting less energy to repairing a damaged professional identity or seeking ways to feel good about themselves in their jobs. Perhaps some of the editors would not have performed effectively and would have had to accommodate themselves to a new role or be replaced. But they would have had an opportunity to learn from experience, an experience that others in the organization could have observed as well. As it was, the employees in the existing editorial group were left thinking that they were supposed to work harder than ever, but that they were not seen as competent to lead or contribute to new missions of the organization.

The Four Basic Questions:
The Flip Side of the Coin

This article has tried to shift the attention of managers from the behavior of the leader to a set of questions that are presumed to exist in the minds of the followers. What has been emphasized here is the idea that by shifting the focus in this way, managers can use these questions as guides in deciding what to do. Having a usable conceptual system seems important for managers in light of the trend toward more complex theories of leader behavior. The conceptual framework offered here reflects a situational or contingency approach with the four questions representing a synthesis of the many aspects of the situation. We have proposed that managers concentrate on providing answers to the four questions. Informed, sophisticated managers should be aware of different behavioral approaches, and should attempt to observe their own behavior as well as draw conclusions from their analysis of the situation. However, consciously focusing attention on doing what is more or less intuitively seen as necessary to provide answers to the four questions, and doing so with a set of objectives squarely in mind, gives managers a good chance of arriving at an approach that is both appropriate and effective.

15

Critical Factors in Leadership Succession

GIL E. GORDON
NED ROSEN

Many research studies treat leadership as a timeless dimension. We are often led to believe that the leader somehow appears in the group or organization and either stays forever or quietly slips away. Very little or no attention is paid to the effects of group history on the new leader, nor is much mention made of the various aspects of the succession process itself, e.g., where the new leader comes from, how the leader is selected, whether there is a mandate for change or a need to maintain the status quo, what happened to the former leader, and so on. Moreover, the continuing discussion between social psychologists and sociologists about the amount of impact a leader can have would seem to lead naturally to the succession issue for study, but it has not.

While there is not a great deal of literature related to either of these two points, there is enough to warrant a brief review of the major works. From this literature, as well as from the group process literature in general, the next step will be an attempt at specifying some of the major variables associated with succession processes. These will be discussed and systematized. Finally, we will suggest a possible measurement strategy that may prove useful.

Review of the Literature

Case Studies

Gouldner's *Patterns of Industrial Bureaucracy* (1954) is a well-known study which deals with a gypsum plant whose former manager had run

Reprinted by permission of the authors and publisher from *Organizational Behavior and Human Performance*, vol. 27 (1981): 227–254.

the operation in a loose, lenient fashion. Rules were commonly broken, and abuses of policy and regulations were widespread; this pattern was so deeply built into the plant that the worker's beliefs about how the plant should be run revolved around this leniency pattern. The parent organization's concern for production led to the replacement of the manager with a new person from outside the plant. The new manager's alternatives were either to "act upon and through the informal system of relations" or "utilize the former system of organization in the plant," relying on the enforcement of preexisting rules and regulations as the way to increase production. Given his complete isolation from the existing social system, among other reasons, the successor chose to fall back on the authority vested in his role, with the net result being increased tension and stress in the plant.

In contrast with this study, Guest's study (1962b) of an auto plant showed the successor confronting a somewhat similar situation with an entirely different strategy. In *Organizational Change*, the new plant manager worked through the existing organizational hierarchy, using informal contacts with subordinates as a primary tactic. First, through casual contacts "on the floor" and later through what Guest calls "institutionalized interactions" the new manager accumulated vitally needed technical knowledge and learned about needs of subordinates, two processes that helped guide future actions.

It is tempting to attribute the contrasting actions and outcomes in both of the above cases to some basic personality differences between the two successors. But as Guest has written, there also are a number of "institutionally derived pressure differences" (Guest, 1962a, p. 53) between the two cases that could more adequately explain the outcomes than could a trait approach to leadership. This matter will be examined in depth in a later section.

Basic personality influences appeared to prevail in a third study reported by Salaman (1977). In this instance a *small* but highly successful manufacturing firm which was dominated by a highly charismatic, authoritarian leader continued to be influenced even after his retirement.

Organizational Correlates

A major theoretical paper, "Administrative Succession in Formal Organizations" by Grusky (1960), examines the degree of instability promoted by succession, and analyzes the process from the point of view of the formal organization as a whole as well as from the viewpoint of the successor's small-group role system. Grusky also worked on the relationship between organization size and succession rate (1961), as did Kriesberg (1962), and both found succession rate to be directly related to organization size. This finding was reexamined by Gordon and Becker (1964) who found the size succession rate relationship to be much less clear. Kriesberg's reply (1964) to Gordon and Becker mentions that historical factors, interindustry differences, and technology differences probably all confound the relationship. It should be noted that retirement policy differences also may have an impact here.

Birnbaum (1971) calls attention to still other aspects of the succession process. He argues that colleges and universities, when selecting new presidents, utilize a succession process ". . . that operates to limit organizational conflict and maximize organizational stability." Th y do this, according to Birnbaum, by two techniques: (1) avoiding vertical promotions from within which presumably prevents interunit conflict from being acted out in the succession process; and (2) by selecting candidates who have been socialized by prior experience in other institutions having characteristics similar to the one doing the recruiting. For example, a large state university would recruit a new president from among the administrative ranks or faculty of another large state university rather than from a community college.

Birnbaum supports his argument in two ways. First he reviews published data showing that by comparison to private industry, colleges and universities are much more likely to select their chief executive from outside the organization, while administrators within higher education below the presidential level have a modal pattern of promotion from within. (See Newcomer, 1955, Hodgkinson, 1970, Bess & Lodahl, 1969.) Second, he presents supporting data from his own study of sending and receiving institutions involved for 76 college presidents in the state of New York. These data are supportive of his argument about candidate socialization in other, but similar institutions.

Finally, Birnbaum nicely articulates the importance of the status/ institutional prestige exchange involved when colleges and candidates seek a presidential match. He points out that the prestige ranking of an institution may be critical to the candidates *and* the institution in the presidential selection process.

Actuarial Studies

Grusky's study of managerial succession in baseball teams (1963) was probably the first major examination of succession at the smaller than total organization level. He found through a statistical study that teams with the poorest won-lost records had the higher rates of succession. Rather than explaining this simply by saying that team owners will fire the manager when he does not produce, Grusky's rather elaborate analysis encompasses many internal *and* external factors ranging from team popularity to managerial role strain. The issue was taken up by Gamson and Scotch (1964) who, after a different type of analysis, claimed that Grusky's explanations were inadequate. They posited a "ritual scapegoating no-way causality theory," which generally suggested that the manager's impact is minimal, and that his firing is a ritual act only. Grusky's reply (1964) introduced the dimension of inside/outside source of the new manager to the analysis, thus adding strength to *his* interpretation. Recent popular writings by sportswriters and big-league baseball players indicate that the Gamson and Scotch "minimal manager impact" view is not necessarily accurate. (See the sports pages of the Cleveland *Plain Dealer*, June 8, 1977 for a discussion of Frank Robinson's problems as the first major league Black manager.)

Allen, Panian, and Lotz (1979) extended the Grusky–Gamson and Scotch analyses and debate with a statistically sophisticated study of baseball managerial succession over a 54-year time span. Using path analysis, they concluded:

1. There is a negative relationship between past team performance and the frequency of managerial succession.
2. ... teams resorting to succession during a season performed worse during the prior season than teams resorting to succession between seasons.
3. ... teams resorting to outside succession performed worse during the prior season than teams resorting to inside succession.
4. The frequency of managerial succession is negatively related to subsequent team performance.
5. In general, succession between seasons is more likely to improve team performance than succession during a season.
6. ... inside succession is less likely to disrupt team performance than outside succession.

Probably their most important finding, however, is that *past* (prior year) team performance is the best predictor of future performance (current year) and accounts for much more variance than managerial succession or player personnel changes. However, it is rare that a team can be redeveloped and substantially improved in only one season, and the *quality* of the personnel changes (players and managers) may well be more important (and interrelated) than the number of such changes.

Another study in the same general tradition of Grusky and Gamson and Scotch has been reported on coach succession in college basketball teams (Eitzen & Yetman, 1972) for more than 100 college teams over a 40-year time span. Overall, this study concluded that coaching changes make no difference in team effectiveness.

Helmich (1974) studied the relationship between the rate of predecessor turnover among presidents and both promotional origin and leadership behavior in a sample of 140 manufacturing companies in the petrochemical industry. His hypothesis that infrequent replacements of predecessors in key administrative positions give rise to a greater desire for organizations to seek new leaders from outside rather than inside was not supported by the data. The data do suggest that frequent replacements of prior administrators tend to give rise to the development of an authoritative, task oriented leadership style during the successor's initial period in office. (Style was measured by self-report questionnaires—ASO/LPC.)

Two other actuarial studies (Lieberson & O'Connor, 1972; Salencik & Pfeffer, 1977), using multiple criteria and moderator variables, attempted to assess the influence of chief executive changes on major organizational variables. Lieberson and O'Connor studied sales, net earnings and profits for 167 corporations in 13 industries over a 20-year time period; leadership changes were defined as the selection of a new president or chairman of the board. Salencik and Pfeffer studied the impact of mayors on municipal budgets. On their face, the findings from both studies suggest that changes in leadership have stronger impact on some performance criteria than on others, and that the relationships are moderated by organizational and industry variables. Both studies present data suggesting that the chief executive's impact accounts for very little criterion variance. On the other hand, Weiner (1978) has replicated the type of organizational analysis employed by both Lieberson and O'Connor and Salencik and Pfeffer, and experimented with alternate statistical procedures. She demonstrates that the percentage of criterion variance accounted for by leadership is strongly affected by the nature of the statistical procedure used in analyzing the data. Her study, aided by insightful conceptual analysis, contradicts the earlier research and clearly indicates the need for an alternate statistical and measurement methodology for studies of this type (total organization). According to her findings in this paper and one other (Weiner and Mahoney, 1979), the chief executive has substantial impact on some major organizational variables.

Aside from other limitations in actuarial-statistical studies, which by definition are based exclusively on historical records without benefit of observation and interviews, such research fails to take into account the parties' intentions and perceptions when each change is made—all the manager (or coach) replacements are treated equally in such analyses. Obviously this research strategy incorporates error variance because managing changes are made for different reasons at different times. Moreover, the purely actuarial type of analysis does not differentiate between interim or acting appointments on the one hand, and more permanent appointments on the other. Such distinctions have strong motivational implications which may have important effects on group process and performance one way or another. Some of the findings from baseball studies may be explained by just such a distinction since manager successions *during* a baseball season are more likely to be of an interim or acting nature than changes between seasons. Moreover, league rules strictly control player personnel changes during a season; most major player changes therefore occur between seasons. Since managerial changes of a permanent nature are more likely between seasons also, and may or may not be influenced by the new manager, some of the statistical analyses reviewed earlier probably are confounded.

More important, the effects of a manager change may require two or three seasons to materialize; a significant performance change in the first season after a succession is unrealistic to expect in most cases. A remarkable experiment by Merei (1958) bears on this argument. He formed groups among relatively passive nursery school children and permitted them to play for several sessions with fixed sets of toys and games in a fixed physical environment. In time, each group developed its own traditions and rituals, i.e., who played with what objects, ways of doing things, and even unique language. Once such traditions were formed, Merei added an acknowledged leader to each group, another child about 1½ years older and who previously had been found to be dominant among these same children in the larger nursery school setting. All of these leaders tried to "take over" the group to which each was introduced. Most of them failed in their attempts! In Merei's words, ". . . the group absorbed the leader, forcing its traditions on him." One leader did succeed, but only after three others, on successive days, had softened up the group! Merei's account of the different leadership strategies tried by these young children makes fascinating reading; Machiavelli would have been impressed.

From this rather arduous debate and accumulated data, two categories of interesting questions emerge: first, what are the characteristics of the leader—alone and in the context of a group—which bear on the effectiveness question, and second, what is the nature and impact of structural, higher-level decisions and processes which may set the limits for the leader's actions and influence attempts? Hall notes in his discussion of leadership (1972, p. 259) that "Grusky's argument that external and internal pressures for success affect performance is directly in line with the evidence presented by Gouldner and Guest. The kinds of personnel available are modified by the social system of which they are a part."

Laboratory Studies

Grusky (1969a) outlined a laboratory method in which simulated business firms were set up, each having 48-min life histories, a general manager, two assistant managers, and four "employees." The latter were confederates; all were students. Only the two assistant managers had any face-to-face contact with the four assembly workers. The general manager was informed about their work by the assistant managers. The quantity and quality of their work actually were preprogrammed by the experimenter. Succession was created by transferring managers from one organization to another at the completion of phase four of eight phases. The organizations were manipulated by a feedback mechanism as to be effective or ineffective. In one line of inquiry, some general managers alone were reassigned to a different organization while others were told to select one of their two assistant managers to accompany them and assist them in their new assignments. Criterion measures were developed out of Bales's interaction observation categories.

Among other findings, Grusky reports that when an ally accompanied the executive into his new assignment both the executive and his lieutenant, *during the transition period,* "eagerly tried to integrate the inherited assistant manager into the staff social structure." (The inherited assistant manager was the one left behind by his previous manager when he selected an ally and moved to another organization.) Grusky goes on to say, ". . . the overtures to the inherited assistant manager did not meet with complete success. . . . the pattern of interaction and support changed drastically in the final phase, when both the manager and the ally interacted more with each other than with the inherited assistant manager." Eventually, the assistant brought along by the executive became *the* trusted second in command, and the inherited assistant was relegated to a less significant role.

In brief, despite the artificialities required by the need for experimental control, and despite the short time period involved which one normally would expect to mitigate against clear results, Grusky produced some provocative findings with his experimental procedure. The procedure has good potential for more elaboration and research. We are not so sure, however, that he is really simulating "organizations" in the laboratory; the social entities involved look more like structured small groups to us, operating in a simulated organizational context. The setting is realistic, however, and has obvious relevance to the real world.

Grusky also has reported (1969b) data from variations on the above design bearing on inside vs outside succession. The findings illustrate commonly observed phenomena associated with these two strategies, and once again demonstrate the potential utility of the lab experiment for studies in this area.

One study designed to measure the effects of *membership* changes on performance of a laboratory task has interesting implications for leader succession, particularly in light of the explanation Grusky put forth about baseball succession. Trow (1960, p. 260) states that the effects of member succession on team performance may be "heavily

conditioned by other variables," and lists such influences as the characteristics of the successors, the characteristics of the task and the way
it is traditionally organized, the environment of the organization, and
the ratio of internal mobility to outside recruitment. He concludes by
saying that "to whatever extent the leadership of a group is held
accountable for performance, the causal relationship may also run in
the other direction, the level of performance determining the rate of
[member] succession."

Another laboratory study (Hamblin, 1958) took a different approach.
He hypothesized that (1) leaders will have more influence during experimentally induced crises than during noncrisis periods, and (2) that
groups informally tend to replace their existing leader if s/he does not
have a solution to the crisis problem. The results supported the hypotheses, and may be seen by some as support for the scapegoating
explanation of succession (Gamson & Scotch, 1964). Note than unlike
baseball managers who are replaced by higher level administrative actions
(sometimes in response to player pressures), Hamblin's leaders were
"replaced" by subordinates. Therefore, the groups' actions may better
be interpreted as problem-solving behavior; informal leaders often emerge
in task groups to compensate for the inadequacies of the formal designated
leader.

A few laboratory studies, also using college students as subjects in
contrived groups, have been addressed to questions concerning the origin
and method of selecting the new leader. (The organizational literature
tends to focus on the inside vs outside dimension, although this is an
oversimplification of a more complex issue.) Goldman and Fraas (1965)
report from such an experiment that followers more readily accept a
leader who has "proven" himself—on the task itself. Results from a
different experiment concerned with leader origin did not support
Goldman and Fraas (Daum, 1975) and suggest that in some circumstances
promotion from within might be dysfunctional.

Hollander and Julian (1978), well known for both theory and research
on leadership questions, review an extensive set of programmatic laboratory studies conducted by them and their students. Some of their
research has a strong bearing on succession. Among other things, they
found significant interactions between method of selection, perceived
competence, and various measures of leader behavior in relation to the
group. They found that ". . . the appointed leader without strong en-
dorsement appears by comparison to be far weaker [than elected leaders]
as a source of influence." They add, "while we had consistent confirmation
of the leader's perceived competence as a significant determinant of his
acceptability and influence, we also found that this relationship was
affected by the followers' perceptions of the leader's motivation. In the

first experiment, for example, there was a significant interaction between the leader's perceived competence and his perceived interest in the group's activity." (Some of the Julian and Hollander data, by the way, corroborate earlier [1950s] findings by Carter, Cattell, and Stice, summarized by Gibb [1969].)

Perhaps of most relevance for this review,

> These (Hollander & Julian) data also indicate that the newly elected leader is more influential in the phase just before he takes over than when he does become the leader. The contrast is sometimes quite dramatic. Furthermore, even a not-too-successful leader is later seen more favorably than his successor, thus suggesting an initial handicap for the successor that somehow must be overcome. Succession therefore offers promising leads as an area for further study.

Experimental Field Studies

In addition to the above laboratory studies, there are three experimental field studies that have implications for the study of succession. First, Jackson's research consisted of making experimental changes in leadership of long-established maintenance groups in a telephone company (1953). Based on member attitude survey scores, three pairs of leaders were switched, each pair consisting of a leader whose group score was above the mean and one whose group score was below the mean. Post-test measures indicated attitude changes in the expected direction, toward the mean in each of the six cases, demonstrating the impact of the new leader on group process. Though this study may have some methodological shortcomings, e.g., regression effect, there is one very interesting result. Jackson (1953, p. 40) cites one group whose men appeared to become

> emotionally disturbed by the transfer of foremen. This seemed to affect the men's ability to make objective evaluations. Not only was their resentment directed against top management (in a section of the attitude survey), but it was reflected in an exaggeratedly low score in response to its new foreman, who thus became a scapegoat.

Jackson explains this by saying that the men were highly attached to the previous supervisor, a situation caused in part by an apparently unclear perception by the men of the limits of company-foreman and foreman-subordinate relationships. The point that Jackson fails to recognize is the *cause* for this close relationship. In this organization, succession was *not* a regular occurrence. Each of the experimental groups' supervisors had been with their groups for 6 months minimum and in several cases much longer. The pretext for the experiment was the company's desire to broaden and develop the experience of the supervisors. This raises the issue of perceived legitimacy of succession for reasons other than death, relocation, etc., and the related issue mentioned by Grusky (1964) and others about the possible outcomes of frequent and regularized succession. These include the limitation of personal authority and the transference of authority to the position, rather than to the incumbent, among others.

A longitudinal study by Lieberman (1956) adds another dimension to the succession issue. Lieberman posited that if a person is placed in a new, unfamiliar role, he will tend to take on or develop attitudes that meet the expectations associated with that role. He found that production workers chosen as foremen became more favorable toward management, and that workers elected as shop stewards shifted toward the union in their attitudes. A concomitant change in behavior that came with role change raises the question of the applicability of reference group theory (role change leads to reference group change, which leads to attitude change then behavior changes) or dissonance theory (role change leads to behavior [i.e., job function] change, leading to attitude change to maintain consistency) in explaining the process. In either case, the implications for succession seem clear: the new leader is not going to function totally independently of his sponsors and of how those around him expect him to function, be they his subordinates, superiors, or peers. Those expectations in turn are at least partially conditioned by the prior experience of those three groups with the *previous* role occupant.

The final study to be cited here is one in which the impact of foremen on attitudes and performance of their groups was assessed by simultaneously changing supervisors, on short notice, in several factory work groups (Rosen, 1969, 1970). The experimental basis for the reassignments was work group preferences for the various foremen. The most noteworthy initial reaction to this rather dramatic leadership succession which involved an entire production department was a pronounced performance increase for the entire department; all of the groups showed an initial increase. Additionally, over a period of time the previously stable rank ordering of the groups' performance levels was destroyed and a *new* rank order gradually emerged—a much different result than reflected in the baseball-manager and basketball-coach studies. (Unlike the athletic team managerial succession studies, the factory study involved changing *all* the managers [n=7] at the same time.)

Rosen (1969) adopts a systems approach to group behavior in explaining his data, and notes that "the perceived technological-administrative skills of the foremen seemed to assume greater importance after the . . . reassignment. This finding suggests that the new foremen were judged [by their subordinates] at least partly on their ability to help the group re-establish equilibrium following the foreman reassignments." While Rosen notes that personality, described as pleasantness-unpleasantness, was a critical element in the process to reestablish equilibrium in the group, the technical-administrative skills finding highlights the role of task competence as a necessary ingredient. This is important in that it shows once more that the leadership succession problem, at least at lower organization levels, cannot be avoided simply by developing a corps of seemingly interchangeable "leaders" who can master any situation, a strategy built into many organizations' management staffing policies. The results of this study, by the way, to some extent parallel Hamblin's and Julian and Hollander's laboratory studies discussed earlier. All of these studies focused on follower reactions to leadership succession, and indicate that leaders are not accepted by their group unless their behavior is instrumental in the group's behalf.

The furniture factory foreman rotation experiment also suggested some additional matters relevant to leadership succession as a process. One of these involves a concept known as "status consensus on the leader" within a group. The data suggest that the extent to which group members, over a period of time, come to an agreement (consensus) on how they evaluate a new leader relates to group effectiveness. Rosen (1969) explained this as follows:

> The results of this . . . experiment, coupled with the "conformity" literature and other research bearing on status consensus, suggest that leadership status consensus . . . may be a direct index of group equilibrium. Thus, if group members cannot reach substantial internal agreement on their attitudes toward and perceptions of their formal leader, the group would be classified, by definition, as out of equilibrium, especially if the group's task requires that the formal leader perform significant functions. . . . Concomitantly we are likely to find low morale or cohesion, which, for interdependent task groups, probably will affect adversely the coordination of members' efforts and the strength of individuals' motivation toward formal goals.

Finally, interviews with the foremen themselves, following the experiment (pp. 131–137), indicated that some of them employed different strategies than others when they first "took command" of their newly assigned groups. For example, some held a meeting with their new charges while others did not. The interviews coupled with direct observations of their on-the-job behavior reflect leader style dimensions reported by both Guest and Gouldner, which in turn may influence the development of status consensus within a group. The different strategies used by the "new" foremen also suggest that they had differential degrees of awareness and different interpretations of the succession process implications. See, also, Merei (1958) in this regard.

Summary of Findings from Empirical Literature

The empirical literature on leadership succession, reviewed above, is based on case studies of individual successions, actuarial studies of large numbers of successions, laboratory studies of selected aspects of the process, and a few field experiments in natural settings. A small amount of survey research also was found to bear on the problem. The following are what we believe to be some of the more interesting points which have reasonable justification in the accumulated evidence; included with some of these points is a bit of editorial commentary.

1. Although the effects of an individual leader are constrained by organizational imperatives, the personality and style of a predecessor can create lasting effects making change by a successor difficult to achieve.

2. There is some evidence that leadership succession rate (frequency) varies with organizational size, although the relationship is not always found and appears to be moderated by various organizational and technological factors. (This finding is consistent with other research on the relationship of labor turnover to group size—leader succession may be viewed as a special case of labor turnover.)

3. Several extensive actuarial studies of managerial succession in athletic organizations, especially professional baseball, have produced a mixed set of data. It may be reasonable to conclude, tentatively, despite methodological shortcomings in such work, that: (a) past performance of a team or unit influences rate of succession; (b) some managerial replacements are made for ritualistic reasons, but different reasons apply to different cases. Some reasons have no clear relationship to performance; (c) too many managerial replacements in too brief a period can be disruptive to a unit.

4. Frequency of executive-level succession in business organizations may influence the development of an authoritarian, task-oriented leadership style during the successor's initial period in office. This may reflect a perceived mandate, or it may reflect the successor's feelings of insecurity, in an unstable work environment.

5. Chief executive succession in corporations may have a stronger impact on some performance criteria than on others (e.g., sales, net earnings, profits), and the relationships are moderated by a variety of organizational and industry variables.

6. The succession process at the chief executive level in institutions of higher education appears to be managed in such a way as to minimize organizational conflict (with exceptions, of course). Successors are frequently chosen from outside but similar organizational cultures. Additionally, institutional prestige of the two organizations involved is important. (Both points might also apply to other professional organizations such as hospitals, research and development units and possibly public utilities.)

7. Crises in group effectiveness can produce leader "replacement," or pressure for leader replacement, by the rank-and-file.

8. Followers frequently more readily accept (grant referent power to) leaders who have proven themselves on the group's task, or on one perceived to be relevant. Most of the systematic evidence comes from the laboratory, but there is considerable anecdotal evidence from military experience and from the corporate world; moreover, the phenomenon can occur at any organizational level, although it *may* be less likely at higher levels.

9. Promotion from within to positions of leadership, a common organizational practice, is not necessarily functional. Some evidence suggests that succession from outside the organization produces better results. The matter needs more research.

10. Among college-student laboratory subjects, elected leaders appear to have more influence than appointed ones. And, those perceived as competent at the group's task also have more influence (see Paragraph 8 above). These relationships, however, are moderated by member perceptions of the leader's motivation vis à vis the group and its work. Since many college students end up in work organizations, this line of research may have significant implications for work motivation.

11. An intriguing finding in one laboratory study is that newly elected leaders are more influential in the phase just before they take over than afterwards. One wonders if there is a parallel phenomenon in work organizations.

12. Newly appointed leaders do not function totally independently of their sponsors and of how those around them expect them to function. The "politics" involved have not been studied systematically by many psychologists, to our knowledge.

13. The way in which succession is introduced can make a difference in outcomes. In contrast to the customary one-at-a-time leadership succession, one study shows sharp improvement in performance following a simultaneous reassignment of several foremen on short notice; another suggests that succession with an ally produces different outcomes than succession alone.

14. Different leaders employ different strategies upon assuming command, which raises as yet unanswered questions regarding their reasons, the group process effects, and related change and performance outcomes.

15. Internal group consensus on the leader appears to be a useful operational measure that relates to group equilibrium, cohesion, and performance, at least in some tasks and motivational circumstances.

The reader might note that most of the points summarized above can be recast in terms of replacing *any* member of a group or organizational unit. For example (Paragraph 14), different *new members*, whether leaders or not, employ different strategies upon joining a group. Or, past performance of a unit influences rate of *member*, not just leader, succession (Paragraph 3[a]). Indeed, the replacement of any key member, including the leader, of a well-integrated group has potential implications for the group's effectiveness, group process, and a variety of indirect costs. Ziller (1965) has treated this topic in considerable depth. The magnitude of succession effects will depend on individual differences, group resources for coping, the technological and psychological significance of the leader's role, and so on.

The leader's role, in our judgment, continues to deserve special theoretical and research attention, despite what is said in the previous paragraph, for several reasons. For one thing, formal organizations are highly sensitized to leadership phenomena and are structured accordingly. For another, society has a right to place greater ethical and social role demands on people occupying leadership positions than on rank-and-file members. For both reasons we believe it would be unrealistic to treat leadership roles as "just" another role within the group having no special conceptual interest. Finally, the evidence clearly shows that leaders can, and often do, make a difference. The task is to discover why and under what circumstances.

Introductory Comments on the Development of a Succession Model

From the preceding literature review it should be clear that there has been no major effort to study the dynamics of the entire succession process. More has been done with the after-effects of the succession, i.e., how did the group adapt and respond to the new leader (Rosen, 1969; Jackson, 1953, for example). It is the writers' belief that an integral part of the succession process is that which occurs *prior* to the successor's arrival; the forces that are set in motion when the fact of an impending succession is made known deserve attention on their own.

One general statement about these forces should be made at this point. While the framework for studying them might be quite stable from situation to situation, there may be one factor—the reason for the succession—that acts as a moderating variable in determining how that framework will be applied. There is a wide range in the reasons for succession to occur; Grusky (1960, p. 107) classifies these into two sets of circumstances. First, there are reasons that tend to be controlled more or less directly by the organization, such as promotion, demotion, or dismissal. Second, Grusky notes that other reasons, such as death, illness, or voluntary movement to a better job tend to be "environmentally controlled." There also are leaders who "step down" (from dean to teaching again, for example) after a fixed term of office. Intuitively, it seems that these circumstances might evoke different succession dynamics. The counterargument, however, is that the difference might only be temporal, in the sense of the reaction time of the led. Under the circumstance of succession due to death, for example, these succession processes may only happen more quickly as compared to a more planned succession due to promotion, where the dynamics might occur gradually. The use of the word "gradually" here implies that the succession process does in fact consist of some set of identifiable events that occur in a somewhat regularized fashion. This assumption is certainly open to question, but it is the writers' contention that this is in fact the case.

A second possible moderator is position level in the organization. The succession literature deals with anything from three-person laboratory groups (Hamblin, 1958) to first-line supervisors (Jackson, 1953) to plant managers (Guest, 1962b) and corporate presidents (Lieberson & O'Connor, 1972). Here again, the question deals with the commonalities of the process across situations. It would appear that there are many common elements in the succession processes; the differences come about in terms of degree. For example, the number of people in the role set of the president is larger than that of the foreman; the number of people involved in the succession dynamics therefore is also greater. It should be noted that the level in the hierarchy is not necessarily the only factor that affects the degree of impact, since there are lower-level employees who have large and complex role sets.

Succession Dynamics

The process of succession will be divided into two phases for this analysis. First, there is a set of events that occur prior to the actual arrival and entrance of the successor to the group. Second, there is a set of events that occur once the successor has taken over the position and begins to act. While these two are treated separately here, it is obvious that (1) the postarrival factors depend in part on the prearrival factors, and (2) the postarrival factors in part may condition (and even somewhat become) the prearrival events for the next successor, if there should be another.

Phase I—The Prearrival Factors

1. The first element is "successor characteristics." These are the actual characteristics of the successor as well as the group's perceptions of them (independent of successor functioning in the new role), and they include such things as:

(a) Age, education, sex, race, prior employment.

(b) Skills and abilities, especially those that are group and situation relevant.

(c) Aspirations and motivations—how does this new job fit into his/her other career goals; is s/he perceived to be using this job as a "stepping stone"; what is his/her promotion record, etc. The relevance of these varies by position.

(d) The successor's orientation, as a function of specialty, past experience and training, etc. Is s/he a "marketing type," a "finance type," a "company man," a "builder," a "hatchet man," etc.?

(e) "Inside" or "outside" status—this relates to the previous position of the successor relative to the group. The definition of the boundary is less than certain: the person who comes in from another organization is an outsider, and the person coming from within the group is an insider; everyone else's status cannot easily be determined except by the group itself. Here, perhaps more than anywhere else, the group's perceptions are what count, since it is *their* definition that is important. The new plant manager in Gouldner's study (1954) was an outsider, yet this fact alone was not as important as the fact that the organization members did not perceive it as legitimate to bring in an outsider. In other systems, perhaps the military, outside status may be the accepted norm, and would not necessarily have the same impact as in Gouldner's case.

(f) Prior knowledge—related to (e), the extent to which this person and his/her managerial style, values, and so on are actually known to the group, and vice versa. This is important in itself, since being an insider does not necessarily imply that the group is familiar with the successor and his or her style.

This last point brings up the issue of actual versus perceived characteristics. Since we are concerned here with the prearrival events, the fact that there may be a discrepancy between the actual and the perceived (especially in such areas as (c) and (d), above) is important information in itself. The possible hypothesis from this section is that the closer the actual and perceived characteristics match (independent of evaluation of these characteristics by the group), the greater the likelihood of a smooth relationship developing *after* the successor's arrival. For example, if a marketing group accustomed to successors being former salesmen is not informed that their new leader is from finance, the shock value of that realization when s/he arrives is likely to introduce some disruption in the system. The disruption would be *independent* (at least initially) of their evaluation of the ability of financial people to manage them.

2. The second element is the *group's experience with succession in general.* Some of the dimensions here are:

(a) The extent to which leadership change is an expected, somewhat routine process in the context of the group. In other words, what kinds of experience has this group (or similar groups) had with leadership change? This includes frequency, desirability, outcomes, etc.

(b) If succession *is* somewhat routine in the group, why is this so? The reasons may include the presence of a rotation/training program for managers, fixed terms of office, chronic problems with the group that have made it a "problem child," poor selection and placement procedures that have resulted in the wrong people being hired and/or placed into this group, and so on.

(c) Following from (a) and (b), what connotation does the succession of leadership for the group have? Based on their experience or experiences of similar groups, does it connote an impending "dead-wood" trimming, a preparation for major change in the tasks, or has their experience been "neutral," such that it has none of these affective overtones, positive or negative? This one dimension may be less relevant in those successions due to death or other "environmentally controlled" causes as compared to other causes, but not completely so. Much anecdotal evidence points up the case where a manager or supervisor has become so politically entrenched that death or retirement are the *only* events that will permit succession to occur. Here, there may have been literally years of personnel and policy changes to be made and this sudden succession may very well conjure up some substantial emotions and anxieties in addition to kindling hopes for new achievements.

This last element also raises the question of "how much is too much?" That is, if succession has become *so* regularized by design (such as in military organizations), what impact does that have on the group? One critical element here is that of the task. The task may have initially required high interdependence between the leader and the group's roles, yet due to the high rate of imposed succession the group has managed to structure itself to minimize the leader's role in the task. In this way the group minimizes retraining problems with new leaders. In this case not only is the successor coming into an empty job but s/he is also facing some strict norms of noninterference in general. However, if the group is not able (or willing) to circumvent the high succession problem like this, then succession in general has an extremely negative connotation.

One possible hypothesis in either of these areas of disruptively rapid succession is that the impact of the "successor characteristics" above is less problematic than in cases where the leadership role has been preserved. In the former case, the successor may be totally unconventional in many respects, but the group might ignore this completely as long as it can function autonomously. In the latter case, the successor could be the most intelligent and competent person available, but the fact that s/he must be broken in and trained in this complex (by the group's standards) role is so disruptive in general that his or her qualities may go unnoticed.

In summary, the frequency of succession may be an important intervening variable when studying the impact of succession on group process. A highly regularized pattern of leadership change can put much stress on a given successor as well as increasing the problems of integrating him or her into the group. One implication of this is that the highly touted management development program of rotation through four to six positions in 2 years may add much to the trainee's breadth, but be highly dysfunctional for the organization in general.

The two major prearrival elements mentioned above are highly variable across instances of succession, almost by definition. There is a major learning process involved in the sense that each instance of succession in a group (even if it happens only once) becomes part of the group's cumulative experience. Added to this is the possibility that changing membership over time will possibly upset or redefine this base of knowledge.

3. The screening procedure is the third element of the prearrival factors:

(a) To what extent did the group have a part in selecting the new leader?

(b) Was a "favorite son or daughter" within the group passed over in the decision outcome? If so, will s/he remain in the group after the new leader arrives, or otherwise be in a position to hamper the newcomer's efforts?

(c) Where will the former leader be, functionally speaking, in relation to his/her successor? For example, if the former leader is being promoted one level up in an organizational framework that includes his former unit, he remains in a position to influence what happens before and after his replacement arrives.

(d) Were outside agencies (executive recruiters) utilized for recruiting purposes? Assessment centers?

Different kinds of organizations, and even different units within the same organization, utilize different strategies for selecting/replacing leaders. In some, the group proposes a candidate, after due deliberation (which may or may not reflect a democratic process), who subsequently is accepted and legitimated by a higher level official. In other instances, candidates are proposed by the higher level official to the group for comparisons and evaluations, but the decision resides with the administration. And, of course, there are many variations. Thus, 3(a) above suggests many possible alternatives, all of which may have implications for group effectiveness. The previously described laboratory research barely scratches the surface.

Paragraph 3(b) above represents a potentially confounding factor. If someone in the group were counting on the next promotion, had good reason to expect it, and subsequently lost out to another person, there are a number of possible implications for the transition period. Such persons, and their friends, may become problems for the new leader.

Paragraph 3(c) above raises another complication similar to 3(b). In this instance, the former leader's promotion actually makes the new leader's appointment possible. The promoted former leader may actually select a successor personally, thus directly influencing group expectations and the future course or direction of the group. For example, if a person with a known reputation is selected, that reputation plus the obvious connection between the two appointments will signal the group as to the prospects for change, business as usual, or a general tightening of the ship. Under 3(c), the former leader also retains power beyond the appointment of a successor because s/he probably will have considerable influence over budgets and related matters. If the former leader is promoted into a separate chain of command, on the other hand, the new leader may have greater flexibility.

Paragraph 3(d) suggests the possibility that thoroughness and objectivity in the screening process might influence subsequent succession phenomena. For example, it has long been known that difficult entrance requirements can influence the attractiveness of a group or organization. Reliance on elaborate procedures such as assessment centers for screening may create motivational sets among those who pass muster and among their prospective subordinates and superiors.

4. The fourth element is the new leader's mandate:

(a) What expectations or plans for the unit's future are held by higher level administrators? Do they wish to expand it, improve it, cut it back, or maintain the status quo? (This ties in with 3(c) above).

(b) What functional changes are intended in the departed leader's role responsibilities? For example, will the successor be expected to assume the same set of responsibilities, or will the role be divided between two or more people? Structural changes of this nature often accompany managerial successions. The successor may be given either more or less responsibility than the predecessor had.

(c) What bargaining concessions have been granted the successor to induce his or her acceptance of the position? Here we are speaking of new resources, or control over resources not necessarily enjoyed by the predecessor.

It seems reasonable to expect that matters such as those described above will have an impact on leader effectiveness following a succession. Moreover, such matters also are frequently involved in managerial/ coaching successions in athletics; the actuarial types of studies reviewed earlier do not and cannot take such matters into account and therefore do not provide much insight into the actual effects of leadership succession and their reasons.

In summary, this rough outline of prearrival factors was presented to point out that there are significant attitudes, effects, and possibly behaviors evoked even before the successor actually arrives. Throughout this section there has been only one mention of the successor's prearrival conditions. The perspective has been that of the group, relating and reacting to this previously inactive "successor." This, of course, is not a complete picture; it is entirely likely that the successor performs this same kind of mental inventory based on *his or her* perceptions, knowledge, past experience, and so on. The successor may even actively seek out potentially useful prearrival information about the group.

The point to remember, however, is that in the prearrival period, it is probably likely that some group members are doing as much or more to ready themselves to respond to this new situation (even if the designated successor happens to be one of them, incidentally) than is the successor. What better time to request a policy or strategy change, pay raise, assignment change, work load change, etc., than when a new leader arrives on the scene who may not necessarily be tied by precedent or the previous leader's biases?

Phase II—The Postarrival Factors

This section will deal with aspects of the succession that occur once the successor has formally assumed his or her new position and is physically located in the new job. At this point the discussion will focus on those aspects of group process dealing mainly with the integration of the successor into the group. There is a point beyond which the successor loses his/her newness, and the events after that point, while important, do not come within the scope of this paper. The relevant factors are as follows:

1. The first element is the *mutual observation process*—here, the successor and the group both have a chance to check out the other in terms of accuracy of perceived or expected characteristics. This process is not unlike the first half-hour of a blind date that has been arranged by a third party; both sides get the chance to see what the other is like. This is an ongoing process that becomes more and more complicated over time, including such things as:

(a) Comparisons with the past—Gouldner cites the prevalence of the so-called "Rebecca Myth" (1954, pp. 79–83), in which the past plant manager is to an extent idealized by some of the workers, despite the fact that he was disliked while present. These comparisons can range from halo-type personality assessments to very specific differences in actions (see later section).

(b) Getting acquainted—specifically, the sending, receiving, and evaluating of role expectations for both sides that will set the stage for future action. This is especially important in cases where the successor is known to and/or knows the group, as in the Lieberman paper (1956), and there is a question of incompatibility between the successor's old and new roles. The group whose member is made supervisor is not familiar with that person in this new role, and there is a period of learning involved on both sides (Katz & Kahn, 1966, pp. 171–198).

In reference to both (a) and (b), it is difficult to say specifically what characteristics or actions of the predecessor will be used for comparison purposes; one would think that the favorable aspects of the predecessor would be most salient in some cases and unfavorable aspects in others. The confounding factor here, of course, is that a supervisor need not act in the same way toward each subordinate; in fact, the extreme case of the popular predecessor who was "all things to all people" can make *any* successor's job extremely difficult.

2. The second element is the *successor's actions and reactions*. This category obviously is broad enough to cover almost anything, but hopefully it will be useful here. The concern here is with specific behaviors by the successor in response to the expectations of his/her superiors and subordinates, such as:

(a) Coping with the immediate problem of gathering information—the successor, if brought in from outside, very simply does not have the regular sources of information (task- and social-related) needed to manage the group. This has been fully discussed in the Guest and Gouldner books, and Grusky notes that the combination of authority inherent in the successor's position and strangeness not only socially isolates the successor who happens to be an outside man, but it simultaneously closes him off to important informal sources of information about the organization (or group). This, in turn, slows down the process by which the successor is socialized and, therefore, reinforces his position of isolation (1960, p. 108).

This problem is highly variable in importance and complexity, depending on such things as the nature of the group's task, group size, linkages with other groups, and other factors. It is also conditioned by many things such as the presence or availability of the predecessor to aid in the transition, perceived capability and attractiveness of the successor to the group, presence of external threats to the group as a whole that makes rapid integration of the successor desired by all, and so on.

Whatever combination of events and circumstances exists, it appears from the literature that two basic courses of action are open to the successor: the use of existing social networks to gather and disseminate information, or the more drastic step of replacement of key personnel and/or increased formalization or bureaucratization where the use of existing mechanisms is not feasible or desirable. The decision to rely predominantly on either of these responses is not necessarily completely a function of the relationship of the successor to that group at the present. For example, historical factors such as the pattern of indulgence at Gouldner's gypsum plant, or the fact that the new plant manager in Guest's study was not under pressure from his superiors to institute bureaucratic routines and use disciplinary measures can affect the outcome. This process leads to another possible hypothesis: given *only* the prearrival factors mentioned before, it should be possible to predict what type of response will be most prevalent in the successor's initial actions. This is not to imply total constraint on the successor; the implication is only that if, for example, the successor's work group has prejudged him positively (or neutrally), and he is not under severe pressure to improve performance, he will be less likely to resort to formal rules and sanctions to effect his integration into and leadership of the work group.

(b) Coping with discrepancies between the successor's and the members' path-goal perceptions—this is a rather complex problem that, while not peculiar to succession, is important here given what was said earlier about the match between perceived and actual characteristics of the successor at the prearrival stage. An example here might be helpful: at the prearrival stage in a succession, imagine a situation where the work group has experienced much succession in supervisors due to that job's role as an entry-level to management, "trial-by-fire" position. Therefore, the group has learned to perceive every successor to this position to have high aspirations, and they have learned that his/her performance (particularly against the budget) is the criterion for his/her promotion (goal) or dismissal. The fact that both the new manager and the group understand this situation to be a fact of life would predict that the integration process would be relatively smooth. Now, what would happen if a new successor comes along with a different path-goal configuration:

(i) The successor believes in the human relations philosophy learned in college, and, contrary to all previous supervisors, believes that a supervisor does *not* have to walk all over the workers to perform well against the budget?

(ii) Alternatively, the successor believes that s/he can prove worthy of promotion not primarily by keeping costs down, but by proposing new ways to do the group tasks even if they are expensive?

Both situations in this lengthy example have the same core issue: the successor's perceptions of the correct means to a commonly recognized end (promotion) are not the same as those of the subordinates which have developed over the course of prior successions. This path-goal discrepancy goes one step further than just being a problem in role conflict or unclear role expectations. This situation may be common enough to warrant special treatment; in any event the net effect is that the group has been thrown a curve, and the members' responses in this situation may be a key element in the study of their succession dynamics.

3. The third element here is the *power and influence source*—this too is a broad category that has at its heart the basic question of the role and capabilities of a leader in general, and it overlaps and/or is dependent on almost everything said before. The debate and confusion over the meshing of authority, power, and influence will be avoided here as much as possible, with one major exception. It would appear that the succession process would be an excellent place to test the manner in which formal authority, power, and influence come into the leadership process. For example, using the French and Raven model (1959) of power as a starting point, a succession study would allow tests of the following:

(a) The sources of power *perceived* to be held by the successor before arrival; specifically, how much do the actions of the predecessor affect the perceptions of the successor's ability to mediate rewards and sanctions?

(b) Over time, how do the successor's sources of power (perceived and actual) change? What difference does it make for the functioning of the group? How does this relate to the successor's choice to use "formal" or "informal" means to gather information and carry out duties, as discussed earlier?

These are only two of the many questions that come up when studying power and influence. In an attempt to add at least a minimal amount of order to this, one possible theoretical model to understand the process of power and influence attempts and actions will be proposed which is far from revolutionary.

Given what was said before about all the prearrival conjecturing and evaluation that goes on, and the vast literature on leadership, it seems reasonable to assume that a successor often must "work his/her way" into a group. A group may initially go only so far as to grant "headship" (Gibb, 1969) status to the successor. Specifically: (1) the influence resources that accrue to the leader must be derived from his/her formal organizational position, and (2) the influence attempts of the leader must be perceived as being legitimate *because* of the formal organizational position (Schmidt, Kochan, & DeCotiis, Note 1). In other words, when the successor first is appointed, the nature of the superior-subordinate relationship often is that of an organization chart: person A by virtue of occupying the box labeled "supervisor" has been endowed by the organization with the right to legitimately attempt to influence (and control) the group that occupies another box on the chart labeled "work group."

The dependent variable, then, is the degree to which the successor does become, over a period of time, the "capital L" leader of the group. In Gibb's (1954) somewhat glowing and meaningful terms, "Leader and follower must be united by common goals and aspirations and by a will to lead, on one side and a will to follow on the other, i.e., by a common acceptance of each other. The leader must be a member of the group, and must share its norms, its objectives, and its aspirations." Assuming that it is not totally fallacious to expect the goals of the leaders and the led to coincide to a degree, the above definition (labeled as "leadership") can be used as one end of a continuum for which the organization chart relationship (or "headship") is the other. In the Gouldner (1954) work, for example, the new plant manager never really did move away from a "headship" position. It was only by putting in his own lieutenants that he was able to get cooperation, but this can hardly be described as a case of voluntary acceptance by the led. In the Guest (1962b) study, the successor did in fact move toward the "leadership" pole of the scale, with positive results.

At this point it is imperative to reinforce what has been said earlier about avoiding the "great man" approach to leadership succession; it is clearly not safe to say that the successor in the white hat can move more toward the "leadership" pole than can the successor in the black hat. The hat the successor wears is often determined by what Guest called "institutionally derived pressures" (1962a, p. 53) such as community pressures, traditions of inside successors, and the like. But since this paper has come full circle at this point without really settling the "constrained behavior" versus "individual abilities" debate, it is now time to attempt to put both in perspective. Unfortunately this will be somewhat of a familiar "satisficing" solution to the debate, and is similar to the position of Hall (1972) mentioned earlier.

Quite simply, the "constrained behavior" notions probably act to set the parameters within which the "individual abilities" notions take effect. Take, for example, the "headship-leadership" continuum mentioned above. Those ominous "institutionally derived pressures" are important, but only in the sense that they probably limit (at least initially) how close the successor might ever expect to get to the "leadership" pole of the continuum. The presence of those pressures does not mean that the new manager will *never* be able to rely on referent or expert power as sources of influence attempts, nor does it mean that s/he will *never* be perceived as anything but an outsider, in the Gouldner sense. Conversely, the absence (or more properly, the relative absence) of these pressures does not connote instant "leadership," common goals, shared norms, and the like. These environmentally based factors tell us what the anchor points of that "headship-leadership" continuum are, and perhaps even how much movement we might reasonably anticipate. Within those parameters the successor can bring to bear knowledge of attitude change, motivation, group dynamics, and the like.

An Alternate Model

The "prearrival/postarrival" model utilized above for analyzing leadership succession dynamics represents a convenient way to conceptualize and categorize the many events and phenomena that interact with the process. There is at least one other model, however, that some researchers and theoreticians may find more appealing. That is, the leadership succession process can be conceptualized in terms of "situational favorableness" for the new leader on his/her way in. The strategy would maintain the long-standing linkage of leadership and group dynamics initially emphasized by Cecil Gibb (1954) and operationalized in recent years by Fiedler (1967). Such a conceptualization would require, for research purposes, the development of an operational measure of situational favorableness going much beyond the one used in the Fiedler contingency model. The following is an illustrative and admittedly incomplete list of guideline or issue questions regarding the succession situation; these, in turn, can generate specific questionnaire or interview format items and eventually produce one or more scales. In other words, the following list is meant to be provocative, not operational. A fully operational statement is beyond the scope of this paper, and may even be premature. We are not even sure, as yet, if all the questions bear strongly on succession processes; directionality of their answers also is not yet known:

1. Is the group's motivation toward goal(s) high and in the same direction as the new leader's?
2. Does the new leader have power, and from what sources?
3. Is the group organized or motivated to resist the new leader (say, because of past bad relationship between group and organization or because of vested interests)?
4. Does the group possess requisite skills and other resources, or is it in a position to obtain them or develop them quickly through replacement, trade, purchase, training, renting, or hiring?
5. Is the group organized into a flexible role structure permitting easy role modification, experimentation, and task reassignment?
6. Is the applicable reward system congruent with group values?
7. Is there a facilitative organization climate surrounding the group: (a) supportive, encouraging, prideful, patient, or (b) mildly hostile, which can energize a "we'll show you we can do it" attitude within the group?
8. Do group size and member locations, schedules, and communications technology enable the new leader to observe members, interact with them, and make timely adjustments?
9. Is the group's task challenging, or does task completion lead to feelings of achievement?
10. Is there an "overlooked" rival leader still in the group, or a former leader of the group still meddling in its affairs?
11. Is the former leader a hero to be lived up to, or a bad act which is easy to follow?
12. What is the group's performance level relative to possible ceiling effect at the time of succession—is there room for easy progress?
13. Are there any rules, policies or laws that have differential effects on different groups and that may put this group at a disadvantage?
14. Are the levels of cohesion and conformity pressures within the group functional for high performance?
15. What is the reputation of the new leader preceding his or her arrival?
16. Is there a history in the group of self-government coupled with an established standing committee system and parliamentary procedures not easily avoided by the new leader?
17. Is the group's membership overloaded with senior level people?
18. Are the group's goals and pathways to those goals known and clear?

19. Have crucial policy/strategy decisions been made, goals set, or technology set in place that cannot be changed immediately after succession because of budgetary, legal, or supply constraints or because of the competitive costs that would be incurred?

Analysis of data based on derivatives of the above questions and others could produce one or more situational favorableness scales from which hypotheses may be generated about leadership succession. Assuming for our present purposes only, one, overall dimension, some of the more obvious hypotheses might include:

The more favorable the situation for the new leader,

1. the more rapidly s/he will be accepted by the group;
2. the more likely there will be an early performance improvement by the group;
3. the longer the new leader will remain in the group;
4. the easier it will be to introduce other changes to the group;
5. the easier it will be to recruit a subsequent leader.

The first task confronting us, however, is one of instrumentation. Operational measures and experimental paradigms are sorely needed. Systematic case studies (Jauch et al., in press) also would be instrumental in developing our knowledge of this important problem area. Moreover, such research might benefit from being grounded in a developmental context. Specifically, Rosen (1981) has postulated elsewhere that groups go through evolutionary stages and that different leader characteristics, skills, and functional emphases fit better in some stages than in others. If this is so, it probably follows that leader succession will have different implications and effects at different stages of a group's developmental history.

Finally, we would like to make a plea for leadership succession research as a substitute for more traditional studies of leadership. It seems to us that cross-sectional studies of groups and leaders during periods of relative equilibrium cannot reveal the full range of variation and complexity that are part of any social system. We believe this paper has made it clear that many of the truly critical phenomena occur before the leader comes on the scene and immediately thereafter. It is during such periods that old allocation of resource battles are fought over again, ideological divisions temporarily suppressed come to the fore, performance standards are reevaluated, role responsibilities are redefined, and new goals are set. The leader's effectiveness or lack thereof will be more visible during such a period, and the tactics that make a difference are more likely to be observable than in quieter times. In short, there is a great deal to be gained from focusing leadership studies during periods of change thereby encompassing organizational, situational, and leadership variables simultaneously. It also may prove useful to study systematically what happens to exleaders in various types of organizations—in some societies Kings losing their grip were murdered (Frazer, 1947).

References

Allen, Michael, Panian, Sharon, & Lotz, Roy. Managerial succession and organizational performance: A recalcitrant problem revisited. *Administrative Science Quarterly.* 1979, **24**(2), 167–180.

Bess, James, & Lodahl, Thomas. Career patterns and satisfactions in university middle-management. *Educational Record,* 1969 (Spring), 220–229.

Birnbaum, Robert. Presidential succession: An inter-institutional analysis. *Educational Record,* 1971 (Spring), 133–145.

Daum, Jeffrey. Internal promotion—a psychological asset or debit. *Organizational Behavior and Human Performance,* 1975, **13**, 404–413.

Eitzen, D. Stanley, & Yetman, Norman. Managerial change, longevity, and organizational effectiveness. *Administrative Science Quarterly,* 1972, **17**, 110–116.

Fiedler, Fred. *A theory of leadership effectiveness.* New York: McGraw-Hill, 1967.

Frazer, J. G. *The golden bough.* New York: Macmillan Co., 1947.

French, John, & Raven, Bertram. The bases of social power. In D. Cartwright (Ed.), *Studies in social power.* Ann Arbor: University of Michigan, 1959. Pp. 150–167.

Gamson, William, & Scotch, Norman. Scapegoating in baseball. *American Journal of Sociology,* 1964, **70**, 69–70.

Gibb, Cecil. Leadership. In G. Lindzey (Ed.), *The handbook of social psychology.* Reading, Mass.: Addison-Wesley, 1954. Vol 2, pp. 877–920.

Gibb, Cecil. Leadership. In G. Lindzey and E. Aronson (Eds.), *The handbook of social psychology.* Reading, Mass.: Addison-Wesley, 1969. 2nd ed., Vol. 4, pp. 205–282.

Goldman, M., & Fraas, L. The effects of leadership selection on group performance. *Sociometry,* 1965, **28**, 82–88.

Gordon, Gerald, & Becker, Selwyn. Organization size and managerial succession: A reexamination. *American Journal of Sociology,* 1964, **70**, 215–222.

Gouldner, Alvin. *Patterns of industrial bureaucracy.* New York: The Free Press, 1954.

Grusky, Oscar. Administrative succession in formal organizations. *Social Forces,* 1960, **39**, 105–115.

Grusky, Oscar. Corporate size, bureaucratization, and managerial succession. *American Journal of Sociology,* 1961, **67**, 261–269.

Grusky, Oscar. Managerial succession. *American Journal of Sociology,* 1963, **69**, 72–76.

Grusky, Oscar. Reply. *American Journal of Sociology,* 1964, **70**, 72–76.

Grusky, Oscar. Succession with an ally. *Administrative Science Quarterly,* 1969, **14,** 155–170.(a)

Grusky, Oscar. Effects of inside vs. outside succession on communication patterns. *Proceedings of the 77th Annual Convention of the American Psychological Association,* 1969, 451–452. (b)

Guest, Robert. Managerial succession in complex organizations. *American Journal of Sociology,* 1962, **68,** 47–54. (a)

Guest, Robert. *Organizational change.* Homewood, Ill.: Irwin-Dorsey, 1962. (b)

Hall, Richard. *Organizations: structure and process.* Englewood Cliffs, N.J.: Prentice-Hall, 1972.

Hamblin, Robert. Leadership and crises. *Sociometry,* 1958, **21,** 322–335.

Helmich, Donald. Predecessor turnover and successor characteristics. *Cornell Journal of Social Relations,* 1974 (Fall), 249–260.

Hodgkinson, Harold. *Institutions in transition, a study of change in higher education.* Berkeley: Carnegie Commission on Higher Education, 1970.

Hollander, Edwin, & Julian, James. Studies in leader legitimacy, influence and innovation and A further look at leader legitimacy, influence, and innovation. In Leonard Berkowitz (Ed.), *Group processes.* New York: Academic Press, 1978.

Jackson, Jay. The effects of changing leadership of small work groups. *Human Relations,* 1953, **6,** 25–44.

Jauch, L., Osborn, R., & Martin, T. Structured content analysis of cases: a complementary method for organizational research. *American Management Review,* in press.

Katz, Daniel, & Kahn, Robert. *The social psychology of organizations.* New York: Wiley, 1966.

Kriesberg, Louis. Careers, organization size, and successions. *American Journal of Sociology,* 1962, **68,** 355–359.

Kriesberg, Louis. Reply. *American Journal of Sociology,* 1964, **70,** 223.

Lieberman, Seymour. The effects of changes in roles on the attitudes of role occupants. *Human Relations,* 1956, **9,** 385–402.

Lieberson, Stanley, & O'Connor, James. Leadership and organizational performance: A study of large corporations. *American Sociological Review,* 1972, **37,** 117–130.

Merei, F. Group leadership and institutionalization. In Eleanor Maccoby, T. Newcomb, & E. Hartley (Eds.), *Readings in Social Psychology* (3rd ed.), New York: Holt, Rinehardt & Winston, 1958. Pp. 522–532.

Newcomer, Mabel. *The big business executive.* New York: Columbia Univ. Press, 1955, p. 20.

Rosen, Ned. *Leadership change and work-group dynamics.* Ithaca, N.Y.: Cornell Univ. Press, 1969.

Rosen, Ned. Open systems theory in an organizational sub-system: A field experiment. *Organizational Behavior and Human Performance,* 1970, **5,** 245–265.

Rosen, Ned. *Groups at Work.* Unpublished manuscript, 1981.

Salaman, Graeme. An historical discontinuity: From charisma to routinization. *Human Relations,* 1977, **30**(4), 373–388.

Salencik, G., & Pfeffer, J. Constraints on administrative discretion: the limited influence of mayors on city budgets. *Urban Affairs Quarterly,* 1977, **12,** 475–496.

Trow, Donald. Membership succession and team performance. *Human Relations,* 1960, **13,** 259–269.

Weiner, Nan. *Situational and leadership influence on organization performance.* Working Paper Series (WPS 78-1), College of Administrative Science, The Ohio State University, January 1978.

Weiner, Nan, & Mahoney, Thomas. *A model of corporate performance as a function of environmental, organizational, and leadership influences.* Working Paper Series (WPS 79-72), College of Administrative Science, The Ohio State University, October 1979.

Ziller, R. C. Toward a theory of open and closed groups. *Psychological Bulletin,* 1965, **64**(3), 164–182.

Reference Note

1. Schmidt, Stu, Kochan, Thomas, & DeCotiis, Thomas. *Leadership, headship, and superior-subordinate relations.* Unpublished paper, University of Wisconsin, Madison, Wisconsin, 1972.

16

The Status of
Black Leadership:
Implications for Black
Followers in the 1980s

KING E. DAVIS

Almost since the start of the involuntary immigration of West Africans
to the North American Continent, a confluence of economic, political,
ethical, and racial inequities have created a climate for, as well as
stimulated the growth and development of, forms of black leadership,
followers, organizations, and movements. Concomitantly, this same set
of inequities served to stimulate debate and confusion regarding the
overall functions of black leaders, the goals of black organizations, and
the extent to which black people participate as followers. As a result
of these polemics, black leaders, followers, and organizations, while
needed and supported by black populations (and validated by their West
African heritage), often tend to be viewed as unnecessary or subversive
by white populations (Hinds, 1979; Kerner, 1968; Ross, 1978; and
Theohavis, 1978).

Some critics of black leaders (Washington, 1978) promulgate the
generalization that black leaders, followers, and organizations are "communist inspired." This generalization has been used to rationalize unconstitutional governmental investigation, surveillance, and disruption.
In numerous instances, surreptitious efforts have been made (such as
those authorized by J. Edgar Hoover) to discredit black leaders (most
notably Martin Luther King, Jr.), reduce their stature among their

Reprinted by permission of the publisher from *Journal of Applied Behavioral Science* 18:3
(1982):309–322.

followers, and destroy their organizations ("As Charges Mount Against the FBI," 1976; Gayle, 1980; McClory, 1979; and Washington, 1978). Some observers (Clark & Wilkins, 1973; Washington, 1978) propose that the covert activities of the FBI contributed directly to the deaths of several black leaders.

The United States Constitution, nonetheless, supports and encourages private citizens to organize and petition the government for change (Nelson, 1968). The realization that government officials, charged with protecting constitutional rights and guarantees, could ignore the constitutional rights of black leaders, followers, and organizations underlies the fear that often surrounds efforts by blacks to organize.

Faced with these dilemmas of unconstitutional opposition, black leaders, followers, organizations, and movements were profoundly changed between 1968 and 1980. The most significant events in this recent history are the death of Martin Luther King, Jr., the shift in ideologies from protesting to conciliatory, a drastic change in the amount and source of operating capital (Davis, 1980), the intrusion of the FBI into activities of black organizations, and the ascendance of materialistic values and the doctrine of individualism.

Purpose and Substantive Questions

The purpose of this essay is to postulate and explore a range of basic questions that help to expand the conceptual framework for understanding the historical, current, and future direction of black leadership, followership, organizations, and movements.

1. How is black leadership defined and to what extent do the parameters and characteristics of black leaders differ from those of black followers, organizations, and movements?
2. What confluence of factors appears to be related to the growth and development of black leaders, followers, organizations, and movements?
3. What issues and factors tend to influence the black leadership role?
4. What is the nature of the relationship among black leaders, followers, and organizations?

Definitions of Major Terms/Concepts

Stogdill's work (1974) reminds us that there are innumerable definitions of leadership and suggests the need to offer tentative definitions of black leadership, followership, organizations, and movements.

Black leaders are able to identify and respond to the problems, policies, conditions, and needs that determine (or are inimical to) the quality of life of black people. As a result, such leaders are able to develop, implement, and evaluate probable solutions, as well as stimulate a following of black people who are moved toward eliminating or modifying the problems, policies, conditions, or unmet needs. This definition of black leadership is similar to the general definition developed by Burns (1978), who stresses the importance of conceptualizing leadership as a reciprocal relationship between leaders and followers, circumscribed around the meeting of needs. Based on Burns's leadership typology (transforming *vs.* transactional), one can conclude that while leaders in the society at large may fit either type, the needs and experiences of the black population may dictate a greater emphasis on transformational leadership, with high moral standards.

Weber's treatment of leadership (see Coser, 1971), while it emphasized charisma and authority, also defined leadership as basically a functional relationship between leaders and followers. In that Weber proposed that the leadership role derived from the followers' basic beliefs about the goals that were proposed for achievement, however, Weber's view differed from Burns's.

Black followers, on the other hand, are stimulated by and sensitive to a problem, policy, condition, or need that influences (or is inimical to) the quality of life of black people. As a result, these followers voluntarily respond to and follow the direction charted by (or mutually arrived at with) black leadership. Implied here is the notion that black followers must have the opportunity to select among leaders. Burns (1978) and Stogdill (1974) imply that there are some endemic problems associated with the leader/follower relationship in those instances where the leader is self-appointed, appointed by groups outside the followers, or motivated by factors other than the needs of the followers.

Black organizations are viewed as the formalized mechanisms through which the relationship, interaction, support, energies, resources, plans, activities, and philosophies of black leaders and followers develop collectively toward the achievement of identified goals and needs.

Black movements represent the combined activities, responses, resources, and plans of several organizations, groups of followers, and leaders aimed generally at eliminating a problem, policy, or condition (i.e., segregation) that is viewed as inimical to the quality of life of all black people in the country or within a given region.

Factors Giving Rise to Black Leadership/Status

Gunnar Myrdal (1944) has proposed that the American propensity to form and join associations is not circumscribed by race. In fact, he found that blacks tended to be more frequent participants in specific social organizations and associations than whites. While Myrdal's classic treatise does propose a relationship between Americanization and participation, we must look further for an understanding of what factors give rise to the development of black leadership.

Burns (1978) proposes a complex of factors that relate to leadership development. He suggests that such factors as personal motivation, awareness of societal need, early psychological experiences, and family characteristics combine to stimulate a desire for leadership on the part of a prospective leader. Stogdill (1974), in his review of the literature on leadership, identifies six different perspectives that are viewed as explanations for leadership development.

While Burns and Stogdill focused on leadership development in the larger society, Thompson's (1963) assessment of black leadership development identifies two major factors: the leader's recognition of unmet social needs and the persistence of inequity in the distribution of opportunities.

Each set of factors cited by Burns (1978), Stogdill (1974), and Thompson (1963) helps to expand our perspective on the personal and societal factors that influence leadership. It appears that at least four interrelated factors help explain why specific persons are selected for leadership roles in black communities.

The first of these factors is the absence of political equity (Thompson, 1963). Political equity involves a complex set of issues and conditions related to one's right to vote, opportunity to hold public office, or be assured equitable representation in accord with the laws of the nation. Governmental analysis (Kerner, 1968) established that black populations were often denied access to the political arena, and black populations were denied the most basic right accorded to American citizens under the Constitution and the Bill of Rights. It is hypothesized that there is a direct correlation between the extent (and activity) of black leadership, followers, and organizations and the degree to which black populations have equitable or reasonable access to the political system (that is not to suggest that there would not be a process of black leadership and a distinct cädre of black followers in a system in which rights were distributed equitably). One could surmise that the concerns of black leadership, in a more equitable system, would be with substantially different issues.

While there have been significant and visible increases in various aspects of black access to the political institutions of U.S. society (e.g., elected officials, increase in registered voters), black leaders continue to educate followers about the need for efforts to ensure that their gains are not dissipated by conservative policies (Williams, note 1). The continued presence of political inequities is a prime factor in the maintenance of black organizations such as the Voter Education Project and the Joint Center for Political Change (Thompson, note 2).

A second factor giving rise to black leaders and followers is the absence of adequate economic opportunity. Only minimal changes in the distribution of wealth in the United States have occurred since the mid-1940s (Brimmer, note 3). While there has been an increase in the income of black populations, Hill (1981) points out that significant black progress is more an illusion than a reality. Government studies (Coleman, 1977) point out the continuation of serious inequities in economic status between blacks and whites.

A third fact is continued violence against black people and a failure on the part of government to respond to the need for police protection in black neighborhoods (Kerner, 1968; Conyers, 1981).

The fourth factor giving rise to black leadership is the historical absence of access to various public accommodations. Racially segregated schools, parks, and transportation (most overt in Southern states) were the most visible inequities in the society and became the primary stimuli for the emergence of such black leaders as Martin Luther King, Jr., his civil rights followers, and the Southern Christian Leadership Conference (SCLC).

While the absence of access to public accommodations (now largely resolved) was a significant issue that helped to solidify black leadership and followers, the tendency to characterize black community problems in relationship to this singular issue may have inadvertently skewed the civil rights movement, and its leadership, from other substantive issues. For example, if black leaders and followers (as well as white supporters) tend to conceptualize the major dilemmas of the black population in terms of public accommodations, whenever the semblance of these rights are obtained (right to vote, school integration, nonsegregated transportation) the thrust of leadership and organization becomes blunted and the willingness of individuals to function as followers subsequently declines.

Since other substantive issues that face black populations are less visible, black leadership may experience a considerable decline in following after concrete goals are achieved. For example, in the historical *Brown vs. Board of Education*, the five suits in the case were conceptualized as a problem of separate and yet inherently unequal school facilities, resources, and opportunity (Jones, 1979). It seems appropriate to view the Topeka case multidimensionally and to include as a major problem the concentration of decision making, since the appointive process did not allow for black participation on the school board, which had the ultimate local authority to decide regarding the distribution of school resources and facilities. To a great extent, this concentration of decision making has not changed in Topeka or in other cities that were characterized by segregated school systems.

Each of the factors cited here suggests that a key to understanding the historic development of black leadership and followers has been the failure of the U.S. government (and society) to provide black citizens with rudimentary rights, guarantees, and protections covered by the Constitution and the Bill of Rights (Kerner, 1968). In effect, representative government has failed historically to meet the human needs and civil rights of blacks, thus stimulating the need for alternative leaders and movements within the black population.

This major expectation helps clarify the linkage between black leaders and their followers and organizations and why black leaders, oriented toward social change, continue to emerge. One could hypothesize that the nature of black leadership, followers, organizations, and movements would change logically in direct proportion to substantive changes in the distribution of resources and the long overdue implementation of constitutional guarantees.

Factors That Link Black Leaders, Followers, and Organizations

Given the relative constancy of institutional inaccessibility and the inveterate maldistribution of resources and decision making, reciprocal expectations between black leaders and followers may have changed only minimally over the past 350 years.

While one cannot deny that the interrelationship between leaders and followers and the process of leadership development appear to be universal in all human groupings (Burns, 1978), there seems to be a unique role demanded of leadership in groups that are oppressed, denied, or alienated from those societal institutions that determine the quality of life (Hamilton, 1981). The leaders of oppressed groups are faced inevitably with the formidable goals of social change and redistribution of decisions and resources (Burns, 1978) while leaders of numerically, militarily, and economically dominant groups have a less formidable task of managing resources and opportunities in such a way as to maintain the status quo.

Few studies have examined in detail the nature of the dynamic internal relationship between black leaders and followers. A few studies (Thompson, 1963; Bowens, note 4) have explored the impact that personal charisma has in stimulating followership. Only limited work, however, has been devoted to the identification of independent variables related to black leader-follower relationships.

The variables that are proposed here are seen as being of value in understanding the ubiquitous forces that guide, reinforce, maintain, or destroy black leader-follower relationships once they are stimulated by broader societal forces. These variables are also potentially useful in understanding shifts and modifications in such relationships. For example, it is proposed that reduction in any one of the variables has the potential of producing significant changes in leader-follower relationships and subsequently in black organizations and movements. For example, a decline in trust between black leaders or followers is only one variable that would impair the functional relationship between black leaders and their followers and would inhibit the functioning of black organizations.

It should be recognized that the maintenance of these variables is not simply a function of black leaders, followers, or organizations. Numerous forces, some external to black communities, have the potential for enhancing or reducing these interactive variables and thus the qualitative nature of the relationship between black leaders and followers. Several writers highlight these variables and more clearly identify their relationship to changes in the direction of the black movement as well as the relationship between black leaders and their followers (Gayle, 1980; Hamilton, 1981; Staples, 1976; and Washington, 1978).

The nature of the relationship between black leaders and followers is believed to be influenced by a complex of variables:

1. Identification of mutual problems and a resulting sense of injustice;
2. Group identity and need for a sense of community;
3. Mutual support;
4. Mutual respect;
5. Mutual trust;
6. Shared expectation of change;
7. Communication patterns and methods;
8. Recognition of the need for reciprocity;
9. Recognition of interdependency;
10. Shared world view.

Status of the Black Movement

While considerable controversy surrounds the current status of the black social change movement, the general opinion appears to be that the black movement for social change has altered its strategies, foci, and lost its momentum (Newman et al., 1978).

The focus of the black movement from the 1940s through the 1970s was toward elimination of the barriers to black access to public services. Supported by extensive media exposure, the black movement appeared raucus, forceful, and overwhelming. It could not be ignored. The movement had the effect of stimulating heterogeneous participation since it promised active involvement and observable results in using the stated aims of democracy to improve the quality of life of blacks.

The black social change movement succeeded in eliminating overt oppressive barriers that had plagued black Americans for centuries. Simultaneously, the black movement propagated similar movements for rights among the aged, women, Chicanos, Native Americans, and Asians. The key to understanding the black movement, then as well as now, was the role played by the cädre of black leaders whose charisma and vision stimulated many others to follow.

Following 1970, the black social change movement abandoned its confronting strategies. Black leaders and their followers marched rarely after 1970. Militant black men and women stopped carrying weapons and shouting for black power. Gone were the oratory, charisma, vision, and the publicity. The black movement became significantly less visible, less vocal, and more intensely involved in building political and economic power at the local level. The black leadership role became equated with political leadership (Williams, note 1). Black gains became equated with increases in the numbers of black office holders. Some observers attribute the significant shift in the black movement to a decline in black leaders.

For example, Brown (1981) suggests that the black movement, as previously known, is near extinction. In his analysis, Brown asserts that the inactivity of the black movement in 1981 is related to an absence of moral and intellectual black leadership, chosen by black people. Brown's essay concludes that blacks are now a leaderless people: therefore, there are no organized followers. Current "black leaders" according to Brown have been chosen by white elites; these black leaders lack the vision and commitment for social reform. Brown espouses the position that power is the most dynamic ingredient in the relationship between leaders and followers. Thus, the black movement, if it is indeed inactive, has become so because black people have failed to use their power creatively, collectively, or accurately in the selection and monitoring of leadership.

Washington's (1978) conclusion is similar to that of Brown's (1981), while her interpretation of the causes of the phenomenon differs. Washington's careful analysis of the status of the black movement attributes its character to the insidious activities of the Federal Bureau of Investigation. She also proposes that the major impact of the FBI's activities has been to decrease the number, assertiveness, and effectiveness of black leaders. The secondary impact of FBI activity has been to reduce the extensiveness of black participation.

In a 1980 survey of its subscribers, *Black Enterprise* (Clemmons, 1980) sought to determine whom blacks identify as their leaders. In addition, the journal's staff sought to determine the extent to which blacks participate in traditional black organizations. The results of this survey suggest that there is no unanimity among blacks surveyed relative to their identified leaders. Other than Jesse Jackson, who was chosen by 33% of the respondents, black persons did not identify one leader. The study also suggests that blacks no longer participate to any significant degree in traditional civil rights organizations.

Stogdill's (1974) descriptive work can be used to support Washington's and Brown's observations. According to Stogdill, organizational dormancy is a frequent occurrence in social movements that experience a precipitous change in leadership. Until new leadership emerges, organizations and groups curtail their external activities and invest more energy in forming a protective internal unit designed to ensure organizational survival. The emphasis on socio-political development vis-à-vis confrontation in the black movement is consistent with this view.

Observers have raised questions about the extent to which black followers participate, about their motivation for participation, and about the extent to which these factors differ from those that characterize white populations (ACTION, 1974; Lenski, 1961; Olsen, 1970; and Orum, 1966). Buckley (1980) postulates that there is a schism between black leaders and their followers, while Raspberry (1980) stimulates questions about the process through which black leaders formulate meaningful associations. Hamilton (1981), on the other hand, provides a more substantive analysis of the parameters of black leadership and dispels the myth that black leaders are unaccountable to their followers.

Three major conclusions can be drawn:

1. Black Americans in 1982 believe that they have fewer national leaders whose charisma or plans stimulate them to challenge the extant social system. Black leadership appears more diffuse among a relatively large number of individuals in politics, business, and religion.

2. Black populations do not participate as actively in traditional or non-traditional black organizations as was the pattern prior to 1970. Black participation, membership, and support of traditional black organizations have declined while participation in social and fraternal organizations appears to have increased.

3. Black organizations have experienced significant declines in their operating capital, and the sources of their revenue have shifted. In the post-1970 period, a number of the traditional black organizations have experienced reductions of up to 90% of their operating capital (Davis, 1980). The newer black organizations have collapsed after losing all funds. Funds to support black organizations in the post-1970 period

have shifted from predominantly black to predominantly white corporate sources (Jordan, 1981).

It seems clear that the most significant factor accounting for the current status of the black movement is the performance of black leaders. A review of the factors that influence black leadership may help increase our understanding of the future of the black movement.

Factors That Influence Black Leadership Performance

Throughout the history of blacks in the United States, a number of superlative men and women have become black leaders: Prosser, Vesey, Turner, Brown, Revels, Tubman, Washington, Garvey, Dubois, Carver, King, Malcolm X, and many others (Bennett, 1961). A review of the histories of these leaders reflects a combination of factors and conditions that influenced their overall performance (in some instances, actually heightening their performance while in other instances, performance was delimited). These factors remain important and may help explain the future direction of black leadership and followers.

One of the most significant factors that has continued to inhibit and influence black leadership is the widespread presence of threats (physical, economic, psychological), some of which have been sanctioned by government (Washington, 1978) and tolerated by the general public (Ginsburg, 1969). Publicity about black leaders, their goals, and strategies has resulted in extreme hostility as well as resistence and aggression (Lincoln, 1967). These feelings have erupted in numerous acts of violence aimed at local and national black leaders. The shooting of Vernon Jordan is the most recent in a series of attacks on black leaders.

The alleged involvement of the FBI in the deaths of several black leaders (Washington, 1978), the general failure of the courts to prosecute persons for violence against blacks, as well as the historical use of violence as a means of resisting social change, seem to have created a climate that reinforces violence against blacks in general. As a result, one can predict that the level of violence aimed at black leaders on the national and local levels is likely to increase.

Jeff (note 5) suggests that violence against black men and women has been used systematically to curtail their efforts to promote social change. As conditions within the economy result in a decrease in real income and jobs, attacks on black leaders tend to increase. Ginsburg's work (1969) implies that violence against blacks has been prevalent in the United States for an extended period. Ginsburg concludes, however, that such violence is often indiscriminate and based on psychological as opposed to economic factors.

During the years from 1960 to 1980, numerous charismatic local and national black leaders died prior to their chronological period of highest influence (Washington, 1978). In each instance, the deaths of these leaders (most notably, Malcolm X, Martin Luther King, Jr., Whitney Young, and George Wiley) left organizations without leaders who had similar influence on their followers, supporters, or detractors.

In some instances, while black organizations simultaneously experienced significant increases in funds (occasioned by a leader's death) major funding declines followed in subsequent years (Davis, 1976; Palmer, 1977). At least two organizations (Southern Christian Leadership Conference and Welfare Rights Organization) did not seem to recover and have not produced leaders or movements of the same or similar intensity. The deaths of Howard Thurman, Roy Wilkins, J. Philip Randolph, and Elijah Muhammed also produced profound changes and gaps in their organizations and the overall black movement.

The loss of significant black leaders over the past 20 years has had a profound influence on the number of black followers and supporters and has left black organizations with a leadership crisis (Burns, 1978, and Stogdill, 1974). At no other point in their history have blacks had such a cumulative loss of significant national leadership, covering the ideological spectrum, in such a short period of time. Obviously, this loss, when combined with the incarceration of such activist leaders as Huey Newton, Stokely Carmichael, Rap Brown, and Angela Davis, forces a period of readjustment and realignment of black leadership, followers, organizations, and the thrust of the black movement.

It is this current period of adjustment and realignment that is interpreted as the black leadership crisis. As used here, the term crisis is consistent with the conceptualizations of Caplan (1974), Burns (1978), and Stogdill (1974). A crisis is a phase of development in which there is a potential for enhanced functioning or dysfunction. The postcrisis direction that is taken depends on the capacity of the organism to withstand temporary dislocation and excessive stress and on the extensiveness of its support system. Given the historical strengths of the black movement, one could reasonably predict that this current crisis will be resolved in the direction of an emergence of new black leaders.

The black leadership role has also been influenced by the way in which other related issues have been handled. On one hand, some black leaders have historically been selected by whites (or predominantly white media) and given the responsibility for increasing the participation and compliance of other blacks (followers) with the status quo. Simultaneously, other black leaders were self-appointed or "chosen" through a somewhat informal group process and were charged with the responsibility of devising proactive methods and strategies to challenge the system in which rights were abrogated. The latter leadership posture included the effort to increase the probability that other blacks (followers) would oppose the extant system and contribute to its demise and replacement by a more equitable order. These two widely divergent approaches to the development of black leadership provide the basis for the trichotomous ideological approaches to social change that characterize black movements: assimilation, protest, and nationalism. To some extent, these three philosophical perspectives and tactical idioms continue to be reflected in black leadership styles and organizational climate of the 1980s.

The third factor that influences the performance of black leadership is the adequacy and sources of their financial support. In recent years, the annual revenue of traditional black organizations has not kept pace with inflation (Davis, 1980). In other instances, the organizations have experienced drastic reductions. For example, in the period between 1968 and 1974, the revenue of the SCLC declined by 90% (Davis, 1980). The revenue of the National Association for the Advancement of Colored People (NAACP) declined by 49% within one year (Davis, 1980). While other traditional black organizations have also experienced significant declines in their income, the decline in revenue for nontraditional black organizations (the Black Panthers, U.S., Core, [Student Nonviolent Coordinating Committee] SNCC) has been so drastic that the organizations are near bankruptcy. Besides the National Urban League, none of the traditional or nontraditional black organizations receive support from local charities such as United Way. In addition, black organizations have rarely been able to utilize payroll deduction plans to raise operating capital.

As a result of their fiscal dilemmas, numerous black organizations have been forced to curtail their programs, limit their growth, and concentrate more of the organizations' activities toward generating funds. In addition, their leaders have sought to increase the amount of their annual budget that comes from sources outside the black community. Currently, the majority of the funds to support the Urban League, PUSH, the Black Caucus, and several other black organizations are provided by corporations and government grants (Davis, 1980; Jordan, 1981; Edley, note 6).

Interests of major funding sources influence the positions taken by some black leaders and the programs operated by their organizations. Such interests are likely to result in demands that black leadership use more conciliatory strategies that have a gradual impact on the status quo (Weingarten, note 7). Such gradualism, however, may be incongruent with the type of transformational leadership needed by excluded populations (Burns, 1978). Finally, the tactics employed by black leaders whose finances are provided by groups other than their followers may be inconsistent with those tactics that have been shown to promote social change (Newman et al., 1978). Thus, many black leaders appear to operate in a fiscal/philosophical/tactical dilemma in which the activities supported by their funding sources increase the schism between black leaders and their followers and decrease the probability that the needs (social change) of the followers will be met.

Threats against black leaders are compounded by the absence of viable mechanisms to ensure their physical safety and their economic independence. Given the obvious risks associated with black leadership in this country, such stress may divide the energies and resources of black leadership and direct a significant proportion of these energies away from the movement toward the assurance of a degree of personal safety.

The protracted crisis in black leadership has stimulated black followers and organizations to ponder the efficacy of singular leaders' models and the need for mechanisms for selecting, protecting, and supporting black leadership in the 1980s.

Conclusion

As one looks retrospectively at changes in black communities over the period between 1960 and 1980, two interrelated conclusions can be drawn relative to black movements: on one hand, the myriad of inequities that have historically precipitated black social change movements continue. The form of these inequities has changed: they are less overt while remaining pernicious.

On the other hand, there have been substantive changes in all phases of the black movement: many traditional black leaders have died; alternative leaders have not yet attracted and sustained a following; followers have declined numerically, and in some instances, have attached themselves to organizations whose strategies are more conciliatory than confronting.

The black movement, however, is far from moribund. As long as oppression persists, it is likely that the black social change movement will continue to function, even though it changes form and direction. The question for this decade is not whether the black movement will survive, but what form and ideological direction it will take.

A confluence of societal conditions and events are useful in identifying and predicting the direction the black movement may take in the remaining years of this decade. The most significant condition that seems likely to influence the black movement is the increasing severity of the economic status of the nation in general and the black population in particular.

Rising unemployment for black youths, men, and women will produce increasing pressure for change.

The most significant events thus far in the decade have been the election of Ronald Reagan (with the majority of black support for Jimmy Carter), the defeat of a number of liberal Democratic members of Congress, and the systematic dismantling of a number of programs and policies that provided jobs, financial stability, and access for black populations and organizations.

Without continuing government assistance, and in some instances, protection, there is a high probability that black economic gains will quickly dissipate. Black populations interpret the conservative shift in the country as inimical to their needs. They see civil rights legislation, such as the Voting Rights Act, imperiled, and with that threat fear the loss of constitutional guarantees gained only recently. Without protective legislation, blacks foresee direct peril to the quality of their lives and their very survival. Such predictions portend a significant shift in the dormant state of the black movement.

These economic, psychological, and physical threats against the black population suggest that many needs of blacks remain unmet. According to Stogdill (1974), Burns (1978), and Thompson (1963), the most significant stimulus for leadership arises out of such unmet needs. Given conditions in the black community, one can predict with some assurance that black populations will identify and empower new leadership. Concomitantly, potential leaders will begin to assert their plans and solidify their relationship with potential followers, thus legitimating their leadership position.

A variety of efforts will be made to identify new black leaders. While *Black Enterprise, Ebony,* and other publications have conducted polls to identify black leaders, it seems more probable that new leaders will be those persons, regardless of their ratings in the polls, who can demonstrate that their plans and approaches are useful in meeting the needs of the black population.

I suggest that the black movement will be reformulated in the 1980s because of persistent unmet needs. The new movement will reflect increased participation and greater effort to form supportive coalitions. It is also likely that the black movement will be more characterized by a federation of black organizations and leaders than heretofore. Furthermore, the demands of potential black followers will stimulate new and more assertive leadership whose activities and programs must be aimed at economics as opposed to civil rights and policies. Black followers, however, will have to increase their financial support to ensure that their leaders are less vulnerable to cooptation and physical attack.

Conditions suggest that the new black movement will focus on securing economic rights, access, and employment. While the struggle to secure some level of economic parity and redistribution will take a variety of forms, black leadership and followers would be wise to build on the lessons learned from the progress black populations made in the 1960s. A review of that era shows clearly that there is a direct relationship between the level of black protest and the level of black progress. When black leaders and followers protested the inequities of their lives, conditions improved. When protest and confrontation declined and the movement focused on obtaining political office, as has occurred over the previous decade, black progress declined in direct proportion.

Given these realities, one can predict a resurgence of a black movement characterized by protest, confrontation, economic pressure, and an independent cädre of transformational leadership.

Reference Notes

1. Williams, E. *Voting, Black participation and the right.* Paper presented to the Congressional Black Caucus Legislative Weekend, September 25, 1981.

2. Thompson, G. *Black voter participation.* Paper presented to the Congressional Black Causus Legislative Weekend, September 25, 1981.

3. Brimmer, A. *The road ahead: Outlook for blacks in business.* Paper presented to the Association for the Study of Negro Life and History, October 9, 1972.

4. Bowens, J. *Building viable black organizations.* Unpublished dissertation, Union Graduate School, West, Los Angeles, 1977.

5. Jeff, M. F. *Black on black homicide.* Unpublished dissertation, Tulane University School of Social Work, New Orleans, La., 1979.

6. Edley, C. *Proceedings, Seventh Annual Conference of the Association of Black Foundation Executives.* St. Louis, Missouri, May 1977.

7. Weingarten, S. *Rationale for corporate giving.* Doctoral dissertation, Brandeis University, Waltham, Mass., 1961.

References

ACTION. *Americans volunteer.* Washington, D.C.: U.S. Government Printing Office, 1974.

As charges mount against the FBI. *U.S. News and World Report,* April 5, 1976, 3–34.

Bennett, L. *Before the Mayflower.* Baltimore, Md.: Penguin, 1961.

Brown, T. Tony Brown's Journal. *Journal and Guide,* July 18, 1981, p. 8.

Buckley, W. Are blacks misrepresented by their leaders? *Virginia Pilot,* December 4, 1980, p. A-14.

Burns, J. M. *Leadership.* New York: Harper & Row, 1978.

Caplan, G. *Support systems and community mental health.* New York: Behavioral Publications, 1974.

Clark, R., & Wilkins, R. *Search and destroy*. New York: Harper & Row, 1973.

Clemmons, J. G. Survey of black leadership. *Black Enterprise*, 1980, *11*(1), 53–55.

Coleman, S. *Income disparities between blacks and whites*. Washington, D.C.: Congressional Budget Office, 1977.

Conyers, J. Police violence and riots. *The Black Scholar*, 1981, *12*(1), 2–5.

Coser, L. A. *Masters of sociological thought*. New York: Harcourt, Brace, Jovanovich, 1971.

Davis, K. E. *United Way and the black community in Atlanta*. Washington, D.C.: The Youth Project, 1976.

Davis, K. E. The financial survival of black organizations. In L. Yearwood (Ed.), *Black organizations: Issues on survival techniques*. Washington, D.C.: University Press of America, 1980. Pp. 145–156.

Gayle, A. *Richard Wright: Ordeal of a native son*. New York: Anchor Press/ Doubleday, 1980.

Ginsburg, R. *One hundred years of lynchings*. New York: Lancer Books, 1969.

Hamilton, C. V. On black leadership. In R. Hill (Ed.), *The state of black America*. New York: The National Urban League, 1981. Pp. 239–263.

Hill, R. B. The economic status of black Americans. In R. Hill (Ed.), *The state of black America*. New York: The National Urban League, 1981. Pp. 1–59.

Hinds, L. *Illusions of justice: Human rights violations in the United States*. Iowa City: School of Social Work, 1979.

Jones, L. *From Brown to Boston (Vol. I)*. Metuchen, N.J.: Scarecrow Press, Inc., 1979.

Jordan, V. Alphas make payment on one-million dollar pledge. *Journal and Guide*, August 26, 1981, p. 11.

Kerner, O. *Report of the national advisory commission on civil disorders*. New York: Bantam Books, 1968.

Lenski, G. *The religious factor: A sociological inquiry*. New York: Doubleday, 1961.

Lincoln, C. E. *The Negro pilgrimage in America*. New York: Bantam Books, 1967.

McClory, R. Agent provacateur. *Chicago Magazine*, February 1979, 7–16.

Myrdal, G. *An American dilemma*. New York: Harper & Row, 1944.

Nelson, T. *The right of revolution*. Boston: Beacon Press, 1968.

Newman, D. K., Amedei, N., Barbara, L. C., Day, D., Kruvont, W., & Russell, J. S. *Protest, politics, and prosperity: Black Americans and white institutions 1940–1975*. New York: Pantheon Books, 1978.

Olsen, M. Social and political participation of Negroes. *American Sociological Review*, 1970, *35*, 682–697.

Orum, A. M. A reappraisal of the social and political participation of Negroes. *American Journal of Sociology*, 1966, *72*, 32–46.

Palmer, E. The United Way and the black community in Atlanta. *The Black Scholar*, 1977, *9*(4), 50–61.

Raspberry, W. The black founding fathers meet in Philadelphia. *Virginia Pilot*, December 4, 1980, A-15.

Ross, C., & Lawrence, K. *J. Edgar Hoover's detention plan: The politics of repression in the United States 1939–1976*. Jackson, Miss.: Anti-Repression Resource Team, 1978.

Staples, R. *Introduction to black sociology,* New York: McGraw-Hill, 1976.
Stogdill, R. M. *Handbook on leadership.* New York: The Free Press, 1974.
Theohavis, A. *Spying on Americans.* Philadelphia: Temple University Press, 1978.
Thompson, D. C. *The Negro leadership class.* Englewood Cliffs, N.J.: Prentice-Hall, 1963.
Washington, I. The FBI plot against black leaders. *Essence Magazine,* October 1978, 70–73, 97–104.

17

The Role of Mentors in Developing Leaders for Academe

KATHRYN M. MOORE

Mere unassisted merit advances slowly if—what is not very common—it advances at all.
—Samuel Johnson, Letters, 1741

At most colleges and universities, many persons in key decision-making positions—deans, vice presidents, and presidents—have achieved those positions largely because someone older, wiser, and more powerful saw in them a spark of leadership ability and encouraged them to develop that ability.

Dean D. is such a person. He completed graduate school in the early sixties and took a teaching position at a small, well-respected university. His work was challenging, and he rose to the rank of full professor by the time he was in his mid-thirties. He was content to labor away in his own specialty until, while serving on a search committee for dean of his college, he met President X. Professor D. thought it mattered very much what direction the college leadership took, and he told the president so in impassioned detail. A new dean who met most of his requirements was selected, and Professor D. resumed his other duties. But shortly thereafter he was appointed to a universitywide planning task force chaired by the president. Professor D. liked the work and admired the president's leadership style. They had worked closely together for nearly a year when the president called him in. Professor D. was pleased, but not entirely surprised, when asked to take a special assignment as the president's assistant to direct the implementation of the task force recommendations. Two years later Professor D. became Dean D. He and President X. have already discussed several other administrative openings, including a vice presidency at a neighboring institution. To his amazement, Dean D. now finds himself occasionally thinking about becoming a college president.

As this vignette illustrates, mentors often figure importantly in the development of successful college administrators. Levinson, in his work on the life course of adult men, points to the critical role played by an older man who decides to use his experience and power to assist a young protégé, and Kanter speaks of young executives who receive a boost into the fast lane through direct help from a senior colleague.[1] As a result of recent attention on mentoring, talented and ambitious young people with specific career goals have been encouraged to sally forth in search of a mentor as though they were Sir Pellinore in search of the Questing Beast.

Mentoring is important not only on the personal level but also on the institutional level. While the protégés may look upon the mentor as a career enhancer, institutions such as colleges ought to regard the mentor as a valuable talent scout and trainer. Although mentoring in academe has seldom been a formal procedure for developing administrative talent, it can be, and often is, used for this purpose.

This article describes what mentors do and how this informal, idiosyncratic process can be harnessed more effectively for leadership development in academe. The approach suggested is based on a series of intensive interviews conducted with college and university administrators who had indicated on a prior survey that they had one or more mentors. (The survey indicated that only one-fourth to one-third of college administrators had a mentor.)

Each interview revealed an intense, lasting, and professional relationship that changed the protégé's and, often, the mentor's life. Men and women who hold high-level posts in academic administration in a variety of college and university settings were interviewed. Nearly all had earned a Ph.D. or professional degree; many had been faculty members. Thus, they were entering administration after having acquired other kinds of experience. Most often, however, their mentor was the person who supervised them in their first administrative job.

Typically, the mentors were also highly placed: they were usually deans, provosts, presidents, or other high-level administrators. Several protégés reported having more than one mentor, sometimes at the same time. Since leadership development is usually an informal process in academe, the purpose of the interviews was to discover, first, how a mentor-protégé relationship develops and, second, what the benefits and the costs or risks are for both the mentor and the protégé.

How the Mentor-Protégé Relationship Develops

As Kanter has pointed out, competence or high performance is usually not sufficient to gain power or the attention of the powerful. An aspiring administrator has to contribute something important to the organization beyond his or her normal job responsibilities, something that may involve risk and increase visibility. This extra effort may be accidental, coincidental, or deliberately planned, but it must be authentic; that is, it must be a part of the institution's regular activities. As in the case of Dean D. and others, the protégé may serve on a committee with the mentor and make important contributions; he or she may provide previously unknown expertise or the resolution to a problem for which the mentor is responsible; or he or she may develop as a leader in one sphere, such as faculty, and be invited into the administrative ranks by the mentor. The performance of an important and visible task is the usual first step in the formation of a mentor-protégé relationship. Most often it is the mentor who recognizes the talented protégé.

The second phase consists of a number of additional "tests" that may be constructed by the mentor or that arise naturally as the protégé carries out his or her responsibilities. The protégé may even sense that he or she is being "watched" or tested. Usually this phase does not last long because the mentor is by definition a decision maker who considers himself or herself a reasonably good judge of people. Committee assignments, too, can be made with the intent of spotting and nourishing new talent.

The next phase in the development of the mentor-protégé relationship begins when the mentor chooses the protégé to work closely with him or her. The recruitment is selective and specific. Generally the protégé is given a lesser role than the mentor's but one that requires close, often daily, contact with the mentor. (A staff role is ideally suited for this purpose.) Occasionally, the mentor selects the protégé for a major role before the relationship has really developed. This approach is risky for the mentor and usually means the protégé comes highly recommended by trusted colleagues or has developed a credible leadership role in another area of the institution. A high appointment often has a "star-making" quality about it—like Jane Russell being discovered at the Hollywood lunch counter. One protégé with virtually no prior administrative experience moved from a midlevel faculty post to chief academic officer at the behest of the mentor, who was president of the institution.

Such a spectacular rise is less and less likely given the current situation in academe, particularly in light of affirmative action requirements.

But even the invitation to work with the mentor in a lesser capacity usually means increased prestige and status for the protégé. Indeed, the appointment is usually sufficiently different and exciting that the protégé feels—and is seen—as being specially chosen. The power of the selection process is such that, in the words of the protégés, "There is a sense of having hands laid on" and "It is like an ordination." The new appointment has the effect of moving the protégé into the inner circle, not necessarily as a full-fledged member in his or her own right, but under the guise and protection of the mentor.

The competence the protégé is seeking to develop under the mentor's tutelage concerns both doing and being. First, the protégé is given the opportunity to see his or her college or university from the vantage point of the mentor and the inner circle, and to contribute to the institution at that level. This opportunity is special in part because it comes before the time the protégé might reasonably have expected it and at a position level higher than he or she may have anticipated achieving. The mentor's vantage point allows the protégé to see "the big picture," as one person described it, and gives access to the knowledge that flows into and out of the inner circle. Often this information is privileged, special, or even secret. Thus, subtly and not so subtly, the protégé is taken into the confidence of the mentor and the inner circle and so becomes accepted by them.

The protégé is put to work on the tasks assigned by the mentor and the leadership group. The work is real, not an exercise invented for the protégé, although it is not without an element of trail or testing. One protégé who worked with a college vice president described the work: "I was a good staff person: I got things done; I tried out ideas; I filled holes. My ability to write complemented his needs. I listened and I learned a lot. He took the heat, but he got a lot of the work." The mentor calls forth performance from the protégé and assess it for its value or contribution to the college.

Moreover, the protégé becomes the object of work by both himself or herself and the mentor; in other words, the protégé is developed. As one protégé said, "Sometimes we need someone outside ourselves to help us take a look at ourselves, to push us. The mentor says, 'You ought to do this. I'll show you how.' " Another person remarked, "Something special comes from interacting with people who are interested in your career." And another, "It's important for someone to tell you you're on the right track. You feel obligated to keep trying."

The work of developing the protégé takes many forms, depending on the abilities and values of both mentor and protégé. This learning encompasses mundane issues (such as how to dress or how to travel) as well as more important matters—the facts of internal academic politics, and a sense of continuity about the institution and its people. Several protégés reported that they learned how to work with people, especially difficult people, how to control their anger, how to pick their battles, how to judge people, and how to analyze all dimensions of a problem. One person summarized the mentor's influence on his own administrative style: "I always think, What would *he* do? Looking at the issue in this way makes me more objective."

Perhaps the most important thing a mentor does for the protégé is assist in career advancement.[2] The mentor usually trains a protégé with the intention of helping him or her secure a higher position. Some mentors are quite open and specific about their goals for their protégés, and their protégés know they are being groomed for the position of president, provost, or dean. Other mentors leave the exact position open but imply it will be an important one. Having a tangible goal makes creating a strategy to accomplish the goal a logical next step, and many protégés felt their mentors did have a strategy in mind. Such strategy commonly seems to have two components: developing contacts and developing competence.

Developing Contacts: The Colleague System

Numerous researchers have pointed to the critical importance of colleague systems in the professions.[3] Lawyers, doctors, and academicians have all developed important ways of communicating with one another about their specialties, their performance and contributions, and the members themselves. Through these "invisible colleges," as they are sometimes called, professionals carry on important, if covert, work.

Academic administrators are often similarly organized on a campus or even across institutions by virtue of their shared roles, norms, and interests. The labels applied to the inner circle of administrators at an institution—"Old Main types," the "president's kitchen cabinet," the "dean's henchmen" or, in larger terms, "the old-boy network"—usually contain more than a grain of truth. And, indeed, this implied professional homogeneity is generally founded not only on the attributes necessary to perform the common task, but also on similarity of attitudes and behaviors as well as similarity of sex, ethnic origin, and religion.

Such colleague systems are the means by which the mentor gains influence beyond his or her own instituion. The promise of contacts through the mentor is often crucial for the protégé and helps diffuse much of the tension and emotional baggage of the relationship. In particular, the pressure to take the obvious next step—namely, to succeed the mentor—is decreased, thereby making the protégé potentially more useful to the broader organization. The colleague network also allows mentors to expand their sphere of influence, although perhaps at the risk of some loss of power, but many mentors feel that giving up the certain power of naming their own successor for the wider power of placing several protégés in other locations is a satisfactory trade-off. Administrators are no less likely to seek to place protégés than are faculty members. Many presidents, like many senior professors, pride themselves on where their bright, young students have gone and what high positions they have achieved.

The colleague system is centered on one particular kind of relationship, namely, that of professional contemporaries and peers, often former classmates. Shapiro and associates point out that a principal advantage of "peer pals" (the author's term) is helping one another, as young beginners in a profession, learn their role.[4] In the process of sharing their resources and learning, the novices develop a sense of colleagueship that they carry with them as they build their careers. Eventually, when a member of the cohort becomes a mentor to a younger colleague and seeks placement or other assistance for him or her, the mentor can call on colleagues who are former "peer pals." These old and longstanding relationships among peers make up a large part of many mentors' networks. The bonds of this colleagueship are cemented with feelings of friendship and loyalty even though the colleagues may be competing professionally. Several of the protégés interviewed remarked on their mentors' ability to speak fondly of colleagues with whom they competed intensely. This insight into friendly combat proved helpful to the protégés in developing their own competitive styles.

The inner circles of leadership in an organization often function in ways similar to colleague systems. Almost by definition these inner circles are small groups bounded by the constraints of personal knowledge and shared experience. Outsiders are outsiders not so much because of the inner circle's overt desire to be exclusive, but rather because the outsiders do not share a common bond. Within the cohort, that bond is a specific common past; within the leadership circle, it is also a specific common responsibility or role.

One of the ways mentors strive to include protégés in the inner circle is to share with them the informal history of the group and its members and to explain in-jokes and informal norms. By explaining the group's history and the informal culture, the mentor is not simply recounting the past as a series of colorful but useless anecdotes; the past has meaning and potency for the group members primarily as an account of the ways of knowing one another and of establishing trust. Protégés make a serious mistake if they do not take this past-sharing seriously, for this knowledge can be a means of making connections with their mentor's colleagues.

Special Problems Confronting Minorities and Women

Groups in which most of the members share a common bond are not likely to accept persons who do not share the similarities noted earlier. Minority group members and women may have particular difficulties in being selected as protégés. Once selected, they may be subjected to additional stresses. Because a woman is frequently the only female in an all-male inner circle, she may become tagged as the token female. Kanter, Epstein, and others have described quite cogently the dynamics of tokenism in professional settings.[5] The circumstances that help create the protégé-mentor relationship are the same for both men and women, but the woman's status as a token often leads to different results. In particular, the sense of specialness, of being exceptional, that makes a woman protégé feel good about being recognized and selected may also cause her to feel or be treated as though she were an exception to other women, thereby encouraging her to participate in keeping other women out of the group. Moreover, the additional performance demands of being "the only" was often cited by minority and female protégés as a reason why they were not willing to function as mentors themselves, at least in the short run.

Making Contacts

All the mentors helped arrange opportunities for protégés to make contacts and gain visibility with important colleagues, and the effort was usually made deliberately, consciously, and conscientiously. The mentors took their protégés with them to meetings or sent them in their place. They made introductions, wrote letters of nomination or recommendations, and arranged for protégés to receive assistance from colleagues whom they felt the protégés should know or work with. Other teachers and friends may perform these activities for a fledgling professional, but they do not do so with the same forethought or consistency as would a mentor.

Sometimes the mentor explained why a particular meeting or opportunity was being arranged, but the clear assumption of all the protégés was that whatever the mentor arranged would help their careers, at least in the long run. Few seemed to be aware, much less concerned, if the mentor had a personal career strategy to which the protégé's advancement contributed. Most protégés, in fact, were so focused on their own careers that they tended not to be aware of their role in the mentor's game plan or, indeed, how they might be part of an even larger organizational plan.

This narrowness of focus sometimes led to serious difficulties. Particularly sharp criticism was expressed by protégés who, when they turned down an opportunity or position the mentor helped them get, discovered that the mentor was more concerned about the effect their action would have on his or her own status and prestige than whether the position was right for them. In one case, the mentor was so disappointed that he refused to recommend the protégé for any other jobs. The protégé felt the mentor cared little for her own needs but was merely interested in placing another one of "his people" in a prestigious job. "He prided himself on his stable of winners," she said, "and didn't much care for horses with minds of their own."

If the relationship is successful, however, the protégé and mentor can build considerable rapport. They may often be viewed as a team or even as one entity. Several protégés discussed the openness they shared with the mentor and their sense of identification with the mentor (what one person called an "affinity"). Levinson asserts the mentor-protégé relationship is a love relationship.[6] Yet whether or not deep affection exists between the two, the protégé usually feels a sense of loyalty, gratitude, and, often, obligation. Many protégés described their relationship with the mentor in parental terms: "I was like a second son." "He was like a father to me." "I am obligated to him in the same way I am to my parents to do well." The mentors appear to reciprocate many of these same feelings. One mentor summarized his confidence in his protégé: "She speaks for me, and everyone knows it."

Developing Competence: Standards, Trust, and Control

The protégé's development as a leader is seldom direct. The mentor teaches primarily through indirection or by example. Placing the protégé in a learning situation is a common technique. As Epstein has pointed out, mentors usually have three jobs: (1) to see that the protégé knows the standards; (2) to develop knowledge about and trust in the protégé; and (3) to maintain a part in, if not control of, the leadership selection process.[7]

Standards in this context refers to norms of performance and belief that use formal regulations or rules simply as points of departure. Academe is replete with unwritten norms of professional behavior, especially among faculty. The inner circle of administrators may also have generated or adopted a set of expectations for behavior and attitudes among themselves that is part of the institutional culture and essential to the group itself. These expectations may be referred to as "the Siwash way" or the "Wiley philosophy." The leadership group is often a principal custodian of an institutional saga or may become a leadership "cult" if the chief executive is particularly charismatic or has held the position for a long time. The protégé learns what the culture is and so learns how things are done or not done at Siwash.

From the mentor, protégés also learn to meet high requirements for performance. Presumably they could learn low ones as well, but, for the most part, the protégés inverviewed spoke admiringly of the pace and workload of their mentors and clearly judged their own performance by that standard. Many indicated they had adopted higher standards as a result of the mentor's influence. Protégés from the faculty ranks commented on the long hours administrators often work; they came to realize that for many administrators ceremonial and social occasions are usually business occasions as well. By observing the expectations the mentor sets for those reporting to him or her, protégés learn to establish standards for a group and how to deal with those who meet these standards and those who don't. The protégé also learns that establishing performance standards is a leader's responsibility.

Finally, the mentor may stimulate or actively assist the protégé to develop a personal ethic. Most mentors assume their way of behaving is worth learning, or else they would not take on a protégé. The protégé may disagree with the mentor's principles openly or covertly, but the protégé clearly learns by comparing his or her own principles with the mentor's. Exact agreement is often not what the mentor is seeking in any case, despite the pressure a protégé may sometimes feel to conform. Rather, the mentor may be striving to enable the protégé to develop and articulate his or her own standards for making decisions and taking stands.

Like the most primitive villagers, the inner circle of administrative leaders often display a similar sense of tribal loyalty. They build trust and rely on trust among one another so that they can continue to function efficiently and survive. Developing trust is crucial in the mentor-protégé relationship as well, and the protégé must prove himself or herself trustworthy. In simpler civilizations, candidates for leadership would be given specific tasks to test their courage, competence, and trustworthiness. In our complex society and in most of our institutions, this basic process is often disguised or encapsulated within activities with multiple functions. But a basic purpose of the work the protégé performs, in addition to developing the protégé's competencies, is to provide the mentor (and other administrators) with opportunities to test the protégé, to observe how he or she responds in crisis or conflict or under multiple pressures.

Often the mentor has no preconceived notion of how the protégé *ought* to respond within a certain range of competent performance, but rather the mentor is more interested in *how* the protégé responds. Does she get angry and lose her temper, or sulk and grow silent? The mentor knows something the protégé does not, namely, that resolving a particular issue often is less important than the kind of response the protégé is likely to give when a similar issue arises. In this way, then, the mentor gains useful knowledge about the protégé. On occasion the mentor may attempt to correct or instruct the protégé if his or her typical response does not seem to be productive. For example, several protégés interviewed (especially men) had clearly been coached by their mentors about their temper: "I was told it was okay to argue, but I should get mad at my own convenience"; "He taught me how to control my anger and pick my battles"; "I was too quick on the trigger, but I learned to be more cautious."

At times the protégés expressed frustration that their mentors did not teach them more, or were too subtle and indirect. However, the mentors clearly were operating, not to teach the protégés directly (as they expected), but to awaken, test, or exercise their talents. Implicit in this approach is a respect on the mentor's part for the particular talents or "charisma" of the protégé.[8] Thus, while the protégés might learn from example, most mentors prefer not to instruct directly except when absolutely necessary because aspiring leaders must learn to know themselves and to govern by themselves. Through such competencies, a leader gains self-confidence and begins to inspire trust.

In discussing corporate leadership development, Jennings has pointed out that "the central concern of the sponsor who must nominate a successor is what the subordinate will do when he holds the reins in his own hand."[9] He asserts that trust and its subcomponent, predictability, are essential in persons who are selected to lead an organization. But because of the power configuration in the mentor-protégé relationship, the work of trust building is primarily the protégé's. The mentor's own trustworthiness is generally not in question. Ultimately, the mentor can be untrustworthy in regard to the protégé without losing his or her reputation or power. A mentor who has been betrayed can "punish" the protégé, whereas the protégé who has been betrayed cannot "punish" the mentor. Protégés who felt they had been betrayed tended to adopt one of two strategies: they severed the relationship with the mentor, thereby sometimes penalizing themselves more than the mentor; or they endured the relationship but vowed that when they came to power (*a*) they would get even with the mentor personally; or (*b*) they would never do the same thing to others as their mentor had done to them (we called these the Slightly Tarnished Golden Rules of Mentoring).

Members of leadership groups are often engaged in making decisions involving high stakes for the colleges or universities they serve, their own careers and reputations, and those of people dependent on them. Mistakes can be extremely costly. In particular, leaders do not want to be mistaken when they delegate responsibilities or when they recommend a person for a major responsibility. To establish the protégé's predictability, the mentor will seek opportunities to judge the protégé's "ability to handle delicate administrative circumstances with good judgment and throughness."[10] If the protégé has major responsibilities, the mentor can easily observe him or her in action. If, however, the protégé has no such responsibilities, the mentor may have to arrange some opportunities by placing the protégé in charge of task forces, committees, or particular decision areas. Here the power of the mentor's position is crucial: without the mentor's ability to arrange these opportunities, the protégé may not benefit as much as possible from the relationship nor might the mentor learn as much as he or she should. By observing the protégé's performance, the mentor learns whether he or she can confidently defend and justify the protégé's decisions.

Leadership in academe is surely as competitive and political as in any other arena. Woodrow Wilson reportedly once said that he learned about politics from the faculty at Princeton and then went to Washington to practice among the amateurs. Sometimes the other members of the leadership group resist the inclusion of the protégé; sometimes they question the tasks assigned to the protégé or contest the protégé's larger responsibilities. Therefore, the mentor must be both willing and able to defend the protégé.

Both formal and informal judgments about protégés and their performance are a continual responsibility of the leadership group. For this reason the process of trust building is so important. The mentor must know the protégé well in order to defend him or her. The mentor must make a personal judgment about the quality and potential of the protégé's contributions and must know how and in what ways he or she can contribute. Finally, the mentor must believe that the person is worth fighting for; that is, the mentor must *care* about what happens to the protégé, at least professionally. Ultimately, a mentor must be willing, if necessary, to put his or her own reputation on the line for the protégé's sake.

Nearly all protégés interviewed reported that their mentors had defended them or fought for them at some time. Some said their mentors had quite literally saved their jobs or had backed crucial decisions for their sake. One protégé told how his mentor saved his job when, as "a brash young Turk," he had mightily offended the board of trustees. He firmly believed that without his mentor's intervention, he would not be there today. The mentor's belief in and support for the protégé is probably the most crucial aspect of the learning experience for the protégé. Knowledge of such support clearly gives the protégé confidence and self-esteem, not to mention a sense of loyalty.

Robert Frost once said, "Freedom is working easy in the harness." Leaders do work in a harness of social control, but this control is more subtle than their followers know. The mentor's job is to channel the protégé's talent, energy, and drive without destroying these attributes. Once a protégé is given a major leadership role, he or she will have the three most valued and valuable assets a leader can possess: power, resources, and opportunity. In a leadership role the protégé will be less controllable than controlling. Therefore, before allowing a protégé to lead, the responsible mentor will make sure the protégé knows the standards, can be trusted to behave responsibly given those standards, and will act in his or her own way to assure the continuity of the institution and its inner circle. Given these expectations and the high stakes involved, it is not surprising that the mentoring experience itself is uncommon or that it seldom totally succeeds.

Implementing a Formal Administrative Program and Setting Goals

Recently several colleges and universities have expressed interest in establishing mentor programs to aid in the identification and development of promising administrators; some institutions have already established such programs.

From the interviews with administrator protégés and mentors, at least seven elements emerged that ought to be included in any attempt to formalize the normally informal and highly idiosyncratic process.

1. *Accessibility.* Provide for frequent (daily) interaction between mentor and protégés in real work settings, dealing with real problems.

2. *Visibility.* Provide opportunities for protégés to work with other high-level leaders inside and outside the institution and to serve in leadership roles themselves.

3. *Feedback.* Insist that protégés receive careful feedback on their strengths and weaknesses. Correction is as important as praise if the protégé's talents are to be developed.

4. *Recognition.* Sound mentoring requires commitment, time, and skill. Not everyone can or should be a mentor. But when mentoring is done well, its value to the institution and to the protégé deserves special (but not necessarily public) acknowledgement and support.

5. *Allowance for failure.* The intense, personal nature of such relationships can foster uncomfortable situations. Monitor the process and

allow opportunities for both mentor and protégé to bow out gracefully, with their integrity preserved. But do not act too quickly: growth often comes through difficulty.

6. *Openness.* When left to their own devices, mentors often select from a narrow range of persons who possess characteristics similar to their own. A mentor program can correct this tendency by insisting that both mentors and protégés be drawn from diverse pools of talented people.

7. *Commitment.* Mentors, protégés, and their institutions must believe that good can come out of such a relationship and willingly invest themselves in the commitment.

The process of developing a continuing supply of leadership talent is an unending task. Genuine, charismatic leadership talent is rare, but trustworthy talent can be developed. Leaders naturally attempt to maintain their sources of power and influence as long as possible. Thus, mentoring is one way, however imperfect, by which a single leader or a leadership group can help assure continuity and pass on to the next generation a particular brand of leadership for the university.

From the protégé's viewpoint, the process involves a special kind of socialization for leadership roles. From the mentor's viewpoint, the process is one of extending and expanding personal efficacy and influence. And from the institution's viewpoint the process is one of organizing and controlling old and new talent for use by the whole. For all parties the risks are great, but so are the results.

Notes

1. Daniel J. Levinson, *The Seasons of a Man's Life* (New York: Alfred A. Knopf, 1978); Rosabeth Moss Kanter, *Men and Women of the Corporation* (New York: Basic Books, 1977).

2. See Jeanne J. Speizer, "Role Models, Mentors, and Sponsors: The Elusive Concepts," *Signs*, Summer 1981, pp. 692–712.

3. See Stanton Wheeler, "The Structure of Formally Organized Socialization Settings," in *Socialization after Childhood*, eds. Orville Brim, Jr., and Stanton Wheeler (New York: Wiley and Sons, 1966), pp. 53–116; Theodore D. Kemper, "Reference Groups, Socialization, and Achievement," *American Sociological Review*, vol. 33, no. 1, pp. 31–45; Gerald R. Roche, "Much Ado about Mentors," *Harvard Business Review*, January 1979, pp. 14–28; and Eliza Collins and Patricia Scott, "Everyone Who Makes It Has a Mentor," *Harvard Business Review*, July-August 1978, pp. 89–101.

4. Eileen C. Shapiro, Florence P. Haseltine, and Mary P. Rose, "Moving Up: Role Models, Mentors, and the Patron System," *Sloan Management Review*, Spring 1978, pp. 51–58.

5. See Kanter and Cynthia Fuchs Epstein, "Encountering the Male Establishment: Sex-Status Limits on Women's Careers in the Professions," *American Journal of Sociology*, vol. 75, no. 6, pp. 965–82.

6. Levinson, p. 235.

7. Epstein, p. 969ff.

8. See Max Weber, *The Theory of Social and Economic Organization*, ed. and trans. Talcott Parsons (New York: Free Press, 1947).

9. Eugene Emerson Jennings, *Routes to the Executive Suite* (New York: McGraw-Hill, 1971), p. 168.

10. Ibid., p. 170.

18

Leadership:
A Return to Basics

General EDWARD C. MEYER

When I became chief of staff, I set two personal goals for myself. The first was to ensure that the Army was continually prepared to go to war, and the second was to create a climate in which each individual member could find personal meaning and fulfillment. It is my belief that only by attainment of the second goal will we ensure the first.

The most modern equipment in the world is useless without motivated individuals, willingly drilled into cohesive unit organizations by sound leadership at all levels. Expert planning, Department of the Army pamphlets, regulations and field manuals will not of themselves rescue the disaffected soldier from apathetic performance of his or her duty. Neither the soldier nor his comrades will survive the first challenge of either the modern world or of the battlefield outside a climate of active and concerned leadership. Because we are a community, a way of life, we cannot isolate our concern to only one of these environments. Our commitment must be complete if we expect dedication returned in kind.

The clear linkage is that our ability to go to war hinges critically on the quality of leadership within the US Army; leadership, what James MacGregor Burns called "one of the most observed and least understood phenomena on earth."[1]

Napoleon listed 115 contributing qualities in trying to define the essentials of leadership. We have no way of knowing if his description was complete at number 115 or if he was otherwise distracted. Some authorities focus on three, five or 10 aspects, while others, perhaps more wisely, begin and end their list with only one, or describe broad theories about leadership. None of these efforts is complete, yet none of them

Reprinted by permission from *Military Review*, LX:7 (July 1980), pp. 4–9.

is useless either, if they assist the professional who already has a firm grasp on fundamentals to better understand and practice leadership.

Need for a Renaissance

Is there a need for a renaissance in the art of military leadership today? I think so. Not because I sense an Army starved for adequate example, but because the circumstances have been such over the past several decades that confusing models vie for attention. Some are woefully deficient and totally inappropriate for tomorrow's battlefield.

We need to discuss openly the fact that we have been lavish in our rewards to those who have demonstrated excellence in sophisticated business and management techniques. These talents are worthwhile to a leader, but, of themselves, they are not leadership. We need to discuss openly the impact that six-month command tours in Vietnam may have had on the perception of a commander's commitment. Under the circumstances of that war, it may have been unavoidable. In the process, have we eroded essential values?

We need to recognize that we have lived through an era in which this country enjoyed massive nuclear superiority. Previously, it was possible to accept less than optimal decisions in the certainty that very few things relating to land forces could be of critical consequence. That is, given our massive, nuclear advantage, only a madman would have challenged us directly. That is no longer the case. Today, we need sensitivity and backbone beyond that which the past several decades have demanded.

We need a renaissance in the art and practice of leadership because this country cannot suffer through the same agonies in a future mobilization which time permitted us to correct the last time around.

The early maneuvers of 1940 turned a harsh spotlight on the then current "training weaknesses of the Army: lack of equipment, poor minor tactics, *lack of basic leadership in many units, and some inept command leadership by officers of high rank."* [2]

This despite the pre-1940 emphasis of the Regular Army on leadership, administration and technical skills. What was uncovered was a proficient relationship between the leader and the led, rooted in peacetime administration—but insufficiently developed to withstand the rigor of combat.

General George Marshall's strategy was to correct the weakness "by arduous training and by the more drastic solution of eliminating the unfit." [3] We are precisely on that track today. But the climate is somehow different. The leader of the 1940s was training to go to war with his unit for the duration. There was no certainty that at some point he would be plucked out of his situation in adherence to a rigid career development pattern. His career extended only to the bounds of developing his unit so it could survive in combat. He would likely see it through there or at an echelon or two above that unit, still dependent upon its continued excellence.

We would be wrong today to invoke a "for the duration" mentality which excluded preparing the force for its future. That is an essential. But we need to root out those situations where such progression denies full loyalty and devotion to the soldier and the unit.

Despite some of its narrowness, for there was only one way, "the Army way," the Army of World War II was a professional force of immense energy whose traditions were strong and whose values were clear. Service parochialism and narrowness helped to spawn a revolution under Robert McNamara in the early 1960s which sought to rationalize interservice resource demands by the adoption or adaptation of business-oriented management techniques. The intent was that the Department of Defense could and should operate as effectively and efficiently as private enterprise.

Ironically, some of the techniques were ones developed by the military during World War II to achieve high-priority goals in specific sectors of our war machine (strategic bombing, weapons development, anti-submarine warfare).

At no time did anyone say, "Let's have an Army of managers—leaders are passé." However, once the system became firmly entrenched, its power and grasp implied to many that the newly arrived technocrat was an attractive alternative career model. Imperceptibly at first, then with a rush, the traditional focus of leadership slipped for many into the abyss as increasing emphasis was placed on management and specialization. Excellence in its theories and principles became for many an alternative to leadership. Unfortunately forgotten was the fact that employees of Sears Roebuck and Company or General Motors Corporation were not asked to give up their lives for corporate cost-effectiveness!

Leadership and management are neither synonomous nor interchangeable. Clearly, good civilian managers must lead, and good military leaders must manage. Both qualities are essential to success. The size and complexity of today's Army, given no overabundance of resources, requires the use of managerial techniques. Their use is essential if we are to maintain and improve our posture.

Accordingly, such training and practice are important. But the leader must know when and how to apply them, never forgetting that the purpose of an Army is to fight. And, to fight effectively, it must be led. Managers can put the most modern and well-equipped force into the

226   Gen. Edward C. Meyer

field. They cannot, however, *manage* an infantry unit through training or *manage* it up a hill into enemy fire to seize an objective.

Two Lessons

In this context, two lessons are important—first, techniques which work well for the management of resources may prove disastrous when substituted for leadership on the battlefield. Conversely, techniques which work well for the battlefield may prove disastrous when substituted for management. Management and leadership are coequally important—not substitutes for one another.

Strong personal leadership is as necessary today as at anytime in our history. That which soldiers are willing to sacrifice their lives for—loyalty, team spirit, morale, trust and confidence—cannot be infused by managing. The attention we need to invest in our soldiers far exceeds that which is possible through any centralized management system. To the degree that such systems assist efficient operation, they are good. To the degree that they interfere with essential relationships between the unit and its leader, they are disruptive. Management techniques have limitations which leaders need to identify and curb to preclude destructive side effects.

Just as overmanagement can be the death of an Army, so can undermanagement which deprives units of essential resources. Leaders need to be active to identify either extreme, for either can impact on the ultimate success of comitted forces.

The kind of leadership we need is founded upon consideration and respect for the soldier. That thought is not new. Over 400 years ago, Machiavelli's prince was taught that: ". . . in order to retain his fidelity [he] ought to think of his minister, honoring and enriching him, doing him kindness, and conferring upon him honors and giving him responsible tasks. . . ."[4]

Repeated through the ages by others, the message—like an overworked popular recording—may have lost its freshness. Societally accustomed as we are to discarding the old for the cleverness of the new, we weary of redundancy and look for the new buzz word, the new turn of phrase: VOLAR (Volunteer Army), DIMES (Defense Integrated Management Engineering Systems), Zero Defects, Management by Objective, Organizational Effectiveness, and so forth. Again, let me remind you, these are all good management-related programs, but not if they replace the essence of leadership essential to an effective Army.

There are no tricks or gimmicks in the watchwords of General John M. Schofield, and I commend them to you:

The one mode or the other of dealing with subordinates springs from a corresponding spirit in the breast of the commander. He who feels the respect which is due to others cannot fail to inspire in them regard for himself, while he who feels, and hence manifests, disrespect toward others, especially his inferiors, cannot fail to inspire hatred against himself.[5]

This summation of leadership leaves the reader to supply his personal "tag line." The premise involves a cultivated feeling by the leader for the attitudes, needs, desires, ambitions and disappointments of the soldier—without which no real communication can exist.

Leaders cannot, must not, bind themselves to a one-answer, one-method scientology. They must discover the method best suited to motivate and employ *each* soldier. Time and one's earnest interest are necessary regardless of method. The end result is an organization which is ready and willing to follow despite hardship or adversity.

In our business, these are much more prevalent than elsewhere in our society. There are the obvious hardships associated with battle; there are also the hardships of peacetime duty—coping economically in a foreign land, coping with old and run-down facilities, coping with constraints on training resources, to name a few. All these will be accepted and creatively overcome by units whose members sense their leader's genuine interest and commitment to their welfare. Abraham Lincoln said that "You can't fool all the people all of the time."[6] To that, I would add that *you cannot fool a soldier anytime!* The leader who tries chooses a hazardous path.

Types of Leadership

How concern and respect are manifested by each of us is the essence of leadership. Just as there are two types of diamonds—gem and industrial quality—there are two types of leadership. The first type, the gem quality, is functional if we only desire our leadership to appear beautiful. The second, or industrial quality, though not cleaved, faceted and polished, is the more functional because its uses are creative. The Army's need is for the industrial quality, the creative quality of leadership.

Just as the diamond requires three properties for its formation—carbon, heat and pressure—successful leaders require the interaction of three properties—character, knowledge and application.

Like carbon to the diamond, character is the basic quality of the leader. It is embodied in the one who, in General Bradley's words, "has high ideals, who stands by them, and who can be trusted absolutely."[7]

Character is an engrained principle expressed consciously and unconsciously to subordinates, superiors and peers alike—honesty, loyalty, courage, self-confidence, humility and self-sacrifice. Its expression to all audiences must ring with authenticity.

But as carbon alone does not create a diamond, neither can character alone create a leader. The diamond needs heat. Man needs knowledge, study and preparation. The novice leader may possess the honesty and decisiveness of a General Marshall or Patton, but, if he or she lacks the requisite knowledge, there is no bench mark from which that character can take form. A leader must be able to choose the harder right instead of the easier wrong, as it says in the Cadet Prayer, but the distinction cannot be made in practice unless the leader possesses knowledge equal to the situation.

General Patton, once accused of making snap decisions, replied: "I've been studying the art of war for forty-odd years. When a surgeon decides in the course of an operation to change its objective ... he is not making a snap decision but one based on knowledge, experience and training. So am I."[8]

To lead, you must know your soldiers, yourself and your profession.

The third property, pressure—acting in conjunction with carbon and heat—forms the diamond. Similarly, one's character, attended by knowledge, blooms through *application* to produce a leader.

Generally, this is expressed through teaching or training—grooming and shaping people and things into smoothly functioning units. It takes many forms. It begins by setting the example and the day-to-day development of subordinates by giving distinct, challenging tasks and allowing free exercise of responsibility to accomplish the task. It extends through tactical drill, weapons operation and maintenance, operational planning, resource management, and so forth. Finally, it is the imparting of knowledge to superiors, for *they* must digest the whole of their organizations and rely increasingly on judgments from below.

Individual Growth

These three properties, brought together, form, like the industrial diamond, a hard, durable creative leader. As the industrial stone is used to cut glass, drill for petroleum products and even for creation of the brilliant gem diamond, leadership works to create cohesive, ready, viable units through a climate which expresses itself in its concern for the growth of the individual.

Growth in a single dimension, that limited to excellence in applied military skills, is only part of the challenge to today's leadership. Alone, it runs the risk of buying single-dimensioned commitment. Full dedication comes by providing a basis for rounded individual development pertinent to survival in life in its broadest aspects.

Today's soldiers seek to become capable citizens across the four critical dimensions of man. The Army, through its leaders, can assist their development mentally, physically, spiritually and socially, equipping them for survival in and out of uniform. Each soldier meaningfully assisted toward development as a whole man, a whole person, is more likely to respond with his or her full commitment.

The leader who chooses to ignore the soldier's search for individual growth may reap a bitter fruit of disillusionment, discontent and listlessness. If we, instead, reach out to touch each soldier—to meet needs and assist in working toward the goal of becoming a "whole person"— we will have bridged the essential needs of the individual to find not only the means of coming together into an effective unit, but the means of "holding together."

Then, we will have effected a tool capable of fulfilling the purpose for which we exist: our ability to go to war. We can then hopefully influence the decision of those who might be tempted to challenge our nation.

As with all scientific and artistic endeavors, one begins with the basics. We must get back to the established basics of leadership. They provide the foundation from which our Army draws its inspiration, its capability and, ultimately, its effectiveness.

Notes

1. James MacGregor Burns, *Leadership*, Harper & Row Publishers Inc., N.Y., 1978, p. 2.

2. Department of the Army Pamphlet 20-212, *History of Military Mobilization in the United States Army, 1775–1945*, by Lieutenant Colonel Marvin A. Kreidberg and First Lieutenant Merton G. Henry, Department of the Army, Washington, D. C., 1956, p. 606.

3. Ibid.

4. Niccolo di Bernardo Machiavelli, *The Prince*, 1513.

5. Speech by General John M. Schofield to the Corps of Cadets, U.S. Military Academy, West Point.

6. Lincoln to a caller at the White House, in Alexander K. McClure, *Lincoln's Yarns and Stories*, J. C. Winston Co., Chicago, Ill., 1904, p. 24.

7. General of the Army Omar N. Bradley, "Leadership," *Parameters*, Winter 1972, p. 7.

8. Edgar F. Puryear, *Nineteen Stars*, Green Publishers Inc., Orange, Va., 1971, p. 382.

Part 4

LEADERSHIP:
A PERSONAL QUALITY

Clearly, the importance of certain leader traits should not be understated; at the same time, the significance of those traits is dependent upon the specific leadership situation. Personality issues are important elements in our lives whether we are followers or leaders. Many researchers have studied motivations, values, and skills in an attempt to link traits of successful leader behavior to selected situations where leadership is called for. In addition, aspects of personality are being discovered that may be pivotal to the influence processes attributed to effective leadership.

Our main concern is with individual differences—those traits that make us unique human beings. Whatever the traits may be that are associated with good leadership, there are some overriding truths that cannot be ignored: First, generic stereotypes are inappropriate, as well as improbable. Second, where one person succeeds as a leader others may easily fail, even though their backgrounds and life experiences are similar. Third, timing or knowing when to act is as important as possessing success-linked traits; being in the right place at the right time can be a matter of luck or it can be the result of careful planning. Fourth, the things we admire most in a person may or may not be a factor in their success as a leader.

In Chapter 19, Edwin Hollander and Jan Yoder review the literature in an attempt to compare men and women as leaders, considering issues such as leader style, situational influences, and leader effectiveness. The authors conclude that leadership historically has been a masculine concept, and as women are increasingly assuming leadership roles in politics, business, education, and the armed forces, it is important for us to know more about gender-related similarities and differences in leadership behavior. Too often, according to the authors, we use sex role stereotypes as if they were actual behaviors because we fail to see the behavior of women as a function of a particular context rather then as a characteristic of gender.

In a similar vein, Warren Bennis declares in "False Grit" (Chapter 20) that the idea that one has to be macho to get ahead in today's organizations is just that—false grit. He argues that it is time to move beyond sex roles and sex differences to a more sophisticated understanding of women and men in organizations. We must recognize the organization as a culture that governs behavior. Success depends greatly upon being able to diagnose the organizational culture and then develop the flexibility to respond and initiate within that structure; there is nothing sex-related about it. It is a grave error, according to Bennis, to fall into the trap of attributing leadership success to toughness or softness, assertiveness or sensitivity, masculinity or femininity, or to any other set of arbitrary criteria. As more women assume critical leadership roles, he hopes that such stereotypes will disappear.

In "Charismatic and Consensus Leaders: A Psychological Comparison" (Chapter 21), Abraham Zaleznik distinguishes between the charismatic leader, who generates strong feelings and appears as a distinctive personality, and the consensus leader, who is an outgrowth of bureaucracy and is difficult to distinguish clearly as a person. Zaleznik believes that the personality traits of both types of leaders have been too often disregarded and that those who argue that a leader's role is defined by the situation ignore the significance of personality characteristics that determine how an individual responds. Many leaders, according to Zaleznik, find themselves in trouble when shifting events demand modes of action that lie outside their normal personal style. This adds credence to the view that successful leader traits are indeed a function of a given situation. Charisma is an individual quality that is as much a reflection of the followers as of the leader's personality.

A personal quality most often found in successful leaders is creativity. Morgan McCall, Jr., conjectures about creative leaders in Chapter 22. He lists some hypothetical descriptions of creative leaders: crafty, grouchy, dangerous, feisty, contrary, evangelistic, prejudiced, and spineless. He goes on to suggest that despite these "horrible" characteristics, creative leaders have a great sense of "play." Playfulness, according to McCall, does not necessarily lead to creativity, but successfully creative organizations have a great deal of fun because there is nothing more exciting than to succeed at what you are doing. This is an interesting view of leader behavior that seems to be characteristic of entrepreneurial organizations. But we all know that for many of us, work is not all "fun." Hard work is, perhaps, a quality more often rewarded, particularly in bureaucratic organizations.

In "How Do Leaders Get to Lead?" (Chapter 23), Michael Lombardo of the Center for Creative Leadership draws upon Tom Wolfe's *The Right Stuff* to make the point that if having the capability to become a leader is considered more important than having the opportunity to develop and demonstrate those talents, then many managers may never have a chance. By creating opportunities for more young managers and by avoiding premature decisions on whether someone will be allowed to pursue a management career, organizations can increase their chances of developing the best possible leaders for the future. For a variety of reasons, many who have the "right stuff" will never be allowed to accumulate the background experiences or learn skills that would enable them to show it. Lombardo suggests that before deciding that some managers don't have it, existing leaders ought to answer the question "Have they ever been in a position where they could show it?"

Finally, John Heider's "The Leader Who Knows How Things Happen" (Chapter 24) is adapted from Lao Tzu's sixth-century B.C. Chinese text, *Tao Te Ching*, on how to rule a kingdom and lead a wise life. In these selections Lao Tzu addresses himself to the concerned, thoughtful leader, the wise leader who "knows how things happen." This ancient voice provides an interesting counterpoint to the twentieth-century thinking we are more familiar with.

One of the reasons it is so hard to make value judgments about leader effectiveness is the complex interaction between individuals and their various situations. A person may be an effective lay leader in the church but be relatively ineffective in a business setting. The personality is the same; only the situations are different. We may find creativity encouraged in some places and discouraged in others. Perhaps we need to test the personal qualities of our would-be leaders in a variety of situations and only then evaluate the results and decide who the leaders really are.

19

Some Issues in Comparing Women and Men as Leaders

EDWIN P. HOLLANDER
JAN YODER

Leadership historically has been a masculine concept. For a long time, the study of leadership was largely based on research with men, sometimes with women, and rarely with both. Since most of the leaders who have been studied are males, entrenched sterotypes about the leader role as a male domain still persist (Lockheed, 1977; McGregor, 1967). However, as more women become leaders in politics, business, universities, and the armed forces, there has been a greater impetus to do research on gender-related similarities and differences in leadership behavior.

In light of the growing interest in studying women and men as leaders, this paper provides a selective review and organization of pertinent work in this area with a view toward making suggestions for future research. There have been some notable earlier reviews of work in this area, for example, O'Leary's (1974) comprehensive treatment of women in managerial roles. Here, our intention is to emphasize the basis for conceiving future studies of gender similarities and differences in leadership behavior, which at least may avoid some of the pitfalls and limitations of past research endeavors.

We propose that three major factors—role expectations, leader style, and situational influences—are especially important in affecting lead-

Reprinted from *Basic and Applied Social Psychology*, 1:3 (September 1980), pp. 267–280, by permission of the authors and publisher.

ership. Within this framework, we review illustrative findings about gender differences in leadership behavior and make suggestions about how researchers might better study leadership behavior by examining leader role, style, and the situation. We begin with several points of context.

Background

In comparing women and men, studies have taken two different approaches. The first of these is investigation of sex-role stereotypes when individuals have not had any interaction with those being evaluated. For example, McKee and Sherriffs (1957) found that males were rated more favorably than females on a variety of measures by both males and females. Heilbrun (1968) examined differences in instrumental and expressive behaviors of males and females and found that females were rated more expressive than instrumental in their behavior by both males and females; on the other hand, males were rated as being expressive and instrumental by both males *and* females. In their well-known study, Broverman, Vogel, Broverman, Clarkson, and Rosenkrantz (1972) found that the male stereotype was loaded on items of competence and the female stereotype on items of warmth and expressiveness.

The second area of investigation of male-female differences has looked at differences when subjects have been in an interactive situation. These situations have included dyads, triads, and larger groups. Some of these studies have been concerned with same-sex groups, and others have investigated differences in mixed-sex groups. Experiments such as those by Bond and Vinacke (1961) and Strodtbeck and Mann(1956) have found male performance tending to be exploitative and competitive, and female performance to be more accommodative and tension-reducing. In addition, both leaders and followers rated male leaders as being more concerned with task performance than were female leaders of groups of male military cadets working on two experimental tasks (Rice, Bender, & Vitters, 1980).

Although results such as these conform to Bales' and Slater's (1955) long-standing distinction between the task role, associated with the father, and the socioemotional role, associated with the mother, they are by no means conclusive. The existence of such gender differences is not necessarily an indication of a predetermined quality of masculinity and femininity (cf. Heine, 1971). Rather, gender distinctions in leader behavior are a function of role expectations, style, and situational characteristics, which we now consider sequentially in greater depth.

Leadership Role

In groups of mixed-sex composition, women generally are less likely
to be the leader and are less inclined then men to see themselves as
leaders or seek that role (Eskilson & Wiley, 1976). Viewed in the larger
perspective, sex-role expectations undoubtedly underlie these results. In
fact, the stereotype distinction between the mother and father roles in
the family, noted earlier, can play a part in producing the usual findings.
This is no accident, because the stereotype of the father as the task
specialist and the mother as supporter is still relatively entrenched.
Experimenters and subjects alike are affected by it, despite the obvious
fact that mothers perform tasks, and give direction, just as fathers can
be emotionally supportive. Indeed, the concept of androgyny seems
especially relevant to recognizing this overlap (see Deaux, 1976).

Nevertheless, as already indicated, there is a body of research evidence
that directly indicates or implies that people generally expect the leader
role to be filled by a man (Inderlied & Powell, 1979). For instance, in
a study by Schein (1973), replicated by Massengill and DiMarco (1979),
male middle managers rated women in general, men in general, or
successful middle managers on their overall characteristics, attitudes,
and temperaments. On 60 of these 86 items, men and managers were
rated similarly; on only eight items were women rated as being similar
to successful middle managers. Furthermore, Megargee (1969) found
that, regardless of the dominance of the woman, she is unlikely to
become leader when a man is available. Additionally, women are not
expected to use power in direct, "leader-like" ways (Johnson, 1976).
Finally, Eskilson and Wiley (1976) found that male leaders were more
likely to choose themselves as the future leader of the group than were
women. In sum, neither women nor men usually expect women to
occupy the leader role (Lockheed, 1977).

Other results, from a study by Hollander and Neider (note 2) indicated
a comparable sex-linked finding. Critical incidents showing good or bad
leadership were obtained from male and female respondents. Males
rarely mentioned female leaders in either the good or bad categories.
On the other hand, female respondents gave many more incidents
showing bad leadership with female leaders than with male leaders.
For good leadership, the female respondents mentioned male and female
leaders about equally. The interpretations of these results were that
women may have had more experience than men with female leaders
and that women may be more critical of female leaders.

For some women, a basic concern may be whether or not the leadership
role is appropriate for them. Although an ineffectual male leader may
have to cope with a stronger sense of failure for mismanaging his

assigned role than would a failing woman (Jacobson & Effertz, 1974), a successful female leader must cope with the fact that societal attitudes do not favor her strivings for success in this role (Pheterson, Kiesler, & Goldberg, 1971). Hence, women, unlike men, often are obliged to deal with the fact that their success in the leadership role is not valued (Gold, 1978). However, a key question is: Valued by whom?

O'Leary (1974) has pointed out that managerial success of women may be inhibited not only by pressures that are external to the woman but also by attitudes held by the woman herself. Regarding the latter, a successful woman may encounter role conflicts basic to her own self-concept. O'Leary says that:

> To the extent that a woman perceived herself as possessing both the masculine attributes associated with probable successful competitive achievement and interests in marriage and family considered appropriately feminine, she might experience role conflict. If the conflict between competing goals was sufficiently strong, the existence or mere anticipation of such a dilemma might result in the suppression of achievement striving [p. 816].

Thus, the finding noted earlier—that women infrequently seek the leadership role (Eskilson & Wiley, 1976)—may be attributable both to external factors, such as sex-role stereotypes and attitudes unfavorable to female leadership, and to internal factors, such as role conflict.

Is there any evidence to indicate that such external barriers to the feminine leadership role exist? Bowman, Worthy, and Greyser (1965) reported that a large proportion (41%) of businessmen looked with some disfavor on employing female executives. This bias appears to rest more upon fears concerning role violations than upon doubts about the competence of women. Schein (1973) found that competence, creativity, and intelligence were judged by male middle managers as important characteristics for a successful manager to possess, and no sex differences were reported for these qualities. In other words, competency, creativity, and intelligence did not differentiate the male and female roles. In addition, Bass, Krusell, and Alexander (1971) found that male managers rated female supervisors as being just as capable as their male counterparts. However, this last study revealed that managers persist in believing that women do not make good supervisors because women are less dependable than men and women violate norms concerning deference (Jacobson, Antonelli, Winning, & Opeil, 1977). Men simply believe that another man would be uncomfortable working as the subordinate of a woman (Cohen, Bunker, Burton, & McManus, 1978).

It should be noted, however, that there is some evidence from research indicating that men are satisfied with the task structure and team interaction of a group led by a woman, especially if the woman exhibits a high need for dominance (Bartol, 1974). Rosen, Jerdee, and Prestwich (1975) presented a national sample of male managers and executives with various scenarios concerning either a female or male employee. The results reflected the expectation that married female executives are not capable of balancing the responsibilities of both career and home and that a woman should forsake her own career advances if these conflict with her husband's professional interests. This latter expectation further reduces confidence in the dependability of a female executive. One consistent and interesting result in two studies is that these discriminatory attitudes were found to be strongest among young male executives (Bowman et al., 1965; Schein, 1973).

In sum, there is compelling evidence that both women and men are less inclined to expect women to function in the leadership role. "In fact, both men and women executives strongly agree that a woman has to be exceptional, indeed overqualified, to succeed in management today" (Bowman et al., 1965, p. 15). If expectations about the leadership role influence leadership behavior, and if that role is seen as not feminine, then women with traditional sex-typed attitudes can be predicted to perform less well as leaders than women not inhibited by this stereotype. Research findings do bear out this prediction. Using field dependence as a measure of conformity to sex-role stereotypes, Lockheed (1977) found that field-dependent women were less active and influential in field-dependent groups than field-independent female leaders of field-independent groups. Yerby (1975) found that mixed-sex groups with positive attitudes toward female leadership were most receptive to the female leader and exhibited a greater tolerance for disagreement within the group. Thus, for a woman to perform effectively as a leader in today's society, she must redefine either her feminine role or the leadership role. O'Leary (1974) presents a useful discussion about how this internal role conflict can be resolved, with a consideration of the consequences of these resolutions.

A methodological note should be added to the conclusions from these studies. Although such research yields important initial results regarding the impact of sex-role attitudes in influencing leadership behavior, leader and follower attitudes are confounded. What would happen, for example, if a field-independent woman led a field-dependent group? Sex-role attitudes of followers and the leader should be combined factorially in future research.

Leadership Style

Leadership style refers to the personality characteristics of the leader that are most typical across situations. Observations of female leadership styles by Kanter (1977) led her to conclude that individual differences are more noteworthy than gender differences. On the other hand, Deaux (1976) suggests that although women and men are equivalent in their need for achievement, men seek to succeed more on tasks whereas women seek to achieve interpersonal successes. Also, in the research by Eskilson and Wiley (1976), women were found to exert more activity directed toward creating positive group affect than did men. Men, on the other hand, concentrated more than women on exhibiting recognizable leader behaviors. Vinacke (1969) contends that, when allocating resources, women focus on maintaining harmonious relations, whereas men concentrate on the quality of an individual's performance. Relatedly, Leventhal (note 3) argues that men value task performance and women stress affilitative goals. Yet if Fiedler's (1965) least-preferred co-worker (LPC) scale is a differentiator of the task-oriented leader (low LPC) from the socioemotional leader (high LPC), it is surprising to discover a report of no significant difference in the mean LPC scores of men and women (Chapman, 1975). Furthermore, Offerman (note 5) has recently presented evidence that strongly suggests the susceptibility of the LPC score to situational variability, including cross-sex differences resulting from group composition.

Denmark (1977) has pointedly concluded that:

> Many of the assumptions that women managers are basically different from men are just not supported by data. The one difference investigators generally agree upon is women's greater concern for relationships among people; this should be considered a plus in terms of leadership effectiveness. Alleged sex differences in ability, attitudes, and personality have been based on sex-role stereotypes, rather then empirical observations of women leaders [pp. 110–111].

Therefore, style can be construed to be more a matter of individual differences than of sex differences (cf. Bartol, 1974; Bartol & Wortman, 1979; Brenner & Greenhaus, 1979; Day & Stogdill, 1972). This point is elaborated later in relationship to leadership effectiveness.

There is, however, an acknowledged problem when the style and demands of a role are in conflict. In an experiment mentioned earlier, Megargee (1969) examined this issue. He paired men and women who scored either high or low on dominance and then asked each of the four pairs to select a leader. In the case of high-dominance woman paired with low-dominance man, a component of leadership style—dominance—predicts that the woman will become leader. In contrast, the leadership role demands a male leader. When this pair was actually asked to select a leader, the woman was most likely to make the decision, more frequently than in any other pair. Most notably, in 91% of the cases, she appointed the man as the leader. Thus, even when a woman's leadership style conforms to role prescriptions regarding leadership, she may defer to the role demands and avoid leadership behavior.

Situational Influences

There is evidence to indicate that several situational factors can still operate to prevent women who have overcome role conflicts from exhibiting leadership behaviors. Under other conditions, these factors can facilitate the reduction of role conflicts so that women become leaders. A review of the literature indicates that the sex composition of the group, attitudes of followers, the type of task employed, the success or failure of the group, and how the leader attains his or her status are the most important situational factors.

If one views leadership as a transactional process, leaders both influence and are influenced by their followers (Hollander, 1978; Hollander & Julian 1969). Therefore, the sex composition of the group is an important variable; it will affect measures not only by itself but also in an interaction with the sex of the leader (Ruble & Higgins, 1976). For instance, regarding the former proposition, group composition has been shown to influence disclosure and risk-taking patterns. All-female groups disclose more about "people other than self" and "self and feelings" than mixed-sex groups (Kraft & Vraa, 1975). In both individual and group conditions, all-female groups were most cautious, mixed-sex groups exhibited intermediate caution, and all-male groups were most likely to take risks (Bauer & Turner, 1974).

Group composition has also been shown to be an important variable because it interacts with the sex of the leader. Female leaders were equally effective and leader-like in performance leading two men, two women, or a mixed-sex group. However, male leaders exhibited the most leader-like behavior and highest performance output when leading two men, and least with a mixed-sex group (Eskilson & Wiley, 1976). Yerby (1975), who studied only females as leaders, reported that a mixed-sex group of two males and two females was most satisfied with the group, whereas an all-male group led by a woman was least satisfied. Groups with same-sex leaders reported a better group atmosphere than groups led by opposite-sex leaders, but no differences were found in productivity

(Bullard & Cook, 1975). In sum, the evidence clearly indicates that an important independent variable in studying leadership is the sex composition of the group.

Again, a transactional approach would predict that the attitudes of followers will influence group processes. Rice et al. (1980) formed 72 four-person groups of male military cadets at West Point that completed two tasks under the leadership of a male or a female cadet. Followers were assigned to groups so that half the groups were composed of followers with liberal attitudes toward the rights and roles of women and the remaining groups held traditional attitudes. When the followers held egalitarian attitudes, they responded similarly to male and female leaders. However, traditional groups felt that the group atmosphere was more positive when the leader was male than when the leader was female. Traditional followers attributed a woman's success to luck and a man's success to hard work and member cooperation. Male-led groups performed slightly better than female-led groups. Clearly, followers' attitudes have an important impact on group processes.

Another variable, which seems to have been largely ignored in the research and commentary on leadership, is the sex-typing of the task. If a task is perceived to be either masculine or feminine, it is likely to influence how men and women respond to it (Makosky, note 4). For example, women conformed more than did men on items viewed as stereotypically masculine, but women conformed as much or less than did men on neutral and stereotypically feminine items (Sistrunk & McDavid, 1971). Maier's (1970) role-playing paradigm in which women play Gus, the foreman, Jack, Walt, and Steve, working on a job assembling fuel pumps, is a case in point. It is unlikely that a woman would find it appealing to play Gus and to work on a task involving assemblage of gas pumps. Despite this incongruity, this method has been used repeatedly (Sashkin & Maier, 1971; Yerby, 1975). Eagly (1970) also had women playing Mr. O'Brien, the social worker, in the Johnny Rocco case.

Although men have, at times, been shown to do better at spatial tasks than women (Maccoby, 1966), both Lockheed (1977) and Eskilson and Wiley (1976) utilized tasks requiring these skills. This is certainly likely to stack the deck against women. Indeed, Deaux (1976) has said that the choice of a task itself creates the potential for a sex bias to occur, possibly by influencing task clarity (Ruch & Newton, 1977) or role ambiguity (Bartol & Wortman, 1979). Future research ought to consider this variable by studying leaders' performance with favorably and unfavorably sex-typed tasks, or at least, to try to neutralize their effects by employing non–sex-specific tasks, such as the signal-detection task reported by Clement and Schiereck (1973).

When group members are engaged in a task with an objectively measured task goal, success or failure in achieving that goal becomes important and may influence perceptions of female and male leaders. For example, Jacobson and Effertz (1974) found that both male and female followers evaluated a failing male leader more harshly than an equally ineffective woman. When devising a task for the study of leadership, it is important to consider the perceived sex-typing associated with that task as well as the experience of success or failure that it may generate.

Also important to note are the effects on the performance of female and male leaders associated with being appointed or emerging as a leader (cf. Darley, 1976; Denmark, 1977). In the Eskilson and Wiley (1976) study, for example, women who thought that they had become the leader because they exhibited task-relevant skills demonstrated greater performance output and acted more leader-like than women who had been randomly appointed. In contrast, male leaders were not found to be affected by the apparent process that led to their attainment of the leader role. Reinforcing a woman's perceptions of her leadership capabilities by pointing to her competency with the task may legitimize leadership behavior for her that otherwise violated her sex-typed stereotype of the leadership role.

One problem in studying appointed or emergent leadership is the constraint that women emerge as leaders in an election less often than do men in mixed-sex groups. An exemplification of this is seen in the research of Fallon and Hollander (note 1) in which groups composed of two women and two men could elect a leader at the outset. There was a clear tilt in favor of males being elected more often than females.

Leadership Effectiveness

Leadership behavior has been operationally defined in many ways. A review of the literature shows that researchers studying leadership processes have measured leader's and followers' satisfaction (Bartol & Wortman, 1976; Maier, 1970; Yerby, 1975), followers' reactions to the leader (Bartol, 1974; Day & Stogdill, 1972), the productivity or effectiveness of the group on some objectively evaluated task (Bullard & Cook, 1975; Eagly, 1970), the individual's and the group's risk-taking (Bauer & Turner, 1974), disclosure patterns (Aries, 1976; Kraft & Vraa, 1975), leader influence (Eskilson & Wiley, 1976; Maier, 1970), and the leader's performance of task-relevant acts (Eskilson & Wiley, 1976). One difficulty in reviewing this body of research is created by the diversity of dependent measures employed. It is risky and confusing to compare findings of one study with those of another study that used different measures. In addition, the use of one measure (e.g., group satisfaction) may bias the results in favor of women, whereas another measure (e.g., task effectiveness) may produce results that favor men. The obvious solution to this problem is the use of multiple-criterion measures.

The measures listed above appear to fit two categories of leadership behavior that earlier research has defined: consideration and initiating structure (Halpin & Winer, 1957). The first factor, consideration, deals with the establishment and maintenance of a positive group climate. The latter factor, initiating structure, measures those aspects of the leader's behavior dealing with goal setting and attainment. As Hollander (1978) points out, these factors are not opposites but are both indicative of effective leader behavior. The use of these two general measures in future research would help to define the concept of leader behavior in richer terms and make the results of several programs of research more comparable.

We come now to the basic issue that often is at the core of comparisons between women and men in leadership roles: Are women or men equally or more effective as leaders? The psychological literature seemingly provides us with contradictory answers to this question (Brown, 1979), for some of the reasons already delineated. Studies show that women played a less dominant role when a task was unstructured than when it was structured (Maier, 1970), male leaders exhibited more leader-like behaviors than did their female counterparts (Eskilson & Wiley, 1976), and field-dependent women were less active and influential than men (Lockheed, 1977). On the other hand, studies using self-ratings of leadership (Bartol & Wortman, 1976) and subordinates' descriptions (Bartol, 1974; Day & Stogdill, 1972) indicate that there may be few job-related and personality differences (Brenner & Greenhaus, 1979) between female and male leaders. Additionally, the sex of the leader was not related to either leader behavior or subordinates' satisfaction in two organizations (Osborn & Vicars, 1976).

There appear to be two distinct approaches to answering this question concerning differences between men and women as leaders: (1) assign women and men the role of leader, keeping various extraneous factors constant, and compare the leader's and group's effectiveness; or (2) examine the leader's and group's reactions to actual leaders, such as male and female managers, teachers, military cadets, and so on. The former procedure addresses the question of whether women, in general, can be as effective as male leaders. The second method asks if women who chose to be leaders are as effective as men who also chose leadership roles. In other words, the second approach restricts itself to actual leaders and is therefore limited in its generalizability. However, this approach may provide a more realistic picture of women who are succeeding in the leadership role, given the current attitudinal barriers to the occupational achievement of women.

These two approaches characterize the two sets of conflicting research results previously discussed. Research supporting gender differences in leadership behavior sampled the general population of women, and studies finding no gender-related differences in leadership behaviors sampled the population of actual female leaders. These two groups are not equivalent (Darley, 1976; Foster & Kolinko, 1979). Thus, the seemingly contradictory evidence presented may have been created by the differences between the populations being studied.

Osborn and Vicars (1976) have also noted the contradictory nature of these two domains of research findings, and they proposed that an artifact may reside in the type of setting employed. The set of findings noting gender differences in leadership behavior arose from short-term laboratory studies. Field studies, on the other hand, revealed no consistent gender differences. These authors argue that in the short-term laboratory experience, stereotypes influence subjects' behaviors. Since the leadership role is seen to be primarily a masculine one, men "perform" better than women. In contrast, actual job experience may mediate stereotyping effects (Deaux, 1976), reducing sex biases against women in actual leadership positions. Both explanations, involving selection of setting, are theoretically feasible. Studies showing differences in the characteristics of successful female leaders, and women in general, would be supportive of the first proposal. Osborn and Vicars (1976) suggest longitudinal studies to verify their speculation. In either case, future research in this vein is clearly indicated.

What causes some women to choose to be leaders and to lead effectively while other women are apparently less successful? We have proposed that leadership role, style, and situational characteristics are the relevant factors and that they influence the leadership behavior expressed or inhibited in women and men in ways that are clearly complex and highly interactive. In further work, personality characteristics that define leadership style need to be more closely identified. Situational variables and sex-role attitudes of leaders and followers must be considered by future researchers. The effects of these factors on the leadership behaviors exhibited by all women and men leaders must be explored, especially in regard to effectiveness, which itself needs attention in specifying appropriate criteria (cf. Larwood & Lockheed, 1979).

Some Conclusions

Clearly, there are complexities associated with studying the behavior of women and men in mixed-sex groups that need to be confronted.

Among those general points touched on here are: (1) the too-ready use of sex-role stereotypes as if they were actual behaviors; and (2) the generalization of findings from dyads to larger groups. Other considerations that require attention are the sex-biased nature of the different group tasks used, and the failure to see the behavior of women as a function of the particular context rather than as a characteristic of gender. With this last consideration goes the need to recognize the mediating effects of the self-concept on the behavior of women thrust into what may be less familiar roles with men.

All of this leads to the conclusion that more must be done to gain an accurate picture of the behavior of women and men together in groups. We do need additional studies in this area, to be sure, but these must be done with greater sensitivity to the samples used and the methods employed. More rigor in this effort will help to enrich our knowledge of groups and help to bring realities to the fore that have long been obscured by myths.

Reference Notes

1. Fallon, B. J., & Hollander, E. P. *Sex-role stereotyping in leadership: A study of undergraduate discussion groups.* Paper presented at the meeting of the American Psychological Association, Washington, D.C., September 1976.

2. Hollander, E. P., & Neider, L. L. *Critical incidents and rating scales in comparing "good"-"bad" leadership.* Paper presented at the meeting of the American Psychological Association, Toronto, August 1978.

3. Leventhal, G. S. *Reward allocation by males and females.* Paper presented at the meeting of the American Psychological Association, Montreal, August 1973.

4. Makosky, V. P. *Fear of success, sex-role orientation of the task, and competitive conditions as variables affecting women's performance in achievement-oriented situations.* Paper presented at the meeting of the Midwestern Psychological Association, Cleveland, April 1972.

5. Offerman, L. *Esteem for least-preferred co-worker as a function of leader sex and group sex composition.* Paper presented at the meeting of the Eastern Psychological Association, Hartford, April 1980.

References

Aries, E. Interaction patterns and themes of male, female, and mixed groups. *Small Group Behavior,* 1976, 7, 7–18.

Bales, R. F., & Slater, P. E. Role differentiation in small decision-making groups. In T. Parsons et al. (Eds.), *Family, socialization, and interaction process.* Glencoe, Ill: Free Press, 1955.

Bartol, K. M. Male versus female leaders: The effect of leader need for dominance on follower satisfaction. *Academy of Management Journal,* 1974, *17,* 225–233.

Bartol, K. M., & Wortman, M. S. Sex effects in leader behavior self-descriptions and job satisfaction. *Journal of Psychology,* 1976, *94,* 177–183.

Bartol, K. M., & Wortman, M. S. Sex of leader and subordinate role stress: A field study. *Sex Roles,* 1979, *5,* 513–518.

Bass, B. M., Krusell, J., & Alexander, R. H. Male managers' attitudes toward working women. *American Behavioral Scientist,* 1971, *15,* 77–83.

Bauer, R. H., & Turner, J. H. Betting behavior in sexually homogeneous and heterogeneous groups. *Psychological Reports,* 1974, *34,* 251–258.

Bond, J. R., & Vinacke, W. E. Coalitions in mixed-sex triads. *Sociometry,* 1961, *24,* 61–75.

Bowman, G. W., Worthy, N. B., & Greyser, S. A. Are women executives people? *Harvard Business Review,* 1965, *43,* 14–17.

Brenner, O. C., & Greenhaus, J. H. Managerial status, sex, and selected personality characteristics. *Journal of Management,* 1979, *5,* 107–113.

Broverman, I., Vogel, S. R., Broverman, D. M., Clarkson, F. E., & Rosenkrantz, P. S. Sex-role stereotypes: A current appraisal. *Journal of Social Issues,* 1972, *28,* 59–78.

Brown, S. M. Male versus female leaders: A comparison of empirical studies. *Sex Roles,* 1979, *5,* 595–611.

Bullard, P. D., & Cook, P. E. Sex and workstyle of leaders and followers: Determinants of productivity. *Psychological Reports,* 1975, *36,* 545–546.

Chapman, J. B. Comparisons of male and female leadership styles. *Academy of Management Journal,* 1975, *18,* 645–650.

Clement, D. E., & Schiereck, J. J. Sex composition and group performance in a visual signal detection task. *Memory and Cognition,* 1973, *1,* 251–255.

Cohen, S. L., Bunker, K. A., Burton, A. L., & McManus, P. D. Reactions of male subordinates to the sex-role congruency of immediate supervision. *Sex Roles,* 1978, *4,* 297–311.

Darley, S. Big-time careers for the little woman: A dual-role dilemma. *Journal of Social Issues,* 1976, *32,* 85–98.

Day, D. R., & Stogdill, R. M. Leader behavior of male and female supervisors: A comparative study. *Personnel Psychology,* 1972, *25,* 353–360.

Deaux, K. *The behavior of women and men.* Monterey, Calif.: Brooks/Cole, 1976.

Denmark, F. L. Styles of leadership. *Psychology of Women Quarterly,* 1977, *2(2),* 99–113.

Eagly, A. H. Leadership style and role differentiation as determinants of group effectiveness. *Journal of Personality,* 1970, *38,* 509–524.

Eskilson, A., & Wiley, M. G. Sex composition and leadership in small groups. *Sociometry,* 1976, *39,* 183–194.

Fiedler, F. E. The contingency model: A theory of leadership effectiveness. In H. Proshansky & B. Seidenberg (Eds.), *Basic studies in social psychology,* New York: Holt, Rinehart & Winston, 1965.

Foster, L. W., & Kolinko, T. Choosing to be a managerial woman: An examination of individual variables and career choice. *Sex Roles,* 1979, *5,* 627–634.

Gold, A. R. Reexamining barriers to women's career development. *American Journal of Orthopsychiatry*, 1978, *48*, 690–702.

Halpin, A. W., & Winer, B. J. A factorial study of the leader behavior descriptions. In R. M. Stogdill & A. E. Coons (Eds.), *Leader behavior: Its description and measurement*. Columbus: Ohio State University, Bureau of Business Research, 1957.

Heilbrun, A. B., Jr. Influence of observer and target sex judgments of sex-typed attributes. *Perceptual and Motor Skills*, 1968, *27*, 1194.

Heine, P. J. *Personality in social theory*. Chicago: Aldine, 1971.

Hollander, E. P. *Leadership dynamics: A practical guide to effective relationships*. New York: Free Press/Macmillian, 1978.

Hollander, E. P., & Julian, J. W. Contemporary trends in the analysis of leadership processes. *Psychological Bulletin*, 1969, *76*, 387–397.

Inderlied, S. D., & Powell, G. Sex-role identity and leadership style: Different labels for the same concept? *Sex Roles*, 1979, *5*, 613–625.

Jacobson, M. B., Antonelli, J., Winning, P. U., & Opeil, D. Women as authority figures: The use and nonuse of authority. *Sex Roles*, 1977, *3*, 365–375.

Jacobson, M. B., & Effertz, J. Sex roles and leadership perceptions of the leaders and the led. *Organizational Behavior and Human Performance*, 1974, *12*, 383–396.

Johnson, P. Women and power: Toward a theory of effectiveness. *Journal of Social Issues*, 1976, *32*, 99–110.

Kanter, R. M. *Men and women of the corporation*. New York: Basic Books, 1977.

Kraft, L. W., & Vraa, C. W. Sex composition of groups and pattern of self-disclosure by high school females. *Psychological Reports*, 1975, *37*, 733–734.

Larwood, L., & Lockheed, M. Women as managers: Toward second generation research. *Sex Roles*, 1979, *5*, 659–666.

Lockheed, M. E. Cognitive style effects on sex status in student work groups. *Journal of Educational Psychology*, 1977, *69*, 158–165.

Maccoby, E. E. Sex differences in intellectual functioning. In E. E. Maccoby (Ed.), *The development of sex differences*. Stanford, Calif.: Stanford University Press, 1966.

Maier, N. R. Male versus female discussion leaders. *Personnel Psychology*, 1970, *23*, 455–461.

Massengill, D., & DiMarco, N. Sex-role stereotypes and requisite management characteristics: A current replication. *Sex Roles*, 1979, *5*, 561–570.

McGregor, D. *The professional manager*. New York: McGraw-Hill, 1967.

McKee, J. P., & Sherriffs, A. C. The differential evaluation of males and females. *Journal of Personality*, 1957, *25*, 356–371.

Megargee, E. I. Influence of sex roles on the manifestation of leadership. *Journal of Applied Psychology*, 1969, *53*, 377–382.

O'Leary, V. E. Some attitudinal barriers to occupational aspirations in women. *Psychological Bulletin*, 1974, *81*, 809–826.

Osborn, R. N. & Vicars, W. M. Sex stereotypes: An artifact in leader behavior and subordinate satisfaction analysis? *Academy of Management Journal*, 1976, *19*, 439–449.

Pheterson, G. I., Kiesler, S. B., & Goldberg, P. A. Evaluation of the performance of women as a function of their sex, achievement, and personal history. *Journal of Personality and Social Psychology*, 1971, *19*, 114–118.

Rice, R. W., Bender, L. R., & Vitters, A. G. Leader sex, follower attitudes toward women, and leadership effectiveness: A laboratory experiment. *Organizational Behavior and Human Performance*, 1980, *25*, 46–78.

Rosen, B., Jerde, T. H., & Prestwich, T. L. Dual-career marital adjustment: Potential effects of discriminatory managerial attitudes. *Journal of Marriage and the Family*, 1975, *37*, 565–572.

Ruble, D. N., & Higgins, E. T. Effects of group sex composition on self-presentation and sex-typing. *Journal of Social Issues*, 1976, *32*, 125–132.

Ruch, L. O., & Newton, R. R. Sex characteristics, task clarity, and authority. *Sex Roles*, 1977, *3*, 479–494.

Sashkin, M., & Maier, N. R. Sex effects in delegation. *Personnel Psychology*, 1971, *24*, 471–476.

Schein, V. E. Relationships between sex role stereotypes and requisite management characteristics. *Journal of Applied Psychology*, 1973, *57*, 95–100.

Sistruck, F., & McDavid, J. W. Sex variable in conforming behavior. *Journal of Personality and Social Psychology*, 1971, *17*, 200–207.

Strodtbeck, F. L., & Mann, R. D. Sex role differentiation in jury deliberations. *Sociometry*, 1956, *19*, 3–11.

Vinacke, W. E. Variables in experimental games: Toward a field theory. *Psychological Bulletin*, 1969, *71*, 293–318.

Yerby, J. Attitude, task, and sex composition as variables affecting female leadership in small problem-solving groups. *Speech Monographs*, 1975, *42*, 160–168.

20

False Grit

WARREN G. BENNIS

There's a mythology of competence going around that says the way for a woman to succeed is to act like a man. One proponent of this new "man-scam" is Marcille Gray Williams, author of *The New Executive Woman: A Guide to Business Success*, who advises women to "learn to control your tears. Mary Tyler Moore may be able to get away with it, but you can't. Whatever you do, don't cry." Women in increasing numbers are enrolling in a variety of training and retraining programs which tell them that if they dress properly (dark gray and dark blue) and talk tough enough (to paraphrase John Wayne, "A woman's got to do what a woman's got to do"), they'll take another step up the ladder of success. Which explains why training programs for women (and men too) have become a booming growth industry.

What we see today are all kinds of workshops and seminars where women undergo a metaphorical sex change, where they acquire a tough-talking, no-nonsense, sink-or-swim macho philosophy. They're told to take on traits just the opposite of those Harvard psychoanalyst Dr. Helen H. Tartakoff assigns to women: "endowments which include the capacity for mutuality as well as for maternity . . . for creativity as well as receptivity. In short," she sums up, "women's feminine heritage, as caretaker and peacemaker, contains the potential for improving the human condition."

Ironically, men are simultaneously encouraged to shed the same masculine character traits that women are trying to imitate through their own form of nonassertiveness and in sensitivity training programs. So it's O.K., even better than O.K., for old Charlie to cry in his office. How marvelous. How liberating. Women impersonate the macho male stereotype and men impersonate the countermacho stereotype of the women.

Reprinted with permission from *Savvy*, 1:6 (June 1980), pp. 43–47.

It's time to move beyond "sex differences" and "sex roles," beyond the myths of female and male impersonations, to a more sophisticated understanding of women in organizations. Instead of retraining women *as individuals* to acquire appropriate dress or assertiveness, we have to face up to the organization as a culture—as a system which governs behavior. For, according to research findings, the impact of the organization on success or failure is much greater than that of personality characteristics—or, for that matter, sex differences.

This realization avoids the "blame the victim" approach which explains executive success in terms of individual dispositions (whether created by temperament or socialization). The villains of the piece turn out to be complex organizations, whose power structures and avenues for opportunity routinely disadvantage those people not particularly sophisticated about how such organizations work. More often than not, those people are women, since they tend to have had less experience in learning the ropes of organizational life. This perspective suggests a different kind of strategy for the elimination of sex discrimination than the "sex roles" school of thought. Instead of retraining women (or men, for that matter) and trapping all concerned in a false dream, it's necessary to take a look at the very nature of complex organizations. It is these systems and the roles within them that women must understand. And it is, at bottom, these complex organizations which should bear the burden of change, not the women subjected to weekend bashes where male-chauvinist Pygmalion games are played to the tune of "Why Can't a Woman Be More Like a Man?"

Alfred North Whitehead cautioned us wisely: "Seek simplicity and then distrust it." To put it kindly, the trouble with too many sex-difference, sex-role training programs is that they seek simplicity but forget to distrust it. And no wonder. Simplicity is easier. It's easier to transform individuals than to transform creaky, complex systems with their bureaucratic sludge and impenetrable webs of self-interest. It's a lot easier to change an Eliza Doolittle than Victorian England's class structure. The trouble is: When Eliza returns to her old habitat in Covent Garden, the old familiar behaviors return almost immediately, and everything she learned from Professor Higgins is extinguished in days. This "fade out" effect has occurred wherever individuals are trained or re-educated outside the organizational context. What's easier can be dangerously off target.

When I discussed this with Boris Yavitz, Dean of Columbia University's Graduate School of Business, he told me, "What I fear is that women will try to take on the attributes of men in a wrong-headed attempt to disprove the old stereotypes." The women he sees in his program have all the intellectual equipment necessary for success in business; they're motivated, directed, purposeful. "We never set out eight years ago to bring in women by making it easy," says Yavitz, "and yet in the last eight years our female enrollment has increased from 5 percent to 40 percent of the school. We are holding exactly the same standards we have always held, and the women are doing superbly." As they are, by the way, in all top graduate schools of management. M.I.T. accepts from 25 percent to 40 percent as do Harvard, Stanford, Chicago and Wharton, the bastions of management-education excellence in this country. Women's competence is well documented. From all reports, they are capable on the job—and, Yavitz adds, "They prove their competence without the need for sporting hair on their chests."

Organizations, thankfully, are too complicated for the popular delusion of simplicity and certainty, the false-grit tunnel vision of a John Wayne. The fact is that there is no one set of rules, of programmed behavior, dress or skills that can apply to women or men in their attempts to succeed. Perhaps the most convincing documentation of this point is a study of 1,800 successful managers recently completed by The American Management Associations (A.M.A.). From this study, a profile emerges: Effective managers are social initiators; they anticipate problems and possible solutions. They build alliances, bring people together, develop networks. Their competencies cluster in several areas: *social-emotional maturity* (composed of such traits as self-control, spontaneity, perceptual objectivity, accurate self-assessment, stamina, adaptability); *entrepreneurial abilities* (efficiency, productivity); *intellectual abilities* (logical thought, conceptual ability, the diagnostic use of ideas and memory); and *interpersonal abilities* (self-presentation, interest in the development of others, concern with impact, oral communication skills, the use of socialized power, and concern with relationships).

The A.M.A. study is, without question, some of the most complete, systematic research ever undertaken on the attributes of the good manager. I see nothing in its findings that would give men or women (with whatever "natural endowments" one attributes to sex roles) an edge. I would also wager that most astute observers of the managerial landscape would agree with the study. Yavitz, for one, describes the effective manager as possessing "the ability for true communication— I don't mean the glib view, that you're communicating when you make a great pitch." He insists that two-way communication is imperative:

A manager must be perceptive, must understand what she's hearing, and then be able to convey the ideas clearly to others . . . must be flexible enough to acknowledge that there are competing constituencies and must be sensitive enough to listen to the emotion and spirit behind the words as well as to the content . . . and she must be able to synthesize what she's heard, to put together something as close to the optimal solution as possible, something that makes sense.

The manager must be able to persuade, explain, convince others why this solution is more sensible and beneficial for the whole cluster of constituencies than another solution. I surmise that a high sense of responsibility and commitment, ability to cope with ambiguity, and a continuing sense of curiosity and willingness to learn are critical attributes for the successful manager.

Does either sex have a monopoly on the constellation of traits identified by the A.M.A. research or by Dean Yavitz?

A better explanation of success, it seems to me, is that those who are favorably placed in organizational structures are more likely to be successful, independent of gender, than those less favorably placed. By "favorably placed" I mean: 1) having the support of one's subordinates, 2) having clear goals and a similarly clear path to them and 3) being empowered by the organization with appropriate means to reward and punish one's subordinates. When these conditions are present, we have what scholars refer to as "situational favorableness."

Complex organizations vary enormously. Specifically, they vary with respect to their "cultures." Some organizations are formalistic in nature, rigid, hierarchical; others are collegial, relying on agreement and consensus; while still others tend to be personalistic, concerned with the self-actualization of their employees. Within organizations, too, there can be great cultural differences. Just compare Bell Telephone's Murray Hill Labs with its international headquarters at Basking Ridge, New Jersey. It's hard to find a man without a beard or with a tie at the Bell Labs at Murray Hill, and equally hard to find a man without a tie and with a beard at Basking Ridge. Table 1 contrasts the values and behavior of three types of organizational systems.

Success depends greatly on being able to diagnose the particular organizational culture within which one is embedded and to develop the flexibility to respond and initiate within that structure. There's nothing sex-related about it. All that's required are the knowledge and the personal skills that most famous of all salesmen, Professor Harold Hill of "The Music Man," expounded: "Gotta know the territory."

From Hobbes to Freud, the special character of Western (most especially American) development has been an awareness of the heterogeneity of human experience and an accentuated consciousness of the power of the individual to overcome or shape his circumstances. As Isaiah Berlin

TABLE 1. Three Types of Organizational Cultures

	Formalistic	*Collegial*	*Personalistic*
Basis for decision	Direction from authority	Discussion, agreement	Directions from within
Form of control	Rules, laws, rewards, punishments	Interpersonal, group commitments	Actions aligned with self-concept
Source of power	Superior	What "we" think and feel	What *I* think and feel
Desired end	Compliance	Consensus	Self-actualization
To be avoided	Deviation from authoritative direction; taking risks	Failure to reach consensus	Not being "true to oneself"
Time perspective	Future	Near future	Now
Position relative to others	Hierarchical	Peer	Individual
Human relationships	Structured	Group oriented	Individually oriented
Basis for growth	Following the established order	Peer group membership	Acting on awareness of self

shows in his *Russian Thinkers,* the Russian tendency has always been for the system—always the senior partner to self-affirmation—to move toward hegemony. In the United States, that partnership has been reversed, with self-affirmation in the ascendence. There is, as Mounier, the French political writer, has warned us, a "madness in both those who treat the world as a dream and . . . a madness in those who treat the inner life as a phantom." To apply this to systems, there are those who view organizations as mirages, with no reality except that which we give them. This is one kind of madness. The other madness is that of those, like the Russians and some *echt* Marxist thinkers, who will not deal with, or even recognize, aspects of their personality, dispositions, if you will, that stem from our inner souls, or private lives. For the sake of our collective sanity, we must recognize the validity and reality of each—by organization and personality—for without that total embrace, our perspective will be dangerously skewed.

In any case, it would be a grave error to fall into the trap of underestimating the power of organizations and conceiving of executive success as dependent on toughness or softness, assertiveness or sensitivity, masculinity or femininity. That popular delusion has already caused too much damage, both to individuals who are impersonating males and females, and to the institutions for which they work.

21

Charismatic and Consensus Leaders: A Psychological Comparison

ABRAHAM ZALEZNIK

One of the outgrowths of industrialization and the development of bureaucracy is the consensus leader. Unlike his opposite, the charismatic leader who generates strong feelings and appears as a distinctive personality, the consensus leader is difficult to distinguish clearly as a person.

The consensus leader would seem to fit the outlines of the antihero who, while a "common man" figuratively speaking, does have the distinction of being able to survive the rigors of institutional politics. The questions for psychoanalysts, historians, and political scientists interested in the relationship between personality and politics center on understanding the character structure of the survivor who becomes leader through the control of consensus mechanisms. What manner of man is the consensus leader? How do the charismatic and consensus leaders differ in personality structure and dynamics? To what types of pathology are charismatic and consensus leaders vulnerable; and if these pathologies differ, how can the underlying patterns of conflict and defense be explained? How do pathological manifestations affect the pattern of leadership and do these manifestations have consequences for the decisions made by these two types of leaders?

Sociologist David Riesman, *et al.* in *The Lonely Crowd: A Study of the Changing American Character* (1950) found two types of national character they called the "inner-directed" and the "other-directed." Briefly, the

Reprinted from *Bulletin of the Menninger Clinic*, 38:3 (May 1974), pp. 222–238, by permission of the author and publisher.

inner-directed person relies on his own beliefs and ideas to guide his thoughts and actions. The other-directed personality depends on the views of others to determine his response. This distinction can be taken as a point of departure for examining and comparing charismatic and consensus leaders in an effort to answer the questions I have posed.

The Charismatic Leader

The psychoanalytic study of charismatic leadership began with Freud's (1895) early work on hysteria and the nature of the influence one person can have on another, especially when deep emotional attachments are unilateral. At the root of hysterical symptoms is the unconscious love an individual feels for another—a love that can progress from fantasy to idealization of the object. All children pass through such phases in their love of their parents in which fantasy compels the child to center his emotional ties on the loved parent. These ties are the basis for influence on thoughts and feelings, intimately affecting character through the mechanisms of incorporation, identification, and imitation. If one cannot have the loved object, one will try to be like him, to gain his approval, and in all respects meet his standards and expectations. To be sure, maturation modifies and transforms an individual's attachments; therefore, the leader and the led experience many different types of relationships, ranging from the deep and sometimes pathological to the purely objective and rational.

The concept of charisma and its applications to leadership and authority were originated by the German sociologist Max Weber (Parsons 1947). He used charisma in the religious sense as a spiritual quality, an inner light, which resulted from divine revelation and conversion. As applied to leadership, "it is the charismatically qualified leader as such who is obeyed by virtue of personal trust in him and his revelation, his heroism or his exemplary qualities so far as they fall within the scope of the individual's belief in his charisma." In its more general application, charisma refers to any combination of unusual qualities in an individual which are attractive to others and result in special attachments, if not devotion, to his leadership. John F. Kennedy had such qualities, as illustrated by his ability to attract crowds during his presidential campaign, and as especially evidenced in the "jumping" phenomenon demonstrated by young girls in the crowd who would jump up and down and squeal with delight over his appearance, much like the crowd response to a "teen-age rock idol." Certainly, Kennedy's appeal grew substantially during and following his performance in the famous debates with Nixon. Although it is not clear what unconscious and preconscious imagery the debates evoked in the minds of the electorate, it does seem clear that they petrified Mr. Nixon. The legend grew into the imagery of Camelot, with the brave and fearless band of brothers kept together by the youthful leader, ready to take on all challengers and overcome all obstacles in "getting America moving again."

A somewhat different quality of charisma appeared in the person or the image of Charles de Gaulle (Hoffman & Hoffman 1968). France in defeat was an aberration awaiting a leader to restore her to her proper place in the constellation of nations. De Gaulle was aloof and distant, yet heroic in the depth of his conviction that France must not only be served but must also follow the path of greatness.

Franklin D. Roosevelt presented still another type of charismatic leader. Instead of aloofness and elitism, this patrician conveyed a sense of pragmatism in facing the terrifying effort to overcome economic paralysis at home and a new kind of tyranny abroad. With a voice which evoked symbols to which individuals from diverse groups and backgrounds could relate, Franklin Roosevelt forged a new coalition in American politics, drawing together the liberal/intellectual, the blue collar worker, the farmer, and the ethnic minorities. Studies of his presidency have yet to grasp how he elicited loyalty from such diverse groups and from whence came the wellspring within his personality which fed his capacity for communication.

The list of illustrations of charismatic leaders could easily be expanded to include individuals with other types of personalities; yet, all had the capacity to secure the emotional ties of others to themselves. Gandhi, for example, embodied both the earlier conception of charisma as a spiritual quality and the modern preoccupation with the revolutionary personality. The study of developing nations suggests, as in the case of India, that the transition from the tribal feelings and the orientation to village and clan on the one hand to the attitudes of nationhood on the other frequently turns on the presence of a charismatic individual. The list of such personalities is long and includes Sukarno in Indonesia, Nkrumah in Ghana, Nasser in Egypt, and, of course, Mao Tse-tung in China.

To discover what makes for the successful emergence of such charismatic leaders, one must look at the interface of psychology and history. Erik Erikson (1958, 1969) is pioneering in the new field of psychohistory with his inquiry into Martin Luther's late adolescent identity crisis and with his more recent study of the emergence of Gandhi's *satayagraha*, or passive resistance, in leading the workers of the Ahmadabad textile mills out on strike.

Those generalizations that can be made from the psychohistorical study of these great leaders seem to center on the fusion of great personal and historical conflicts. For Martin Luther, the personal issue was loyalty to his father and obedience to authority. His father, knowing the new secular careers offered possibilities for upward mobility, wanted his gifted son to study law. Yet, because of deep oedipal conflicts, young Luther could neither accede to his father's wishes nor rebel in an outright way. Rebellion against his father became possible when he entered a monastery to follow the priesthood, for he could then submit to the overriding code of obedience of another authority figure. However, such a compromise could not stabilize the conflict for long, and the issue of rebellion or submission escalated from the authorities in the monastery to the Pope and ultimately to God. Erikson says this crisis resulted in a series of transformations which cannot be easily explained by sublimation or the neutralization of energy. Instead, the nature of the transformations can only be understood by a close look at the individual's endowments, the demands of narcissism, and, above all, the nature of historical change, where personal conflicts provide the media for communication between leader and led. Luther was not alone in his doubts about obedience, particularly in accepting intermediaries in man's relationship with God. The emergence of strong princes and the resulting conflict between secular and religious authority gave Luther some powerful allies in his struggle to which he attracted the masses through his personal eloquence and the message that good works are a sign of predestined salvation.

As mentioned earlier and as alluded to in the previous example, the study of charismatic leadership must start with the origins of influence and the forms of psychic disequilibria which arise in early object ties. Here, Riesman's (1950) designation of the "inner-directed" personality may be applied to the charismatic leader. Such a leader has a highly developed and well populated inner life as a result of introjecting early objects and later identifying with objects, symbols, and ideals which have some connection to the introjects. The imagos, or internal audience, exert a powerful influence on the leader and form the basis for the ties he establishes with the masses.

The study of Charles de Gaulle illustrates how introjects work in the development of a charismatic leadership style. Stanley and Inge Hoffmann in their paper "The Will to Grandeur: de Gaulle as Political Artist" (1968) correlate de Gaulle's majestic sense with the quality of his internal audience which he projected upon France. De Gaulle's introjects established his sense of independence which he manifested in school and later in his career; but this independence did not involve rebellion against his parents. As the Hoffmanns show, de Gaulle remained deeply attached to his parents; even so, he was able to transform this attachment into an idealized relationship with France. To de Gaulle, authority transcended men and ordinary human relationships so that when an individual submitted, it was to ideals. Therefore, he avoided conventional compliance, as demonstrated in his dealings with Pétain, and later with Churchill and Roosevelt. For these latter two, de Gaulle remained a perplexing and vexing figure, seemingly without power but enormously absorbed in and directed toward one overriding goal—restoring France to her rightful place in the constellation of nations. De Gaulle was able to bide his time in England during the war, personifying France in waiting. He was also able to withdraw, accept defeat, and sustain himself through his imagos, awaiting the call to power in 1958. Once in power, he acted decisively to extricate France from Algeria without waiting to test for consensus and acceptance.

This capacity to wait and accept passivity, then to act and move assertively would seem to depend upon the sustaining effects of benevolent introjects, for such self-assurance must come from being at one with these inner images. From this integration, the charismatic leader secures his sense of being special, and here the relationship to mother appears significant. In Freud's words, "A man who has been the indisputable favorite of his mother keeps for life the feeling of a conqueror, that confidence of success that often induces real success [Jones 1953, p. 5]." However, this statement does not completely explain how introjects function for creative individuals in all fields. Some transformations take place in which the sense of being special and the attachment to early objects as introjects are related to social and historical reality with both a past and a future.

To understand this transformation requires a look at the types of psychopathology manifested in the lives and works of charismatic leaders. The psychopathology of the charismatic leader is straight out of Shakespeare. Megalomania, paranoia, all the massive psychic upheavals fit for a King Lear are still valid indicators of how great men fall ill. Although the examples are many, there are still too few good analytic studies.

Studies of Adolph Hitler (Erikson 1950; Langer 1972) serve as counterpoints to studies of charismatic leaders who secure and communicate visions of the future—visions which mobilize and focus the forces of change in society. In contrast, Hitler's life and work exemplify the return to primitive modes of thinking and acting. Only a charismatic leader of this kind could link his own primitive fantasies to a nation's potential for regression, with history as witness to the almost unbelievable outcomes. For a partial explanation, we must again look at the nature of the introjects and their origins in personal history and development.

Hitler was possessed by an internalized audience which mirrored unsettled yet intense attachments to his parents. To begin with, Hitler had doubts about his own origin and legitimacy, and there was also some question about whether his father was born of an illegitimate relationship—both of which found expression in his obsession with a pure race. Hitler's father, who died when the boy was 13 years old, was 23 years older than his mother. Hitler had either witnessed or was obsessed by fantasies that his father beat his mother. In any case, Hitler's relationship to his father was distant, which left him not only with a hatred for his father but with an insecure feeling about what it means to be a man. This hatred became the basis for his hatred of the Jews; he projected upon the Jews what he hated in himself, and he set out to destroy them.

Hitler's incestuous love for his mother, who also died during his adolescence, provided the emotional reservoir which fed his desire for a "pure" reconstructed and unravished German nation. This love of mother and nation remained deeply erotic—untransformed sexuality and aggression—and became the motive power for his sadism. However, Hitler retained a two-sided view of his mother—the earthly, warm, seductive side and the powerful "iron virgin" (to use Erikson's term). The latter became his, and ultimately Germany's, ideal for the nation. The quality of these introjects and the inability to fuse the contrasting images of his parents led to his intense, hysterical love affair with the German people—an affair conducted at the expense of humanity and perpetuated by an inability to tame impulses which once unleashed only destroyed.

Although it is seemingly a long journey from the nature of influence in the parent-child relationship to the structure of power relations in political life, the conceptual links—love and sexuality on the one hand and aggression on the other—are reasonably clear as illustrated in the previous examples. In the cohesive political structure, the direction of love toward a leader or some representation, such as an ideology or a totem, serves to bind members to each other (Freud 1921). If, at the same time, the group's aggression is dampened or is directed toward some external object (e.g., toward tasks to be achieved or toward the representation of some common enemy who in real or mythological terms threatens the group's survival), then the structure is preserved. This classic model of group cohesion may also describe a condition of object surrender, where the followers hand over their egos to the leader and remain susceptible to his commands and directives. They submit in order to preserve their love of the leader, and whatever esteem they experience comes from the sense of devotion to the ideals and causes established in the leader's image.

The study of charismatic leaders invariably is a study of change, specifically the relationship between personal and historical change. Undoubtedly in all generations there are potential charismatic figures who never appear on the stage of history. Individual conflicts and attempts at their resolution remain purely personal events until great historical crises call forth new definitions of self-interest. When established authority structures begin to crumble, seldom is only one segment of society affected; the effects are visible in the family, community, religious institutions, universities, and, of course, government. Therefore, more than one charismatic leader appears at one time. The great depression of the 1930s and World War II pushed many great men forward both to generate and resolve crises. Similarly, the demise of these great men brought about a new era. There has been no genuinely charismatic leader in the United States since Franlkin Roosevelt (although John Kennedy had some attributes of such a leader). Likewise, in Great Britain after Winston Churchill, the succession of leaders has been a product of close political infighting, reflecting the problems of alliance (rather than crisis) politics. Even in the great dictatorships, the mantle has not been passed to another individual as often as to a coalitional or bipartite leadership structure. When the last of the charismatic leaders of World War II, Charles de Gaulle, relinquished power, his successor, Georges Pompidou, exemplified the type of leader who arises from the anonymity of bureaucratic function to the top position as a result of consensus politics.

The Consensus Leader

The consensus form of leadership has deep roots in the American national character, for Americans seem to have a basic distrust of charismatic leaders. The nation which began with the overthrow of authority had to establish a legacy in which authority of all kinds (not the least of which is paternal) was suspect. In addition, the experience of overpowering nature with technology has produced a sense of optimism which is peculiarly American—an optimism which produced a system in which a man is judged by *what* he does rather than *who* he is. Status by achievement rather than ascription, furthermore, supports a peer group culture built on the dual images of pragmatism and egalitarianism.

With this foundation which rejects the paternal image and charisma, the question of leadership is ambiguous. The types of leaders (political as well as institutional) who have gained power in the United States present a new personality configuration in which the idealized image, as well as the problematic image, is that of brother and peer rather than father. The philosophical basis for this new personality configuration can be found in the works of George Herbert Mead (1934) and Charles Horton Cooley (1956). In their theory and philosophy, they based the formation of the American character on the conscious assessments and acceptances of others. In other words, character is defined by an individual's memberships and roles. That group formations occur within the fabric of society and that there is an interrelationship between groups and institutions led these theorists to conclude that the American ego belongs to society. Because control of aggression is central to the types of constraints groups exert upon individuals, the taming of destructive impulses is assured by the individual's unwillingness to risk the impoverishment and possible ostracism which would be his lot if he violated group codes. Libido is less troublesome since group relationships have absorbed and ritualized unconscious homosexual impulses; yet, overt aggression, such as competitiveness, status striving, and outright attempts to secure dominance and control, runs counter to the ideology of primary group ties among brothers.

On the whole, our understanding of the psychology of the consensus leader is limited. Such leaders do not generate much interest among psychobiographers; besides, anonymity is a characterological trait of consensus leaders and accounts in no small measure for their successful rise to power. The consensus leader's classical tactic is to establish his position in the center of the political spectrum and gradually to widen the power base, isolating the opposition outside the consensus structure. Centrists tend to be followers rather than leaders of opinion. They avoid substantive positions for as long as possible and, instead, concentrate their energies on procedure.

One of the striking characteristics of consensus leadership is the relative absence of strong emotional bonds between leader and follower. The leader is the first among equals; and calculated self and group interests are the ties that bind men to the structure. However, men are willing to compromise in order to reach some satisfactory consensus in which interest groups neither win nor lose. Therefore, in a sense, dependency in consensus structures is masked, for the polity is mutually dependent; and the leader, if anything, is more dependent on his followers than they on him. This reversal of the usual dependency pattern is especially marked in complex bureaucracies where the leader knows less about any particular issue than selected subordinates. What a chief executive brings to policy making is more a sense of timing than expertise.

As a case example, let us look at Lyndon Baines Johnson as senate majority leader and as president of the United States (Geyelin 1966). Although there is little doubt that history will judge him brilliant as majority leader and more equivocally as president, Johnson exemplified the consensus style of leadership in his ability to bring together diverse points of view and personalities in the Senate even (or perhaps especially) under a president from the opposing party. Johnson liked to quote the prophet Isaiah, "Come, let us reason together," condensing the complex of calculated interests of senators and their constituencies. He could reason, mediate, and persuade more adroitly when his own position was either unformed or genuinely neutral. He also functioned for consensus when he brought forth the political IOUs which he amassed by doing things for others. Given the tradition of compromise and the avoidance of win-lose tactics in the Senate, many senators found Johnson's actions in keeping with their own desires to avoid polarization and exaggerated contentions.

That Johnson performed so brilliantly as majority leader suggests that he experienced the self-enhancement which occurs when the demands of a job and the psychological dynamics of the individual are in almost perfect harmony. In his early years as president, Johnson turned the grief of the nation into a national sentiment to fulfill a program in civil rights and domestic reform which the fallen hero had been unable to accomplish. However, Johnson's decisive victory in the 1964 election gave him power in his own name, providing a mandate for his style of leadership while, at the same time, signifying rejection of his opponent who seemed to evoke extremist images (particularly on issues of war and peace). Yet, what occurred over the next four years prompts a number of questions: Did Johnson's personality change, and did he abandon the consensus style for an arbitrary and autocratic position which was out of keeping with national sentiment? Or, did his problems as president reflect the limitations of the consensus style of leadership?

The Vietnam War was a product of consensus politics and does not reflect a change either in Johnson's style of leadership or his personality (Halberstam 1972). The choices were to stay out and let the fate of the Indochina peninsula go its way or to launch an all-out military operation to secure the existence of South Vietnam. Although the American people were not prepared for the second course, the first course of action, to stay out, aroused fears about the domino effect in Southeast Asia. The Washington bureaucracy and the power structure were fearful about the public reaction to the fall of a new territory to a communist government, for they were still sensitized by public reaction to the events in China in 1949. Therefore, the compromise, or the consensus position, was to respond with enough force to tip the balance in favor of South Vietnam while, at the same time, avoiding not only the classical economic argument of guns versus butter but also the decisions accompanying mobilization for warfare. Events largely have indicated that these decisions reached through consensus were unwise; and the military operations of 1972 suggest that our government under President Nixon was still entrapped by the consensus approach. Therefore, one of the limitations of the consensus approach to leadership is that the accumulation of individual compromises in decision making can and often does result in a rigid, extremist position.

In its most highly developed form, consensus leadership is a product of large-scale corporations and works especially well when goals are explicit and measurement of outcomes is equally clear-cut. To a striking degree, policy initiatives come from below and are debated and modified long before they reach the attention of or become identified with the consensus leader.

An extreme example of consensus as a mechanism and style of leadership is the Japanese system of *ringisei*. Policy proposals are debated at lower levels of management and only move to higher levels of authority when a consensus has been reached with each participant signifying his agreement by initialing the policy documents. When the policy initiatives finally reach the chief executive, his role is purely symbolic—attesting to the consensus. The consensus leader in Japan, a position usually reserved for elder statesmen, is like a grandfather (to use the analogy of kinship structures); in less extreme cases, the consensus leader functions as an older brother, in contrast to the charismatic leader as a parental figure.

The particular strengths of the consensus style are in the individual's capacity to form alliances initially with a small number of individuals and then progressively to gain wider participation in decision making by distributing power throughout the hierarchy and by encouraging initiatives from below. Such alliances and participative structures would be impossible to sustain without the consensus leader's orientation to peers and his sensitivity to their motives and interests. These characteristics were outstanding features in the personality of one of American industry's great corporate innovators.

A recent history of Pierre Du Pont's corporate leadership (Chandler & Salisbury 1971) traces the evolution of the Du Pont Corporation and General Motors as a product of consensus leadership. Pierre Du Pont came to power with two cousins, Coleman and Alfred, who collectively succeeded the older generation of Du Ponts. When Coleman, the older cousin, lost interest in the corporation, Pierre and Alfred became contenders for leadership. Pierre's strategic position in dealing with the financial affairs of the corporation placed him in the best spot for assuming leadership, in contrast to Alfred's narrow specialization in the manufacture of gunpowder. Given his position and personality, Pierre found it congenial to encourage initiative from below and to solidify a coalition with subordinates by appealing to their interests and motives. Alfred, on the other hand, experienced his isolation as somewhat consistent with his defenses and could not put together a workable coalition to counter Pierre.

Among the personality attributes which suited Pierre for consensus leadership were a sense of attachment and responsibility to subordinates. This trait he developed early in life, perhaps as a result of his father's premature death. Pierre became a surrogate father to his younger siblings; in fact, they called him "Dad." However, as surrogate, he avoided the emotional and behavioral characteristics of the strong and even autocratic father. He was truly an older brother. His attachment to peers both in his family and in the Du Pont Corporation probably accounts for the fact that he did not marry until late in life and that he never had children.

To maintain a consistent attitude of caring, responsibility, and attachment to peers the consensus leader must moderate both libido and aggression. If the libidinal charge is too intense or insufficiently disguised, excessive anxiety would be aroused in others and would result in the dissolution of group formations. Perhaps more significant in understanding the consensus leader's character structure is the fate of aggression. The aggression must be low-key, directed outside the group (if manifested at all), and, in general, limited in the degree to which aggression is actually experienced by both the consensus leader and his group. Understanding of the vicissitudes of aggression suggests that the consensus leader apparently experiences excessive guilt in containing, if not resolving, the oedipus complex and must maintain reaction formation as an ego defense. Although both guilt and reaction formation sustain the consensus leader's intense sense of responsibility toward his group, these affective repressors account for the frequency with which such leaders appear bland, opaque, and gray in demeanor and personality. However, those individuals for whom reaction formation and guilt are such prominent aspects of their psychic experience occasionally lose control and often react with anger that is disproportionate to the provocation. On the other hand, when anger may be genuinely used in the service of action, it seems to them that such an expression is beyond the range of permissible behavior.

All of these formulations concerning the consensus leader are familiar in relation to the outcomes of the infantile oedipus complex. Although these formulations are valid, I believe they are somehow incomplete. Therefore, a more specific look at the nature of psychopathology in consensus leaders must be taken.

Those who opt for corporate and political leadership are very bright people, ambitious, upwardly mobile; yet, with all their intellectual gifts, they persist in magical beliefs about performance and accomplishment. These fantasies begin with the person's sense of having *been* special, of winning the oedipal struggle. As long as one maintains the sense of being special, he will not fall into the predepressive or detached and affectively isolated state so aptly presented in Albert Camus' *The Stranger* (1946). The loss of this sense of being special occurs when there is some setback which causes a leak in the narcissistic reservoir. The disruptions in self-esteem may also occur in what Elliott Jacques (1965) described as the "mid-life crisis." Individuals who have achieved substantial success are beset with the disappointments associated with the failure of reality to live up to expectations; this condition leads to regressive longings and the wish to return to the idyllic states encapsulated in preoedipal fantasies. The defense against these longings is built into adaptation to reality. These individuals owe their success to their capacity to establish a fit with some social reality and, in this sense, function through hyperadaptation and excessive activity.

Consensus leaders seem to lack stable, benevolent, and well-integrated introjects. The explanation for this inner impoverishment in personality is that in early development the individual experienced disruption in object ties, particularly in separation from mother and in his reactions to the birth of younger siblings. When such disruptions occur, there may be a precipitous and premature reach for new objects, bypassing the mental process of turning inward to fantasy and recovering the object through internalization and identification. The consequences of such a pattern of development can be found in cognitive and affective modes—the "radar effect" of turning outward, or field dependency.

Subject and Audience: The Theater of Leadership

I want to engage in one further comparison of charismatic and consensus leaders—one that is particularly appropriate during a season of political campaigning. During a campaign, we become exquisitely attuned to and consequently manipulated by the stagecraft of politics. Both the consensus and the charismatic leader employ a form of theatrics in the way they present themselves to an audience and in evoking the actions and reactions they seek. However, this similarity is superficial and misleading. The consensus leader's performance tends to utilize role playing as a form of acting, while the charismatic leader's performance is a renewed dramatization, merging (if only momentarily) the internalized audience and the real audience.

The charismatic leader has a continuous dialogue with his internal images which are joined episodically with the external audience. For this reason, the observer in initially observing charismatic figures has the experience of standing outside a dramatization. The appeal is voyeuristic; the fascination is being a witness to the unfolding of a personality which occurs as though the actor were performing unobserved. This feeling of watching from the outside permits both the performer and the audience to relax their defenses, to "suspend disbelief," and to allow their emotions to surge and to join with those of others. Once joined, the distance between performer and audience suddenly disappears. The audience is on the inside, having lost the separation of self and objects which characterizes rational thought in which intellect and emotion are split off. Within the audience, the images of parents as protectors and love objects surface in a collapse of time—a merging of past and present. The orator now has a hold on his audience. If he is a demagogue, he can seduce them into ignoring reality; and, instead of creating a future, he re-creates a past in a mythological form in which scapegoats are presented to focus hatred and to mislead. If the charismatic leader is in communication with benevolent images, he appeals to a future—a new reality that is an unexpected combination of intellect and emotion which transcends the limits of narrow rationality. (After all, it was narrow rationality that led the United States into Vietnam and later sought to extricate us with our original purpose intact and the rules of power unchanged.)

The Hoffmans (1968) further explain the charismatic leader's dramatizations in terms of the warmth the leader seeks. For the charismatic leader, as in the case of de Gaulle,

> The warmth he needs is not the intimacy of equals, but the support and sympathy of the led. The "melancholy" that is the accepted price of domination, that willing sacrifice of ordinary human relations, becomes intolerable and leads to "ill-explained retreats" only when the *leader's* soul becomes engulfed by what Clemenceau . . . called its worst pain: cold—the indifference or hostility of the led. The warmth he needs is public [p. 854].

For the consensus leader, the mass audience provides little warmth and, in fact, is an object of mistrust, a feeling which parallels his reaction to his internal audience. His inner images are vague, illusory, and contradictory. Consequently, they provide little warmth and support for the consensus leader's sense of self-esteem, and even less substance for projecting a collective belief or idea onto the public. The consensus leader in politics, therefore, uses a type of role playing rather than dramatization.

Role playing is a very calculating method of communicating ideas to an audience and requires a structure made up of three parts: a stereotyped image, an audience of one, and the player. The stereotype must be easily recognized and simply presented, e.g., Mr. Nixon's famous "Checkers" speech in which he evoked the stereotype of the naive but honest son who is the victim of oppression at the hands of a powerful aggressor.

The audience of one and the player both accept the stereotype but maintain it as an object outside of themselves. They avoid close identification with the stereotype, since otherwise it would arouse too much emotion which is unacceptable both in the psychology of consensus and in role playing. The emotional level can also be kept down by preventing the audience of one from merging with a collective audience— "playing it cool" is the key.

Of course, television is ideally suited for role playing. Besides being a "cool medium," it prevents the audience from forming bonds with one another or directly with the player. Technically, television maintains distance between the stereotype, the audience of one, and the player.

When this structure is established with a low-keyed emotional tone, the role play can be brought to its conclusion. Here the player tries to present himself as a peacemaker, a preserver of law and order, a reformer, a protector of property, a friend of the disadvantaged, or any of the other political images. It is even possible in concluding the role play to disguise a policy or decision by presenting the opposite image. If the president is about to undertake major air bombardment in Indochina, then the conclusion of the role play is to present himself as a peacemaker and negotiator, which may have been the purpose behind Mr. Nixon's decision to "blow the cover" on Dr. Kissinger's secret negotiations with the North Vietnamese. If he is about to take action which will probably displease the right wing of his consensus position, then predictably it is timely for a role play to evoke recognizable stereotypes and self-presentations in line with conservative choices.

The consensus leader through indirectness and the capacity to manipulate through role playing seeks to enlarge and control the center of the political spectrum and to prevent it from fragmenting into many interest groups. While this capacity may be successful in being elected to office, the cost for the consensus leader and consequently his constituents is potentially high. He seldom experiences the peace of mind which comes from the security of purpose, the commitment to deeply held convictions, the realization that he is master of his own house. For too long he has sought to control the insecurities of the sibling and the competition of peer relationships through maneuvering and adjustment to the outside world.

Conclusion

The personality traits of both charismatic and consensus leaders have been too often disregarded. It has been argued that a leader's role is defined by the situation. However, this argument ignores the significance of personality characteristics which determine how an individual will respond. Any leader will act or react in ways consistent with his personal style and will resort to his habitual modes of managing internal and external conflict. I cannot offer a definitive answer to the relative weight of situational and personal factors in determining decisions. However, I believe the personality factors have been underestimated in their capacity to determine how a chief executive acts upon the constraints and opportunities available to him. In fact, many leaders discover themselves in trouble when shifting events place a burden on their defensive apparatus because these events demand modes of action which lie beyond the leader's personal style.

For example, many of the problems Woodrow Wilson experienced in his relationship with the Senate after the negotiation of the peace treaty resulted from a shift in group psychology—from attachment to the strong leader to the urge to equalize power consistent with peer group attitudes. Had Wilson been able to adapt to the requirements of this new consensus psychology, he might have salvaged the treaty and the League of Nations. But Wilson reacted like the father under attack from rebellious sons. Under these conditions of stress, he resorted to his appeal to the masses, his favored coalition, and bypassed leaders in the Senate for whom consultation was both necessary and desirable in their quest for a new distribution of power. The appeal to the masses failed, and Wilson was unable to shift his presidential style, a fact that contributed (at least in part) to his subsequent stroke and incapacitation (George & George 1956).

In the various phases of a lifetime, in the progression from infancy to old age, the decisive event in adulthood, for which the early years are preparation, is the change from being the son and peer to being the father and leader (at least in the family if not in organizational or elective politics). However, this progression seems to have been interrupted culturally as well as politically. The emergence of the fraternal ideal as the substitute for the heroic father has created a standard which only adds to the anxieties under which the transition from son to father takes place. But there is a limit to how effective cleverness, adroitness, and flexibility can be in circumventing reality and anxiety. When this limit is reached in the cyclical currents of group psychology, the turn may well be toward the leadership of a charismatic man who knows how to wait.

References

Bion, W. R.: *Experiences in Groups and Other Papers.* New York: Basic Books, 1961.

Camus, Albert: *The Stranger,* Stuart Gilbert, trans. New York: Knopf, 1946.

Chandler, A. D., Jr. & Salisbury, Stephen: *Pierre S. Du Pont and the Making of the Modern Corporation.* New York: Harper & Row, 1971.

Cooley, C. W.: *Social Organization.* Glencoe, Ill.: Free Press, 1956.

Erikson, E. H.: *Childhood and Society.* New York: Norton, 1950.

_____: *Young Man Luther: A Study in Psychoanalysis and History.* New York: Norton, 1958.

_____: *Gandhi's Truth on the Origins of Militant Nonviolence.* New York: Norton, 1969.

Freud, Sigmund (1895): The Psychotherapy of Hysteria. *Standard Edition* 2:255–305, 1955.

_____ (1921): Group Psychology and the Analysis of the Ego. *Standard Edition* 18:69–143, 1955.

George, Alexander & George, Juliette: *Woodrow Wilson and Colonel House: A Personality Study.* New York: Day, 1956.

Geyelin, Philip: *Lyndon B. Johnson and the World.* New York: Praeger, 1966.

Halberstam, David: *The Best and the Brightest.* New York: Random House, 1972.

Hoffmann, Stanley & Hoffmann, Inge: The Will to Grandeur: de Gaulle as Political Artist, *Daedulus* 97(3):829–87, Summer 1968.

Jacques, Elliott: Death and the Mid-Life Crisis. *Int. J. Psycho-Anal.* 46(4):502–14, 1965.

Jones, Ernest: *The Life and Work of Sigmund Freud,* Vol. 1, New York: Basic Books, 1953.

Langer, W. C.: *The Mind of Adolph Hitler: The Secret Wartime Report.* New York: Basic Books, 1972.

Mead, G. H.: *Mind, Self and Society from the Standpoint of a Social Behaviorist,* C. W. Morris, ed. Chicago: University of Chicago Press, 1934.

Parsons, Talcott, ed.: *Max Weber: The Theory of Social and Economic Organization.* New York: Oxford University Press, 1947.

Riesman, David, *et al.: The Lonely Crowd: A Study of the Changing American Character.* New Haven: Yale University Press, 1950.

22

Conjecturing
About Creative Leaders

MORGAN W. McCALL, JR.

I will frankly admit to you that both the terms creative and leadership confuse me. I have learned to be relatively comfortable with some of the ambiguities and outrages of leadership research, but I have always been afraid to confront the nebulousness of creativity, much less to try to put creativity and leadership together. So it is my hope to share a few thoughts with you, not based in science. Abraham Maslow once said that "science is a means whereby noncreative people can create." So I will avoid data. My intention here is to stir up some controversy, and I think that is almost assured. I am certainly not giving prescriptions; in fact, maybe you should do the opposite of what I suggest if you want to be a creative leader.

In preparing for this talk, I drew heavily on Karl Weick (1974, 1976, 1978) and Michael Cohen and Jim March (1974), who to me are among the most creative of the social scientists writing today. I'll try to give them credit where it is due. I also drew on John Steinbeck (1962) who is one of the most creative persons whom I have ever encountered in print. And finally, I drew on David Ogilvy (1965) who is the head of a major advertising firm and has written some very interesting things.

What I am going to be talking about is leaders in organizations. I am going to be talking about managers, administrators, presidents, foremen, supervisors; I am not going to be talking about the research and development types, or isolated staff specialists, or independent creative people. What I am going to do is to try to reflect on what creative leadership might be in a nonreflective, fast-paced, constrained, goal-oriented system. In a real live organization what can creative leadership possibly mean?

Reprinted by permission from *The Journal of Creative Behavior*, 14:4 (1979), pp. 225–234.

I think one way to start is with the Second Law of Thermodynamics. Entropy is a natural law that things tend to run down, fly apart, return to their natural disorganized state. One way to look at managers is as manifestations of negative entropy, because managers are the glue that keeps systems from flying apart, running down, and disorganizing.

Cohen and March studied the presidents of 42 universities. What they had to say about the lives of those people is relevant to other managers as well. They described them as reactive, parochial, conventional, and living an illusion (Cohen & March, 1974). By reactive, Cohen and March could be talking about Warren Bennis (he was then President of the University of Cincinnati) who described some 500 interest groups with which he had to deal. Most of his job was reacting to the demands and concerns of other people. By parochial, they mean that if you look at where college presidents come from, you discover that they have similar backgrounds, similar experiences, and relatively narrow views of the world. If you look at upwardly mobile corporate managers, some of those same characteristics apply. They mean conventional in the sense that many people have expectations about what a president, or manager, or chief executive officer will do; people have certain expectations of what leaders will do and they tend to be conventional expectations. Leaders will handle the budget, will administer, will be fair, and so forth. Finally, the illusion Cohen and March write about is that presidents think they have a lot of control, when the reality is that presidents have only modest control over events. The main things affecting universities are far beyond the power of any individual to do much about. They may be things as esoteric as the birthrate 20 years ago. And the same thing is true for leaders of corporations, and particularly for the President of the United States.

Leaders work in an environment that sees creativity as a threat, especially creativity defined as a deviant response. The deviant response is something that could ruin an organization as easily as it could move it forward. So organizations tend to be designed for survival, not for creativity. And managers are imbedded in an organization that runs contrary to most of the things that we know about creativity. In fact, most organizations might have a sign that says "stamp out creativity." Many organizations deal with creativity by isolating it, controlling it, judging it, and, at times, even eliminating it.

What is a creative leader in this kind of environment, and what is that creative leader trying to do? It is probably useful to describe a simple series of steps that creative leaders are involved with. One thing that they are trying to do is generate, or stimulate others to generate original, creative ideas, and so come up with new processes, new ways of doing things. The second thing that they have to do as managers is to find out somehow what all these ideas are, collect them in some way, and then evaluate them, because in an on-going organization you can't just let ideas float around indefinitely. Then, having evaluated and picked a few of them, creative leaders have to convince the organization that an idea is worth the investment and worth the trouble to implement. Now that is a very simple model, not profound; but I would suggest to you, for the sake of heresy, that there are already so many ideas, and so much information, and so many different opinions running around in organizations that the real challenge of creative leadership is in the last two steps. Nonetheless, there is some value in trying to produce more ideas; so how might we describe one of these creative leaders in an ongoing organization? I am going to describe creative leaders as being crafty, grouchy, dangerous, feisty, contrary, inconsistent, evangelistic, prejudiced, and spineless. (I'm indebted to Karl Weick [1976] who used a similar series of adjectives to describe organizations.) Let me try to justify these descriptions one at a time.

Crafty

My feeling is that creativity itself, and certainly the evaluation of whether something is good or bad, involves a value judgment. If I were to put up six pieces of modern art and ask you which were creative and which were good, I would get a lot of differences of opinion. So the first thing about creativity is that, because value judgments are involved, people will disagree about whether an idea is good or bad, or whether it is even creative. The second aspect is that organizations are political systems. The evidence is overwhelming; all of you live in organizations, and you see the political activities all around you. So you put those two together, and you have a value judgment being made in a political system. That is why I suggest to you that creative leaders are crafty. There is a good deal of cunning involved, first in helping others to create something, and, second, in being able to create something oneself in a political environment. This means that leaders out there who are creative are, in fact, able to negotiate very well; they are able to circumvent constraints; they are very sensitive to the tactical issues involved in the use of power. Although power is a different topic, I don't think you can talk about creative leadership in organizations without talking about power, because power is unevenly distributed; and whether or not the people who are trying to push through a creative idea have power is going to make a lot of difference in their effectiveness. The literature on power includes a variety of tactics, some subtle, some blatant—and I suspect that creative leaders are well versed in how to use the power that they have.

Another interesting aspect of craftiness is that, in organizations, managers have to survive failures. We have interviewed a lot of managers, and we have discovered that a manager is usually permitted one or two boners. After that he or she is in trouble. The nature of creativity requires taking a series of half-baked ideas, pushing for them, and getting them implemented. Because of power structures, if creative leaders are to survive, they have to be able to disassociate with failures and associate with successes. Thus, creative leaders are probably manipulative, even Machiavellian. They probably use structure, create structure, disband structure, and change structure. They probably also use people; in short, they are probably extremely political.

Grouchy

I suspect that complacency is the enemy of creativity. There has been a lot of research done on the issue of satisfaction, and some people have claimed that if your employees are satisfied, your employees will be more productive. The accumulated research evidence is heavily against that. There are few consistent relationships between the satisfaction of individual employees and their productivity. Sometimes the relationship is negative, sometimes it is positive, but most of the time there is no relationship at all. In fact, when there is a causal relationship between employee satisfaction and performance, it usually goes the other way: high performing employees are more satisfied; more satisfied employees are not necessarily more productive. So I would suspect that our grouchy, creative leader can be quite demanding and controlling, and may, in fact, have exorbitant standards.

This brings us to the issue of complaints. One of Maslow's interesting suggestions is that the number of complaints in an organization is relatively constant; that no matter how good you are to people, the number of complaints will remain the same. What happens is that complaints will change in level. Karl Weick elaborated on this idea when he suggested that we consider the level of complaint in an organization. If people are complaining about conditions of work and job security, you have a relatively low level of complaint going on in your organization. However, if people are complaining about not getting praised, or about threats to their self-esteem, then you have a higher level of complaint. It means you have evolved as an organization. Weick goes on to say that in the effective organization, a large number of complaints focus on perfection, truth, beauty, and other higher ideals. To give you an example of what I mean, I'll quote from Maslow (cited by Weick, 1976):

To complain about the garden programs in the city where I live, to have committees heatedly coming in and saying that the rose gardens in the parks are not sufficiently cared for, is in itself a wonderful thing; because it indicates the height of life at which the complainers are living. To complain about rose gardens means that your belly is full, that you have a good roof over your head, that your furnace is working, that you are not afraid of bubonic plague, that you are not afraid of assassination, that the police and fire departments work well and many other pre-conditions are already satisfied. This is the point, the high level complaint is not to be taken simply like any other complaint. It must be used to indicate all the pre-conditions which have been satisfied in order to make the height of his complaint theoretically possible.

So we may have some grouches out there who are trying to keep people from being complacent by moving them to a different level of noncomplacency, if such a thing is possible.

We have done some research using Mintzberg's ten managerial roles. One, leadership, concerns what is called "consideration and initiating structure" in our jargon, and means creating a warm, supportive climate for subordinates, structuring their work, and setting goals. This is the only one of the ten roles negatively related to both level in the organization and promotion rate within the organization in a sample of 2,700 managers. I suspect that creative leaders are, in fact, a bit grouchy, that they do prod people, and that they probably won't worry as much about the satisfaction of their people as might be suspected.

Dangerous

From an organizational perspective, creative leaders are indeed dangerous. As I said before, creative ideas are something new, something untried, something different that a leader is going to get implemented. In most organizations implementing a major new idea means millions of dollars, new plants, commitments for years ahead. So new ideas represent a threat to organization survival. Take, for example, a new technology. An organization taking advantage of new technology may have to build a plant before they even know if the new product will sell. Failure might sink the organization; success could make it great. Maybe that is why research and development tends to be isolated on a hill somewhere. In most companies they do that; they build a little cage and put all their creative people in it, and then when an idea comes out they take it back to the management committee and evaluate it in the cold light of day-to-day realities. But creative leaders can be dangerous because they tend to take risks first and ask questions later.

From an organizational point of view, the unpredictability of this can be disturbing.

Feisty

I suspect that creative leaders deliberately create conflict—not to increase competition necessarily but to create sparks that contain ideas. If you have ever read Oliver Wendell Holmes, you may remember the notion of the dice and marbles (Weick, 1974). You can take two positions and visualize them as dice. They have sharp corners and they are very distinct. The noncreative leader takes a rasp and files all the sharp corners off so that they roll around, and anybody who wants to can roll them. In fact, some people have argued that compromise is the worst possible strategy because the result is the most inane parts of two ideas—the parts that everybody can agree on; you lose what was really dramatically different about them. I suspect that creative leaders, rather than trying to suppress conflict, sometimes generate it and often try to control and direct it. The real challenge is to make that conflict useful.

Another reason that creative leaders may be feisty is that in an organization, it is tough to get resources, so they are fighting for resources and the power to implement ideas. To protect people out there having weird ideas takes a lot of work—it takes some fighting. Some of the managers that we talked to, the ones that struck us as creative, markedly loved to straighten out messes, to get involved in conflicts, and make conflicts productive.

Contrary

By contrary I simply mean that some of the creative leaders out there must be contrary to our laws of human nature. Let me give you five of these contradictions out of Cohen and March (1974). Creative leaders might treat:

1. goals as hypotheses;
2. intuition as reality;
3. hypocrisy as transition;
4. memory as an enemy; and
5. experience as theory.

Most of us like to have a concrete goal, something that we are working for; but apparently some people, who are a little bit more creative than most of us, treat goals as hypotheses. They are not wedded to a particular point of view, a particular thing that they are after.

As for treating intuition as reality—intuition can be viewed as an excuse for doing something you can't justify. However, creative leaders see it as a real factor and will go on a hunch. As I said before, they will take a risk and see what happens: they'll learn by experience.

Creative leaders treat hypocrisy as transition. Now there is a thought-provoking idea. Most of us in our lives try to balance our attitudes and values with what we do. We are uncomfortable when we believe one thing and do a different thing. We try to balance. It is called "cognitive balance" in the jargon. If I like Mary, and Mary likes John, then I want to like John—because if I don't I have an imbalance. Cohen and March argue that when people behave differently than they believe they are ripe for change. And there is good research evidence to say that behavior creates attitudes, not the reverse. What you think is a poor predictor of what you do, but what you do is an excellent predictor of what you will eventually think. So creative leaders may be out there trying to get people to behave differently and, in so doing, may be creating new values.

Memory is treated as an enemy. Habit, folklore, and myth are as prevalent in organizations as anywhere else, so creative leaders try not to be susceptible to them. And finally, creative leaders treat experience as a theory. They act before thinking rather than think before acting. So there are five ways in which creative leaders may be contrary.

Inconsistent

We envision managers having things highly integrated, with lots of rules, processes, and control. The survival of the organization depends on its different pieces being interdependent and being controlled and being watched. However, creative leaders may try to keep the system flexible so the different pieces can do different things. John Steinbeck (1962) has talked about that, and he puts it in terms of integration. As we integrate organizations—make them more interdependent, more controlled—we drive out the possibility that different parts of the organization can do things differently. Steinbeck says:

> We thought that perhaps our species thrives best and most creatively in a state of semi-anarchy, governed by loose rules and half-practiced mores. To this we added the premise that overintegration in human groups might parallel the law in paleontology that over-armor or over-ornamentation are symptoms of decay and disappearance. Indeed, we thought, over-integration *might be* the symptom of human decay. We thought: there is

no creative unit in the human save the individual working alone. In pure creativeness, in art, in music, in mathematics, there are no true collaborations. The creative principle is a lonely and an individual matter. Groups can correlate, investigate, and build, but we could not think of any group that has ever created or invented anything. Indeed, the first impulse of the group seems to be to destroy the creation and the creator. But integration, or the designed group, seems to be highly vulnerable.

He then goes on to give some examples which suggest that we don't want integrated systems, and then says:

Consider the blundering anarchic system of the United States; the stupidity of some of its lawmakers, the violent reaction, the slowness of its ability to change. Twenty-five key men destroyed could make the Soviet Union stagger, but we could lose our Congress, our President, and our general staff and nothing much would have happened. We could go right on. In fact we might be better for it.

In any case I suspect that creative leaders might have to fight the urge to integrate, to solidify, to make everything interdependent. They want to keep the pieces loose enough so that they could lose a few and the organization would still survive.

Evangelistic

Karl Weick once said, "Leaders are evangelists, not accountants." By that he meant that creative leaders manipulate symbols for the rest of the organization. If you walk into an organization that is bottom-line oriented, what you are walking into is a symbol; this is the way we punctuate reality in this organization, this is the reality we strive for. Creative leaders create the myths and symbols by which other people operate. In that sense, they are evangelists, preaching a cause, saying it is alright to be creative, saying that the organization prefers this to that, using a reward system to make people who do something bizarre-but-effective a symbol for the whole organization. It is the suggestion box raised to a level at which it becomes a symbolic part of the people in the organization.

Prejudiced

When I suggest that creative leaders are prejudiced, I don't mean sex bias or race bias; they may or may not be prejudiced in those ways. I do suspect, though, that creative leaders are prejudiced about competence. They use it and discriminate with it. If they have different kinds of people, they match them to jobs so that the creative ones are not mixed in with the Philistines. There is some evidence in the leadership research that leaders rarely treat all of their subordinates the same way. They have in-groups and out-groups, and when you look at their relationships with individual subordinates, they are, in fact, discriminating. There is a quote from Ogilvy that I want to share with you. At one time he worked in a French kitchen and apparently the head chef was a real tyrant. Ogilvy (1965) said this about him:

> M. Pitard did not tolerate incompetence. He knew that it is demoralizing for professionals to work alongside incompetent amateurs. I saw him fire three pastry cooks in a month for the same crime: They could not make the caps on their brioches rise evenly. Mr. Gladstone would have applauded such ruthlessness; he held that the first essential for a prime minister is to be a good butcher. M. Pitard taught me exorbitant standards of service.

While creative leaders are prejudiced, they are not at all egalitarian. This idea has been expanded on by Craig Lundberg (1978) who has talked about Lieutenants, about how effective leaders in organizations find an ally with whom they work closely. They may exclude others; they may fight the selection system. So I suggest that any creative leaders out there would be far from egalitarian or participative in the way they make decisions.

Spineless

One of the crucial things about living in a complex organizational environment and being able to deal with it is to be a listener, an absorber, a monitor. The data we have indicates a positive correlation between monitoring information and promotion rate in the organization. In a recent essay, Karl Weick (1978) makes a point about managers being a media. To demonstrate this point, he uses a contour gauge. You can set it down on a corner, press on it, and you'll come away with a precise image of the corner. Weick elaborates on this analogy by pointing out that each one of the little spines in the contour gauge operates independently of the others. In much the same way, he says, creative leaders are out there absorbing all kinds of different things, but not necessarily connecting them. The interesting irony of all this is that creative leaders are also able to act. They can turn their absorbing, monitoring functions around and use all that differentiation to make something happen. It is almost like being on the other side of the contour gauge when you push it down.

So, these are some hypothetical characteristics of creative leaders: they may be crafty, grouchy, dangerous, feisty, contrary, evangelistic, prejudiced, and spineless.

I suspect that some of the creative leaders in organizations would appear two-faced to an outsider, because on the one hand, they are playing the traditional organizational game so that they can stay in the system and continue to do something with it, while on the other hand they are moving ahead, gaining credits, and being generally outrageous.

Finally, I believe that people have fun in organizations in spite of these "horrible" characteristics of creative leaders. My proposition would be that success is the fun. Playfulness does not necessarily lead to creativity, but successfully creative organizations have a great deal of fun because there is nothing more exciting than to succeed at what you are doing.

Let me close by reminding you that I started out with Cohen and March describing managers as reactive, parochial, conventional, and living an illusion. Because I think there are many oxymorons in creative leadership, and because the nature of creativity is making opposites fit and frames of reference clash, what we really may be talking about is reactive reflection, broad parochialism, unorthodox conventionalism, and solid illusions.

References

Cohen, D. & March, J. G. *Leadership and ambiguity.* NYC: McGraw-Hill, 1974.

Lundberg, C. The unreported leadership research of Dr. G. Hypothetical. In McCall, M. & Lombardo, M. (eds.), *Leadership: where else can we go?* Durham, NC: Duke University Press, 1978.

Ogilvy, D. M. The creative chef. In Steiner, G. A. (ed.), *The creative organization.* Chicago: University of Chicago Press, 1965.

Steinbeck, J. *The log from the sea of Cortez.* NYC: Viking, 1962.

Thomas, L. *The lives of a cell.* NYC: Bantam, 1974.

Weick, K. E. Reward concepts: dice or marbles. Presented at the School of Industrial and Labor Relations, Cornell University, Ithaca, NY, 1974.

Weick, K. E. On re-punctuating the problem of organizational effectiveness. Paper presented at a conference on organizational effectiveness at Carnegie-Mellon University, Pittsburgh, 1976.

Weick, K. E. The spines of leaders. In McCall, M. & Lombardo, M. (eds.), *Leadership: where else can we go?* Durham, NC: Duke University Press, 1978.

23

How Do Leaders Get to Lead?

MICHAEL M. LOMBARDO

The question of whether leaders are born or made has vexed organizations throughout history. Even though about 75 percent of management development directors say real development occurs on the job, there is evidence that most organizations allow this development to occur for only a chosen few.

If having the skills and capabilities to become a leader is not as important as the opportunity to develop and demonstrate them, then many managers never have a chance.

The Early Years

A young man might go into military flight training believing that he was entering some sort of technical school in which he was simply going to acquire a certain set of skills. Instead, he found himself all at once enclosed in a fraternity. And in this fraternity, even though it was military, men were not rated by their outward rank as ensigns, lieutenants, commanders, or whatever. "The world was divided into those who had it and those who did not." This quality, this "it," was never named, however, nor was it talked about in any way.

—Tom Wolfe,
The Right Stuff

Organizations usually separate those who have "it" from those who do not during the early years of a career, and in so doing organizations favor as their future leaders young managers who demonstrate skills

Reprinted by permission from *Issues and Observations*, 2:1 (February 1982), pp. 1–4.

and abilities they bring with them to the job. Abilities to work with others, handle conflict, analyze problems, run a meeting, set priorities and so forth are looked for early, and, if seen, can lead to anointment as a high-potential or fast-track manager. If the manager has the right background as well (e.g., an MBA and past positions of leadership), the odds of being dubbed a rising star increase further.

Organizations put confidence in this rite of anointment to reduce risk. The question of future leadership is a matter of survival. With the vicissitudes of competition, regulation, and the economy, businesses can't afford added uncertainty in the promotion of leaders.

To insure a steady stream of competent leaders, organizations therefore select and hone managers who demonstrate certain skills early. Since learning a management job takes about two years and learning a business takes several decades, organizations take the least risk possible. Although young managers cannot quickly understand the business, they can quickly demonstrate the skills necessary to learn it.

In short, it's easier to teach the objective components of business than it is to teach the murky clusters of behavior called skills, or even more difficult to teach abstractions like judgement.

There is more than logic to support the selection of future leaders from among the managers who demonstrate leadership skills early. In Bray and Howard's 20-year study of AT&T managers, there was a shocking finding: The average manager does not improve in managerial abilities over time. There is no evidence that managerial experience is a good teacher of management.

Critics can say that this finding holds for average managers but that those who get to the top are anything but average. Or they might attack the assessment center data on which the Bray and Howard findings are based, contending that the skills and abilities measured are too global to pick up the subtle learning and the refinement of skills that take place over 20 years. A manager who excelled in defining problems 20 years ago may have since developed subtle questioning techniques and ways of turning a problem inside out that a straightforward rating of "clearly defined the problem" might miss.

Still, there is the nagging suspicion that managers who have the skills to begin with have an edge that time only increases. Although most managers in the study indeed changed, becoming both more occupationally and family-oriented, less dependent on others, and more interested in achievement and influencing others, their skills didn't change much. Even for successful managers, interest in personal development and interpersonal skills tended to sag, but (and this is the source of the suspicion) their skills started higher and stayed higher than did the skills of those who were less successful.

It may be that even eventual leaders don't learn many new skills from experience. Instead, they bring their skills to the job, and, as some executives have insisted, rise to the top because their capabilities blossom when they are confronted with new situations. With this view, a manager who jumps in and handles a nasty conflict does so because the requisite skills are waiting within until they are needed.

The Self-Fulfilling Prophecy

If success as a leader were as simple as having the right skills and seizing opportunities to demonstrate them, this view of leadership development could be compelling. But even more important than having the right skills is having the right jobs. Once noticed, fast-movers get into, or are placed in, challenging jobs where they spend more time on projects involving top management, and work for managers who are themselves moving up.

This combination of access to the counsel of top management, working for a highly-regarded manager, and having a core job gives fast-movers the four edges that matter most:

- They learn the business more quickly.
- They learn the perspective of top managers on the business.
- They learn which kinds of jobs and experiences compose the core of the business.
- They more often have a highly-placed mentor to nudge and guide them.

As a result of being seen and being good, the highly-regarded move fast. Leaving their first position in less than two years (according to Veiga), they broaden their perspective with cross-divisional experiences and become expert in one segment of corporate operations.

While not as obvious as being knighted, there is apparently a self-fulfilling prophecy generated whereby success breeds success. By the third year or almost always by the third level of management, potential leaders have been spotted and from then on are exposed to jobs that provide experience relevant for higher-level jobs.

These experiences create expanding opportunities for high-potential managers to learn things far beyond management skills. One group of successful executives, reflecting on the significant learnings in their careers, came up with the following list:

- *Learning to delegate.* Many managers do it all until they pass middle-management, rarely delegating or keeping subordinates adequately informed. Once they become executives, however, a change in outlook must be made: Rather than enjoying doing something, executives must enjoy seeing it done. There must be a letting go of hands-on control in favor of in-out advice.
- *Learning how to get advice.* Many managers excel at aggressively seeking information and taking charge. Executives must learn how to communicate the need for advice and information, and how to listen to others' concerns.
- *Setting life goals.* Although managers may conduct their lives by just letting things happen, executives must learn to make career and life decisions based on specific, incremental goals.
- *Discovering strengths.* To take advantage of the opportunities that come to them, executives must learn what it is they are good at doing.
- *Dealing with adversity.* Executives must learn not to over-analyze the past when they are confronted with a failure. They must quickly understand what went wrong, accept responsibility for their part in the failure, and then move on.
- *Struggling with change.* Executives must learn how to take on new and demanding roles, to deal with a changing organization, new technology, and changing societal norms.

Managers not seen by their organizations as fast-trackers face a different experience. They leave their first position later (3–4 years), and often work in peripheral units for so-so managers. Although they, too, change jobs often, the pattern of their moves is less coherent.

They often switch across functional lines, garnering assignments that hinder the development of long-term business contacts (their network) and make it difficult to master any one segment of the business. (The opportunity to learn marketing or manufacturing or legal affairs in detail is critical to later success. In one study, presidents and board chairmen spent as much as two-thirds of their careers in the *same* function.)

The experiences that non-fast-trackers are exposed to are more narrow and specific. They learn how to implement decisions, set procedures, and master the technical side of management systems, but rarely do they have the opportunity to learn or practice the kinds of skills mentioned by more successful managers.

Haves and Have Nots

A man either had it or he didn't! There was no such thing as having most of it.

—Tom Wolfe,
The Right Stuff

Whether by nature or by nurture or by both, by about the third level of management, groups of "haves" and "have nots" form in many organizations. For the "haves," their past opportunities have helped them to develop patterns of behavior that are seen as effective in their present jobs and they remain eligible for the top.

For the "have nots"—those who lacked some of the skills to begin with—their problems have been compounded by dead-end, low-visibility jobs which further hinder the catching up they need to do. Real differences now exist between the groups, differences that were there to begin with and that have been exacerbated by later experiences. (See Table 1.)

For the "have nots," a self-defeating pattern emerges: They only listen long enough to categorize a problem, then they shoot from the hip with a standardized solution. If the problem reappears, thornier than ever, they waffle and shunt it off to a committee or they go to the other extreme and attempt to overwhelm the problem with a barrage of solutions. At no time do they stop and ask the questions that might tell them what the problem really is.

For the "haves," the essential difference is an ability to break set, to go against the grain of habit. Many managers who become successful embody an oppositeness of nature that enables them to pause long enough to listen to the music of organizational problems, heads craned for that one funny note, then, once they understand what's going on, to act quickly to hammer out the lyrics.

The Right Stuff?

. . . the idea was to prove at every foot of the way up that pyramid that you were one of the elected and anointed ones who had "the right stuff" and could move higher and higher and even—ultimately, God willing, one day— that you might be able to join that special few at the very top, that elite who had the capacity to bring tears to men's eyes, the very Brotherhood of the Right Stuff itself.

—Tom Wolfe,
The Right Stuff

Such divergent patterns beg the question of "Are these groups really

TABLE 1

Have Nots	Haves
Creatures of habit; tend to wing it based on what worked previously; management by cliché ("never fire-fight"; "the key to management is delegation")	Analyze each situation; may appear inconsistent because seemingly similar situations in fact aren't
Consistently err at the extremes of behavior—they may never get into detail, or may become obsessed with all details	May get into fine detail on one problem and totally ignore detail on the next; act according to the nature of the problem, not the nature of their habits
Work on whatever comes up (12 problems at once in one study)	Spend a third to a half of their time working on one or two priorities
Lack boldness; hesitate to make decisions on complex problems	Involve lots of people, listen to different views of the problem, play with ideas; once mind is made up, act quickly
Don't seek enough advice or help (limited network of contacts)	Extensive network of contacts who might be located anywhere inside or outside the organization
Personal and work-related blind spots resulting from inadequate feedback (e.g., believe they are superb delegators while their subordinates believe the opposite)	Job interests are balanced with family, friends, and other interests that provide helpful feedback

different or did they grow to be this way?" Or more simply, "Is there such a thing as the right stuff?"

There may well be. The problem is no one knows what the right stuff is, since it is the result of both the nature and the nurture of managers.

Most administrative and interpersonal skills are learnable, so these cannot form any unique set of talents. Conceptual abilities, however, are developed fairly early in life and although they can be modified a little, no one has as yet figured out how to improve them dramatically.

Teaching good judgement, or the ability to break set, or the ability to pick key problems, or the courage to make unpopular decisions is not something that can be reduced to simple formulas. Such abilities are terribly complex, and require dealing with ambiguity as a matter of course.

If there is such a thing as the right stuff, it probably lies in a certain comfort with the unknown, and in the ability to make sense of the discordant notes that most of us never even hear. But even if we assume that such an ineffable quality exists, many managers never get much opportunity to show it. Perhaps more important, they may never have had the life experiences that create the credentials that make them visible.

So What?

The point is this: By creating opportunities for more young managers, and by avoiding premature decisions on managerial careers, organizations can increase their chances of developing the best possible leaders for the future.

For a host of reasons, many managers who may have the right stuff will not have the background experiences and skills that will enable them to show it. Blacks, women, and "late-bloomers" are frequently mentioned as three talent pools who may have had inadequate opportunities to develop.

Here are some suggestions for ways to create opportunities for more managers.

- Have a committee of executives address the question, "What should our leaders look like 20 years from now?" (Otherwise, organizations run the risk of promoting only those managers who fit the model of leadership in use 20 years ago.) Decide what developmental experiences the leaders of the year 2000 could benefit from.
- Besides the traditional emphasis on skills and business training for young managers, conduct symposia on the significant events and major learnings of successful executives. These symposia should be small, informal, and conducted by the executives themselves.
- Many organizations have coaching and counseling programs for managers. Organizations could benefit from an executive mentoring program as well. Assign each management recruit to a mentor who meets with the recruit at least once a month for lunch. Ask the mentor to advise the recruit on the recruit's most pressing problems, at the same time injecting top management's perspective into the discussions. Besides getting advice, recruits may be able

to learn the business more quickly and understand how successful managers attack problems.

- Give young managers who have lightly-regarded bosses a chance to work with an effective role model at least part of the time.
- Before deciding that some managers don't have it, answer the question, "Have they ever been in a position where they could show it?"

None of these suggestions will produce miracles. Nor will they create wheat from chaff. They may, however, produce some pleasant surprises.

24

The Leader Who Knows
How Things Happen

JOHN HEIDER

This article consists of twelve chapters of Lao Tzu's *Tao Te Ching*. I have adapted these chapters for group leaders, psychotherapists, and other human-potential educators.

According to tradition, *Tao Te Ching* was written in sixth century B.C. China by Lao Tzu, a state librarian and sage. Myth and history mingle in this tradition.

Tao Te Ching is very short: eighty-one chapters, each no longer than a single page. There are many translations of *Tao Te Ching*. I have included in this article an annotated list of six translations for the reader who wishes to compare my interpretation of Lao Tzu with more literal versions of the same chapters.

I have selected twelve of the original eighty-one chapters of *Tao Te Ching* in order to focus on Lao Tzu's approach to leadership. Other chapters, not presented here, deal with metaphysics (how things happen) and ethics (how to live in accordance with how things happen).

Lao Tzu addressed himself to the sage or to the wise ruler. Here his words are for the wise leader, the leader who knows how things happen.

John Heider, "The Leader Who Knows How Things Happen," *Journal of Humanistic Psychgology*, 27:3 (Summer 1982), pp. 33–39. Copyright © 1982 by the Association for Humanistic Psychology. Reprinted by permission of Sage Publications, Inc.
Author's Note: Chapter numbers and titles: The chapter *numbers* used here are the same as those generally used in other versions of *Tao Te Ching*. The reader can compare this rendition of Chapter 9 with Chapter 9 in any of the translations listed in the reference section. The chapter *titles* are my own: not every version of *Tao Te Ching* uses titles for individual chapters.

Chapter 9: A Good Group

A good group is better than a spectacular group.

When leaders become superstars, the teacher outshines the teaching.

Also, very few superstars are down-to-earth. Fame breeds fame. Before long they get carried away with themselves. They then fly off center and crash.

The wise leader settles for good work and then lets others have the floor. The leader does not take all the credit for what happens and has no need for fame.

A moderate ego demonstrates wisdom.

Chapter 11: The Group Field

Pay attention to silence. What is happening when nothing is happening in group? That is the group field.

Thirteen people sit in a circle, but it is the climate or the spirit in the center of the circle, where nothing is happening, that determines the nature of the group field.

Learn to see emptiness. When you enter an empty house, can you feel the mood of the place? It is the same with a vase or pot; learn to see the emptiness inside, which is the usefulness of it.

People's speech and actions are figural events. They give the group form and content.

The silences and empty spaces, on the other hand, reveal the group's essential mood, the context for everything that happens. That is the group field.

Chapter 17: Like a Midwife

The wise leader does not intervene unnecessarily. The leader's presence is felt, but often the group runs itself.

Lesser leaders do a lot, say a lot, have followers, and form cults.

Even worse ones use fear to energize the group and force to overcome resistance.

Only the most dreadful leaders have bad reputations.

Remember that you are facilitating another person's process. It is not your process. Do not intrude. Do not control. Do not force your own needs and insights into the foreground.

If you do not trust a person's process, that person will not trust you.

Imagine that you are a midwife. You are assisting at someone else's birth. Do good without show or fuss. Facilitate what is happening rather than what you think ought to be happening. If you must take the lead, lead so that the mother is helped, yet still free and in charge.

When the baby is born, the mother will say: we did it ourselves.

Chapter 26: Center and Ground

The leader who is centered and grounded can work with erratic people and critical group situations without harm.

Being centered means having the ability to recover one's balance, even in the midst of action. A centered person is not subject to passing whims or sudden excitements.

Being grounded means being down-to-earth, having gravity or weight. I know where I stand, and I know what I stand for: that is ground.

The centered and grounded leader has stability and a sense of self.

One who is not stable can easily get carried away by the intensity of leadership and make mistakes of judgment or even become ill.

Chapter 31: Harsh Interventions

There are times when it seems as if one must intervene powerfully, suddenly, and even harshly. The wise leader does this only when all else fails.

As a rule, the leader feels more wholesome when the group process is flowing freely and unfolding naturally, when delicate facilitations far outnumber harsh interventions.

Harsh interventions are a warning that the leader may be uncentered or have an emotional attachment to whatever is happening. A special awareness is called for.

Even if harsh interventions succeed brilliantly, there is no cause for celebration. There has been injury. Someone's process has been violated.

Later on, the person whose process has been violated may well become less open and more defended. There will be a deeper resistance and possibly even resentment.

Making people do what you think they ought to do does not lead toward clarity and consciousness. While they may do what you tell them to do at the time, they will cringe inwardly, grow confused, and plot revenge.

That is why your victory is actually a failure.

Chapter 43: Gentle Interventions

Gentle interventions, if they are clear, overcome rigid resistances.

If gentleness fails, try yielding or stepping back altogether. When the leader yields, resistances relax.

Generally speaking, the leader's consciousness sheds more light on what is happening than any number of interventions or explanations. But a few leaders realize how much how little will do.

Chapter 46: Nothing to Win

The well-run group is not a battlefield of egos. Of course there will be conflict, but these energies become creative forces.

If the leader loses sight of how things happen, quarrels and fear devastate the group field.

This is a matter of attitude. There is nothing to win or lose in group work. Making a point does not shed light on what is happening. The need to be right blinds people.

The wise leader knows that it is far more important to be content with what is actually happening than to get upset over what might be happening but isn't.

Chapter 56: The Leader's Integrity

The wise leader knows that the true nature of events cannot be captured in words. So why pretend?

Confusing jargon is one sign of a leader who does not know how things happen.

But what cannot be said can be demonstrated: be silent, be conscious. Consciousness works. It sheds light on what is happening. It clarifies conflicts and harmonizes the agitated individual or group field.

The leader also knows that all existence is a single whole. Therefore the leader is a neutral observer who takes no sides.

The leader cannot be seduced by offers or threats. Money, love, or fame—whether gained or lost—do not sway the leader from center.

The leader's integrity is not idealistic. It rests on a pragmatic knowledge of how things work.

Chapter 60: Don't Stir Things Up

Run the group delicately, as if you were cooking small fish.

As much as possible, allow the group process to emerge naturally. Resist any temptation to instigate issues or elicit emotions which have not appeared on their own.

If you stir things up, you will release forces before their time and under unwarranted pressure. These forces may be emotions which belong to other people or places. They may be unspecific or chaotic energies which, in response to your pressure, strike out and hit any available target.

These forces are real. They do exist in the group. But do not push. Allow them to come out when they are ready.

When hidden issues and emotions emerge naturally, they resolve themselves naturally. They are not harmful. In fact, they are no different from any other thoughts or feelings.

All energies naturally arise, take form, grow strong, come to a new resolution, and finally pass away.

Chapter 62: Whether You Know It or Not

A person does not have to join a group or be a wise leader to work things out. Life's process unfolds naturally. Conflicts resolve themselves sooner or later, whether or not a person knows how things happen.

It is true that being aware of how things happen makes one's words more potent and one's behavior more effective.

But even without the light of consciousness, people grow and improve. Being unconscious is not a crime, it is merely the lack of a very helpful ability.

Knowing how things work gives the leader more real power and ability than all the degrees or job titles the world can offer.

That is why people in every era and in every culture have honored those who know how things happen.

Chapter 72: Spiritual Awareness

Group work must include spiritual awareness, if it is to touch the existential anxiety of our times. Without awe, the awful remains unspoken; a diffuse malaise remains.

Be willing to speak of traditional religion, no matter how offended some group members may be. Overcome the bias against the word "God." The great force of our spiritual roots lies in tradition, like it or not.

The wise leader models spiritual behavior and lives in harmony with spiritual values. There is a way of knowing, higher than reason; there is a self, greater than egocentricity.

The leader demonstrates the power of selflessness and the unity of all creation.

Chapter 81: The Reward

It is more important to tell the simple, blunt truth than it is to say things that sound good. The group is not a contest of eloquence.

It is more important to act in behalf of everyone than it is to win arguments. The group is not a debating society.

It is more important to react wisely to what is happening than it is to be able to explain everything in terms of certain theories. The group is not a final examination for a college course.

The wise leader is not collecting a string of successes. The leader is helping others to find their own success. There is plenty to go around. Sharing success with others is very successful.

The single principle behind all creation teaches us that true benefit blesses everyone and diminishes no one.

The wise leader knows that the reward for doing the work arises naturally out of the work.

References

Bynner, W. *The way of life according to Lao-tzu*. New York: Capricorn Books, 1962.

Witter Bynner lived in China for a time; he loved the Chinese. His scholarship is less important than his spirit. I must have bought ten copies of this version. He wrote it in 1944, a dark time for China.

Feng, G., & English, J. *Tao te ching*. New York: Knopf, 1972.

Both of these authors lead awareness groups. Their language is contemporary and clear. Jane English's photography and Gia-fu Feng's calligraphy evoke the spirit of Tao better than any commentary.

Medhurst, C. S. *The tao-teh-king*. Wheaton, IL: Theosophical Publishing House, 1972.

The language of this cranky old 1905 translation seems more remote than Lao Tzu himself. I like this commentary. He can relate *Tao Te Ching* to Western religious and cultural traditions. Medhurst is spiritual.

Schmidt, K. O. *Tao te ching*. Lakemont, GA: CSA Press, 1975.

Schmidt is a German metaphysical writer. He knows and loves the mysteries. His rendition makes sense. In both teaching and in understanding Lao Tzu, I have relied on Schmidt most. He is often inaccurate.

Suzuki, D. T., & Carus, P. *The canon of reason and virtue*. La Salle, IL: Open Court Publishing, 1974.

This translation is clear. Scholarship and commentary are very helpful. In addition, the entire text is presented in printed Chinese characters. Only Arthur Waley seems as reliable to me.

Waley, A. *The way and its power.* New York: Grove Press, 1958

Witter Bynner said, "Arthur Waley's [Lao Tzu] is painstakingly accurate and scholarly but difficult for any but scholars to follow." Difficult, but worth it. I use Waley when I want to get close to the original. I trust him most.

Part Five

LEADERSHIP:
AN UNCERTAIN FUTURE

Leaders will take us from where we are today to where we will be tomorrow; they will continue to influence our destinies as they have for centuries. Perhaps our concern with leadership reflects a need to be assured that our leaders will take us *where we want to be*, individually and collectively. That would certainly explain the persistence of our inquiry into the nature of leadership, particularly our efforts to identify, select, and train the leaders of tomorrow.

The problems of leadership have not, perhaps, changed all that dramatically over the years. Changes in society have always created new vacancies for which there have always been numbers of leader candidates. It's true that life is more complex, but so are the technological tools we have for making the most of our lives. Historical reviews do not suggest that there are fewer (or more) able leaders today than in the past. Medieval peasants no doubt yearned as fervently for a good leader to solve their economic and social problems as we do today. The fact that early man had neither the inclination nor the ability to study leadership makes the analogy even more poignant.

Interestingly, research aimed at discrediting trait theories of leadership has failed to eliminate personal attributes as part of successful leadership. Contemporary writers are once again looking at vision, self-confidence, ego involvement, power, and even humor as being necessary to assure strong leadership in the future. Headship, administration, management, and executive decision making concentrate on the status quo; we've honed the tools, techniques, training programs, and incentive systems of that status quo to a fine edge. But leadership must also deal with the uncertainties and surprises of the future. The pace at which we are rushing into the future has intensified our drive to secure competent leadership for today.

"Wanted: Corporate Leaders" (Chapter 25) provides a short but powerful example of contemporary thinking on leadership. Walter Kiechel states that vision and culture-building are the keys to success. In his view, leadership is a psychological phenomenon based on a strong ego and a sense of commitment and born of some timely crisis situation. His suggestion that we must train leaders for the future merely confirms the pressures we all feel.

In Chapter 26, Michael Maccoby traces the development of leadership in our society and describes the leadership needs of the 1980s. He addresses the management phenomenon but then focuses on the changes in our society in terms of technology and values, noting the narrowing gap between leaders and followers, and asserting that good development of followers will yield the effective leaders we seek. According to Maccoby, the primary tasks of leaders are understanding motives for and resistance to change and establishing operating principles that build trust, facilitate cooperation, and clarify the significance of the individual within the common purpose. He concludes by asking us to be more aware of the dynamic nature of our society, which demands that we pursue collective rather than individual goals.

One of the most significant readings in this volume is Chapter 27, John W. Gardner's essay from 1965, "The Antileadership Vaccine." Most striking are his concerns with the dispersion of power and our failure to cope with the "big questions." Gardner suggests that the antileadership vaccine is inherent in our educational system and the structure of our society, resulting in a lack of confidence in the leadership role. In training people for leadership, we often neglect the broader moral view of shared values, thus inhibiting vision, creativity, and risk-taking. After reading this essay, you may well ask, "What's next?"

Robert K. Mueller takes an action orientation in Chapter 28, "Leading-Edge Leadership." His view of leadership is based on the scientific, technological, political, economic, social, and cultural forces at work today. Reaffirming the long-run nature of leadership, Mueller cites five critical leadership issues: (1) intellectual operations involving innovation and communication; (2) power and group dynamics; (3) abstractions of order, disorder, causation, and change; (4) technological forces; and (5) ethical, legal, and religious spheres of sentient and moral power. This chapter captures the truly eclectic nature of the leadership role.

We still have not defined leadership in a precise way, but each of you probably remains firmly convinced that you know good leadership when you experience it. Perhaps if we were able to articulate a specific logic for the leadership process, the "magic" of leadership would cease to exist. Regardless of our lack of exacting definitions, we will continue to seek leaders and to try and decipher what it is that produces the leaders we need.

25

Wanted: Corporate Leaders

WALTER KIECHEL, III

It's in the air, trend spotters, just about ready to precipitate in the swirling clouds of economic change and rain down on us in a thousand articles and speeches. It's behind much of the business community's fascination with Lee Iacocca. It has something to do with why *In Search of Excellence*, a study of what authors Thomas J. Peters and Robert H. Waterman, Jr., describe as America's best-run companies, has sold over 300,000 copies and become a No. 1 best-seller nationwide. It's there just below the surface of all the talk about fostering entrepreneurialism inside the large corporation.

This soon to be very hot subject is leadership.

At the mere mention of the word, your eyes might reasonably glaze over, iced with recollection of too many politicians promising a new tomorrow, too many unread books with the big L in the title, too many after-dinner exhortations by football coaches who should never have been permitted to doff their windbreakers and eschew their gum. Wake up. This time there may actually be something there.

Item: In an interview a young associate professor at one of those ultra-prestigious business schools announces that when he completes his latest tome on corporate strategy—a bandwagon he's been riding for five years—he proposes to devote himself full-time to the study of leadership. And where will be begin his research? "The military academies," he replies.

Item: Executive recruiters, asked what qualities their client companies are seeking in a candidate for a top job, report that they're hearing our old friend "charisma" a great deal more than they used to. "Vision"

Reprinted by permission from *Fortune*, May 30, 1983, pp. 135–140.

also seems in increasing demand; while the headhunters aren't sure precisely what the term means, they sense that is has to do with new and much-sought-after skills in motivating people.

Item: In 1981 Matsushita Electric Industrial Co. endowed a chair in leadership at the Harvard Business School—the first professorship devoted to the subject to be established at any major business school. In preparing students to deal with the flesh-and-blood variable in the business equation, these institutions have traditionally taught organizational design, human behavior in different organizational contexts, maybe a bit of labor relations—the skills, in short, that would be called on in planning and administering a bureaucracy.

In February, after casting about hither and yon for an expert on leadership, Harvard awarded the Matsushita professorship to Abraham Zaleznik, already the holder of another endowed chair at HBS and one of the faculty members who had helped raise the money from the Japanese company. Zaleznik, a lay psychoanalyst with a private practice he conducts from beside a couch in his campus office, is the author of an award-winning 1977 article arguing that the psychology of leaders differs dramatically from that of managers. The article raised the hackles of many of Zaleznik's colleagues at the institution formally named the Graduate School of Business Administration.

Most of the interesting thinking about leadership these days—and the punch such thinking has, way beyond the usual pep-rally bromides— has its roots in this notion that, psychologically, managers and leaders are very different cups of tea indeed. Zaleznik claims no monopoly on the idea. He sees it reflected, for example, in the distinction James MacGregor Burns makes in his book *Leadership* between transformative leaders who change the course of events, and transactional ones, who without much emotional involvement get things done through contractual relationships within some sort of organizational structure. Other academics trace the idea back to sociologist Max Weber, who argued that charismatic leaders launch enterprises, only to give way to bureaucrats who take over the running of them.

The experts who of late seem to make the most sense of the leader-manager distinction are (hold onto your hats and your prejudices) Freudians—men like Zaleznik and Harry Levinson, the Menninger Foundation-trained psychologist whose Levinson Institute seminars are perhaps the only forum that routinely brings together businessmen and clinicians. The title of Levinson's seminar for corporate officers is, and has been for 14 years, "On Leadership."

Just more psychohumbug? It may seem to the casual observer that the Freudians are on the run, pilloried in everything from trendy books such as *Psychoanalysis: The Impossible Profession* to movies—the recent

Lovesick, for example, in which Dudley Moore plays an analyst caught up in the toils of countertransference (that is, he falls in love with a patient). Ach, the followers of Sigmund rejoin, you have to distinguish between our underlying theory and our therapeutic techniques. Did any other theory survive the new-therapies-and-psychobabble explosion of the 1960s and 1970s with as much of its explanatory and predictive power intact?

Much of Freudian doctrine, you may recall from the psychology course you took in college to buck up your average, revolves around a sort of tripartite division of the psyche—into id, ego, and superego. According to the Freudians, it is the particular and characteristic way that these three act and interact within the leader that sets him apart from others, including the manager. Recognizing how these psychodynamics work and consciously trying to ape some of the resultant behavior may even make your own bureaucratic style more inspiring.

In just about everyone, the theory goes, the id is a bubbling, seething stew of instinctual energies, often energies of the randiest or most aggressive sort, all of which in a civilized person are usually kept unconscious. The superego, by contrast, incorporates what our parents and society have taught us about being good; it rewards us psychically for a job well done and also bestows that attribute essential to middle-class life, a sense of guilt. Finally, there's the ego, largely conscious and always caught up in mediating between the other two parts and outside reality. Thus, in Freudian theory, "Man is basically a battlefield," in the felicitous words of the British psychologist Donald Bannister, "a dark cellar in which a well-bred spinster lady and a sex-crazed monkey are forever engaged in mortal combat, the struggle being refereed by a rather nervous bank clerk."

For the leader, though, the internal struggle seems in some ways less bitter, less divisive. In him, the psychologists speculate, that harsh, nagging component of the superego that we commonly call the conscience isn't quite as punitive as it is in other folks. This lets him more readily admit into consciousness the impressions, energies, and associations that bubble up from the id. Asked for his definition of vision, Zaleznik replies, "It's the capacity to see connections, to draw inferences that aren't obvious, that are unprecedented." Some businessmen call it the ability to see around corners as the leader peers into his company's future. It's a talent that has come to seem all the more valuable as the pace of technological and economic change quickens.

This isn't the only element in the leader's vision, however. Perhaps because he has less energy invested in the conscience, he channels more into another component of the superego, the ego ideal. The ego ideal is the image of what he wants himself, and by extension his organization, to be. This vision, which he strives constantly to achieve, is perhaps the most powerful motivational tool in the leader's kit. It gives him a consistent sense of who he is and what he's after, a sense that he can, by words and example, invite others to share in.

As Harry Levinson parses the psychodynamics at work, the leader's pursuit of an ego ideal enables him to frame a transcendent purpose for his organization. (Zaleznik prefers the slightly less highfalutin formulation "enduring goal.") This purpose usually includes within it the perpetuation of the organization, and hence necessarily entails taking a long-term view. Since merely staying alive isn't by itself all that beckoning an ideal, the transcendent purpose will commonly be cast in more inspiring terms—making the best computers in the world, say, or the best cars.

While your typical manager-bureaucrat tries to get people to do things for money or out of fear, the leader invites his co-workers to identify their pursuit of an ego ideal with his own, and with the transcendent purpose of the organization. If the purpose is sufficiently lofty, this identification infuses their work with meaning, meaning beyond just making a living. Hitting your profit targets each quarter probably isn't much of a transcendent purpose.

Without a transcendent purpose understood and enunciated from on high, the company's direction is at the mercy of the winds of corporate fad and fancy. Shall we become a conglomerate tomorrow?

If all this seems a bit mystical for your taste, try thinking of it in terms of that concept much in vogue nowadays, corporate culture. What, at bottom, is a corporate culture but a set of shared values, values that get reflected in behavior and, in the best cases, further everyone's pursuit of a common end? Each of the well-managed companies listed in *In Search of Excellence*, it should be noted, has a strong culture.

In interviews, authors Peters and Waterman observe that in most cases the culture seemed to be the creation of a strong leader who hammered away at a message to his organization for years. He might be someone who started the company, or who was present almost from the beginning—Tom Watson at IBM—or, considerably less often, someone who rose through the ranks to get the top job, from which bully pulpit he instilled the gospel in a previously less than excellent company— Rene McPherson at Dana. It's enough to make you slightly suspicious of those consultants who offer to help you build a strong corporate culture around your current wimpy management.

The leader's strong ego ideal, coupled with an active but not hypercritical conscience, has other effects on how he gets along with peers and subordinates. Because his aggressive energies are channeled into the pursuit of a goal larger than himself, when Joe the plant manager lashes out against him in a rage, he won't retaliate in kind. Indeed, if he's the McCoy, he'll probably find some way to help Joe direct his megatonnage against the common task.

The Freudian's typical manager, by comparison, has a conscience that's always keeping score and just maybe poisoning the wellsprings of self-confidence with guilt. All het up with nowhere to go—no very bright ideal to pursue—his aggressive energies will be sluiced into attacks on himself and those around him: he'll distrust his own competence and theirs. The result is corporate politics at its least productive: turf battles, a boss rivalrous toward subordinates and unwilling to help them along, demoralization in all its senses. While the leader devotes himself to getting the job done, the manager worries about "how am *I* doing"— he is a careerist.

The Freudians, as you may imagine, tend to think that the way that we get along with our boss has much to do with how we fared with Mama and Dada. We bring to our dealings with the guy in the corner office feelings of dependency and a need for affection. You scoff: *Affection and dependency—we don't allow those at my company.* No, in the corporate world it's known as seeking recognition, feedback, support. Members of the baby-boom generation, perhaps because they've had to compete to be singled out from their too-numerous peers for so long, are becoming famous for demanding this warm stuff quite explicitly.

The leader—secure, serene in his commitment to task, and looking for people to help him accomplish it—does a better job handling these demands than your average manager. Which, with the accession of baby-boomers to more and more managerial jobs these days, may in part account for why companies seem suddenly to be seeking leader types to yoke the boomers' energies to a corporate purpose. He doesn't just tolerate, he actively encourages all those would-be entrepreneurs in the company skunkworks.

Not that this fabled leader is any kind of cupcake. Because of his overriding commitment to the common goal, and because he's less hung up about his own aggressiveness and others', he can be utterly forthright in telling people when they're not performing up to the mark. If all else has been tried, he can even fire them with a clearer conscience than is common among bureaucrats. Such forthrightness does, however, present special problems for women who would be leaders. Because subordinates expect deep down that the woman who happens to be their boss will be, if anything, more supportive and affectionate than a male—more like Mom—and because women build some of these same expectations into what they demand of themselves, it may be two generations before many women can act as freely, as unconstrainedly, in a leadership role as a man might, at least in Harry Levinson's view.

There are, of course, other problems with this model of a leader, beginning with the question whether any of these paragons actually exist out there in the world. The Freudians are distinctly reluctant to cite examples on the current corporate scene—who knows what his early childhood was like, and whether he really fits the model? Moreover, can the typical large company, with its entrenched bureaucracy, accommodate such a wild man? Probably only if the pain—the pressure from foreign competitors, the inability to overcome economic stagnation—is great enough.

Even if a company were positively hungry for one of these men on horseback, it isn't clear where it would find him. Can leaders be trained, can some latent potential for acting in accordance with the leader's particular psychological makeup be brought out in, say, the average MBA candidate? "We don't know," confesses Harold J. Leavitt, a professor of organizational behavior at Stanford. "We never can tell until we try." Harvard's Zaleznik warns that any attempt to identify potential leaders early in their education and give them special training will have to withstand charges of that most un-American of sins, elitism.

But then, we may not have that much choice if we're going to compete globally with societies that seem to do a better job of fostering and giving rein to leaders. If the prospect gives you pause—and it should— you might want to dwell on the thought that the first endowed chair of leadership in this country bears the name of one Konosuke Matsushita, a peasant's son who in his lifetime managed to build the 33rd-largest industrial corporation in the world.

26

Leadership Needs
of the 1980s

MICHAEL MACCOBY

Today, the ideal image of both leader and character in America is in question. We are unclear about what is best in us and what it takes to bring it out. I believe this confusion has resulted from a lack of fit between old styles of leadership and changes in technology, work, and national character.

There are two interrelated aspects of the leader's role. One has to do with the functions of leadership, which may range from inspiring to disciplining, from mediating to commanding. The second has to do with presenting an image, a model that others want to emulate if not imitate. This image draws out and integrates shared traits of character in the leader's constituency (the social character). The ideal leader should bring out the best in people, supporting the ideal character of a particular culture and historical period. When an individual in a position of leadership has the wrong traits or presents an image discordant with the times, that leader's constituency will lack inspiration.

Both the ideal character and the functions of leadership have changed historically, because of economic and social transformations. I believe that there is a crisis of authority, a questioning of its legitimacy, because neither the functions of leadership nor the image of the leader fit the needs of large organizations, especially business and government, in an age of rights, limits, new values, and a changing concept of productivity, which have not yet crystalized into a new ideal character. Nor have universities understood this change and provided the education needed for leadership.

Reprinted with permission from AAHE (American Association for Higher Education) from *Current Issues in Higher Education*, 1979, no. 2, pp. 17–23.

During the past 200 years, there have been three different types of ideal social character in America. These images represent traits adaptive to the dominant modes of production at different periods in our history. By modeling these traits, especially the positive ones, the leaders have both performed the changing functions of leadership, and at the same time projected an image that others copy, thus adapting the social character to the changing styles of production.

The three ideal character types have been: the *independent craftsman* (from the late 18th century to the Civil War), the paternalistic *empire builder* (from post–Civil War to the 1950s), and the *gamesman* (from 1960 to the present). Obviously, these are Weberian ideal types. Not only are real leaders and followers mixtures of these types, but all three exist today in positions of leadership.

The Ideal of the Independent Craftsman

The ideal of the independent craftsman fit America of the late 18th century, where more than 80 percent of the workforce were self-employed—mainly as farmers, craftsmen, and small businessmen. Jefferson's vision of an egalitarian democracy was built on the basis of economically independent individuals who had the disciplined virtues of experimental farmers and craftsmen.

It was Benjamin Franklin who expressed these virtues, and by omission also pointed to negative traits in the craftsman character, which are the opposites of the positive ones. The virtues Franklin described included moderation, silence, orderliness, resoluteness, thriftiness (frugality), industry, sincerity, justice or fairness, temperance or "coolness of head," cleanliness, imperturbability (tranquility), chastity, and humility ("I cannot boast of much success in acquiring the *reality* of this virtue," wrote Franklin.[1])

These are traits that served a businesslike, male-dominated society of independent craftsmen. Unlike Jefferson's, whose concept of virtue included a developed heart as well as a disciplined mind, Franklin's list of attributes has no place for what have been considered the feminine virtues—charity, love, kindness, compassion, tolerance, and generosity. The negative traits of the craftsman's character not mentioned by Franklin include obstinacy (the negative of resoluteness and diligence), stinginess (the negative of thriftiness), and the inability to cooperate (the negative of imperturbability, taciturnity, and of the rugged individualism so admired in a young nation of refugees from authority).

It was difficult to find any leader to satisfy such individualists. It took George Washington, a leader with exceptional qualities of courage and humanity as well as the craftsmanlike traits of the experimental farmer, to inspire cooperation among the founders of the country, who were more attuned to Franklin's individualistic virtues than to Washington's paternalism and magnificence. Reverence for "the father of the country" was ambivalent at best for many who prized independence above all. The image of Washington as Cincinnatus, returning to his plow after leading the army, did not reassure those who feared monarchy and the establishment of a new aristocracy in America. Washington, in turn, did not romanticize his followers. His description of the continental army in 1775 should be instructional for those who bemoan the deteriorization of the "work ethic": "Such a dearth of public spirit and want of virtue, such . . . fertility in all the low arts to obtain advantages . . . such a dirty, mercenary spirit pervades the whole."[2]

Although, in the first part of the 19th century, Andrew Jackson and Abraham Lincoln appealed to more ambitious traits in the new entrepreneurs and risk-taking frontiersmen, the character of the independent farmer-craftsman-small businessman remained the dominant ideal until after the Civil War. In the early 1830s, Tocqueville wrote that big business could endanger the spirit of equality in America by producing a new elite. In fact, the acceleration of the industrial revolution, the exploitation of technology and resources, and the construction of new organizational pyramids in the post–Civil War economic jungle favored the rise of a new leader and a new ideal character.

The Ideal of the Empire-Builder

As organizations grew more powerful, self-employment declined (by 1970, it included only 8 percent of the workforce).[3] The new leader had to have the entrepreneurial skills and toughness to build industries and to survive in a competitive jungle. He had to manage the flood of new immigrants who wanted work. Today, from a different, socioeconomic and cultural perspective, we emphasize the negative traits of the empire builders: exploitation, domination of the weak, the crushing of rivals, greed. Andrew Carnegie, unique among robber barons because he had a conscience, justified his predatory career by philanthropy and an appeal to social Darwinism; but he betrayed those who got in his way, even his closest business partner, Henry Clay Frick. As an old man living in New York City, Carnegie sent a messenger down the street to Frick's house, saying that since they were now old, he would like to meet Frick one last time and forget the past. The reply was, "Tell Mr. Carnegie I'll meet him in Hell."[4]

There was also a positive side to the industrial patriarch, as expressed by Carnegie's philanthropy and the even greater paternalism of entrepreneurs like Thomas Watson of I.B.M., who protected loyal followers in their industrial baronies with job security. Such leaders could be trusted because they owned the business and stood by their personal principles. This image of the ideal, responsible patriarch was supported by a new ideal social character, which was described by novelist Horatio Alger.

The heroes of Horatio Alger became the models for success in a society increasingly dominated by big business. In contrast to the conservative, self-contained and taciturn craftsmen, Alger's heroes, like Ragged Dick, are smart-talking, tricky, and entrepreneurial. They are liberal spenders with a taste for elegance.[5] They are poor, but tough and honest, neither mean nor lazy. Dick works hard and charges more than the other boys for his shoe shines, because his service is better. In a way, the heroes of Horatio Alger represent the successful barons' version of an inner-directed climb from poverty that justifies subsequent riches. In his model of a success story, there is generally a paternal figure around to recognize the hero's virtues and give him a chance to rise further in big business. The climber and the patriarch need each other. In a symbiotic sense, the hero's lack of a father expresses the change in both the culture and the social character needed for success. Ambitious boys must seek new fathers who have mastered the new challenges, leaving behind their own less adapted fathers (as was the case with Andrew Carnegie, whose father was an unsuccessful craftsman).

The paternalistic leader probably appealed more to the immigrants at the turn of the century, to new Americans in need of a Godfather, than to the still-independent craftsmen who were being forced into increasingly routinized factory jobs. The struggle against the paternalistic jungle fighter was led by unions. Women joined the battle; first to gain the right to vote, then for equal rights and respect at the workplace. The civil-rights and the anti-war movements also challenged and weakened traditional patriarchal power and the image of the lion-like jungle fighter as ideal leader.

The challenge to patriarchy has not been limited to the United States. Throughout the world, revolutions against the old orders and increased demands for rights by those—women, youth, minorities—who were dominated by old men in power have de-legitimized traditional authority. The automatic respect once commanded by parents, priests, professors, and presidents now must be earned. Even in Japan, a society that was considered an example of patriarchy at its strongest, where the group dominates the individual, studies now show a decline in respect for parents, with new desire by the young for "ikigai," self-realization.

The Ideal of the Gamesman

In the United States, as the social character became more self affirmative and the spirit meritocratic, a new image of leadership appealed to Americans—that of the gamesman. Adventurous and ambitious but fair and flexible, the gamesman reminded Americans of an earlier, more exciting, anti-bureaucratic frontier spirit, of Jacksonian capitalism before the era of industrial empires and robber barons.

The arrival of the gamesman image of leadership coincided with the election of John F. Kennedy as president. Kennedy promised to invigorate a country gone flabby under the leadership of a tired paternal figure. His New Frontier energized the electronics and aerospace industries, which were also discovering they needed gamesmen to lead teams of specialists in research and development of new systems.

The gamesman has become the dominant model for leadership in America. Unlike the paternal leader who demanded deference, the gamesman enjoys challenge. With a boyish, informal style, he controls subordinates by persuasion, enthusiasm and seduction rather than heavy and humiliating commands. Fair but detached, the gamesman has welcomed the era of rights and equal opportunity as both a fair and an efficient climate for moving the "best" to the top.

In retrospect, Abraham Lincoln, who lived between the ages of craftsmanship and industrialism, appears to have been the prototype of the meritocratic gamesman of the technotronic age. "His ambition was a little engine that knew no rest," said his law partner, William H. Herndon.[6] He was impatient; bored by lack of challenge, he rode the circuit compulsively. Although moved by a sense of justice, he was self protective and detached, a political realist and strategist who tailored his speeches to different audiences in the north and south of Illinois. Frederick Douglass criticized Lincoln's lack of feeling for blacks, saying he was "entirely devoted to the welfare of white men," but he also said that Lincoln was "the first great man that I talked with in the United States freely, who in no single instance reminded me of the difference between himself and myself, of the difference of color."[6]

Unlike most gamesmen, who remained addicted to the exhilaration of winning, Lincoln, as Richard Hofstadter points out, "was chastened and not *intoxicated* by power."

Lincoln was not merely ambitious. He was also, Herndon testified, "a man of heart." The modern gamesman, unlike the robber barons, is not a hard-hearted power seeker; but few approach Lincoln's qualities of heart. Most gamesmen are detached, ungenerous, and uncompassionate, even though they are fair. The typical gamesman feels it is dangerous to open one's heart. Emotion, feeling, and compassion may cloud strategy and weaken the will to win.

The positive traits of the gamesman—enthusiasm, risk-taking, meritocratic fairness—fit America in a period of unlimited economic growth and hunger for change. The negative traits of manipulation, seduction, supercareerism, and the perpetual adolescent need for adventure were always problems, causing distrust and unnecessary crisis. They have become serious liabilities in this period of limited resources, when the team no longer can be controlled by promises of more, and productivity requires a higher level of trust and cooperation.

In universities, gamesman leaders took over in the 1960s and supported the idea of making the academic game fairer, not only on the grounds of justice, but on the grounds that affirmative action would bring out the best in people. In a period of retrenchment, where the need is for greater concern for the common good, gamesman leaders become helpless against employee groups, which often select jungle-fighter leaders to protect their interests. The university then becomes a battleground for departments and/or unions fighting for a lion's share of scarce resources, at the expense of rational planning or mutual concern with educational policy and the needs of students.

In business, such a deterioration of common purpose would lead to bankruptcy. David Riesman believes that it will hasten the failure of private colleges, but that since no state university has ever been closed, there is not even the threat of survival to balance the domination of interest groups.[7]

The Leadership Problem Today

The gamesman does not provide the leadership needed by organizations in this era of limits, because he has no vision of development beyond winning. Many people are turned off by his careerism and lack of compassion for those who are not winners in the meritocratic game. The gamesman runs and rationalizes the organizational pyramids. He may even make them fairer, but he does not transform them. He offers no alternative to what Burton Bledstein calls "the vertical vision of life."[8] He does not appeal to responsibility or a sense of service, but to winning and a sense of glory. He promises that no one will have to sacrifice if everyone plays his position well, but this is not always the case. In a world of shrinking resources, people must be prepared to make difficult choices; but without responsible paternalists at the top, who is there to care about the common good? Who will protect the weak from the strong? God the father, the paternalistic god, is replaced by what the movie *Star Wars* popularized as "the Force"; the spirit of justice and compassion gives way to a winning attitude. As fewer are able to win, more see the game as each against all.

Many employees within the meritocratic pyramids in business and government today lack the spirit to do their work properly. This is sometimes called a "morale problem," which leaders blame on the decline in "the work ethic" or a failure in "communications." This implies either that people are to blame or that the problem can be solved mechanically. I believe the problem goes deeper: it is one of both a changing American character and confusion in the ranks of leadership, which do not fully understand the change.

In *The Gamesman*,[9] I cited the symptoms ("difficulties") checked by a significant percentage of successful managers. Many were individuals moving up the corporate ladder to positions of leadership. Their symptoms indicated anxiety, guilt, and depression. Managers were anxious about constantly being rated, about how they were doing and about whether or not they were really needed, and about controlling impulses—including criticisms—that might get them in trouble. They felt guilty about giving too much, about betraying their best impulses and values to get ahead. And they were depressed by the friendless, deadening atmosphere resulting from competition and repression of feelings. Some who consciously were satisfied with work reported unconscious disturbances, such as dreams of being buried alive or of offices filled with corpses. That is indeed a profound problem in morale and communications, starting at the top.

The problem of leadership in large organizations today, in an age of limits, is how to create organizational goals that will bring out the best in workers who are becoming increasingly skeptical and self affirmative, more interested in enjoying life than any generation in American history. These are people who adapt to career requirements, but who rebel, often unconsciously, against wasting their lives in dehumanized bureaucracies.

Social and Character Changes in America

The change in American social character appears to be the result of two broad currents. One is the transformation of traditional rural to modern urban values, based on revolutionary changes in technology, increased education and the disappearance of a sense of independence rooted in self employment. The other, as noted, is the decline of patriarchal authority, based on new demands for human rights. These are, of course, trends. Some people, especially in rural areas, still fit into the older patterns. But increasingly, as studies by Daniel Yankelovich and the National Opinion Research Corporation show,[10] the new values are becoming dominant and determine attitudes at work, and unless leaders understand them, they may bring out the worst rather than the best in the emerging social character.

One of the most significant social changes in America in this century has been the migration from farms and small towns to cities. Traditional rural values included fundamentalist religious beliefs and an ethic of hard work and self-sacrifice for the family. The modern urban individual is skeptical about religion and oriented to self rather than family. Technological advances have lessened the prevalence of back-breaking jobs and stimulated new desires for entertainment. Education has encouraged more people to aspire to higher status. Freed somewhat by technology and affluence from the tyranny of necessity, individuals of all classes have broken old taboos and chased experiences that in the past were the exclusive property of the rich. From a psychoanalytic point of view, sexual liberation and the permission to consume rather than save have undermined the main mechanisms of the traditional uptight, hoarding character. *The negative traits are narcissistic—self-centeredness and greediness. The positive traits are increased concern and responsibility for self-development, learning, and health.*

The disappearance of self employment is in large measure a result of the demise of the family farm and the small-town services that supported it, with the corresponding growth in large organizations. Gone with self employment is the comforting idea that if one does not like work in the organization, one can always go out and start a business. Increasingly, the sense of independence is rooted in one's technical and managerial skills, rather than ownership of a farm or a business. *The negative traits associated with this change are careerism and self marketing; the need to sell oneself, to make oneself an attractive package at the expense of integrity. The positive traits are flexibility and tolerance, and the ability to understand and cooperate with strangers.*

The decline in patriarchy, due both to urban values and the many challenges to the domination of the father and the boss, results in the demand for rights and the demand that leaders justify their actions, as opposed to the demand for protection—although many people are like adolescents who want both.

For organizations, *the negative side of this trend is the crisis of authority. Lacking respect for traditional bosses and angry at the impersonality of large, anonymous organizations, employees become experts at beating or sabotaging the system. The positive side of this trend is a critical, questioning attitude, the wish for maturity and mutual respect, to be involved, to have a say, to contribute to a principled organization.*

●   **New Concerns for Leaders**

How do these issues translate into the pressing immediate concerns of leaders?

More is demanded from leadership now than in the age of paternalism or of unlimited economic growth. The combination of increased competition, the need to innovate and cut costs, new technology and materials, changing government regulations, and changing attitudes of workers demand a higher level of leadership in organizations than ever before. The primary tasks of leaders are to understand both motives and resistances to change, and to establish operating principles that build trust, facilitate cooperation, and explain the significance of the individual's role in the common purpose. What brings out the worst in employees, including middle and lower levels of management, is a sense of powerlessness due to the size of the workplace and anonymous authority that treats everyone like a part in a large machine. Insecurity, suspicion, rumor, and a sense of injustice grow in organizations where employees do not understand the reasons for decisions and do not have a say in how work is organized and evaluated.

In my experience, only a small minority of workers have a negative character structure that is immune to good leadership and the resulting peer pressure to cooperate. This is a generation prepared to communicate and responsive to reasonable explanations. Leadership will bring out the best in the emerging American character only by welcoming the positive aspects of character, and by establishing a moral code that appeals to the common good and meets needs for participation, personal development, and equity. The trust earned by the best paternalists can be achieved by the modern corporate leader only by establishing constitutional principles in the workplace. Only within such a constitutional system will the task of leadership become easier as responsible followers accept some of the functions of leadership and the discipline of responsibility.

Yet there is a tendency, well known to psychoanalysts, for an individual who is at a point in life that demands further growth and maturity to regress, to seek a solution in a more comfortable but unrealistic image. Many organizational responses to new values of self concern and individual rights may be what Erich Fromm called escapes from freedom,[11] attempts to recreate the paternalistic Godfather or to set up a foolproof, unbeatable, craftsmanlike control system (anonymous authority) that will be fair and authoritative, because it allows no human error (or responsiveness). These ill-fated solutions play on the ambivalence in people, the conflict between the conscious wish for autonomy and yearnings for protection and dependency.

The day of the patriarch is over. Nostalgic leaders want deference, but lack the responsiveness and personal concern for their employees of paternal leaders who own their own companies. Employees want their rights and resent autocratic leadership, but at the same time want to avoid rational discipline and complain that leaders don't care about them. For many leaders and followers, the ideal of "participative management" (that vague, quasi-ideological term which does not mean voting or representative democracy, but only makes sense if it involves participative study of problems within a structure of strong, rational authority) is that of the boss-parent talking directly to the workers, at the expense of middle managers who are seen as the ambitious, uncaring older siblings. A number of programs in government and business based on this illusion that paternalism can coexist with a society of rights and obligations have resulted in the undermining of the managerial structure, raising expectations that cannot be met and eventually fomenting cynicism on all levels.

Within industry, especially the large technology-creating companies, change in product design, technology, and jobs is constant. Competition increasingly demands higher quality and lower costs. From managerial levels on down, effectiveness requires responsibility and teamwork, which cannot be controlled by authoritarian management. How does management develop the higher levels of trust and involvement that will increase quality and effectiveness, when traditionally this type of concern for people is associated with paternalism? It is not easy to do.

I recently attended a meeting of top and middle managers of a large company. The chief executive exhorted the managers to show more concern about employees, to "communicate" with them and develop a spirit of teamwork. He pointed to evidence of employee complaints that management was not listening to them. Other speakers claimed that improved communication has significantly increased productivity in other companies. The chief executive ordered the managers to report back in six months with results. Privately, the managers complained that they were getting contradictory messages. They were being asked to be more concerned, but were being evaluated by their ability to produce the right numbers. They were being asked to trust people, but the company was investing in new technology to monitor and control workers. They were being ordered to listen to the workers, but no one was listening to them. Why did the managers not complain? Obviously, the problem of trust was not limited to workers.

I recently also attended a meeting of supergrade managers at a large government agency. Following the requirements of the Civil Service Reform Act, they were developing complex new personnel systems. The legislation institutes a Senior Executive Service, which is supposed to make government more effective by increasing the executive's control over the Civil Service through bonus incentives and easier firing of "incompetent" employees. The civil servants, in turn, were responding by using the letter of the law to construct mechanisms and red tape to protect themselves from the arbitrary exercise of executive power.

Before the passage of the legislation, this group of senior civil servants had been trying to achieve a higher level of cooperation among themselves. They had recognized that the overly competitive, hierarchical system impeded communication and collaboration among departments. Personnel systems bring out the worst in bureaucrats by supporting an adversarial atmosphere, increasing distrust among civil servants and between them and the public they are supposed to serve.

The mission of public service, which is what originally motivated the best civil servants to a career in government, often becomes buried beneath the fears of losing one's place, being treated unfairly, and not getting ahead. The new legislation, while intended to improve government, in fact emphasized the vertical vision of life, which conflicts with concern for people, both within and outside the bureaucracy. Defensive behavior on the part of bureaucrats against the jungle fighters and gamesmen at the top produces more red tape.

Some leaders believe that since it is impossible to please everyone, the only possible recourse is to muddle through. There are others who grasp at any new technique that promises results; their only goal is survival.

New Models of Leadership

During the past seven years I have been working with and studying leaders in business, unions, and government who are trying to develop new models of organization that bring out the best in people. These individuals are convinced that by balancing concern for people (humanistic values) with attention to mission (economic values), it is possible to design better organizations. Some of them were moved to make changes by problems of morale and productivity that demanded response. Others have moved not out of immediate necessity, but from the conviction that change would improve the lives of their employees, and ultimately the quality of work. Given their different goals and the constraints of the market, technology, culture and social character, both the designs of the organization and their styles of management have varied.

However, these leaders share two personal characteristics that may be essential for a new model of leadership which will bring out the best in the emerging social character.

(1) They have developed or are developing a philosophy of management which is rooted in a concern for their workers and resentment of wasted human potential. This rooted conviction, in contrast to a rigid ideology, provides a basis for pragmatic experimentation and satisfaction in step-by-step gains. Although most of these leaders share the gamesman's respect for strategy and tactics, they do not suffer the need for perpetual adventure and drama.

These leaders can stand back and let others share the functions of leadership but are able to assert authority on issues of principle, articulating these principles in terms of essential values. They are prepared to defend their values against power. They approach conflict strategically, and they are prepared for retreat when necessary. Their principles provide them the deep sense of security necessary to compromise, but they do not lose sight of their goals.

(2) They are students of the organizations they lead and are willing and able to "problematize" both the mission (definition of the product or service) and the control systems. They take time from the tiring managerial tasks of responding to crisis to question whether the mission serves society and individuals. They are not willing to gain power or money by appealing to the worst in people. They are engaged by the task of analyzing and reconstructing the organization.

These leaders find that they need help in articulating a philosophy that expresses a progressive spirit in the organization, in developing a rational structure of participation or consultation that avoids anarchy, and in understanding conscious and unconscious resistance to change. It is at this point that, as a participant researcher, I have been able to help some of these leaders.

To conclude, despite the real stresses of leadership and the valid complaints of those in positions of authority, there is no shortage of would-be leaders who do not inspire or lead, either because they maintain outmoded styles of leadership or because their only goal is their own survival. If we are to develop a more productive democratic society, what we need are leaders in business, government, and higher education who are able to bring out the best in a changing national character. Although a new model of leadership has not yet crystalized, a few such leaders exist, and they are usually working against the main trends in organizations and education. They are contending not only with individuals or groups that do not want to give up power and control, but also with a heavy, depressed collective spirit, a deadly mixture of anxiety, competitiveness, hopelessness, and secret guilt about self betrayal for career and comfort.

It will be possible to lead the organizations of the 1980s, but there is a shortage of both the kinds of leaders needed and the education they require. If adequate leadership emerges, it will be largely through on-the-job, social research and development. Leaders will develop higher levels of trust and teamwork if they participate with those they lead in studying organizational problems, experimenting with solutions, and evaluating alternatives according to both economic and human (moral) criteria.

Notes

1. Jesse L. Lemisch, ed., *Benjamin Franklin: "The Autobiography" and Other Writings,* New York: New American Library, 1961, p. 104.

2. James Thomas Flexner, *Washington, The Indispensable Man*, Boston, Little Brown, 1974, p. 73.

3. United States Census figures.

4. Joseph Frazer Wall, *Andrew Carnegie*, New York: Oxford University Press, 1970, p. 764.

5. Horatio Alger, Jr., *Ragged Dick and Mark, the Match Boy*, New York: Collier Books, 1962.

6. Richard Hofstadter, *American Political Tradition*, New York: Vintage Books, 1948.

7. Personal communication between author and D. Riesman.

8. Burton Bledstein, *The Culture of Professionalism: The Middle Class and the Development of Higher Education in America*, New York: Norton, 1977.

9. Michael Maccoby, *The Gamesman*, New York: Simon and Schuster, 1976.

10. See Daniel Yankelovich, "The New Psychological Contracts at Work," *Psychology Today*, May 1978, pp. 46–50; M. R. Cooper, B. S. Morgan, P. M. Foley, and L. B. Kaplan, "Changing Employee Values: Deepening Discontent," *Harvard Business Review*, January-February 1979, pp. 117–125.

11. Erich Fromm, *Escape from Freedom*, New York: Rinehart, 1941.

27

The Antileadership Vaccine

JOHN W. GARDNER

It is generally believed that we need enlightened and responsible leaders—
at every level and in every phase of our national life. Everyone says
so. But the nature of leadership in our society is very imperfectly
understood, and many of the public statements about it are utter nonsense.

This is unfortunate because there are serious issues of leadership
facing this society, and we had better understand them.

The Dispersion of Power

The most fundamental thing to be said about leadership in the United
States is also the most obvious. We have gone as far as any known
society in creating a leadership system that is *not* based on caste or
class, nor even on wealth. There is not yet equal access to leadership
(witness the remaining barriers facing women and Negroes), but we
have come a long, long way from the family- or class-based leadership
group. Even with its present defects, ours is a relatively open system.

The next important thing to be said is that leadership is dispersed
among a great many groups in our society. The President, of course,
has a unique, and uniquely important, leadership role, but beneath him,
fragmentation is the rule. This idea is directly at odds with the notion
that the society is run by a coherent power group—the Power Elite, as
C. Wright Mills called it, or the Establishment, as later writers have
named it. It is hard not to believe that such a group exists. Foreigners
find it particularly difficult to believe in the reality of the fluid, scattered,

Reprinted from "The Antileadership Vaccine" by John W. Gardner, Carnegie Corporation
of New York annual report essay, 1965.

shifting leadership that is visible to the naked eye. The real leadership, they imagine, must be behind the scenes. But at a national level this simply isn't so.

In many local communities and even in some states there *is* a coherent power group, sometimes behind the scenes, sometimes out in the open. In communities where such an "establishment," that is, a coherent ruling group, exists, the leading citizen can be thought of as having power in a generalized sense: he can bring about a change in zoning ordinances, influence the location of a new factory, and determine whether the local museum will buy contemporary paintings. But in the dispersed and fragmented power system that prevails in the nation as a whole one cannot say "So-and-so is powerful," without further elaboration. Those who know how our system works always want to know, "Powerful in what way? Powerful to accomplish what?" We have leaders in business and leaders in government, military leaders and educational leaders, leaders in labor and in agriculture, leaders in science, in the world of art, and in many other special fields. As a rule, leaders in any one of these fields do not recognize the authority of leaders from a neighboring field. Often they don't even know one another, nor do they particularly want to. Mutual suspicion is just about as common as mutual respect— and a lot more common than mutual cooperation in manipulating society's levers.

Most of the significant issues in our society are settled by a balancing of forces. A lot of people and groups are involved and the most powerful do not always win. Sometimes a coalition of the less powerful wins. Sometimes an individual of very limited power gets himself into the position of casting the deciding ballot.

Not only are there apt to be many groups involved in any critical issue, but their relative strength varies with each issue that comes up. A group that is powerful today may not be powerful next year. A group that can cast a decisive vote on question A may not even be listened to when question B comes up.

The Nature of Leadership

People who have never exercised power have all kinds of curious ideas about it. The popular notion of top leadership is a fantasy of capricious power: the top man presses a button and something remarkable happens; he gives an order as the whim strikes him, and it is obeyed.

Actually, the capricious use of power is relatively rare except in some large dictatorships and some small family firms. Most leaders are hedged around by constraints—tradition, constitutional limitations, the realities of the external situation, rights and privileges of followers, the requirements of teamwork, and most of all the inexorable demands of large-scale organization, which does not operate on capriciousness. In short, most power is wielded circumspectly.

There are many different ways of leading, many kinds of leaders. Consider, for example, the marked contrasts between the politician and the intellectual leader, the large-scale manager and the spiritual leader. One sees solemn descriptions of the qualities needed for leadership without any reference at all to the fact that the necessary attributes depend on the kind of leadership under discussion. Even in a single field there may be different kinds of leadership with different required attributes. Think of the difference between the military hero and the military manager.

If social action is to occur, certain functions must be performed. The problems facing the group or organization must be clarified, and ideas necessary to their solution formulated. Objectives must be defined. There must be widespread awareness of those objectives, and the will to achieve them. Often those on whom action depends must develop new attitudes and habits. Social machinery must be set in motion. The consequences of social effort must be evaluated and criticized, and new goals set.

A particular leader may contribute at only one point to this process. He may be gifted in analysis of the problem, but limited in his capacity to communicate. He may be superb in communicating, but incapable of managing. He may, in short, be an outstanding leader without being good at every aspect of leadership.

If anything significant is to be accomplished, leaders must understand the social institutions and processes through which action is carried out. And in a society as complex as ours, that is no mean achievement. A leader, whether corporation president, university dean, or labor official, knows his organization, understands what makes it move, comprehends its limitations. Every social system or institution has a logic and dynamic of its own that cannot be ignored.

We have all seen men with lots of bright ideas but no patience with the machinery by which ideas are translated into action. As a rule, the machinery defeats them. It is a pity, because the professional and academic man can play a useful role in practical affairs. But too often he is a dilettante. He dips in here or there; he gives bits of advice on a dozen fronts; he never gets his hands dirty working with one piece of the social machinery until he knows it well. He will not take the time to understand the social institutions and processes by which change is accomplished.

Although our decentralized system of leadership has served us well, we must not be so complacent as to imagine that it has no weaknesses, that it faces no new challenges, or that we have nothing to learn. There are grave questions to be answered concerning the leadership of our society. Are we living up to standards of leadership that we have achieved in our own past? Do the conditions of modern life introduce new complications into the task of leadership? Are we failing to prepare leaders for tomorrow?

Here are some of our salient difficulties.

Failure to Cope with the Big Questions

Nothing should be allowed to impair the effectiveness and independence of our specialized leadership groups. But such fragmented leadership does create certain problems. One of them is that it isn't anybody's business to think about the big questions that cut across specialties— the largest questions facing our society. Where are we headed? Where do we *want* to head? What are the major trends determining our future? Should we do anything about them? Our fragmented leadership fails to deal effectively with these transcendent questions.

Very few of our most prominent people take a really large view of the leadership assignment. Most of them are simply tending the machinery of that part of society to which they belong. The machinery may be a great corporation or a great government agency or a great law practice or a great university. These people may tend it very well indeed, but they are not pursuing a vision of what the total society needs. They have not developed a strategy as to how it can be achieved, and they are not moving to accomplish it.

One does not blame them, of course. They do not see themselves as leaders of the society at large, and they have plenty to do handling their own specialized role.

Yet it is doubtful that we can any longer afford such widespread inattention to the largest questions facing us. We achieved greatness in an era when changes came more slowly than now. The problems facing the society took shape at a stately pace. We could afford to be slow in recognizing them, slow in coping with them. Today, problems of enormous import hit us swiftly. Great social changes emerge with frightening speed. We can no longer afford to respond in a leisurely fashion.

Our inability to cope with the largest questions tends to weaken the private sector. Any question that cannot be dealt with by one of the special leadership groups—that is, any question that cuts across special fields—tends to end up being dealt with by government. Most Americans value the role played by nongovernmental leadership in this country and would wish it to continue. In my judgment it will not continue under the present conditions.

The cure is not to work against the fragmentation of leadership, which is a vital element in our pluralism, but to create better channels of communication among significant leadership groups, especially in connection with the great issues that transcend any particular group.

Failure of Confidence

Another of the maladies of leadership today is a failure of confidence. Anyone who accomplishes anything of significance has more confidence than the facts would justify. It is something that outstanding executives have in common with gifted military commanders, brilliant political leaders, and great artists. It is true of societies as well as of individuals. Every great civilization has been characterized by confidence in itself.

Lacking such confidence, too many leaders add ingenious new twists to the modern art which I call "How to reach a decision without really deciding." They require that the question be put through a series of clearances within the organization and let the clearance process settle it. Or take a public opinion poll and let the poll settle it. Or devise elaborate statistical systems, cost-accounting systems, information-processing systems, hoping that out of them will come unassailable support for one course of action rather than another.

This is not to say that leadership cannot profit enormously from good information. If the modern leader doesn't know the facts he is in grave trouble, but rarely do the facts provide unqualified guidance. After the facts are in, the leader must in some measure emulate the little girl who told the teacher she was going to draw a picture of God. The teacher said, "But, Mary, no one knows what God looks like"; and Mary said, "They will when I get through."

The confidence required of leaders poses a delicate problem for a free society. We don't want to be led by Men of Destiny who think they know all the answers. Neither do we wish to be led by Nervous Nellies. It is a matter of balance. We are no longer in much danger, in this society, from Men of Destiny. But we *are* in danger of falling under the leadership of men who lack the confidence to lead. And we are in danger of destroying the effectiveness of those who have a natural gift for leadership.

Of all our deficiencies with respect to leadership, one of the gravest is that we are not doing what we should to encourage potential leaders. In the late eighteenth century we produced out of a small population a truly extraordinary group of leaders—Washington, Adams, Jefferson, Franklin, Madison, Monroe, and others. Why is it so difficult today, out of a vastly greater population, to produce men of that caliber? It is a question that most reflective people ask themselves sooner or later. There is no reason to doubt that the human material is still there, but there is excellent reason to believe that we are failing to develop it—or that we are diverting it into nonleadership activities.

The Antileadership Vaccine

Indeed, it is my belief that we are immunizing a high proportion of our most gifted young people against any tendencies to leadership. It will be worth our time to examine how the antileadership vaccine is administered.

The process is initiated by the society itself. The conditions of life in a modern, complex society are not conducive to the emergence of leaders. The young person today is acutely aware of the fact that he is an anonymous member of a mass society, an individual lost among millions of others. The processes by which leadership is exercised are not visible to him, and he is bound to believe that they are exceedingly intricate. Very little in his experience encourages him to think that he might some day exercise a role of leadership.

This unfocused discouragement is of little consequence compared with the expert dissuasion the young person will encounter if he is sufficiently bright to attend a college or university. In those institutions today, the best students are carefully schooled to avoid leadership responsibilities.

Most of our intellectually gifted young people go from college directly into graduate school or into one of the older and more prestigious professional schools. There they are introduced to—or, more correctly, powerfully indoctrinated in—a set of attitudes appropriate to scholars, scientists, and professional men. This is all to the good. The students learn to identify themselves strongly with their calling and its ideals. They acquire a conception of what a good scholar, scientist, or professional man is like.

As things stand now, however, that conception leaves little room for leadership in the normal sense; the only kind of leadership encouraged is that which follows from the performing of purely professional tasks in a superior manner. Entry into what most of us would regard as the leadership roles in the society at large is discouraged.

In the early stages of a career, there is a good reason for this: becoming a first-class scholar, scientist, or professional requires single-minded dedication. Unfortunately, by the time the individual is sufficiently far along in his career to afford a broadening of interests, he often finds himself irrevocably set in a narrow mold.

The antileadership vaccine has other more subtle and powerful ingredients. The image of the corporation president, politician, or college president that is current among most intellectuals and professionals today has some decidedly unattractive features. It is said that such men compromise their convictions almost daily, if not hourly. It is said that they have tasted the corrupting experience of power. They must be status seekers, the argument goes, or they would not be where they are.

Needless to say, the student picks up such attitudes. It is not that professors propound these views and students learn them. Rather, they are in the air and students absorb them. The resulting unfavorable image contrasts dramatically with the image these young people are given of the professional who is almost by definition dedicated to his field, pure in his motives, and unencumbered by worldly ambition.

My own extensive acquaintance with scholars and professionals on the one hand and administrators and managers on the other does not confirm this contrast in character. In my experience, each category has its share of opportunists. Nevertheless, the negative attitudes persist.

As a result the academic world appears to be approaching a point at which everyone will want to educate the technical expert who advises the leader, or the intellectual who stands off and criticizes the leader, but no one will want to educate the leader himself.

Are Leaders Necessary?

For a good many academic and other professional people, negative attitudes toward leadership go deeper than skepticism concerning the leader's integrity. Many have real doubts, not always explicitly formulated, about the necessity for leadership.

The doubts are of two kinds. First, many scientific and professional people are accustomed to the kinds of problems that can be solved by expert technical advice or action. It is easy for them to imagine that any social enterprise could be managed in the same way. They envisage a world that does not need leaders, only experts. The notion is based, of course, upon a false conception of the leader's function. The supplying of technically correct solutions is the least of his responsibilities.

There is another kind of question that some academic or professional people raise concerning leadership: Is the very notion of leadership somehow at odds with the ideals of a free society? Is it a throwback to earlier notions of social organization?

These are not foolish questions. We have in fact outgrown or rejected several varieties of leadership that have loomed large in the history of mankind. We do not want autocratic leaders who treat us like inferior beings. We do not want leaders, no matter how wise or kind, who treat us like children.

But at the same time that we were rejecting those forms of leadership, we were evolving forms more suitable to our values. As a result our best leaders today are *not* out of place in a free society—on the contrary, they strengthen our free society.

We can have the kinds of leaders we want, but we cannot choose to do without them. It is in the nature of social organization that we must have them at all levels of our national life, in and out of government— in business, labor, politics, education, science, the arts, and every other field. Since we must have them, it helps considerably if they are gifted in the performance of their appointed task. The sad truth is that a great many of our organizations are badly managed or badly led. And because of that, people within those organizations are frustrated when they need not be frustrated. They are not helped when they could be helped. They are not given the opportunities to fulfill themselves that are clearly possible.

In the minds of some, leadership is associated with goals that are distasteful—power, profit, efficiency, and the like. But leadership, properly conceived, also serves the individual human goals that our society values so highly, and we shall not achieve those goals without it.

Leaders worthy of the name, whether they are university presidents or senators, corporation executives or newspaper editors, school super-intendents or governors, contribute to the continuing definition and articulation of the most cherished values of our society. They offer, in short, moral leadership.

So much of our energy has been devoted to tending the machinery of our complex society that we have neglected this element in leadership. I am using the word "moral" to refer to the shared values that must undergird any functioning society. The thing that makes a number of individuals a society rather than a population or a crowd is the presence of shared attitudes, habits and values, a shared conception of the enterprise of which they are all a part, shared views of why it is worthwhile for the enterprise to continue and to flourish. Leaders can help in bringing that about. In fact, it is required that they do so. When leaders lose their credibility or their moral authority, then the society begins to disintegrate.

Leaders have a significant role in creating the state of mind that is the society. They can serve as symbols of the moral unity of the society. They can express the values that hold the society together. Most important, they can conceive and articulate goals that lift people out of their petty preoccupations, carry them above the conflicts that tear a society apart, and unite them in the pursuit of objectives worthy of their best efforts.

28

Leading-Edge Leadership

ROBERT K. MUELLER

1. Introduction

About the year 1800, the word *leadership* entered the English language. It was and is a sophisticated concept with multiple definitions. Leadership defined as the initiation and maintenance of structure in expectation and interaction may be the meaning best suited for the future manager. New structures can often create new expectations and interactions in group goal attainment and problem solution.

How can a person prepare for such a leadership role? What are the attributes of a 21st century leader? These are elegant questions posed for a fuzzy future. They are important questions for these leaders are just now entering our schools and colleges.

Theories of leadership are many. Future leadership calls for more than logic. Theories run the gamut of great man theories, environmental theories, person-situation theories, interaction-expectation theories, humanistic and exchange theories. Research has shown that effective leaders score high in social service, persuasive, business and intellectual values.

An underlying postulate for the future is that a leader must influence an institution more than it influences him or her. Certainly this activist perspective is the core challenge of leading-edge-leadership. No longer can the leader be only the "wave pushed ahead by the ship" as Tolstoy wrote. Instead, he must become the force behind the movement and the navigator. Sections 2 and 3 describe the turbulent situation and the key issues to be faced in the future.

The true leader is a trumpet that does not give an uncertain sound. He or she tends to be a revolutionist, an innovator and not an evolutionist or traditionalist. This role is distinct from what sociologists call an

Reprinted by permission from *Human Systems Management*, 1 (1980), pp. 17–27. Copyright © 1980 by North-Holland Publishing Company.

executive, manager or administrator. Three key components of leadership thought, beliefs and behavior required to cope with the leading management issues of the future are proposed later in this discussion.

Many years ago Bishop Gore of Oxford, whose total life had been dedicated to education, was asked to make some generalization about students. He said the most striking and unexpected discovery he had made was that, although the natural gifts of people varied enormously, he was convinced that such differences in talent were of little or no value compared with the issue of how a person uses the talent he possesses.

Without strong individual determination, the executive or manager's role is likely to be determined by the organization or by the environment in which the institution finds itself. The challenge is to reverse this equation.

The future leader will need some sense of purpose, an ability to make trade-offs amongst emergent factors and an understanding of the broader aspects of institutional governance.

2. Leading Where and How?

2.1. *The Fuzzy Future*

Futurology, a newly fledged discipline, is having as much trouble establishing itself as fuzzy set theory. None of the three Hellenic coinages for the study of the future have caught on. Jedrzejewski's *stoxology*— the science of conjecture—; the anonymously minted *mellology*—the science of the future—; and Wescott's *alleotics*—the study of change— haven't made it any better. The only purely Latin term for this field was dubbed *futuribles* by Bertrand de Jouvenel. This term has more currency in Europe.

Flechtheim's *futurology* or the slightly less Hellenic *futuristics* focuses mainly on techniques of prediction: determinative, normative and random. The intellectual freemasonry of futurists consists of members who are open to new ideas and often noncompetitive in their relationship to one another.

The purpose of this discussion is not to attempt to forecast or predict a future end-state for managers but rather to identify certain trends and patterns now; the driving forces, impacts, possible swings, events and alternative end-state characterizations. Their implications for the manager 20 to 30 years ahead are profound.

Some basic hypotheses have been made in connection with some recent research at Arthur D. Little, Inc. These identify certain global trends affecting the probable end-state environment for institutions. The requirement, both for more leadership and more management ability is clear. Some of the trends which call for new capabilities are:

(a) The internationalization of political and economic institutions in other than the large industrialized nations.

(b) A growing dependence of developed nations on the availability of key external resources obtainable mainly in less developed countries. The balance of physical survival and economic health versus political relationships is shifting to redress this interdependence.

(c) As developing countries reach a more advanced state, different patterns of government and business relationships enter the international competitive area. This causes increased uncertainty in the conduct of international business and a strong sense that there will be a transition to new patterns of institutions, business, government and international relationships.

(d) A political explosion in the formation and reformation of new nations increases the number of actors on the global stage. A rapid increase in sophistication of these participants is occurring whether they are new governments, political aggregations, culture groups, new private enterprises, new suppliers or consumers.

(e) Basic value systems are changing. There is a strong drive toward egalitarianism resulting from the growth and affluence of developed nations. There is a growth in interdependence among nations. There is also a search by individuals and institutions for a stronger sense of identity.

(f) All of this calls for more clarity (legal, strategic nature, social, political) in the interrelationships of institutions and presages a change in the relative aging of industries and societies.

(g) Relationships and conflicts between fundamental driving forces and systems will gradually develop to provide special incentives and some differentiation. These will be based on self value, egalitarianism and of course market values in free world areas.

(h) The impacts of technology will affect industries, social-economic maturity and the balances between nations and social force systems. These will be a continuing cause for future turbulence.

The presumption that if government, activists, communities, unions and shareowners will only leave the corporation alone, everyone's welfare will be served just doesn't fit the prospective future complex society anymore than it does today.

In recent years, the Faraday type force-fields of hard-science technology occupied man's interest persistently and more effectively than similar force-fields in the softer sciences of sociology, anthropology, political science and psychology. The creations of technology have pushed institutions of the developed world to where different governance concepts and systems are required if corporations are to be effectively managed. This is taking place in the social-political jungle and ambiguous situations in which managers and leaders now find themselves. These situations will become progressively more complex in the future. The leading edges of these force-fields are where the management action must occur.

It seems appropriate that a systems view of such force-fields will continue to be useful. This means an understanding of an orderly arrangement of interdependent activities and related processes. The task of the executive and of the leader is to identify the dominant force-fields, to watch and assess them in an experimental frame of mind. The storm watch of the weather bureau comes to mind as a metaphor. Especially equipped aircraft and crews seek and interact with impending storms, pierce hurricane vortices to size up the forces at work and assess probable impacts for warning purposes.

Suffice it to say, there is a Sargasso Sea of problems ahead for the leading-edge-leader. I suggest that he must be a student of at least six different perspectives. We refer to these as the shifts and trends at the leading edge of the force-fields currently at work in the world. These emergent factors are the subject of Section 3 of this set of notions about leading-edge-leadership.

2.2 Wanted: More Leaders, Fewer Executives

What this prospective future suggests—certainly the need exists to-day—is the need for more leaders and fewer executives. We need persons who can initiate structure in group expectation and show us how to master and motivate institutions and individuals within a complex environment experiencing excessive internal and external stresses and changes.

The interactions, conflicts and increasing rates of change with which we must coexist require the use of new (or venerable) insights and tools of the psychologists and anthropologists [8]. No longer can a "yellow pages manager" pick out from a conventional inventory list, the theme or strategy which is most effective for leadership of an institution.

Balancing artful leadership attributes along with management science will be necessary to achieve useful results in practice. This will occur in the future through many processes which may lack adequate experimental verification today. Whether a leader can also be a manager, a governor, an administrator, an executive, and a professional is doubtful given the turbulence ahead. Political effectiveness, managerial effectiveness and charismatic leadership is an unusual combination of attributes to find in any one individual. Hence the recent trend toward plural management organizational structures.

Walter Lippman once said that "the genius of a good leader is to leave behind him a situation which common sense without the grace of genius can deal with successfully." The 21st century leader will have to first develop a core team of unusually qualified persons who can jointly cope with the problems and uncertainties in the future.

(1) *Eclectic traits and behavior.* Certain leadership and management characteristics have no impact on, or are dysfunctional with respect to, group performance and follower satisfaction. Recognition of these is vital. Determination of leader characteristics and their interaction with followers and with the environment requires an understanding of the leader's and follower's values, judgments, behavioral patterns, personality and vision. Recruitment, development and educational programs will have to recognize these factors.

(2) *Style.* Leadership style can be developed so that it has a favorable impact on groups or followers in terms of adequate satisfaction, group cohesion and group drive. Patterns of behavior and expectation should be flexible with respect to the expected future managerial environment. Oversensitivity developed by such techniques as T-Group training often incapacitate a leader in coping with this job. Experimental work is required to determine specifically what style will strengthen or weaken the retention of a leadership position for each individual and each encountered circumstance.

I visited Yugoslavia about a year after the major political shakeup of the ruling League of Communists of Yugoslavia to try to fathom the contradictory trends in economic reform and attractiveness of the country for foreign investment. At that time, there occurred a striking example of the psychological dominance style of a leader in dealing with the matter of respective roles and mutual trust as we know them in Western industrial countries.

The group of foreign European, American and Asian businessmen with whom I was associated in the visit were deeply impressed with the off-record discussions with President Tito, his ministers and leading figures in the financial, government and business communities. Their complex—to us—concept of free enterprise with stateowned facilities bugged our group for almost a week of free wheeling interrogation and exchange of views.

The authority of the management to reserve funds for growth, for example, rather than to raise the year-end bonus, always bowed officially to a Worker's Council which, it appeared, attempted to act as a board of directors on the one hand and a union group on the other hand. In questioning one of the industrial leaders, we were unable to get to the nub of how he made a basic business decision. The chief manager of one of the largest stateowned enterprises said (with the translator's tailoring of this into three languages) what may be paraphrased as "I just tell the council that's the way it's got to be!"

As a 230 pound, direct-mannered Yugoslavian type of executive-leader that he appeared to be, it was obvious his dynamic personality and personal prestige transcended any artificial, ideological network of constraints. He did not permit these abstract constraints to inhibit a clear resolution of an action in the best interest of the enterprise as might be judged by any Western value system.

(3) *Interpersonal reinforcement of leadership.* This involves consolidating the position with careful use of personal style and attitude characteristics. Techniques vary for large or small companies, for different types of organizations. The interpersonal space factors, commitments of persons to the corporation or profession, the status factors, the management hierarchy, the identity, certain social norms, reference groups and value systems all fit into reinforcement of a leadership position.

The future leader will be aware of these elements and deal with them accordingly. Frequent reorganization of central versus decentral units, ad hoc task force formation, spin-off of separate business enterprise and use of non-uniform incentive schemes are among the obvious variants.

(4) *Political power.* Leadership behavior, personality and the interaction with power are affected differently according to whether a task-pattern or a person-oriented-pattern is involved and whether it provides a low or high powered influence. Seeking power equalization and leader legitimacy with those involved, and resolving role conflicts which occur are important factors in coping with political power.

Organizations have been characterized with respect to the nature of their primary power that often is used to control their lowest ranking participants. Coercive organizations, such as a prison, keep order through threat of physical force. Utilitarian organizations, such as manufacturing or service entities, keep order primarily through monetary rewards. Normative organizations, e.g., churches, professional organizations, learned societies and schools elicit compliance through allocation and manipulation of symbolic awards, e.g., diplomas, licenses, titles and membership status.

Normative organizations tend to demand higher degrees of commitment and allegiance from the members. Charisma is ascribed to the officers or senior participants of the elite group. Use of charismatic power by personal contact, symbols, rituals and the gift of grace may parallel the formal organizational chart as means to relieve the political strain of challenges to organizational hegemony, integration and competition for resources. Charismatic power however cannot be routinized as a source of political power.

(5) *Contingency management.* In recent years, there has been growing acceptance of what is an eclectic use of various theories of comparative organization.

There has been a growing acceptance of contingency management which is also called situational management. This states that the optimum management strategy or practice is contingent upon the real world situation. It has become clear that the classical bureaucratic design, the neoclassical or decentralized design, or even modern structural design such as free-form systems and matrix-setups do not hold up under all organizational situations. In effect, bureaucracy was found unable to cope with dynamic situations. Matrix or free-form designs are not adequately adaptable to situations which require cutbacks and stability. Fred E. Fiedler [1,2] and his associates did early research in the situational approach to leadership. They found that a task-oriented leader is more successful in extreme situations when he has a great deal of influence: i.e., position power is high and the task is highly structured, or alternatively when he has very little influence: i.e., position power is low, and the task is unstructured.

(6) Group survival is dependent upon leader behavior and this has direct but unquantifiable effects on group arousal, group drive, group cohesiveness and productivity. The future leader will be conscious of this dependency and modify his behavior to enhance his own survival and effectiveness. He will employ, inter alia, what has been called the "helicopter factor." This is the ability to rise above the particulars of a situation and perceive it as a whole, in its relation to the overall environment.

Given these attributes of a 21st century leader we can expect to see an emerging change in management style.

2.3. *Future Management Style*

The biologists teach that inefficiency is an extremely important element in the survival of the species. A species will not expand to the limit of its environment if it is to survive. Otherwise the environment would worsen and the opportunity for continued existence is jeopardized. The efficient species simply collapses into extinction whereas the inefficient species possesses reserves. Redundancy and some irrelevance are the sort of elements that a governance system requires in order to survive.

We can look at an institution as such a "repository of redundance in society" to use the phrase of Kenneth Boulding, Professor at the University of Colorado. The task of the leader is to get out of an institution's action as much in terms of human values as he possibly can in proportion to whatever values are put in. Redundancy and vagueness are important reserves in this regard. They are obviously of great value in time of crisis.

One of the outstanding properties of a fuzzy future is its irreducible uncertainty. The ability to make decisions under these conditions is limited. While our techniques could produce projections of the future, we cannot totally trust them. Data needs to be treated as evidence in the same form that a physician treats symptoms and protocol checks when examining a patient. A way to approach the fuzzy future is through adaptability and use of the heuristic process.

In looking at the societal network in which the leader finds himself, we see a finite number of states undergoing transition at discrete instances of time. A societal network will undergo an evolution of its states and may be thought of as a dynamic process. The long-term behavior of the societal network indicates it will either reach a stable state or a periodic pattern of state transitions in which the leader may find himself. An effective leader will be sensitive to these states in the chain-of-being. Instinct and intuitive powers will be vital in this situation.

That instinct plays an important part in leadership is asserted by many experienced persons. The adjective *instinctive* connotes innate, impulsive or spontaneous attitude as a result of behavioral patterns which are mediated by reactions below the conscious level and are conditioned by environment.

The adjective *intuitive* implies direct perception of apprehension without apparent reasoning, or evolutionary behavior patterns. Such "reason in a hurry" is a significant trait in successful leadership. In some instances it may be the result of protracted, long and agonizing groping.

From my observation, a good leader is one who is able to simplify problems. Validation of this is obscure or absent in most studies of leadership and management. The ability to intuitively select significant factors of a situation, without going through the rigor of reducing it through a logical chain of reasoning, identifies leadership talent in a practicing world. This insight apprehends the inner nature of problem situations and is a powerful ability of a leader.

The skill to jump to the crux of a complex matter while the rest of the crowd are still trying to identify the problem is a rare gift of leaders albeit sometimes a risky one. Only exceptional leaders, and few executives or managers, possess this ability to a degree that results in a good batting average for their decisions. Certainly this is an area for future leadership research. First we need to identify the nature of means by which *rapid reification* can be developed. Secondly, we need to integrate and relate a charismatic component with the logical and intuitive attributes which we suggest are vital to leading-edge leadership. This integration is both the key and challenge and is the subject of Section 4.

There is increasing interaction, interdependency and proliferation of institutional units occurring in this sea of socio-technical-cultural-political-individual forces. A free-form organizational style is probably the most likely to survive. Attributes of such a type and the style involved may be characterized by the following:

(1) Organizational fluidity. Work engagements and pursuits of objectives are often carried out in the task force mode spawned from core resource groups.

(2) The center of gravity of the professional or economic cutting edge is placed in a core group of individuals. Beyond this center extends a group of satellite organizations placed in pattern form reminiscent of Buddhists' graphic symbols. This Buddhist concept of a mandala configuration includes certain primary components; a core and an enclosing boundary with a complex of satellites around a center. Some components will have a permanent nature, some exist as interim task forces and others are transient imperatives around the compass of far-flung organizations.

(3) A climate of encouragement of individual priority-setting needs to be present with an increasing degree of freedom in such choices. Appropriate incentives will be available for leading-edge leaders.

(4) More employee mobility will occur between institutions as a more acceptable way of life. The one-company-one-career-one-job ethos will be replaced by professional career changes at all stages of a working life. Increased attention will be given to optimal time for retirement or "repotting" in another career setting.

(5) Peer systems of management with minimum hierarchical structure are more likely to retain the leading-edge leader. He will have to be comfortable and be able to survive within this type management context. Organizational policies will employ more collegial style as distinct from directive style common to most institutional managements.

(6) Increase in service and software activity as distinct from fixed assets and hardware. This will extensively alter the management of resources. Individuals may have to be willing to invest their own time in research and development in the softer socio-cultural areas of corporate activity.

(7) Consciousness of the concept of intellectual property will be raised as a key element in management. In addition to conventional industrial property rights, this concept also involves intangibles such as statutory

and moral rights associated with education, art, and literature which are so important in the further world development.

The bulwark concept of intellectual property in the early 17th century was first set forth in Anglo-Saxon terms in the United Kingdom. The rationale for including incorporeal property under a broad juridicial-trust concept rested on the premise that the main ingredients to progress were the theoretical scientists, the inventors and entrepreneurs. The legal principles say that a society intending to progress must enter into a compact with the inventive and creative members of that society through a legal structure for protecting intellectual property rights.

A future analogy will be society entering into a compact with institutional leaders in order to deal with socio-cultural and techno-economic inventions. Those in responsible charge will need certain political and interpersonal sensitivities, professional talents, visions and experience to apply throughout the development process [6]. As these skills produce socio-technical-economic inventions, their value can be enormous.

(8) An entrepreneurial climate fostered by special incentives will become more common and will encourage innovation. Future organizations will need to allow relative freedom to their staff to spend time on individual entrepreneurial pursuits and projects. Many companies are now struggling with revised compensation schemes to nurture the entrepreneur [7].

(9) There will be more carefully controlled security systems where need-to-know criteria would be strictly observed in order to retain intellectual property values in an enterprise and to keep a competitive edge. Future managers will be skilled in techniques, policies and appropriate communications in order to manage these improved security systems.

(10) Those persons engaged in the governance of institutions will have to permit unusual degrees of freedom and encouragement to leaders, professional staff and administrative managers. This will allow staff to pursue non-conflicting non-sensitive interests on their own time or even part-time. This freedom will help to retain outstanding persons who need to extend their perspectives; continually sharpen intellectual, academic and business capabilities. It will further reduce the dependency on the central-life interest factor for a balanced career.

Given the ten attributes of the future free-form style organizations, the intellectual focus of the leader is likely to be like the Brownian movement, always in motion. Some philosophical arrangement may help to cluster the problems, opportunities, concepts and leading ideas with which a leader must cope.

3. Edge or Hedge?—Emergent Factors

3.1. *Shifts and Trends*

The work at the Center for Social Policy at Stanford Research Institute (among other organizations) has outlined certain consciousness-raising trends for the future [3]. These are not unlike my own postulates for the environment in which leaders will have to manage.

These shifts and trends are popularized in the form of:

(1) *Alternative futures or options.* This includes awareness of the Faustian powers of technological manipulation in shaping the future. New dimensions of human responsibility are emerging for the future in which our managers will function. Job rights, human rights, social cost accounting are examples. Futurism, one of the significant recent intellectual developments along with the systems theory, has provoked a shift from the discipline of the factory and Weberian bureaucracy to more flexible, knowledge-based organizations and a decline in traditional sources of authority.

(2) *Spaceship earth system.* Concern for environment, ecological systems, resource control, an awareness of the biosphere as a life support system. This has been called a revolution in lowering expectations. The expectations are a complex of concerns over limits to growth, the energy crisis, pollution, exhaustion of non-renewable resources. This "revolution" is in direct conflict with the revolution of rising expectations of millions of persons in the developing nations for a higher standard of living.

(3) *Growing international awareness of inequities.* These are caused partly by the rapid advances in transport, communications and the mobility of a managerial elite in taking up residence in non-native environs. People are becoming aware of the need to redress the balance between the less developed areas and those in a greater state of development with a better standard of living.

(4) *Shift towards humanistic and spiritual values.* This includes the movement towards egalitarianism. The shift is manifest in forms of employee discontent, new political and social emphasis on self-determination and in the new styles of management for coping with these trends. The movement to upgrade opportunities for qualified females and minorities is yet another symptom.

(5) *Shortage of meaningful social roles.* Automation, specialization of work to the detriment of personal satisfaction has reduced the meaningfulness of work opportunities. Increase in leisure time and the recent change in retirement age are not the answer to this problem. A world job-shortage by the year 2000 despite a declining birth rate is predicted by the Population Reference Bureau in Washington. The pressure will

be mainly in the developing countries where the search for jobs is already desperate. Between 300 and 500 million persons are already unemployed worldwide with the labor force expected to rise from the current 1.7 billion to 2.5 billion by the end of this century. Research is needed to illuminate solutions for these human needs through meaningful socially responsible work and for self-service new industrial patterns.

(6) *Shift towards a new transcendentalism.* This is manifested by the emergence of widespread interest in new naturalism, religious and spiritual concerns, psychic phenomena and other self-exploratory techniques.

The future leader will have to be aware of the potential impacts of these shifts which are due to cause future problems. The issues include overpopulation, problems of the aged, biological and nuclear hazards, environmental integrity, unemployment, urbanization, excessive energy consumption, rising expectations and rebellion against nonmeaningful work, egalitariansim, and the anticipated consequences of technological applications further widening the gap between the have and have-not regions of the world.

The 21st century leader will be acutely aware of these trade-off equations. Resolution can directly or indirectly impact most enterprises through the changes in life expectancy, geriatric costs, further technical breakthroughs, incentive-motivation changes, work-leisure patterns, health care and other economic and social issues. Sophistication on the part of the leader will be needed in exercising his powers of human choice given this array of today's decisions to make about the future.

3.2. New Leadership Issues

The 21st century leader will be confronted with a large variety of issues as he is today. These sprout from the leading edge of scientific, technological, political, economic, social and cultural forces already at work. The issues seem to fall into five general categories.

(1) *Intellectual operations* involving the acquisition, development and retention of new ideas and concepts including:

(a) The formation of ideas—situations of creativity, invention, discovery, insight, intuition and experience.

(b) Communication of ideas. We often deal in communications with the ambiguous, the unexplained, the unexpected, the unknown, the random event and the entrepreneurial dimension.

(c) Innovation. This embraces societal, personal or market acceptance of new developments which may threaten, enhance or be neutral to the recipient. Institutional rejection of new implants of intellectual variety is as common as in biological transplants.

(2) *Phenomenon of power.* This means the ideas derived from the exercise of volition on the part of power holders. It involves issues of choice, intersocial and group relationships, and decision making:

(a) Power use concerns individuals' trade-off strategies, tactics, authority, risk, change, growth, development, antagonism, discord, conflict, crisis, dilemma, instability, disorganization and behavior. Examples of these problems abound: Arthur D. Little's proprietary studies of government loans to farmers in the Philippines to motivate individuals to develop the agricultural sector, or the personal-social issues involved in the mass distribution strategy and techniques created for introducing contraceptives in India. Determination of private enterprise conflict factors in New Zealand rested on many of the power issues cited above.

(b) Intersocial and group relations. These embrace, along with other things, the classical conflicts of social order. This concerns the use of force by the stronger, guile and fraud by the weaker in a competition for the scarce resources and rewards. Relationships relevant here include alienation, tension, risk, interracial problems and opportunities.

(3) *Abstract relationships,* particularly:

(a) The phenomenon of change. This concerns growth, innovation, development, crises, diversification, discontinuity, instability and mutations. Arthur D. Little's recent study of public policy, tax, legal, financial issues affecting technological innovations in the United States is a prime example of this category. Administration attitudes, regulatory trends and legal constraints were found to be in need of change [4].

(b) Causation. These are the phenomena caused by force, power, perturbation, disorder, tension, conflict and creativity. A private diagnostic study of industrial problems and root causes in financial, production and manpower areas of Argentina involved a critical analysis of the industrial sector. Detailed evaluation of problems and analysis of government policies with their effect on industry produced recommendations on changes in tax, tariff and financial policies.

(c) Order and disorder. The problem situations derive from form, structure, instability, confusion, discontinuity, diversity, discord, tradeoffs and conflict. They afford a particular arena of managerial challenge.

(4) *Materials world.* This concerns the inorganic and organic matter of nature, the physical sciences, energy, and the domains of engineering and technology. Technoeconomic forces are key factors in the future.

(5) *Ethical, legal, religious spheres* of sentient and moral powers. This involves work in many cultures and value systems around the world. An example of constructive work in this category was the impact and linking of cultural change in economic development conducted by Arthur D. Little for the Dominican Republic.

In ancient Greece, a custom prevailed for a time in which a man proposing a law in the popular assembly did so on a platform with a rope around his neck. If his law passed, they removed the rope; if it failed, they removed the platform. In early American Indian tribes, the man who dared represent himself as a rainmaker lived a similar go-no-go existence. If the rainmaker's prognostications failed to come true with at least reasonable accuracy, he was buried alive. The leader today runs a similar risk in maintaining his position and in structuring expectations. It is likely that opinions rather than events would unseat him in times of trouble in the future.

From a pragmatic viewpoint, the keys appear to be personal equilibrium, reasonable goal development, recognition of potential limitations, realism, interest level, self realization and personal fulfillment. What the leading-edge leader needs, however, is some sense of protocol which provides him with a balanced grasp of reasonable knowledge of logical science and humanistic arts. Our conventional education and training programs do not address this need now. Check and balance in making use of logic, emotion and drive is a process little understood by most leaders.

An appreciation of purpose and respect for our place in the scheme of things is the key issue to leading-edge leadership. This will be most challenging. It is a sophisticated component of the mental and emotional baggage the future leader will carry into the 21st century.

4. Leadership and Governance

4.1. Threeness in Governance

Threeness appears in many religious systems as the Holy Trinity of God. The Brahma, Vishnu and Shiva in the Hindu traditions is a triune example. As it seems with all threes, there is an intrinsic movement that shifts the reference point as soon as one tries to pin it down. However, we can at least distinguish a temporal succession. In the trinity of thinker, manager and leader, the thinker tends to be the antecedent to any situation even though often dealing with unreal time. The manager is the successor struggling to administer the present, often without thinking about the future. The leader is the visionary providing immanence to the present and a transcendental drive into the future.

The thinker is usually termed a "professional" in this governance threesome of the future. Most often the manager is the action-oriented producer and the leader is a charismatic visionary providing the expectation and structure. These three components are not necessarily tightly bound together but they exist in a rather relaxed form, often in several persons and in a fuzzy type of relationship.

The asset of ambiguity and the virtue of vagueness surrounding such a future tripartite grouping presents us with the option of three separate roles for governance in the 21st century. One person may aspire to provide all three components. Perhaps more realistically and in the mode of situational management, an individual must select only one (or two) of the three roles since future complexity and dynamics make a triple approach unrealistic in most anticipated circumstances and for most available persons. Like a golfer, the chief executive officer has a bag of clubs. He uses the one most appropriate for the shot he has to make. To be a winner he must:

(a) choose the right club,
(b) be skillful in the use of most of the clubs in the bag,
(c) be better than the others.

Inquiry into the management of such plural human systems requires a transdisciplinary study of principles and methods. Such principles should seek to enhance both the analytical and intuitive faculties of management practitioners. An abstract construct can be helpful to the future practitioner for advancing from simple, well-structured, statistical and deterministic concepts towards the more complex, fuzzy, dynamic and stochastic problems of managing. This process is of course reversible and could go from the complex to the well-structured, simpler state if a leader is capable of reifying the situation.

It has been proposed by Professor Milan Zeleny that the optimal working framework of the human mind changes from the logical, rational, sequential and quantitative (LRSQ) framework to the perceptive, intuitive, simultaneous and qualitative (PISQ) mental framework for approaching managerial problems. The concept is useful both in the present and for the future. This issue is as old as the conflict between Aristotle and The Rhetoricians. In full complexity, Professor Zeleny's framework calls for an inseparable unity between the LRSQ and PISQ ends of an ever shifting continuum of thought [10].

However, with respect to *leadership*, either in the present and certainly more in the future, a third framework of the human mind and soul, *TISC*, could be suggested. This concerns the teleological-ideological, instinctive, spiritual and charismatic attributes of a leader. These may or may not exist in the managerial or the professional affective framework to the same degree.

There is a surprising lack of experimentation, other than rhetoric and opinion, regarding the importance of this dharmic framework in leadership. For example, in the ancient institution of divine kingship, charisma was often gained by special initiation, regalia of office, sumptuary privileges, ascetic practices or auspicious birth. These were recognized signs of merit and power accumulated in previous lives. The modern version of corporate practice, power flow concepts, perquisites, democratic canons and professional management are often antithetical to these charismatic concepts, even though some institutions attempt to recapture their symbolism.

Another ancient notion, the group-soul concept, has always been a part of the tradition of primitive people. It has been demonstrated in the animal kingdom by Marais that the same species have the same instincts (Marais, 1939). The group-soul concept however has been studied and found inadequate for man because of his peculiar individuality in the evolutionary sense. More of such experimentation is needed in the TISC framework of man.

Traits of charisma, instinct, intuition, inspiration, ideology, emotion and will are elusive but key components of mind and soul. They are seminal to our leading-edge leadership postulate and we hypothesize will be the cachet of the 21st century leader. This will not be a new set of attributes. While these traits are vital to leadership today, they will be needed to an even greater extent in the future.

Oliver Wendell Holmes, Jr., once said, "There are one story intellects, two story intellects, three story intellects with skylights. All fact collectors who have no aim behind their facts are one story men; two story men compare, reason, generalize, using the labors of the fact collectors as well as their own. Three story men idealize, imagine, predict. Their best illumination comes from above through the skylight." Leading-edge-leaders will be Holmesian third story persons aided and abetted in their work by one story colleagues and their management subsystems.

Robert A. Smith, III, Organizational Behavior Analyst, NASA ret., has suggested how this holistic integration can take place in his "trichotomy of complex organizations" setting forth three components, the institutional, functional and programmatic in overlapping fields [9]. These are interconnected and revitalized constantly. The programmatic component corresponds to Zeleny's LRSQ component. The functional component representing multiple systems, heterostasis and skills in the professional sense is represented by the PISQ collect of mental processes.

The institutional open system rests on normative principles. According to Smith, it embraces such processes as decision, judication, membership, turnover of elite, program selections, sanctions, awards and objectives. However, it does not capture the TISC transcendental notion suggested previously in this section. This notion is that inspiration, ideology, vision, purpose and design form a balance with the LRSQ and PISQ factors and that certain ends are preordained in nature. Those who deal with leading-edge forces must grasp these notions in a triad of mental frameworks. This is a key to shaping activities towards a worthy purpose, ideological in content, and perhaps religio-philosophical in nature.

Very few persons possess all three sets of attributes as inherited mental equipment. By my definition, the leading-edge-leader will certainly have the TISC component. He may join forces with those who have special logic or intuitive talents for coping with the complex area of conflicts which face institutions in the future. The power struggle deals with survival and immortality of the institution which is being led which endeavors to perpetuate itself through normative principles or canons. These principles can include a pluralistic overview, social transformation, transcendental vision or a capability for continuous self-renewal.

Future leadership will need to include the ability of enhancing an institution or society's capability for such self-renewal on a continuous basis. Thus, the effort becomes a political creation with the orientation in the corporate sense being toward a socio-technological-economic system of purposeful work. In this, the purpose is the long-range outcome and orientation versus focusing on short-term outputs to the system.

The function of managing human systems, then, is the management of conflict by avoidance, dissolution, removal or resolution usually between short-term and long-term needs while at the same time pursuing a process of continuous self-renewal.

4.2. The Challenge

Requirements for effective leadership of corporations are changing rapidly. The complexities surrounding our institutions introduce more legal, strategic, economic, social and political interrelationships than in the past.

New patterns of government and business relations are developing as interactivity and interdependence increase internally.

Value systems of societies and individuals are changing. These are intensified social pressures and confrontations with challenges that most present-day managers have not been trained to meet. The challenge is to deal with the questions in a manner that serves society without compromising the legitimate corporate objectives. This is fast becoming a major requirement for effective leadership and management. Leaders in the future will have to be multi-talented and well-trained. Ability to manage with flexible, plural type hierarchical structures will require new, creative organizational development thinking and planning.

There is also a focus toward egalitarianism in compensation as well as opportunity. All of these forces will call for a new generation of managerial elite to lead our enterprises.

The expectation that our corporations, because they have proven effective in the economic sphere, can bear the responsibility or even be effective instruments for accomplishing new, broader social goals, demands a new set of leadership attributes which have to be developed.

Executives and managers, as persons in positions of leadership and power, must take up part of the responsibility to articulate and move toward social goals. This should be a strategic decision and a positive one. Business corporations cannot be made to adequately approach this challenge in an atmosphere of social guilt and adversary proceedings.

Given this complex situation in which to govern, leadership talent will become an even more valued attribute in the executive suite. A new breed of leaders conscious of the changing forces, conflicts, values and uncertainties will emerge from the ranks well-trained in schools of education and experience. The concept of a triple framework (LRSQ, PISQ, TISC) for conceptual thinking about management and leadership described previously may be a helpful trait to seek in a new managerial elite. Without some special talents, understandings, an enlightened style and philosophy about governance, it will be difficult to initiate and maintain structure in expectation and interaction. Such is the challenge for the leading-edge-leader of the future.

References

1. F. E. Fiedler, A contingency model of leadership effectiveness, in: L. Berkowitz, Ed., Advances in Experimental Social Psychology (Academic Press, New York, 1964).
2. F. E. Fiedler, Personality and situational determinants of leader behavior, Technical Report, Department of Psychology, University of Washington, Seattle (1971).
3. Willis W. Harman, The coming transformation in our view of knowledge, The Futurist (June 1974) 126–128.
4. Arthur D. Little, Inc. and Industrial Research Institute, Inc., Barriers to innovation in industry: Opportunities for public policy changes, prepared for the National Science Foundation (Contracts NSF-C725) (September 1973).
5. Eugene Marais, The Soul of the White Ant, translated by Winifred Dekok (Methuen and Company, London, 1939).
6. Robert Kirk Mueller, Metadevelopment: Beyond the Bottom Line (Lexington Books, Lexington, MA, 1977) Ch. 9.
7. Robert Kirk Mueller, The Innovation Ethic (AMACOM, New York, 1971).
8. R. K. Mueller, The managementality gap in IEEE Transactions on Systems and Cybernetics, IEEE Trans. Systems, Man Cybernet. 3(1) (1979). Published

also in: Robert Kirk Mueller, Ed., Risk, Survival and Power (AMACOM, New York, 1970) Ch. 4.

9. Robert A. Smith, III, National goals, planning and human potential, HSM Human Systems Management 9 (1979) 17–20.

10. Milan Zeleny, Managers without management science?, Interfaces 5(4) (1975) 41.

About the Book and Editors

Contemporary Issues in Leadership
edited by William E. Rosenbach and Robert L. Taylor

The term "leadership" is a relatively recent addition to the language, whereas the root word "leader" has been around for more than six centuries. As a consequence, an abundance of information has been collected about leaders but little is known about the leadership process itself. Although we have been unable to adequately define or measure it, we still seem to know good leadership when we see it.

Rather than accepting the traditional emphasis on the attributes of individual leaders, Rosenbach and Taylor stress the dynamic view of leadership as an influence process whereby one individual affects the attitudes and behaviors of others in efforts to accomplish a common goal. They concentrate on describing the phenomenon of leadership and on identifying what it is that makes a person an effective leader. To what extent, for example, is the ability to lead a product of natural gifts, background, knowledge, training, or personal charisma? How does mastering the skills of followership contribute to successful leadership? What are the differences between headship, management, and leadership? And, perhaps most important, how much of the leadership influence process can be taught or learned?

Both classic and current expressions of our understanding of leadership are included, providing a blend of scholarly and journalistic styles and an interdisciplinary view of the key issues in leadership, at different organizational levels and from a variety of perspectives. The collection is a comprehensive review of the phenomenon of leadership that presents with clarity the challenges that now face leaders and potential leaders who must respond to the demands of advanced communications and technology; it is also a major step forward in understanding how individuals learn to lead effectively and humanely.

William E. Rosenbach is professor and head, Department of Behavioral Sciences and Leadership, United States Air Force Academy. For the past twelve years he has been a consultant, teacher, and researcher in leadership, job attitudes, and organizational effectiveness. **Robert L. Taylor** is the Carl N. Jacobs Professor of Business and associate dean, College of Letters and Sciences at the University of Wisconsin-Stevens Point. In his distinguished career as an Air Force officer, he served in a variety of leadership roles, retiring in 1981 as professor and head of the Department of Management at the USAF Academy.